REAL FOOD, REAL FAST

REAL FOOD, REAL FAST

Comfort Food Classics and Homestyle Meals
Made Healthier with Whole Foods

Susan McQuillian, MS, RDN,
and the editors of **Prevention.**

RODALE.

© 2017 by Rodale Inc.

All rights reserved. No part of this publication may be reproduced or transmitted in any form or by any means, electronic or mechanical, including photocopying, recording, or any other information storage and retrieval system, without the written permission of the publisher.

Prevention® is a registered trademark of Rodale Inc.

Printed in the United States of America

Rodale Inc. makes every effort to use acid-free ♾, recycled paper ♻.

Recipes shown on the cover: *(front, top)* Rosemary-Lemon Doughnuts, page 100; Strawberry-Vanilla Doughnuts, page 102; and Chocolate Glazed Doughnuts, page 98; *(front, middle)* Sirloin and Snow Pea Stir-Fry, page 181; *(front, bottom)* Chocolate Tart with Berries, page 258; *(back, top)* Scallops with Spinach and Bacon, page 209; *(back, middle)* Mexican Bean Soup, page 114; and *(back, bottom)* Egg Brunch Pizza, page 81

Photo credits appear on page 329.

Book design by Christina Gaugler

Library of Congress Cataloging-in-Publication Data is on file with the publisher.

ISBN 978-1-62336-980-4

2 4 6 8 10 9 7 5 3 1 direct mail hardcover

We inspire health, healing, happiness, and love in the world.
Starting with you.

CONTENTS

INTRODUCTION

We all know that eating well is important for your health. But in reality, do you find it difficult to eat well every single day? Food marketers feel your pain. We are bombarded with thousands of advertisements and new products every year, each promising to help you create convenient, tasty meals. But what exactly goes into those shelf-stable, processed foods in the first place? Are they as nutritious as they claim to be? Are we paying a higher price for convenience?

Here's something else to think about. Did you know that letting your kitchen go dormant could shave years off your life? A 2012 study published in the journal *Public Health Nutrition* found that people who cooked at home at least five times a week were 47 percent more likely to be alive after 10 years than the people who relied more on processed foods.

While grab-and-go foods may seem like a good deal, when you break down the real cost, it's generally cheaper—and healthier—to make those same foods from scratch. For instance, a popular brand's microwave bowl of chili costs $3.39 and includes harmful bisphenol A, fake food dye, and industrial meat raised using antibiotics, as well as other questionable additives. You can whip up a batch of gourmet, 100-percent-organic chili from scratch using fresh ingredients, including omega-3-rich, heart-healthy grass-fed beef, for about $2.86 per serving. Cheaper, tastier, organic, and healthier!

If you're not a chili fan, you'll find 12 more recipes that rely on ground beef in this collection, as well as 54 that use real cheese, 26 that use butter, and 13 that use chocolate! That's right. We're talking about more than 190 recipes that use real, wholesome ingredients so you can minimize your exposure to processed foods and potentially harmful additives.

Most importantly, these recipes come together quickly—most in 30 minutes or less—and our 4-week plan will show you how to make changes gradually so your new food habits are more likely to become permanent. Of course, the quality of your meals and how much better you feel when you're eating real, healthy foods may provide all the convincing you require.

Are you ready to start eating well every day? Then let's get started!

CHAPTER 1

THE TRUTH ABOUT REAL FOOD

Would you love to wake up feeling great every morning, enjoy more mental and physical energy throughout the day, look your very best, and actually feel happier? What if a few simple changes could help you with all that *and* increase your odds of a longer, healthy life? The good news is that sound scientific research confirms that making the right food choices can help you make this wish list a reality.[1, 2, 3, 4, 5]

It doesn't matter if you're young or old, male or female, or if you suffer from a chronic condition like diabetes or just occasional heartburn. The equation is the same: The way you eat affects your health, and your state of health affects your quality of life and determines how you function mentally, physically, and socially from day to day.[6, 7, 8] Moreover, if you're interested in making the switch to a better lifestyle, it doesn't matter what type of diet you follow provided it is full of real, healthy foods.

Consider, for example, a study at Yale where researchers compared several different types of popular diets and eating styles, such as Mediterranean, vegetarian, low-carb, and low-fat. The researchers concluded that the healthiest eating plans all have one thing in common: an abundance of "true foods" or real, whole foods that come directly to you, from nature, with very little handling along the way.[9] These eating styles feature real, natural foods—fresh vegetables, fruits, whole grains, nuts, and beans—and keep highly processed convenience foods to a minimum. Regardless of the plan you choose, this basic approach will put you on a path to a longer, healthier, more vibrant life.

Studies have also shown that eating real, whole foods like fresh fruits and vegetables can not only make you healthier, but also happier! In one study published in the *American Journal of Public Health*,[10] researchers looked at the food diaries of more than 12,000 men and women and found that those who increased the amount of fruits and vegetables they ate by eight servings a day over the course of 2 years experienced measurably improved feelings of happiness, well-being, and life satisfaction. In another scientific report,[11] researchers who surveyed more than 500 medical students found that those with healthier eating patterns, including eating more than eight servings of fruits and vegetables each day, also scored higher on happiness surveys. Eight servings may sound like a lot, but remember that a serving size is only $\frac{1}{2}$ measuring cup of cut-up fruits or veggies, or 1 cup (a handful) of leafy greens.

At the other end of the spectrum, studies repeatedly show that when fast foods and convenience foods regularly replace real food in your diet, the result is poor health, often associated with weight gain, and other debilitating and often life-threatening medical conditions.[12, 13, 14]

In *Real Food, Real Fast,* you'll learn how a real food diet can help prevent or manage conditions such as gastrointestinal disorders, high blood pressure, skin problems, chronic inflammation, coronary heart disease, diabetes, cancer, and mood disorders. The conditions vary, but the solution is the same. What follows is a plan to help you switch over to a whole foods diet that includes fun, flavorful, easy-to-prepare recipes, along with science-backed evidence similar to a real food plan recommended by the American Heart Association, American Cancer Society, American Diabetes Association, and other top health and research organizations.

Ready to get started? Let's begin by reviewing exactly why you'll want to limit the amount of highly processed foods in your diet.

THE HARD TRUTH BEHIND HIGHLY PROCESSED FOODS

Most foods in your supermarket can be measured on a scale that ranges from minimally processed to highly refined. Minimally processed foods include products like shelled and roasted nuts, triple-washed and bagged salad greens, natural peanut butter, prepared broth, yogurt, and pre-peeled, pre-cut packaged fruits and vegetables. These are real food products that have been simply pre-prepped to save you time in the kitchen; little or nothing has been done to these foods that you couldn't do yourself with the right tools and a little time.

At the other end of the food spectrum are highly processed products that contain a variety of additives that can affect their color, flavor, texture, and shape, as well as extend their shelf life. Many frozen products, such as breaded chicken or fish nuggets, pot pies, and microwaveable pizza, fall into the highly processed foods category. Likewise, salad dressings, cake mixes, fried and dehydrated ramen noodles with seasoning packets, hot dogs, shelf-stable puddings, soft drinks, and pastry snacks are considered highly processed. And that's just the beginning of a long list of foods that have lost their authenticity. In fact, you'd be hard-pressed

When Our Food Became Unreal

So, just when and how did so much of our food supply become "unreal"?

Between the late 18th and 19th centuries, the Industrial Revolution streamlined heavy labor and introduced food processing methods and means. Canning machines and other technological advances made it possible to supply a wider variety of food to military troops during World War I. But convenience foods for home use, as we know them today, accelerated after World War II. In the early 1950s, frozen, pre-cooked, individually portioned meals in divided metal trays known as TV dinners were first introduced.

The development of artificial flavorings, preservatives, colors, and texturizers made it easy for food manufacturers to produce a wide range of products that could travel long distances and suit just about any taste. Unlimited use of salt, sugar, and fat gave these products plenty of flavor, and ever-improving technology that supported mass production of food resulted in more and cheaper products almost anyone could afford.

Food historians date the beginning of today's absolute explosion of convenience food products back to the 1980s and '90s, when an increase in government farm subsidies led to the overproduction of staple ingredients like wheat and corn. The abundance and easy availability of these and other crops, like soybeans, rice, and sugar, led food manufacturers to develop hundreds of new food products that gave consumers infinite choices at affordable prices. Coinciding with the development of so many new food products that required little more than opening and heating up a package was the arrival of the microwave oven.[15]

to find a single aisle in your supermarket that doesn't contain a wide selection of highly processed and refined food products loaded with added ingredients.

So what exactly is the allure of these questionable food products? In a word: convenience. Even though Americans eat most of their food at home, studies show we devote much less time to preparing fresh food than we did in the past.[16] Researchers say we rely more often on packaged and convenience foods because they're readily available and we believe they are quicker and easier to fix compared to their fresh food counterparts. Bottom line: We're eating less real, whole food and more fake, processed food products. If you need proof, a quick survey of our food-buying habits reveals an interesting story.

The average American household spends about half its total food budget on fast-food and sit-down restaurants, and more than a quarter of its food budget on convenient fast-food products to eat at home, like ready-to-cook and ready-to-eat refrigerated, frozen, and shelf-stable meals and snacks.[17] When you stop and think about it, this is hardly surprising. So many of the products found in the typical sprawling grocery store are so "unreal," they don't even come close to resembling the food they were made from; they are certainly not natural foods.

The funny thing is that most highly processed foods started as real foods that were then mechanically broken down, reshaped, colored, texturized, flavored, and often dehydrated or mixed with extra salt, sugar, or fat. All that before they were chemically preserved and canned, bottled, boxed, or otherwise packaged in ways that allow them to sit in a factory or food store for an extended time until they are purchased. Aside from color and perhaps flavor, strawberry jelly doesn't look anything like the berry it begins with, and it certainly doesn't provide the same nutrients or health benefits. Even the best of cheese powders in a box of mac and cheese hardly resembles a wholesome chunk of Cheddar. It kind of begs the question: Why not stick with the original product? Why not top your toast with fresh sliced strawberries? Why not grate real Cheddar cheese over whole grain macaroni?

Do you fear your wallet will take a hit if you make some of these changes?[18] This may come as a surprise to you since organic and specialized "health" foods often cost more than conventionally produced foods, but a study reported in the professional journal *Family Medicine* revealed that, overall, it is twice as expensive to eat a convenience food diet, especially if you include eating out at fast-food restaurants.[19] The researchers found that the relative cost of a whole food diet was 18 percent of total income, while a convenience food diet ate up a whopping 37 percent, or more than one-third, of income. That's $18 out of every $100 of income spent on a real-food diet versus $37 out of every $100 of income spent on a fast-food diet!

HOW HIGHLY PROCESSED FOODS HARM: THE DISEASE OF CONVENIENCE

So what has been the real impact of the explosive growth of the highly processed foods industry? Alongside the shift in American eating habits that rely on so many pre-prepped and ready-cooked foods,[20] our tastes have changed, too. As a nation, our palates have adjusted to the taste of salty, sugary, fatty, processed foods, and the idea of real, whole, natural foods has become less and less appealing to us. To meet consumer demand, not only have more convenience foods appeared in our supermarkets, but fast-food chains have spread quickly across the country and around the world. In general, the growing appeal of highly processed food requires that good nutrition plays less and less of a role in our food choices.

However, when we examine the result of such compromised food choices, we can begin to see the folly of our ways, so to speak. Poor eating habits and highly processed, fake foods have contributed to an epidemic of obesity that is linked to many health problems.[21, 22] Links between commonly used commercial food additives and chronic health conditions are currently being studied. For instance, researchers speculate that the rise in gastrointestinal, neurological, and other autoimmune diseases is associated with the increased use of salts, sugars, gluten, emulsifiers, solvents, and other industrial products that are often added to commercially produced foods.[23]

As health experts and consumers alike begin to recognize and experience the devastating effects of an unreal diet,[24] we realize we must return to minimally processed, real foods if we want to save ourselves from the crippling effects of obesity and chronic disease. Let's take a closer look at the top diet-related health threats, if you need more convincing.

Metabolic Syndrome

Diet-related conditions such as abdominal obesity, high blood sugar, elevated blood pressure, insulin resistance, high blood triglycerides (fats), and low HDL cholesterol (the healthy form of cholesterol) come with very serious health risks. If you develop three or more of these disorders, you have what doctors call insulin resistance syndrome, or metabolic syndrome,[25] so named because this condition disrupts the metabolic process, or the way your body breaks down food and converts it to energy. The more of these factors you have, the

higher your risk of developing diabetes, coronary heart disease, or stroke.

The symptoms and conditions associated with metabolic syndrome are considered "lifestyle factors" that, to a large degree, can be prevented or managed by making wise day-to-day decisions, like choosing to eat healthy whole foods and getting enough exercise. In fact, a study published in the American Heart Association's journal, *Circulation*,[26] examined the role of the typical American fast-food diet as it relates to metabolic syndrome and concluded that the excess calories from fats and sugars in "junk food" cause inflammation that is associated with obesity, insulin resistance, and other markers of metabolic syndrome.

The Cancer Connection

A review of studies published in the journal *Anticancer Research* concluded that the typical American, or Western, diet—too high in salt, sugar, animal protein, and processed foods and, at the same time, too low in fiber and other important nutrients found in whole grains, beans, seeds, and fresh fruits and vegetables—can put you at higher risk of developing cancer.[27] According to these researchers, being overweight or obese is also a risk factor.[28]

Excess weight is not only associated with the development of cancer but also puts you at higher risk of dying from the disease once it is established. In fact, studies show that diet and obesity are responsible for approximately one-third of all cancer-related deaths in the United States. According to research from the American

Cancer Society, weight loss could prevent 90,000 cancer deaths each year in this country.[29] Weight control, healthy food choices, and physical activity are all associated with reducing the risk of breast, colon, rectal, mouth, esophageal, pharynx, and larynx cancers.[30]

Several commonly used food additives, particularly salts used in food processing, are known to cause cancer in laboratory animals and humans, especially with long-term use. Processed meats, salted fish and vegetables, and overuse of table salt are all linked to cancer of the stomach and gastrointestinal tract. Researchers found that the more salt in the diet, the higher the risk of developing gastric cancers.[31] At the same time, diets with less salt and more fresh fruits and vegetables are associated with reduced rates of gastrointestinal cancers around the world.[32]

The Fire That Burns Within

Inflammation—what you may recognize as pain, swelling, and reddening of the skin—is triggered by your immune system to protect your body against injury or invaders, such as viruses and allergens. You may think of inflammation as a problem mostly associated with skin disorders, asthma, allergies, and joint conditions such as arthritis, but inflammation affects many internal organs and bodily processes. In fact, medical researchers now think that inflammation underlies most chronic diseases, including some of the major causes of premature death: heart disease, diabetes, and cancer.[33] Researchers have also discovered that a diet rich in omega-3 fats found in oily fish, and

certain chemicals found in nonstarchy, deeply colored vegetables, can help treat and prevent inflammation.[34] Flaxseeds, walnuts, and green leafy vegetables also contain fatty acids that are converted to omega-3s in your body, potentially conveying the same protection as fish oils.[35]

Boning Up

News headlines tend to focus on chronic diseases that can directly lead to early death, such as heart disease, diabetes, and cancer, so it's easy to forget about the role of a healthy, whole-food diet in managing your everyday health and preventing or managing debilitating conditions like bone-thinning osteoporosis and other age-related medical problems that may not kill you but can make life very difficult.

One study of elderly Chinese men and women, published in the journal *Osteoporosis International*, found that the more deeply colored fruits, vegetables, or combination of fruits and veggies the men and women ate, the lower their risk of hip fractures due to osteoporosis.[36] Women specifically benefited from eating more vegetables, while men appeared to benefit more from eating both fruits and vegetables. Researchers who reviewed several related studies confirmed the link between mineral-rich fruits and veggies and bone health.[37] Some of these studies singled out dried plums, or prunes, as especially beneficial in preventing and possibly reversing osteopenia, or low bone density that can lead to osteoporosis.[38] The researchers found that dried plums not only help prevent bone loss but also increase new bone formation.

PROCESSED FOODS:
WHAT YOU LOSE FROM WHOLE FOODS

Some global health experts are so concerned about the effects of highly processed foods and beverages on your health that they lump these products with tobacco and alcohol and view them all together as "unhealthy commodities" that can lead to chronic disease.[39] The sky is the limit for the number of convenience food products available in food markets today, and the number only seems to be climbing, so it's up to you to navigate your food choices carefully. The more you understand about the detrimental effects of processing on your food and your health, the better equipped you are to make those choices.

Let's start by taking a closer look at exactly what happens when a whole food is transformed into a processed food product. In a nutshell, many of the methods manufacturers use in cooking or preserving involve exposing foods to heat, light, oxygen, milling, extruding, and other processing techniques that degrade the beneficial nutrients found in whole and minimally processed foods.[40, 41] In contrast, a diet filled with whole, fresh foods is naturally abundant in the crucial vitamins and minerals your body needs to thrive, as well as the special compounds known as phytochemicals that only plant-based foods can provide.

Consider one study among many that looked at the effect of heat processing on the phytochemical levels in kale, spinach, cabbage, and shallots. Just 1 minute of heat processing significantly decreased the total amount of beneficial compounds available in these vegetables.[42] Another study found similar losses when blueberries, which are rich in a type of compound known as anthocyanins, were processed to make blueberry juice.[43] The researchers pressed frozen blueberries and separated the juice from the pulp in order to measure the amount of these phytochemicals in the juice and the amount that remained behind in the berry pulp. Less than one-third of the anthocyanins made it to the juice. While some of the other phytochemicals remained in the pulp, significant amounts were simply lost in the processing.

Something else that's often lost when whole foods become highly processed is fiber.[44] Even though fiber isn't technically a nutrient, it may well be one of the most important dietary benefits we receive from fresh fruits, vegetables, and other plant foods.[45] Once known as roughage and thought to be most useful for preventing constipation, food scientists now know that dietary fiber not only moves food through your intestinal tract but also helps control blood sugar and blood fats, which in turn helps prevent and manage type 2 diabetes and heart disease.[46] Beyond these benefits, researchers also have reason to believe that some dietary fibers play a role in mental health and the immune system by maintaining a balance of beneficial bacteria that live in your intestinal tract.[47]

Of course, thus far we've only covered what

nutrients are lost when whole foods are transformed into highly processed food products. Food manufacturers also rely on a slew of chemical additives to achieve consistent flavor, texture, and shelf life in the products they create. Let's take a closer look at what happens when those other hard-to-pronounce ingredients are added to the mix.

ABOUT THOSE ADDITIVES

What comes to mind when you hear the words *food additive*? You might immediately think about artificial colorings and flavors, preservatives, flavor enhancers, thickeners, anti-caking ingredients, and the like. And while those are certainly some questionable additives, some of the most harmful come in the form of added fats, sugars, and salts. When researchers looked at the food purchases of more than 157,000 American households to determine which foods provided the most calories, they found that more than 60 percent of calories came from highly processed foods and more than 15 percent came from moderately processed foods. Altogether, that's more than three-fourths of each family's total calories coming from convenience food products. More than half the families studied were bringing home enough processed foods and beverages to exceed the recommended daily limits for calories, saturated fats, sugar, and sodium.[48]

Real food contains only naturally occurring sugars, and preparing food at home from "real" ingredients means you can control the amount of extra sugar you eat. Many convenience foods and beverages, on the other hand, arrive on your plate already loaded with added sugars in amounts you can't control. And all that extra sugar can add up quickly and impact your health. In one study of more than 91,000 women, those who drank one or more servings of sugar-sweetened sodas or fruit punch a day were at twice the risk of developing diabetes as those who drank less than one serving per month.[49]

Real foods contain naturally occurring fats that may either be potentially helpful or potentially harmful to your health. You may already know, for instance, that red meat and full-fat dairy products are high in saturated fats, and that excess saturated fat in the diet could contribute over time to higher blood cholesterol levels, clogged arteries, fatty liver, and even some forms of cancer.[50, 51, 52] You probably also know that olive oil, which is rich in monounsaturated fats, may help keep your blood sugar steady, does not significantly increase cholesterol levels, and reduces your risk of heart disease, stroke, and premature death.[53, 54]

Many highly processed foods, on the other hand, contain unnaturally hydrogenated, or hardened, oils, sometimes called trans fats, which have only recently been recognized as unsafe by the FDA. And even as processed food manufacturers are removing hydrogenated fats from their products, they are investigating the use of replacement fat products that would serve the same purpose as hydrogenated fats,

Sugar ID

The food industry relies on sugar—in various forms—the same way you use it at home: to sweeten, enhance flavor, improve texture and color, act as a preservative, produce alcohol, feed yeast in baked goods, and provide balance in acidic products, such as a tomato sauce, lemonade, or vinegar-based dressing. Unfortunately, the food industry abuses sugar's sweetening power. There's just too much sugar added to too many foods and beverages.

You're probably familiar with the sugars most often used in home cooking: white table sugar (granulated and processed raw sugar, or sucrose), brown sugar (white sugar with added molasses, natural flavor, and color), 10X or confectioners' sugar (finely powdered table sugar), honey (sweetener produced by bees that is mostly sucrose), molasses (the thick brown syrup that remains after table sugar is processed), and maple syrup (the sweet, concentrated and purified sap of a sugar maple tree that is also mostly sucrose). But you may not know much about sweeteners commonly used in commercial food processing:[55]

Corn syrup is a thick liquid sweetener made from cornstarch that has been treated with acid, enzymes, and heat. When it is dehydrated, corn syrup is called corn syrup solids.

Dextrose is another commercial name that manufacturers use for sucrose, which you probably know better as white table sugar.

HFCS, or high-fructose corn syrup, is an inexpensive sweetener made from cornstarch that manufacturers use in processed foods and beverages. Similar to regular corn syrup, HFCS is refined to be even sweeter.

Invert sugar is a liquid sweetener made from regular white sugar. It is used to help preserve foods and prevent shrinkage.

Raw sugar is not as highly refined as regular white table sugar; however, several processing steps ensure it is free from dirt, insect fragments, and other debris found in truly raw sugar.

Turbinado sugar is processed in the same way as regular white table sugar, but without the bleaching and anti-caking steps used to produce table sugar.

chiefly to maintain a solid or semisolid form at room temperature in foods like margarine and baked goods. One type of processed fat under consideration is interesterified fat, produced by rearranging the fatty acids in a fat molecule. Although technically these are considered nontrans fats, some researchers are concerned because the long-term effects of interesterified fats on health and nutrition are unknown.[56, 57, 58]

While real foods also contain safe and natural amounts of sodium, highly processed fast foods and convenience foods are notorious for their sky-high levels.[59] Food manufacturers use sodium, in one form or another, to enhance the flavor of their products and act as a preservative. The fact that there is so much salt in so many highly processed foods can be a serious problem for anyone with concerns about high blood pressure, heart disease, kidney disease, or even bone health, since dietary sodium is associated with all of these conditions.[60, 61] Once again, when you choose mostly whole, minimally processed foods and prepare them in your own kitchen, you have control over the amount of sodium in your diet, which is helpful if you want to increase your chances of staying healthy.

Besides the excess sugar, fats, and salt added to so many processed foods, as well as the nutrients that are often removed along the way, any discussion of real versus highly processed food must also consider both the natural and synthetic additives that manufacturers use to change the look, feel, and flavor of their products and allow them to sit unspoiled on supermarket shelves for indefinite periods of time. These would be those mostly unfamiliar names you see at the end of that long string of ingredients listed on many packaged foods.

From time to time, an article surfaces on the Internet that reads "your inability to pronounce a chemical ingredient is not an argument against it." And this statement is absolutely true.

Everything that exists in this physical world has a chemical name; most are difficult to pronounce; and they're not all scary or dangerous. Sometimes the chemical name you read on a food label is an added nutrient. And many additives with chemical or otherwise unfamiliar names are derived from natural sources. Most food additives approved by the FDA are considered safe for most healthy people to eat.

But when a package of frozen fries contains not only the potatoes, vegetable oil, and salt you might use to make them yourself, but also ingredients like dextrose, disodium dihydrogen pyrophosphate, and annatto, it's wise to consider exactly what those additives are. There are potential problems with all additives. Dextrose is an easily absorbed form of sugar that quickly raises your blood sugar levels, which is why it is used to treat hypoglycemia, a condition that poses the risk of dangerously low blood sugar.[62] Disodium dihydrogen pyrophosphate is a common preservative used in meat and vegetable products that, in this case, helps maintain the natural color of the potato while it is in a frozen state. It is a chemical compound made up of sodium and phosphorus, both of which are on the "watch list" of substances to avoid for people with kidney disease, who may need to limit these minerals in their diets.[63] Annatto is another commonly used additive that adds mild seasoning and orange-red color to foods. It may be the least worrisome of the three because it's a natural product, yet it has been known to cause rare but severe allergic reactions in some people. So, while it is an approved additive, it is by no means a completely safe substance, especially for anyone with other known allergies.[64, 65]

If you're looking for a definitive list of additives to avoid, you'd need a separate book to cover all that information. That's one more reason to consider sticking to real food as much as possible—it is simply the safer alternative. However, we've compiled a list of some of the most common food additives you may find on a food label. Here's what to avoid and why:

Aspartame. An artificial sweetener found in "diet" or "sugar-free" products such as diet soda, sugar-free gum, sugar-free desserts, chewable vitamins, cough syrup, toothpaste, and even cereal. Aspartame, along with other artificial sweeteners, has been associated with health problems such as obesity, headaches, and some types of cancer. Mounting research also suggests that artificial sweeteners can lead to an unhealthy balance of bad to good bacteria in our guts, which may affect many other bodily functions, from metabolism to mood.

BHA and BHT. Preservatives found in potato chips, gum, cereal, frozen sausages, enriched rice, lard, shortening, candy, and Jell-O. These are manufactured from petroleum, and the National Institutes of Health reports that, based on animal studies, BHA is a likely human carcinogen; BHT has been linked to cancer to a lesser degree. The FDA considers BHA, which keeps fats from spoiling and is commonly found in potato chips and butter, to be generally regarded as safe. But while low doses may be fine, it's easy to find chips and butter that don't contain BHA, so why mess around?

Brominated vegetable oil (BVO). Safety concerns surrounding this emulsifier, historically used in fruit-flavored sodas and sports drinks, first emerged more than 5 decades ago after scientists linked it to heart and liver damage as well as impaired development. The FDA removed its "generally regarded as safe" status in 1970 but allowed companies to continue using it on an interim basis, pending additional study. Guess what? BVO is still an "interim-allowed" additive in the United States, even though it has since been banned in Europe and Japan. After some intense public shaming, both Coca-Cola and Pepsi agreed to remove BVO from all of their drinks, but it can still be found in many beverages.

Food dyes: blue #1 and #2, red #3 and #40, yellow #5 (tartrazine) and #6. Artificial colors found in fruit cocktail, maraschino cherries, ice cream, candy, baked goods, American cheese, macaroni and cheese, and more. Several of these petroleum-based dyes have been linked to hyperactivity in children and cancer in lab animals.

Monosodium glutamate (MSG). A flavor enhancer found in some Chinese food, potato chips, snacks, cookies, seasonings, canned soup, frozen meals, and lunchmeats. The additive is a common migraine trigger and goes hand in hand with high amounts of sodium—it's 21 percent sodium itself.

Mycoprotein. Though the makers of Quorn, a brand of fake meats popular with vegetarians around the world, claim that its star ingredient—mycoprotein—is a form of mushroom protein, the Center for Science in the Public Interest (CSPI) revealed that it's actually made from a processed mold that does not produce mushrooms, and which may cause "serious and even fatal allergic reactions." In one study, the CSPI found that there are probably more consumers with sensitivities to mycoprotein than there are to other common allergens, like milk or peanuts.

Potassium bromate. A flour-bulking agent found in breads and rolls, bagel chips, wraps, and bread crumbs. An oxidizing agent, it's used to strengthen dough and shorten baking time, but it may cause kidney or nervous system disorders and gastrointestinal discomfort.

Overseeing Additives

The Food and Drug Administration (FDA) falls under the control of the US Department of Health and Human Services and is responsible for the safety of all food processed and sold in US interstate commerce, except for meat, poultry, and eggs, which are the responsibility of the US Department of Agriculture. The FDA also inspects food plants and imported foods, and sets standards for food product ingredients and package labeling. For the most part, we must depend on these government agencies to ensure the safety of all our food, both fresh and processed.

When it comes to food additives, the FDA is responsible for approving both natural and artificial ingredients that are added to commercially processed foods. FDA regulators cannot be completely sure that a food additive is risk-free, so in order to grant approval, they review scientific evidence to determine with "reasonable certainty" that any chemical ingredient or other substance added to a food product will not harm consumers.[66]

Food scientists and health and medical professionals sometimes challenge the reliability of the FDA's testing methods, and they routinely make recommendations for improvement.[67] These experts have questioned the FDA's definition of "harm" and point out that many people, depending on their individual eating habits, health status, and sensitivity to both natural and synthetic substances, are more susceptible than others to experiencing side effects from food additives. Some experts believe that the FDA's current assessment tools may not be able to detect the subtle effects of chemical additives on the human nervous system or immune system, and that the animal studies used to determine safety do not sufficiently reflect human eating patterns. They continue to encourage the FDA to self-evaluate, develop more sensitive and reliable tests, and take advantage of modern technology to assess the safety of both new and some previously approved food additives.

Sodium nitrate. A synthetic preservative found in processed meats like hot dogs, lunchmeats, bacon, and smoked fish. Some animal research suggests that it morphs into carcinogenic compounds in the body, but that's still under debate. Natural sodium nitrates in the form of celery powder, found in many "uncured" meat products, may be safer.

Sulfites. Preservatives and flavor enhancers found naturally in wine and beer and added to soft drinks, juice, dried fruit, condiments, and potato products. The FDA estimates that about 10 percent of the population is sensitive to these sulfur-based compounds, with reactions ranging from mild hay fever–like symptoms to life-threatening anaphylaxis.

Tragacanth gum. Gums are used as thickeners and stabilizers, and they're omnipresent in packaged foods. Created from natural elements found in bushes, trees, and seaweed, they are not absorbed by the body and most of them are probably safe. However, the CSPI points out that they haven't been thoroughly tested, and some alarm bells have been raised—tragacanth gum, in particular, can cause severe allergic reactions.

It's clear that the food choices we face are fraught with challenges. But the good news is that the natural food world provides a rich variety of options. In the next chapter, we'll take a closer look to see exactly how you can turn to Mother Nature's market basket to find all the nutrients you need for optimal health.

CHAPTER 2

REAL FOOD BASICS

True or False: You are what you eat.

Would it surprise you to learn that the answer is a bit complicated? On the one hand, you're obviously not a meatball, a mango, or a bowl of mac and cheese. Those are simply delicious foods you like to eat. But just like those foods, it's true that you are a mix of protein, carbohydrates, fats, vitamins, minerals, and water. It's all there in your body—protein in your muscles; a layer of fat under your skin; vitamins, minerals, various chemicals, and water running through your bloodstream—just as it is in your food. So in that sense, you are pretty much what you eat.

It is well established that, for optimal health, you need to eat a great variety of foods every day, not just for energy, but also for nutrients that keep you healthy and fighting off chronic disease. That means eating from every food group in a variety of forms—both raw and cooked, liquid and solid. For your body to function optimally, you need many different vitamins, minerals, phytochemicals, fibers, and enzymes. And the only way to get these essential nutrients in their natural form—the form your body uses best—is to eat real food.

Of course, real food doesn't come with an ingredient list on its package, and in many cases, it doesn't come in a package at all. Fresh apples, oranges, tomatoes, peppers, mangoes, and broccoli are real because they are whole, unadulterated foods that still contain all their original vitamins and minerals. So how do you know you're getting the right mix of nutrients your body needs? There are several ways to approach this question, so we'll break it down for you and make all the nutrition information you need easier to digest.

NUTRITION 101

Let's start with a quick overview of the information you'll probably recall from that high school health class you took long ago. There are three basic "macronutrient" categories: carbohydrates, proteins, and fats. These are essentially the calorie-dense elements of your food. In a

Anti-What?

With all the nutrition terminology that gets tossed around, it's easy to forget (if you ever really knew) the meaning of some commonly used words like *antioxidant,* which is any substance in food—vitamin, mineral, phytochemical—that protects body cells from oxidative damage. Specifically, an antioxidant puts a stop to normal reactions in your body that can, over time, cause disease. These reactions are called oxidation, and sometimes they produce dangerous molecules known as free radicals that can accelerate cell damage. Antioxidants step in, neutralize free radicals, and significantly decrease the damage that normally occurs. Foods bursting with antioxidants include berries, apples, red grapes, beets, broccoli, cabbage, dark green leafy vegetables, onions, tomatoes, winter squash, green tea, and dark chocolate.

nutshell, your body uses carbohydrates for energy; proteins to grow and repair body parts; and fats to help keep your brain and nerve cells functioning properly, to keep your skin and hair from getting dry and drab, and to help you to absorb fat-soluble vitamins.

Let's go another level deeper, though, to review how the health benefits you get from real foods extend beyond these macronutrients. Real foods contain vitamins and minerals as well as a slew of phytochemicals, which are active substances found only in plant foods. These are known as micronutrients, and these nutritional powerhouses are vital for good health[1] because they may help reduce your risk of developing diabetes, heart disease, some cancers, cataracts, and other age-related and chronic medical conditions.[2] Researchers have identified thousands of different phytochemicals and believe their key benefit is not only related to the special mix of them found in each food, but also the unique synergy that takes place between the phytochemicals and other nutrients in other food.[3]

In other words, when you eat vitamin-, mineral-, and phytochemical-rich whole, fresh fruits, vegetables, grains, legumes, and even nuts, you get a complete nutritional package. Let's take a closer look at the type of real foods you should eat, as well as the food imposters lurking in those grocery aisles, to get a clearer picture.

Focus on the Right Fats

Some dietary fats appear to be better for your health than others, though which ones are the good guys and which are the bad is sometimes hotly debated. All fats make food more flavorful. Fat also helps you feel satisfied after a meal, helps produce hormones, and enables the absorption of fat-soluble vitamins, like D and E. So you need to include some fat in your diet in order to stay healthy. But *some* doesn't mean *a lot,* because too much fat in your diet can ultimately mean too much fat in your bloodstream, leading to health problems like obesity, heart disease, and diabetes.[4]

Major health organizations such as the American Heart Association recommend limiting your saturated fat intake to no more than 5 to 6 percent of total calories. Therefore, if you need about 2,000 calories a day, no more than 120 of them should come from saturated fat, about 13 grams per day, for example, 3 ounces of cooked sirloin steak and 1 tablespoon butter.

When choosing oils, select those with the terms cold-pressed and/or expeller-pressed on their bottles. Cold-pressed oils are pressed at low temperatures, which means they retain all the flavors, aromas, and nutrients that would otherwise be destroyed by heat. Expeller-pressing is another clean way of producing oil: It means that oil was extracted mechanically (i.e., good old-fashioned squeezing) instead of chemically.

It's also worth noting why real foods that are naturally lower in fat are a better choice than foods that have been processed to reduce their fat content. Since the low-fat fad began, Americans have become fatter and sicker. One reason? In most low-fat products, added sugar takes the place of fat, and eating these products can ultimately make you feel hungry and unsatisfied. Further, the types of fats that are removed are sometimes the beneficial ones. For example, many low-fat dairy products have been stripped of conjugated linoleic acid, a healthy fat shown to fight weight gain and cancer. This is just one more reason why it's important to know your fats.

Likewise, as we covered in the previous chapter, industrial fats like partially hydrogenated oils are dangerous. However, monounsaturated fats like olive oil, as well as fat from organic, grass-fed animal products like yogurt, can benefit your heart and brain. In the next section, we'll cover more reasons why meat and dairy products could be healthier choices than you may have been led to believe.

Make the Most of Meats and Dairy Products

Animal products play an important role in a real food meal plan because they contribute important nutrients to the diet. Some of these nutrients, like iron, selenium, vitamin B_{12}, and folate, are not as readily available from plant foods.[5] And plenty of quick and easy-to-cook options exist. Turkey drumsticks, boneless chicken breasts, sirloin steak, peeled and deveined shrimp, and salmon fillets are all examples of real, natural, whole foods that have simply been cut or trimmed for your convenience. Unlike hot dogs, deli-style cold cuts, and other highly processed meat products that have been clearly linked to an increased risk of certain cancers such as colorectal, bladder, and breast,[6, 7, 8] there's no evidence that fresh lean meat, poultry, and seafood, if properly handled and eaten in reasonable amounts, carry any additional risk to your health.

In a study published in the American Heart Association journal *Circulation,* researchers further clarified the effects of meat and processed meats on health by closely examining the scientific literature that linked meat with higher rates of heart disease and type 2 diabetes. After narrowing down more than 1,500 studies, they found 20 well-designed reports that separated the findings for red meat and processed meats. The researchers concluded that there is no link between red meat and heart disease or type 2 diabetes, but that processed meats are associated with a 42 percent higher risk of heart disease and a 19 percent higher risk of type 2 diabetes.[9]

Another study of kidney patients on dialysis found that processed meats, like sausage and ham, significantly raised the risk of high blood pressure.[10] The increased risk was due in part to the high sodium content of these cured meats.

So what is a reasonable amount of real meat in a healthy diet, anyway? The American Heart Association says up to 6 ounces a day of lean meat, poultry, or fish.[11] That's the equivalent of one large or two small servings. The American Cancer Society recommends sticking to lean cuts of meat and smaller portion sizes. They also point out that commonplace salting and smoking methods used in making processed meat products can add potentially cancer-causing compounds to the meat.[12] Maybe it's time to switch off those nacho-flavored meat sticks for a handful of mini carrot sticks!

As for dairy products, this food group offers one of the richest sources of calcium and, when fortified, one of the few good food sources of vitamin D. Like meat, poultry, and fish, low-fat dairy products are also a good source of animal protein. While it's a good idea to use the "all things in moderation" philosophy when it comes to dairy, excellent choices include grass-fed Greek yogurt, milk, and cheeses. If dairy products leave you with an upset stomach or feeling gassy, you may be among the 25 percent of the population who has trouble digesting a sugar found in milk called lactose; look for products labeled lactose-free instead.

Discover the Bean Scene

Legumes—beans, lentils, and peas—are an excellent source of plant protein. And why would you be looking for plant protein? Maybe you are a vegetarian, or you feed a vegetarian, or you just want to cut back on some of the animal protein in your diet. In any case, you need protein every day, and legumes like black beans; kidney beans; pinto beans; chickpeas; green, red, black, or brown lentils; and green or yellow split peas are all excellent choices. Not only do legumes contribute high-quality protein to your diet, but they also provide fiber and phytochemicals that protect against chronic diseases.[13] And if you need another reason to choose legumes to your meals? They are as fast as opening a can or pouch.

Just as it is a good idea to enjoy a wide variety of foods, it is a good idea to mix up the legumes in your diet, too, to get the most benefit. While all legumes supply many of the same essential nutrients, some offer distinct

Feed Your Gut Bugs

A very special community of bacteria and other microorganisms, collectively known as the *microbiota,* lives in your gastrointestinal tract. And that's okay—they're supposed to be there! These "good bacteria" help you digest and metabolize your food, and generally keep your gastrointestinal tract working properly. They even produce nutrients, like the B vitamins, folate, and vitamin K.[14]

Fermented foods like yogurt, kefir, fresh sauerkraut, kimchi, and some aged cheeses contain probiotics, also referred to as live cultures, that are similar to those good bugs in your gut. Eating foods rich in probiotics helps maintain a healthy balance of microbiota. Other foods, like asparagus, bananas, onions, garlic, soybeans, and whole wheat, contain *prebiotics,* substances that nourish probiotics. Together, prebiotics and probiotics, along with your natural gut bacteria, not only help maintain your gut health but may also support your immune system and your overall health, according to researchers.[15]

Researchers have also found reason to believe that eating fermented foods and beverages to maintain a balanced, healthy microbiota has a positive effect on your brain and your mental health.[16] In one small study, participants ate fermented dairy products while another group did not, and then researchers measured the two groups and found notable differences in the brain activity that controls emotion and sensation.[17] In a review of numerous animal and human studies where subjects were given fermented foods, or probiotics similar to those found in fermented foods, researchers repeatedly documented reduced anxiety, depression, and fatigue.[18]

advantages. For instance, chickpeas stand out in the bean crowd for their especially high-quality protein,[19] while black beans lead for having the most flavonols and saponins, phytochemicals that protect your heart and inhibit the growth of cancer cells.[20] One study found that lentils, which offer another type of phytochemical known as phenolic compounds, control enzymes that play a role in fat and sugar digestion, potentially helping to manage both blood sugar and weight.[21] In addition to cholesterol-lowering, antioxidant, and anticancer substances, split peas contain prebiotic nondigestible substances (known by their scientific name as galacto-oligosaccharides) that help maintain the right balance of beneficial bacteria in your colon, or large intestine.[22]

Get Your Guac On!

It turns out that guacamole—yes, guacamole!—can help keep you healthy and reduce your risk of developing some serious medical conditions. Studies published in the *Nutrition Journal*[23] and the *Journal of Agricultural and Food Chemistry*[24] found that avocados, the main ingredient in guacamole, are not only rich in heart-protective monounsaturated fats, fiber, and vitamin E, but they're also loaded with phytochemicals such as lutein and zeaxanthin, which help protect your eyes against age-related macular degeneration,[25] and phytosterols, which reduce the absorption of heart-stopping LDL cholesterol into your bloodstream.[26] As if that's not enough, these researchers also found that avocado eaters are 50 percent less likely than non-eaters to develop metabolic syndrome, a group of medical conditions and symptoms, including high blood fats, high blood pressure, and insulin resistance, that significantly increase the risk of developing diabetes, heart disease, kidney disease, and stroke when they occur together.[27] And to keep it real (and real healthy), just be sure to scoop up your guac with real food dippers like carrot, bell pepper, and celery sticks, and broccoli and cauliflower florets, or spread your avocado mash on whole grain toast.

FRUITS AND VEGETABLES: SUPER REAL FOODS

There's a good reason why foods like pomegranates, dark leafy greens, blueberries, nuts, and avocados make headlines for being "superfoods." It's because they are super-high in essential nutrients and powerful phytochemicals that can protect you from developing high blood pressure, heart disease, cancers, and other medical conditions often associated with aging.

If you've been sipping on pomegranate juice, or sprinkling the fruit's juicy, ruby-red seedpods on your salads, cereals, or yogurt, you may already enjoy some antioxidant-related health benefits that researchers have been delving into for years.[28] Many studies have confirmed that pomegranates prevent the oxidation, or corrosion, of LDL cholesterol in the bloodstream that leads to plaque buildup in the arteries and, ultimately, heart disease.[29] Some newer studies suggest that pomegranates might also help reduce inflammation in the joints that leads to osteoarthritis,[30] while others show that pomegranate has antiviral capabilities that could protect you against herpes, influenza, and other viral illnesses, including strains of norovirus and other forms of food poisoning.[31] That's a lot of healing potential in one small piece of fruit!

Though some of the fruits you may already enjoy might not be as exotic as pomegranates, they are equally powerful sources of protective phytochemicals. Food scientists have discovered that apples, oranges, plums, and strawberries are among the top sources of antioxidants in the American diet.[32] Yes, these common fruits that you may take for granted contain substances powerful enough to fight cancer, heart disease, and other chronic medical conditions.

And let's not forget the super-veggies! Vegetables not only provide essential vitamins and minerals, but they are also excellent sources of phytochemicals. In particular, cruciferous vegetables—broccoli, cauliflower, cabbage, and Brussels sprouts—contain higher than average amounts of glucosinolates, phytochemicals that researchers suspect are powerful warriors in the fight against colorectal, lung, prostate, and breast cancers.[33, 34]

When you choose leafy greens for a salad, soup, or sandwich filling, darker is better because, generally, the darker the leaf, the more phytochemicals and antioxidants it contains. That's why, even though all greens are good greens, kale, spinach, collards, and watercress lead the pack. But that's not the only reason to include a variety of leafy green vegetables in your diet every day. Though their nutritional values vary slightly from green to green, these nutrient storehouses are all loaded with vitamin A (in the form of beta-carotene) to help prevent cancer, vitamin C to step up your immune system, vitamin K to protect your bones and reduce inflammation, and several B vitamins, including folate, which help prevent birth defects and protects heart health.[35]

What Does "Multigrain" Mean on a Food Label?

If one grain is good, "multi" grains must be better, right? Yes, except when all those multigrains are just multiple versions of unhealthy refined grains. And that could be what you're getting when you reach for a loaf of multigrain bread. The FDA has never explicitly stated that anything labeled "multigrain" must contain the whole version of all grains that are used, and food marketers like to use the claim on wheat products because it makes their products seem healthier than they are.

However, "multigrain" isn't always bad; some companies do in fact use whole grains in multigrain breads, cereals, and other baked goods. It just means you must read the ingredient list and make sure the word "whole" precedes every grain listed. Or look for the "100% whole grain" claim. That phrase is regulated by the FDA and would mean that all grains used in the product are whole.

THE GRAIN, THE WHOLE GRAIN, AND NOTHING BUT THE GRAIN

Whole grain foods like quinoa, oats, barley, and bulgur are important sources of dietary fiber. One study showed that eating just three servings, or 48 grams, of whole grain foods each day can reduce your risk of developing several forms of heart disease—including both clogged arteries and stroke—by reducing your blood pressure and blood cholesterol levels. Diets rich in whole grain foods have also been shown to reduce inflammation and improve insulin sensitivity when compared to diets high in processed and refined foods.[36] Researchers have also found that people who eat between three and five servings, or 48 to 80 grams, of whole grain each day are less likely to gain weight.[37]

The results of the Iowa Women's Health Study, a large research study that has followed more than 35,000 women for decades, suggest that you may live longer if you eat fiber from whole grain rather than from refined grain products.[38] When the researchers reviewed the diet records of more than 11,000 postmenopausal women, they found a 17 percent lower rate of death in those who consumed more whole grain fiber than refined grain fiber. Another review of studies investigating the connection between grain foods and diabetes found that a diet high in whole grains and brown rice, but not refined grains or white rice, can help reduce the risk of developing type 2 diabetes.[39] The researchers found similar results when they looked at the relationship between whole grains

and refined grains in the diet and the risk of developing heart disease or cancer, or dying prematurely from any cause.[40] They concluded that eating more whole grains and fewer refined grains reduces your likelihood of dying before your time, not only from heart disease, cancer, or diabetes, but also from respiratory illness or infectious disease.

One of the best reasons to ditch refined grain products and switch to whole grains is the specific phytochemical makeup of whole grains. Phytochemicals are especially concentrated in the bran, one of the outer layers of the grain kernel that is often lost in processing. Like avocados and other whole foods, wheat bran contains lutein and zeaxanthin,[41] phytochemicals that protect your eyesight. Bran is also closely associated with reducing your risk of heart disease, and while the fiber content of bran often gets the credit for this all to itself, researchers now suspect the protective effect may be due to interactions between fiber and phytochemicals.[42, 43]

One study concluded that the phytochemicals in whole grains work best in tandem with those found in fruits and vegetables.[44] So, all you have to do to reap optimal benefits is add a sliced banana or a handful of berries to your breakfast cereal, toss your multigrain pasta with chopped fresh tomatoes or chopped greens, and spread your sprouted wheat toast with mashed avocado or strawberries. Simple and delicious!

Though some of the fruits you may already enjoy might not be as exotic as pomegranates, they are equally powerful sources of protective phytochemicals. Food scientists have discovered that apples, oranges, plums, and strawberries are among the top sources of antioxidants in the American diet.[32] Yes, these common fruits that you may take for granted contain substances powerful enough to fight cancer, heart disease, and other chronic medical conditions.

And let's not forget the super-veggies! Vegetables not only provide essential vitamins and minerals, but they are also excellent sources of phytochemicals. In particular, cruciferous vegetables—broccoli, cauliflower, cabbage, and Brussels sprouts—contain higher than average amounts of glucosinolates, phytochemicals that researchers suspect are powerful warriors in the fight against colorectal, lung, prostate, and breast cancers.[33, 34]

When you choose leafy greens for a salad, soup, or sandwich filling, darker is better because, generally, the darker the leaf, the more phytochemicals and antioxidants it contains. That's why, even though all greens are good greens, kale, spinach, collards, and watercress lead the pack. But that's not the only reason to include a variety of leafy green vegetables in your diet every day. Though their nutritional values vary slightly from green to green, these nutrient storehouses are all loaded with vitamin A (in the form of beta-carotene) to help prevent cancer, vitamin C to step up your immune system, vitamin K to protect your bones and reduce inflammation, and several B vitamins, including folate, which help prevent birth defects and protects heart health.[35]

What Does "Multigrain" Mean on a Food Label?

If one grain is good, "multi" grains must be better, right? Yes, except when all those multigrains are just multiple versions of unhealthy refined grains. And that could be what you're getting when you reach for a loaf of multigrain bread. The FDA has never explicitly stated that anything labeled "multigrain" must contain the whole version of all grains that are used, and food marketers like to use the claim on wheat products because it makes their products seem healthier than they are.

However, "multigrain" isn't always bad; some companies do in fact use whole grains in multigrain breads, cereals, and other baked goods. It just means you must read the ingredient list and make sure the word "whole" precedes every grain listed. Or look for the "100% whole grain" claim. That phrase is regulated by the FDA and would mean that all grains used in the product are whole.

THE GRAIN, THE WHOLE GRAIN, AND NOTHING BUT THE GRAIN

Whole grain foods like quinoa, oats, barley, and bulgur are important sources of dietary fiber. One study showed that eating just three servings, or 48 grams, of whole grain foods each day can reduce your risk of developing several forms of heart disease—including both clogged arteries and stroke—by reducing your blood pressure and blood cholesterol levels. Diets rich in whole grain foods have also been shown to reduce inflammation and improve insulin sensitivity when compared to diets high in processed and refined foods.[36] Researchers have also found that people who eat between three and five servings, or 48 to 80 grams, of whole grain each day are less likely to gain weight.[37]

The results of the Iowa Women's Health Study, a large research study that has followed more than 35,000 women for decades, suggest that you may live longer if you eat fiber from whole grain rather than from refined grain products.[38] When the researchers reviewed the diet records of more than 11,000 postmenopausal women, they found a 17 percent lower rate of death in those who consumed more whole grain fiber than refined grain fiber. Another review of studies investigating the connection between grain foods and diabetes found that a diet high in whole grains and brown rice, but not refined grains or white rice, can help reduce the risk of developing type 2 diabetes.[39] The researchers found similar results when they looked at the relationship between whole grains

and refined grains in the diet and the risk of developing heart disease or cancer, or dying prematurely from any cause.[40] They concluded that eating more whole grains and fewer refined grains reduces your likelihood of dying before your time, not only from heart disease, cancer, or diabetes, but also from respiratory illness or infectious disease.

One of the best reasons to ditch refined grain products and switch to whole grains is the specific phytochemical makeup of whole grains. Phytochemicals are especially concentrated in the bran, one of the outer layers of the grain kernel that is often lost in processing. Like avocados and other whole foods, wheat bran contains lutein and zeaxanthin,[41] phytochemicals that protect your eyesight. Bran is also closely associated with reducing your risk of heart disease, and while the fiber content of bran often gets the credit for this all to itself, researchers now suspect the protective effect may be due to interactions between fiber and phytochemicals.[42, 43]

One study concluded that the phytochemicals in whole grains work best in tandem with those found in fruits and vegetables.[44] So, all you have to do to reap optimal benefits is add a sliced banana or a handful of berries to your breakfast cereal, toss your multigrain pasta with chopped fresh tomatoes or chopped greens, and spread your sprouted wheat toast with mashed avocado or strawberries. Simple and delicious!

Nutty Ideas

Nuts make a great, portable snack, but you can also add them to your diet in other ways. It doesn't matter which nuts you use, so choose your favorites and try some of these easy ways to add more nuts to your meals:

- Stir chopped nuts into hot and cold cereals.
- Sprinkle nuts over a salad or a plain vegetable side dish.
- Add nuts or nut butter to the blender the next time you make a smoothie.
- Top yogurt with nuts and dried or fresh fruit.
- Substitute ground nuts for half of the bread crumbs you normally use to coat chicken cutlets or fish fillets.
- Toss chopped nuts into a stir-fry or cheesy pasta dish.
- Grind nuts to a powdery meal, and use it in place of some of the flour called for in any recipe for muffins, quick breads, piecrusts, and other baked goods. Replace $\frac{1}{4}$ cup of each full cup of flour with this nut flour. So, if the recipe calls for 2 cups of flour, use $1\frac{1}{2}$ cups flour and $\frac{1}{2}$ cup nut meal. Nut flours are also available in stores.

GO NUTS!

If you were to give up pretzels, potato chips, and similar snack foods, could you go nuts instead? Quite literally, the answer is yes! Walnuts, almonds, Brazil nuts, pecans, pistachios, and peanuts help satisfy the need for a crispy-crunchy snack and offer health benefits such as reducing inflammation and high blood fats, thanks to their high levels of healthy fats, phytochemicals, and antioxidants including the mineral selenium.[45, 46, 47] While many studies have revealed the health benefits of individual types of nuts, most common varieties convey a ton of important health benefits, so it is fine to stick to your favorites where nuts are concerned. One study, for example, followed people who ate any types of nuts once a week or less and another group who ate between one and four servings a week. The researchers found that the more nuts or even peanut butter eaten, the lower the chances of dying from heart disease.[48]

AIM FOR THE BEST

As with all things in life, some choices are better than others. In that respect, some foods are superstars among the others. Listed on the next page, you'll find what you need to focus on when it comes to the best foods that keep you healthy.

TO GET THE BEST CARBOHYDRATES

INCLUDE:

- Whole grain and multigrain foods, including flours, unsweetened hot and cold cereals, pastas, breads, and brown rice

- Starchy veggies like corn, carrots, sweet peas, winter squash, potatoes, and sweet potatoes

- Non-starchy fresh vegetables like asparagus, broccoli, cauliflower, cucumbers, peppers, tomatoes, onions, and zucchini, as well as all types of greens like spinach, kale, collards, and lettuce

- Legumes such as kidney beans, chickpeas, black beans, lentils, and split peas (Legumes also double as a good source of plant protein.)

- Fresh fruit such as apples, berries, peaches, bananas, kiwifruit, mangoes, oranges, papayas, and pears

- Limited amounts of natural sugars, including honey, maple syrup, and molasses

AVOID:

- Sweetened breakfast cereals, cereal bars, pastries, pancakes, and waffles

- Candy

- Commercially produced desserts, including cookies, cakes, and pies

- Soft drinks and sweetened tea, as well as fruit-flavored drinks and sodas

- Sugar-laden jams and jellies, as well as condiments with added sugars, such as ketchup and barbecue sauce

TO GET THE BEST PROTEINS

INCLUDE:

- Lean fresh meats and poultry

- Eggs

- Seafood, including fatty fish like salmon, mackerel, sardines, and herring (Fatty fish are a good source of inflammation-fighting omega-3 fats.)

- Tofu, veggie burgers, and other minimally processed vegetarian protein foods

- Grass-fed dairy products such as milk, yogurt, and cheese

AVOID:

- Cured, processed, and otherwise adulterated meat, poultry, and seafood

TO GET THE BEST FATS

INCLUDE:

- Oils rich in monounsaturated fats, especially olive oil, flaxseed oil, and nut oils, such as walnut and almond oil

- Nuts, seeds, and nut and seed butters, including flaxseeds, sesame seeds, almonds, walnuts, cashews, pine nuts, and hazelnuts

- Avocados

- Olives

AVOID:

- Hydrogenated (trans) fats

- Vegetable oils high in polyunsaturated and/or saturated fats, including corn oil, sunflower oil, and soybean oil

- Excess fat of any kind

FINDING BALANCE

So now that we've covered how different foods can pave the best path to good nutritional health, you still may be wondering what the right balance of carbohydrates, proteins, and fats looks like. Exactly how much do you need to eat to ensure optimal nutrition?

The rules are simple, regardless of your eating style and food preferences. There are five basic food groups—fruits, vegetables, grains, protein, and dairy—and you need to eat several servings of food from each group every day to get the nutrients you need to stay healthy. Within the fruit, vegetable, and grain groups—which are all considered plant foods—there are many different foods to choose from. Within the protein and dairy groups, there is also a great variety of both animal-sourced and plant-based options and alternatives. So you can be a vegetarian, you can follow a restricted diet for health purposes, or you can be a meat-and-potatoes type and still get all the nutrients you need. With the food choices available today, both fresh and minimally processed, it's not difficult to adapt a typical one-size-fits-all diet plan to suit your own preferences and needs.

Since you don't want to overeat from any one food group, or miss the important benefits from another, USDA nutritionists and other health experts have devised different ways to help you create a balanced plate of food that includes optimal amounts of different types of foods from each of the five groups. Remember that the broad dietary recommendations that come from the government and professional health organizations are designed for the general public. They are not tailored to individual tastes and food preferences. Use their guidelines to create your own personal diet plan, according to your unique food preferences and health considerations. For instance, if you don't eat meat, you still need the nutrients that come with meat, especially protein and iron. Those nutrients can be found in significant amounts in legumes (beans, lentils, and split peas), tofu, nuts, seeds, and some high-protein whole grains like quinoa and spelt.

You can search health.gov and nutrition.gov for the latest Dietary Guidelines for Americans and other information on eating balanced meals. Organizations such as the American Heart Association and American Diabetes Association provide similar information on their Web sites. But for now, a quick and simple way to understand how to create a balanced plate of food is to visually divide your plate into four equal-size sections and fill each section with a different food from each food group, putting dairy in a separate category (for a glass of milk, a bowl of yogurt, or an ounce or two of cheese that may or may not be combined with other foods on your plate). Include a protein, a grain or starchy vegetable, a non-starchy vegetable, and a fruit (or two vegetables) on the plate itself. Using breakfast as an example, your plate might contain an egg, a slice of whole grain toast, a sliced tomato, and $\frac{1}{2}$ cup of blueberries. Of course, the idea of a divided plate is simply a visual to encompass all the food groups; your blueberries or tomato might be served separately, and your egg may be sitting on top of your toast. Your dairy component might be the cheese in an omelet or yogurt mixed in with the blueberries.

A Natural Rainbow of Nutrients

Another helpful way to navigate your food choices is to think about the many colors reflected in the beauty of a rainbow. Does that seem like a stretch? It shouldn't once you consider how the natural pigments in fresh fruits and vegetables not only give color to these foods but often reflect the different vitamins, minerals, and disease-fighting antioxidants and phytochemicals they contain. Simply put, the more variety of natural color you see on your plate—greens, reds, oranges, yellows, blues, and purples—the more nutrients you are getting in your meal. Different colors, even whites, browns, and beiges, represent different nutrients, different phytochemicals, and different health benefits, so a good mix is essential.

For instance, yellow-orange vegetables are rich in a variety of carotenoids, pigments that provide us with vitamin A and also serve as antioxidants that help protect against heart disease, certain cancers, skin damage from ultraviolet radiation (sunburn), macular degeneration, and inflammation.[49] Green vegetables like broccoli, kale, cabbage, spinach, and collards are not

Name That Phytochemical

Phytochemicals (*phyto* simply means *plant*) are substances found only in plant foods that are not nutrients, like vitamins and minerals, but that have similar protective and healing qualities when it comes to your health. You'll see some of the most powerful phytochemicals in food referred to as phenolic compounds, phenolic acids, polyphenols, phytosterols, flavonoids, anthocyanins, or any one of thousands of chemical names assigned to the individual substances that make up this family of compounds known to promote health, prevent chronic and debilitating diseases, and possibly help heal existing medical conditions.[51] Though chemical-sounding names might make you cringe, remember that everything that exists has a chemical name. What's most important to remember is that these substances are found only in plant foods, and they are most powerful when they work with other nutrients found in the same foods.[52] And some foods, like pomegranates, almonds, broccoli, and avocados, just happen to be loaded with essential nutrients and phytochemicals,[53] so they are considered the superstars of the plant food kingdom.

only rich in vitamin C, but they also contain beneficial carotenoids as well as phytochemicals that can help detoxify cancer-causing substances in your diet and delay or prevent tumor growth.[50] And there's more! Researchers found that dark green, leafy and nonleafy vegetables get top scores when it comes to getting the most nutritional value for your money.

Blue, red, and purple fruits and vegetables, like grapes, blueberries, blackberries, cherries, and red cabbage, get their deep color from flavonoid phytochemicals known as anthocyanins.[54] One laboratory study found that anthocyanins significantly stop the growth of breast cancer cells.[55] A review of other laboratory, animal, and human studies suggests that anthocyanins have anti-inflammatory and antioxidant activity associated with prevention and control of heart disease, obesity, and diabetes.[56] Foods that provide anthocyanins are also rich in vitamins A and C and assorted minerals.

Brown and beige foods, including beans, grains, and nuts, are generally rich in protein, and most are important sources of B vitamins, iron, and other minerals. Like other plant foods, grains and legumes contain a variety of phytochemicals that may help protect against inflammation, chronic disease, and other disorders.[57, 58] In fact, a diet high in whole grain foods can reduce the risk of developing diabetes by up to 30 percent, and the credit goes to their fiber, vitamin, mineral, and phytochemical content.[59] Nuts, the brown-beige foods most known for being rich in healthful fats,

are also good sources of phytochemicals and antioxidants.[60]

Although they are not plant foods and therefore do not contain phytochemicals, dairy products, which comprise most white or yellowish white foods in the diet, are a good source of calcium and, when fortified, one of the few good food sources of vitamin D. Like meat, poultry, and fish, grass-fed dairy products are also a good source of animal protein.

Building a multicolored plate of food helps ensure a solid nutritional base that will help keep you strong and healthy while protecting you from degenerative diseases and also against environmental toxins such as lead, mercury, arsenic, and other heavy metals in the soil, air, water, and even food, which can accumulate in your brain and body over time.[61, 62] And the way to ensure you end up with a healthful variety of color on your plate is to start by adding a wide variety of fresh, real, colorful foods to your shopping cart at the supermarket.

With all of the great evidence about supernutritious, real foods and how they can keep your body healthy and help protect you from chronic diseases and disorders, it's clear that there are countless reasons to include a wide variety of fresh fruits and vegetables, legumes, nuts, whole grains, and high-quality protein foods in your diet every day. Some may say, however, that eating real foods every day is easier said than done. But in reality, nothing could be further from the truth. We'll show you how in the next chapter.

CHAPTER 3

THE QUICKEST WAY TO REAL FOOD

Eating real food every day should be a top priority if you want to help your body operate at its peak efficiency and protect yourself from chronic disease. The nutritional evidence speaks for itself. But how exactly can you make the switch to real foods? Ultimately, you need to focus on two important changes: how you shop and how you cook.

This chapter is designed to give you a good head start in both of those arenas. You'll find everything you need to know about shopping for real food ingredients and exactly what to look for on the Nutrition Facts label to ensure your choices are the best. At the end of the chapter, you'll find a helpful 4-week step-by-step guide to make the transformation complete. But as you might have gleaned, there are many shades of gray to consider when making the shift to a real food lifestyle, so let's begin with a frank discussion of processed food and what you need to ask yourself to determine if the true cost of convenience comes at the right price when you're planning your next meal.

UNDERSTANDING THE REAL PRICE OF PROCESSED FOODS

No doubt about it, convenience foods are here to stay. Processed food is a staple in our society, and even the purists among us are bound to have some canned, bottled, bagged, or otherwise packaged food in our cupboards. The trick is learning to distinguish and choose between real, whole foods and the many processed food products that range between minimally processed and highly processed.

The truth is that every time you cook, you are processing food. When you peel a potato, you are processing that potato, but peeling a whole food

Food Label Lies: "Natural"

The implications of this label can make anyone feel good about their farm-fresh, straight-from-the-tree . . . can of powdered lemonade. Unfortunately, there isn't any official definition of "natural," except when it comes to meat. The USDA has defined "natural meat" as any product "containing no artificial Ingredient or added color and [that] is only minimally processed (a process which does not fundamentally alter the raw product)." Their definition doesn't, however, make any statements about how animals were raised or whether the animals were fed hormones or antibiotics. The FDA, which regulates fruits, vegetables, and most processed foods, doesn't have any official definition for the term when applied to all items on the grocery shelf. Essentially, a product can be as "natural" as the manufacturer would like you to believe and may contain genetically modified organisms (GMOs) and artificial sweeteners like high-fructose corn syrup.

comes under the category of very minimal processing. If you cut up, cook, and mash the potato, and whip in some olive oil, yogurt, salt, and pepper, that's more processing. But it is still a minimally processed food because you started with a fresh vegetable that was simply cooked, seasoned, and eaten soon after it was prepared. When you prepare your own food from scratch, you control the cooking style and the type and amount of seasonings you add, and you also preserve nutrients that are otherwise lost when food sits on a shelf or in a freezer case for months or years.

At the other end of the spectrum, you have a product such as commercially prepared and packaged instant mashed potatoes. Instant potatoes started out as fresh potatoes that were simply peeled, cooked, and mashed, but it was done in a factory many months or even years before your purchase, and the processing didn't stop there.

Those mashed potatoes were mixed with seasonings, preservatives, emulsifiers, anti-clumping chemicals, and possibly artificial flavoring or coloring, rolled into thin sheets, dehydrated until crisp, and crumbled into flakes before they were packaged and sent to the supermarket. You then purchase those flakes and take them home to reconstitute back into something that resembles mashed potatoes. As this example shows, this is a highly processed, very *un*real food?

To cook at home, you may need to rely on many processed ingredients, such as flours for baked goods, prepared broths for soup bases, and sweeteners for desserts. For instance, cornmeal is a processed ingredient you may rely on for baking because you're not able to grow, shuck, remove, and dry kernels of corn, and then grind those kernels to make corn muffins. Few people are. At the same time, commercially baked corn muffins and mixes are often considered highly processed food products because they contain more sugar and fat and less fiber than is healthful, as well as other additives that are used only by food manufacturers.

Consider the ingredient list on a popular corn muffin[1] mix: wheat flour, degerminated yellow cornmeal, sugar, animal shortening (lard, hydrogenated lard, tocopherols preservative, BHT preservative, citric acid preservative), contains less than 2 percent of each of the following: baking soda, sodium acid pyrophosphate, monocalcium phosphate, salt, wheat starch, niacin, reduced iron, tricalcium phosphate, thiamine mononitrate, riboflavin, folic acid, silicon dioxide.

Ask yourself: What's the point of buying a product like corn muffin mix when homemade corn muffins are comparably quick and easy to prepare using less sugar, healthier fats, and higher-fiber cornmeals and flours than most of what you'll find in a typical mix, with no questionable additives? A mix may seem more convenient for you in the short term when you're weighing your options in the grocery aisle because you think you won't have the time to measure the dry ingredients, but think again. In the long run, homemade is a lot more convenient for your health. Try ours on page 105.

Need another example? Next time you pick up a package of frozen breaded chicken nuggets at the supermarket, check the ingredient list and consider whether you're doing yourself any favors. You may count as many as 28 different ingredients in those nuggets,[2] most of which are likely to be chemical preservatives and fla-

vor enhancers, artificial flavorings, texturizers, and color enhancers in the breading. Many of the common additives used in commercially prepared breaded nuggets—salt, sodium lactate, sodium diacetate, sodium acid pyrophosphate, sodium phosphates, to name a few—are forms of sodium, which means they are contributing to the already existing problem of excess sodium in the American diet.[3] In a study that compared a high-additive diet to a low-additive diet, researchers saw an average increase of more than 1,300 milligrams of sodium in the diet that was high in additives.[4] Compare this to our delicious Zesty Orange Chicken recipe that you'll find on page 188, which contains just five all-natural ingredients and can be on the table in 25 minutes, including prep time. And you can control the amount of sodium in nuggets you prepare yourself. Sure, the commercially prepared nuggets are ready to serve in 13 minutes, but isn't your health worth 12 extra minutes? Of course it is!

And what about that humble little box of pancake mix? The ingredient list reads: enriched bleached flour (bleached wheat flour, niacin, reduced iron, thiamin mononitrate, riboflavin, folic acid), sugar, leavening (sodium bicarbonate, sodium aluminum phosphate, monocalcium phosphate), dextrose, dried buttermilk, partially hydrogenated soybean oil, salt, wheat gluten, calcium carbonate, corn syrup solids, sodium caseinate, mono- and diglycerides, lactic acid.[5] Stir in some water and you're ready to go. But in addition to convenience, that mix is giving you three different sugars—sugar, dextrose, and corn syrup solids—and hydrogenated oil, the worst type of fat for your health. Try this instead: Using a from-scratch recipe for pancakes, mix the dry ingredients together the night before and cover the bowl until the morning. Presto! You've made your own mix ahead of time, in minutes, minus the additional sugars, hydrogenated fat, extra gluten, calcium carbonate, sodium casein-ate, mono- and diglycerides, and lactic acid. The next morning, you're in the same time zone you'd be in if you were using a mix. All you have to do is stir in your liquid ingredients, and you're ready to start flipping those cakes!

Even simple ingredients like lemon juice need a reality check. Look at the ingredient list on bot-tled lemon juice. You're likely to see some (or all) of the following ingredients: water, concentrated lemon juice, sodium benzoate, sodium metabi-sulfite, sodium sulfite, and lemon oil. Squeeze a lemon, and all you get is pure, fresh juice. Fresh lemons also provide a flavor bonus: You can grate the outer, colored part of the peel (known as the zest) and add it to drinks, baked goods, soups, stews, and fruit desserts, or sprinkle it on chicken, seafood, or vegetables before cooking.

Of course, additives aren't the only concern when you're measuring a convenience food diet against a real food diet. Food scientists have long known that in addition to eliminating nutrients, processing can sometimes interfere with your body's ability to digest, absorb, and use the nutrients that remain in a food product after its ingredients have been altered.[6]

It's not always easy to determine when that interference begins. After all, some of the initial stages of food preparation, such as cutting or even pulverizing, can help enhance the availability of some nutrients by physically releasing them from the food. This is true whether the processing is done at home or in a food factory. In fact, when your food is raw or minimally processed, your body kick-starts this process by chewing. Beyond basic preparation, however, the nutritional value of food begins to diminish when it is exposed to heat, light, and even air. Lengthy storage of food can also diminish its nutritional value.

At home, you are in charge. You control what happens to your food after the initial process-ing. You decide which cooking method to use; what other ingredients to add, if any; how long to cook your food for it to be both safe and nutritious; and how food is served after it is pre-pared. Of course, in order to accomplish this goal, you'll need to make sure you're stocking up on the right real foods. And the first step in this journey starts with food shopping.

NAVIGATING YOUR CHOICES: HOW TO BECOME A REAL FOOD SHOPPER

Let's begin by evaluating where you shop and what options are available to you. In general, supermarkets have gotten bigger and bigger over time, but their layouts remain pretty much the same. The freshest, "realest" foods—whole fruits and vegetables, meats, poultry, seafood, eggs, and dairy products—are usually on the perimeter, or outer aisles, while processed foods—commercially canned, bottled, boxed, and otherwise packaged products—are distributed throughout the inner aisles. In large, well-stocked supermarkets, you have plenty of choices: Green tea or black? Multigrain bread or whole wheat? Standard milk or hormone-free? Conventionally grown fruits and vegetables or organic? Grass-fed or grain-fed beef?

However, where you shop can make a significant difference in how much packaged versus real food you buy. If you don't have easy access to a large, well-stocked supermarket and a good, varied supply of real, whole foods, you may be buying a lot of your food from convenience stores. If you're spending your food dollars at convenience stores, and buying mostly processed food products, you could be putting yourself at increased risk of weight gain and chronic disease.[7] And you aren't alone.

At least one study[8] found that more people are purchasing packaged foods from warehouse clubs, mass merchandisers, and convenience stores than ever before. Many of the top types of food products purchased at these outlets—commercially packaged snacks, desserts, and soft drinks—are among the poorest sources of nutrition because they are high in calories, sugar, sodium, and saturated fat. Although fresh food can be found in nontraditional food outlets,

supermarkets—especially larger supermarkets—carry the widest selection of healthful foods.[9]

To avoid giving in to so many highly refined, commercially packaged convenience products, see how many of the following real food shopping rules you can follow on your next run to the market:

- Never go food shopping when you're hungry.
- Plan ahead with menus based on simple, real food meals and snacks.
- Use your menu plans to organize the recipes you'll need during the week, and use them to make up your shopping list.
- Stick to that shopping list!
- Shop at farmers' markets, food co-ops, ethnic markets, and health food or specialty stores that sell whole foods like grains, nuts, seeds, and dried beans in bulk.
- At the same time, avoid doing your food shopping at any of the big-box stores that sell "more for less," unless that "more" includes a large selection of fresh foods and not just highly processed convenience foods that are easy to discount in bulk.

Of course, this list is just the tip of the iceberg. Once you are in the store, there are many different issues to consider, so let's keep going.

EATING "CLEAN" AND THE REAL FOOD CONNECTION

When reading various articles about how to make healthy food choices, you may have heard the term *clean eating* used more than once or twice. How exactly do the ideas behind "clean eating" intersect with a real food lifestyle? It may help to know that "clean eating" is a popular catchphrase with no clear origins, but it often goes hand in hand with another popular concept of "green" living, which means choosing a healthier lifestyle that's not only good for you, but good for the environment, too. Clean eating is all about eating real, whole, unadulterated foods—lots of fresh fruits and vegetables—as often as possible, and avoiding processed and refined foods whenever you can, so in essence when you embrace a "clean eating" approach to food, you are focusing on a real food lifestyle.[10]

What does this lifestyle mean in its most practical terms? When you choose to eat clean, the emphasis is on eating more plant protein from foods like beans, lentils, nuts, and high-protein grains and less protein from animal sources, especially those raised in concentrated animal feeding operations or "factory farms." Factory-farmed animals live in very close quarters, have limited or no access to the outdoors, and are typically fed grains and otherwise bulked up before slaughter in order to produce more meat.

This conventional system of raising cows, pigs, turkeys, chickens, and other livestock under such unnatural conditions relies on questionable farm methods that show little regard for animal welfare, the welfare of industrial farm workers, and the communities where these factory farms are located. To help consumers better understand their choices, the USDA certification program ensures food labels accurately reflect how animals are raised. For example, certified free-range chickens and turkeys are given access to the outdoors rather than being caged for 24 hours a day.[11] Grass-fed animals from small farms, such as cattle and sheep, are fed only grass and grass-sourced hay, and sometimes milk, from the time they are weaned from their mothers until they enter our food system. Animals certified under the USDA's grass-fed program have had continuous access to pasture.[12] And meat from cattle that is raised without growth hormones can be labeled "hormone-free" or "no hormones administered," if the USDA is given documentation to prove this is the case. (If pork or poultry is labeled "hormone-free," it must also be noted that by federal law, no hormones are allowed to be used in the raising of any hogs or poultry.)[13]

HOW ORGANIC FOODS FIT INTO THE REAL FOOD EQUATION

Let's take the clean food approach a step further. Should you buy organic food? As we've seen with the other issues you must face when making real food choices, there are many factors to consider.

For one thing, organic farmers fend off insects and other agricultural pests with less toxic means than conventional growers use, so organically grown food comes with less risk of exposure to pesticide residues that may be linked to human diseases and disorders.[14] For another, you may just want to support farmers who take a more thoughtful and environmentally conscious approach than others. Also,

The Produce Buyer's Guide to Secret Codes

Do you read those little stickers attached to each piece of fruit and vegetable you buy? Each sticker contains a code that will help you determine whether a food is organically or conventionally grown, or whether or not it contains genetically modified organisms (GMOs). Though most organic products are labeled as such, you can also look for a five-digit code that begins with the number 9. Conventionally grown fruits and vegetables are labeled with a four-digit code. Any produce that has been genetically modified is labeled with a five-digit code that begins with the number 8. Check it out next time you're in the produce aisle!

"organic" is not just about pesticides. That label also ensures that your food has not been irradiated, hasn't been grown with fertilizer made from sewage, and doesn't contain genetically modified organisms (GMOs).[15]

Studies also reveal nutritional differences between some organically grown and conventionally grown fruits and vegetables. For instance, one study[16, 17] found that organic tomatoes contained at least 30 percent more vitamin C, 24 percent more total phenolic compounds, and 20 percent more of the phytochemical lycopene, which research shows may protect against cancer and heart disease.[18] The researchers noted that organic tomatoes are often smaller in size, but since they are more concentrated in nutrients and phytochemicals, a small organic tomato may provide more vitamins and phytochemicals than a larger conventionally grown tomato.[19] Other researchers have also reported higher vitamin C levels in organically grown leafy green vegetables.[20]

Food scientists who study the differences between organic and conventionally grown strawberries have noted that the organic strawberries are darker and redder than the conventionally grown, and that these physical characteristics indicate higher levels of phytochemicals.[21] Organic strawberries have significantly higher amounts of vitamin C and anthocyanin, the phytochemical that gives berries and other blue-red foods their deep color and is also known to fight inflammation and cancer.[22]

BECOME A LABEL SLEUTH

Before you buy any food that comes in a package, it's always a good idea to take a look at the information provided on its label. Reading food labels can help you make healthy choices because they tell you what ingredients and how many nutrients are in the food you're buying. If you're curious to know more about food that isn't packaged, like fresh fruits and vegetables, you should be able to find the same information on nearby posters or brochures. The only time you may not see a nutrition label is on foods that provide few or no calories and nutrients, like coffee, tea, and spices; foods that are prepared and sold in the store; and foods produced in limited amounts by very small businesses. Though not required by law, some smaller food producers voluntarily provide nutrition information. Here's what you need to focus on:

Check the ingredient list first. Packaged foods, even those that are not required to provide nutrition information, are required by law to list all ingredients, including additives. When you read the ingredient list, remember that ingredients are listed in descending order by weight, which is the fairest way to reflect the given amounts of each ingredient contained in any food. So, for instance, if sugar is the first ingredient listed, there is more sugar in that product by weight than anything else. If the ingredient list on the label of a can of beans says, "water, organic black beans, sea salt," there is more water in that can, by weight, than anything else. That is not necessarily a bad thing, however. Water is heavy. The order of ingredients simply indicates that the water in the can weighs more than the beans; if you were to measure the contents of that can by volume, it would be easy to see that you are getting more beans than water.

20 Sneaky Names for MSG

MSG (monosodium glutamate) is a common food additive that comes in many forms. Studies have shown that the consumption of MSG is linked to headaches,[23] sleep disorders,[24] and even fibromyalgia.[25] It's wise to steer clear of it when you can. When shopping for your Real Food Pantry, make sure to read the labels on foods and keep an eye out for these other names that MSG goes by:

- Autolyzed yeast
- Autolyzed yeast protein
- Calcium glutamate
- Carrageenan
- Glutamate
- Glutamic acid
- Hydrolyzed corn
- Ingredients listed as hydrolyzed, protein fortified, ultra-pasteurized, fermented, or enzyme modified
- Magnesium glutamate
- Monoammonium glutamate
- Monopotassium glutamate
- Natural flavors (ask manufacturers their sources, to be safe)
- Pectin
- Sodium caseinate
- Soy isolate
- Soy sauce
- Textured protein
- Vegetable extract
- Yeast extract
- Yeast food

What Does the Term *Basted* Mean on a Label?

When you see the term *basted* or *self-basted* on a bone-in poultry product like turkey breast or a whole turkey, that means your bird has been injected or marinated with an edible fat, broth, stock, or water, along with spices, flavor enhancers, or other approved food additives.[26] The label must list the basting ingredients, so read carefully! And keep in mind that up to 8 percent of the weight of the raw bird can be basting solution. That means your 15-pound turkey may be closer to 14 pounds of actual bird. Opt instead for a natural or organic bird that's free of this unnecessary basting liquid.

The labels of many highly processed convenience foods have long ingredient lists that include additives with names you may not recognize. These could be preservatives, flavorings, flavor protectors, colorings, emulsifiers, or even added nutrients. Some additives come from natural sources, while others are synthetic.[27] Regardless of their origins, the presence of so many additives is a good sign that you're not looking at a real food, so look for products with the shortest lists. Better yet, stop and consider whether you can put together a homemade version of that food instead.

Review the nutrition facts. The nutrition facts panel found on food packaging labels doesn't tell you anything specific about ingredients or additives, but it does provide some important clues about what's in your food and how much it might help your health by indicating amounts for calories, fats, cholesterol, sodium, carbohydrates, sugars, fiber, and protein. If you are keeping track of any of these nutrients in your diet, you can use these figures to see how much a specific food contributes. The panel also tells you if the food product contributes significant amounts of vitamins or minerals, including vitamins A and C, iron, and calcium.[28]

To best decide if a product fits the nutritional profile you want in the food you eat, look at the serving size listed at the top of the Nutrition Facts panel so you can put the rest of the information into context. If the serving size is ½ cup, for instance, the nutrition information given is for ½ cup of that product. And remember that some seemingly single-serving products actually contain several servings per container, so referring to this information is the only way to know for sure.

Okay, that's simple. Here's where it gets confusing: The nutrition analysis on the panel is based on a 2,000-calorie daily diet. That's because the actual amount of each nutrient you need depends on the number of calories you consume, and 2,000 calories is considered a healthy average amount for many people. However, based on your age, size, and metabolism, you may need either more or fewer calories to maintain a healthy weight, and more or fewer of each nutrient to stay healthy. There's no way the government can make individual recommendations for every American, so they had to pick one number and base everything else on that number. You simply need to understand that the amounts and percentages listed are approximate. Talk with your doctor about what calorie range is right for you so you can evaluate labels with your individual needs in mind.

One of the best ways to use the Nutrition Facts panel is to compare similar products side by side to see if one has a better nutrition profile than the other. Again, check the serving size at the top of each label. Be sure that the information given for each product is based on the same amount of food. Compare the amounts of calories, fat, sugar, and salt in comparable products, and decide which brand is better for your health.

Think about food allergens. More than 160 food ingredients can cause an allergic reaction, but only the foods and food groups that contain one of the proteins that are responsible for 90 percent of all food reactions are required to be listed on food labels.[29] These include milk, egg, fish, crustacean shellfish (such as shrimp), tree nuts (such as walnuts, almonds, and Brazil nuts), peanuts, wheat, and soybeans. You may see these allergens in bold print; for example, a package might proclaim, "Contains milk ingredients."

How Accurate Are Nutrition Facts Labels?

The FDA allows food manufacturers to use averages for the calorie counts, salt content, and fat grams (and any other information on the Nutrition Facts panel) of their foods, and food manufacturers are given leeway to be off by as much as 20 percent. So that 500-calorie frozen dinner you're eating could have as many as 600 calories. If every meal you ate had 100 extra calories, you'd gain an additional 30 pounds this year. Another sticky label? Trans fats. The FDA allows manufacturers to put "0" if the amount of trans fats per serving is below 0.5 gram. That's a quarter of a day's worth, according to nutritionists at the Center for Science in the Public Interest. In fact, 2 grams is what health experts suggest should be your daily limit.

To avoid this problem altogether, avoid packaged foods as much as possible. After all, the foods without Nutrition Facts labels—fruits and vegetables—are the healthiest foods. And when you do buy packaged foods, take a moment to read ingredient labels, not just nutrition labels, to make sure you avoid trans fats. In general, avoid products with partially hydrogenated oils listed. If there's no partially hydrogenated oil, the trans-fat content really is zero.

READING BETWEEN THE LINES: HOW TO UNDERSTAND HEALTH CLAIMS

Food manufacturers love to promote how their product, or an ingredient or nutrient added to their product, will reduce your risk of developing a chronic disease. The FDA allows manufacturers to make certain health claims, such as "a low-sodium diet may reduce the risk of high blood pressure." The agency also allows nutrient content claims, such as "excellent source of calcium and vitamin D" on a container of yogurt or "high in fiber" and "sodium-free" on a package of rolled oats. Of course, these claims must be supported by scientific evidence. You might also see what are known as structure/function claims on food packaging, such as the promise on a box of instant rice that it "supports a healthy heart," but these types of claims cannot mention a disease or symptom. The same package of rice, for example, cannot claim that the product "may reduce the risk of heart disease." Think of these promotional tactics as a tool to grab your attention at the grocery store and get you to take a closer look. But do take a closer look. The only way to know for sure how much real food benefit a processed food may offer is to study the ingredient label carefully.

REAL FOOD, REAL CONVENIENCE

The truth of the matter, and the central idea behind this book, is that packaged foods haven't really cornered the market when it comes to convenience. In every supermarket, you'll find an amazing variety of convenience foods that are also "real" foods—if you know what to look for. In the produce section, for example, you are likely to find peeled, trimmed, and pre-cut fruits and vegetables that are ready to be eaten as is or used as ingredients in a home-cooked meal. In fact, you may be surprised how many *real* convenience foods are available to make meal prep a breeze.

When you're trying to decide if a commercially packaged product is a real food, just take a good look at the ingredient list. If you recognize everything on that list as an ingredient you would use in your own kitchen, or a nutrient, then it's probably safe to say you have something real in your hands. Starting on page 42 are some of the best examples of canned, bottled, boxed, bagged, and otherwise packaged convenience foods that are "real" enough to be added to your shopping list.

- Canned or package prepared low-sodium beans (i.e., black, white, red, and pinto beans, chickpeas, etc.)

- Boxed broths (chicken, vegetable, beef)

- Canned or otherwise packaged tomato products with no additives

- Multigrain pasta, including whole grain couscous and orzo

- Quick-cooking or precooked brown rice and unseasoned rice mixtures
- Quick-cooking or precooked barley
- Whole grain and unsweetened cold cereals
- Quick-cooking oatmeal and whole-grain-based hot cereals
- Shelled nuts and seeds
- Nut butters and seed butters (no additives)
- Frozen fruits, vegetables, and whole grains (no additives or sauces)
- Pre-prepped, or peeled and cut up, fresh fruits and vegetables, including triple-washed salad greens
- Pre-sliced (i.e., for stir-fry) or otherwise pre-prepped fresh meats, poultry, and seafood
- Pre-peeled hard-cooked eggs
- Plain yogurt, kefir, and other dairy products
- Shredded and pre-sliced cheeses
- Peeled garlic cloves

"100 PERCENT Natural" Foods That Aren't

It's one of the most popular label claims around, but there are some surprising ingredients lurking in your "all natural" health foods. Avoid dropping these packaged foods into your shopping cart until you take a closer look:

Almond milk. It seems like a win-win: a low-calorie dairy substitute made from one of nature's nutritional powerhouses. Except there are very few almonds in this mostly water beverage, and pretty much none of their natural goodness—including protein, fiber, healthy fat, and antioxidants—survives the processing into "milk." Instead, what's added is a whole bunch of fortified nutrients as well as thickeners and stabilizers like carrageenan, which scientists warn may cause gastrointestinal inflammation. The same goes for rice milk.

Granola bars. Many granola-bar brands contain processed sweeteners, such as corn syrup, fructose, and invert sugar, and "natural flavors"—an umbrella term for flavors derived from natural sources, but which are often processed in a lab like artificial flavors. Then there's cellulose, an ingredient made from nontoxic wood pulp or cotton, that's added to up the fiber content in your bar. For a far more natural snack, set aside 10 minutes of prep time and bake your own healthy energy bars.

Honey. Nature's perfect sweetener isn't always 100 percent natural. The jarred honeys you'll find in an average grocery store have all undergone various levels of processing, and it's hard to know how much just from looking at the labels. In fact, according to research by Food Safety News, most store-bought honey isn't technically honey at all, because virtually all of the natural pollen has been filtered out. For truly natural honey—and all the

- Grated ginger and prepared horseradish

- Dehydrated chives

- Simple seasonings with a straightforward ingredient list, like reduced-sodium soy sauce, anchovy paste, or hot sauce

Some of the worst offenders in your supermarket—those products to avoid whenever you can—include:

- Frozen complete meals

- Sodas and other beverages with added sugar

- Most canned fruits, vegetables, and meat products

- Sweetened cold cereals

- Bouillon cubes and other high-sodium seasoning mixtures with MSG (Look for natural or organic brands.)

- Bottled salad dressings and sauces

- Flavored, sweetened yogurts and kefirs

- Commercially baked cookies, cakes, pies, and pastries

immune-boosting and allergy-fighting benefits that come with it—head to a farmers' market, where you can buy it raw from local beekeepers.

Nondairy and soy cheeses. Cheese substitutes often contain added colors and flavors to make them more cheeselike. One common ingredient? Carrageenan, a processed carbohydrate that may upset some people's stomachs. Additionally, soy is one of the most common genetically modified crops around—roughly 94 percent of the soy grown in the United States is GMO, in fact—so if you're wary of eating them, make sure you're buying organic.

Veggie chips. It's easy to be tempted by the idea of a crunchy, salty snack food made from real vegetables. But the truth is, most veggie chips (also veggie straws) have very little in common with a real vegetable. They are made mostly from dehydrated corn or potato starch and contain lots of flavoring, and even the color comes from vegetable powder and not the real thing. Some exceptions exist, including Terra brand chips, which really are just sliced, fried, and salted root vegetables. A better choice? Make your own veggie chips (our Zucchini Chips recipe that you'll find on page 302 is downright addictive), or just grab the potato chips like you wanted to do in the first place.

Yogurt. Natural and artificial flavors and processed sweeteners abound in many packaged yogurts, so don't assume that blueberry flavor (not to mention the purplish hue) is coming only from real blueberries. As always, scrutinize the label, and buy grass-fed organic if you want to avoid dairy from cows given artificial growth hormones. Or buy plain yogurt and add in fresh fruit.

REAL FOOD BRANDS WE LOVE

Below is a selection of natural food products we choose for our Real Food kitchens, however the list is not exclusive. Keep an eye out for more brands in your supermarkets. When selecting any products including these brands, read the labels and opt for organic or non-GMO whenever possible. As mentioned earlier, looking for local producers is another great way to get the healthiest products available.

BREADS AND PASTA

- Ancient Harvest
- Bionaturae Organic Pasta
- Dave's Killer Bread
- DeBoles Organic Pasta
- Food For Life Ezekiel 4:9
- Lundberg Family Farms
- Rising Moon Organic
- Rudy's Organic
- Seeds of Change
- Vermont Bread Company

DAIRY/DAIRY ALTERNATIVES
(OPT FOR GRASS-FED IF POSSIBLE)

- Brown Cow
- Common Good Farm
- EcoMeal Organic
- Green Valley Organics
- Handsome Brook Farm
- Happy Egg Company
- Horizon Organic
- Kalona Organics
- Maple Hill Creamery
- Mission Mountain
- Native Forest
- Organic Creamery
- Organic Cow of Vermont
- Organic Valley
- Pete and Gerry's
- So Delicious Dairy Free
- Stonyfield Farm
- Thoughtful Organics
- Vital Farms
- Wallaby Organic

FROZEN PRODUCTS

- Alexia Organic
- Amy's Kitchen
- Cascadian Farm
- Frieda's
- Muir Glen
- Wholly Wholesome
- Woodstock Farms Organics

MEAT, POULTRY, FISH, AND VEGETARIAN PROTEINS
(OPT FOR WILD FISH AND GRASS-FED MEATS IF POSSIBLE)

- Applegate Farms
- Bell & Evans
- Coleman Natural
- Organic Prairie
- Nasoya
- Plainville
- Quinn
- Rocky Mountain
- SoyBoy
- Wild Planet

PANTRY ITEMS

- Ah!laska
- Alvarado Street Bakery
- Alter Eco
- Annie's Homegrown
- Arrowhead Mills
- Bearitos
- Bob's Red Mill
- Earthbound Farms
- Eden Foods
- Farmer's Market
- Flavorganics
- Frontier Co-op
- Hain
- Health Valley
- Imagine Foods

A Menu for Convenience

What if you prepare mac and cheese from a box, toss some greens and tomatoes with bottled salad dressing, and end on a sweet note with, say, a parfait of instant vanilla pudding layered with fresh strawberries and blueberries? Sounds like a relatively well-balanced meal, doesn't it? And one that includes fresh fruits and vegetables! But take a closer look at everything else you're eating:

In addition to an "enriched macaroni product," in a typical box of macaroni and cheese, you're likely to find a package of dehydrated cheese sauce that contains the following 18 ingredients: whey, modified food starch, salt, milk fat, milk protein concentrate, sodium phosphate, calcium carbonate, cellulose gel, cellulose gum, citric acid, lactic acid, calcium phosphate, paprika, annatto, turmeric, enzymes, cheese culture, and xanthan gum.

Your salad dressing is likely a mix of vinegar, water, vegetable oils, sugar, salt, dried garlic, dried red bell peppers, dried onions, xanthan gum, spice, oleoresin paprika, potassium sorbate, and calcium disodium EDTA.

And the ingredient list on that box of pudding mix starts with sugar, continues with modified cornstarch, natural and artificial flavor, salt, disodium phosphate, tetrasodium pyrophosphate, monoglycerides, diglycerides, artificial color, yellow 5, and yellow 6, and ends with the preservative known as BHA.

Quick and easy? Definitely. Healthful and appetizing?

Maybe not so much. Although these unrecognizable ingredients are government approved for safety, do you really want to have them for dinner?

Several additives in these foods—sodium phosphate, disodium phosphate, tetrasodium pyrophosphate—are not only forms of sodium but also forms of phosphorus, a mineral that researchers say is overconsumed in the United States, in part because of its presence in so many convenience foods. An imbalance, or excess, of phosphorus in the blood and in body tissues can interfere with your body's use of calcium and trigger the release of hormones that can damage body tissue and lead to heart disease, kidney disorders, and bone loss.[30]

- Let's Do Organic
- Lundberg Farms
- Newman's Own
- Madhava
- McCormick Organics
- Mediterranean Organic
- Muir Glen

- NaraNatha Organic
- Native Forest
- Nature's Path
- Organicville
- Pacific Foods
- Rice Select
- Santa Cruz Organic

- Simply Organic
- Spectrum
- Walnut Acres
- Westbrae Natural
- Wholesome!
- Woodstock Farms Organics

PRODUCE

- Cal-Organic
- Gourmet Garden
- Earthbound Farms

- Foxy Organic
- Lady Moon Farms
- Olivia's Organics

- Terra's Garden
- Southern Selects

SAUCES, DIPS, AND SPREADS

- Hope Foods
- Amy's Kitchen
- Primal Kitchen
- Stonewall Kitchen

- Coombs Family Farms
- Spectrum Organics
- Annie's Homegrown
- Organic Valley

- Bragg Foods
- Crofter's Organic Fruit Spreads
- Newman's Own Organics
- Organicville

SNACKS

- Cliff
- Country Choice Organic
- Nature's Path
- KIND Snacks

- Hain Celestial Group
- Health Warrior
- Late July Snacks
- Garden of Eatin'

- Green & Black
- Equal Exchange
- Theo Chocolates
- Bob's Red Mill

STORE BRANDS
(HERE IS A SAMPLING OF THE MANY STORE BRANDS AVAILABLE, OPT FOR ORGANIC IF POSSIBLE)

- 365 Everyday Value
- Central Market
- Harris Teeter Organics
- H.E.B
- Nature's Promise

- O organics
- Private Selection Organic
- Simply Balanced
- Simply Nature
- Simple Truth

- Wild Harvest
- Wild Oats

HOW TO CREATE A REAL FOOD KITCHEN

As you become more comfortable navigating the grocery aisles, the second part of adopting a real food lifestyle involves cooking all those real ingredients into simple, healthful meals. Rest assured there are no complicated recipes in this book. You don't have to go to cooking school to learn how to prepare these foods. Nor do you have to stock your shelves with exotic ingredients; you should be able to find everything you need in a well-stocked supermarket. You'll see that whole foods are just as easy to prepare as convenience foods, and that you don't have to be a trained chef to put delicious, healthful food on the table in no time.

Your time is too valuable to spend hours and hours preparing and cooking three meals a day, every day. But what if you could prepare most of your meals from real, minimally processed food, at home, without spending much more time or energy than you would by eating highly processed convenience and fast foods?

Most of the recipes in this book can be on the table in 30 minutes or less; any exceptions can still be quickly prepared but may require some extra unwatched time in the oven, slow cooker, stewpot, or skillet. Recipe ingredient lists are kept as short as possible, but don't forget that an extra seasoning or two can make the difference between a mediocre recipe and a real keeper, and won't take more than a few extra seconds of your time.

The meal plan that you'll find on page 304 and the recipes in this book have been developed to give you real, delicious versions of the foods you and your family love to eat on a regular basis. You'll find recipes for Fresh Fruit Scones and a simple-to-prepare Crustless Breakfast Quiche, as well as many different taco ideas and hearty soups that are sure to become family favorites, like Cod Fish Chowder and Mexican Bean Soup. Even traditional dishes like Chicken Enchiladas and Hearty Red Scalloped Potatoes are included because when you're cooking with real ingredients, nothing is off-limits. Many of the recipes feature a before-and-after analysis highlighting and comparing the nutritional value and number of "nonfood" ingredients in both the real food recipe and a more highly processed, convenience food counterpart you are likely to find in your grocery store or local restaurant.

Studies suggest that cooking skills—or a lack of them—are a huge factor in choosing convenience over nutrition and may also play a role in the epidemics of overweight and obesity and their associated health issues. One study found that people who enjoy cooking are more likely to know how to cook and that those who know how to cook eat more fruits and vegetables and fewer convenience foods.[31, 32, 33] The Real Food, Real Fast way of eating—which isn't a diet, per se, but more of an upgraded eating style—requires no special cooking skills. The menus and recipes herein are designed to be as simple and speedy as possible. You need not worry about special kitchen equipment, hard-to-find ingredients, or learning to do anything more complicated than combining simple ingredients in a skillet or roasting pan.

The Equipment You'll Need

Not only do you need very little in the way of special kitchen equipment, you don't need much equipment at all. The basic equipment that most anyone has in the kitchen is enough to cook Real Food, Real Fast.

Essential Equipment

- Sharp knives: chef's, paring, serrated
- Various size pots, saucepans, and skillets with lids
- Baking sheets and baking pans
- Food processor or blender
- Stand or hand mixer
- Measuring cups
- Measuring spoons
- Steamer
- Grater

- Citrus juicer
- Cutting boards
- Cooking utensils: wooden spoons, flat spatula, rubber spatula, whisk, tongs
- Storage containers for leftovers and make-aheads

Nice to Have

- **Hand blender.** You can insert a hand blender, or stick blender, directly into a pot to puree soups, sauces, and cooked vegetables, as well as into a large glass whenever a smoothie craving hits. In fact, a hand blender is a nice alternative to a regular blender because it requires a lot less time and energy to clean up.

- **Spiralizer.** A spiralizer turns vegetables into a noodlelike "pasta" shape, which allows you to still enjoy your favorite pasta sauces if starchy foods are a concern or if you're trying to get more vegetables in your diet.

- **Slow cooker.** Although it takes hours to cook in a slow cooker, there is relatively little prep and you can cook real, fresh food in an unwatched pot for a wholesome meal that's ready when you are.

YOUR 4-WEEK REAL FOOD PLAN

One of the first things you need to do to make the switch to a real food lifestyle doesn't happen on a plate or in a grocery store. It happens in your mind. To make the switch from a convenience food lifestyle to a real food lifestyle, you must first get used to the idea of change. That means changing the way you think about food as well as changing the way you eat. It's easier to break out of your routine and change your eating habits if you think through these changes and make them gradually, one step at a time. You need to give yourself a little time to adjust to one change before you move on to another. That's why we've broken the Real Food, Real Fast plan down into a 4-week schedule. Start with a week to prepare yourself and get used to the idea of change, then concentrate on changing one meal per week for the following 3 weeks.

Our 4-week plan shows you which foods to avoid and which to include at each meal as you transition to a real food diet. For example, it may seem obvious at this point that your goal is to avoid cream-filled doughnuts and iced cinnamon buns for breakfast, and to eliminate commercially prepared, breaded, and deep-fried foods at lunch and dinner times. But what will you eat instead? We'll help you figure that out!

Week 1: Prepare for Change!

While the food in this book may be fast to prepare, the process of switching over to a real food diet should happen slowly. Changing the way you eat requires changing old habits—many of which may have been ingrained since childhood. It's not an easy job, because most of us like to stick with what's familiar. We are accustomed to eating certain foods at specific times. Our eating habits are so fixed in our day-to-day lives that eating occurs automatically, without much thought. You might keep slipping into old, familiar habits simply because you forget from moment to moment that you're trying to develop new ones.

Take some time this week to think about what you're going to do with your diet, to make plans, and to ease into healthier eating habits, one meal at a time. That way, you will not be overwhelmed by too much change too soon. Remember that most people go through several stages of change before they can make permanent changes,[34] starting with "precontemplation," the stage where you are introduced to the concept of healthier eating but are still in denial about the benefits of giving up, or at least cutting back on, some of your favorite convenience and fast foods. Or perhaps you are clear about the benefits of a real food lifestyle, but you haven't even started to plan any significant changes yet. Even when you move on to the "contemplation" stage of change and start to think, "Well, maybe there *is* something to this real food diet thing," you might still get stuck in this phase before you are fully convinced that switching from highly processed to minimally processed foods is worth the effort and worth what you might perceive as a sacrifice. Once you've had sufficient time to think through this transition, you'll arrive at the preparation stage, where you can earnestly start planning the switchover and what that work entails.

Once you are in the preparation stage, your goal shifts and you should begin to identify specific foods and eating behaviors that need to change, and to take small steps to get the process started. For example, you might start your preparation by getting rid of any highly processed foods in your home; stocking up on new, unprocessed, and minimally processed foods; and thinking hard about your eating habits, perhaps especially your snacking habits. Here's your strategy outline for Week 1:

Clear your pantry, kitchen cupboards, and refrigerator and freezer shelves of any highly processed foods you have in stock. Decide whether any of it is worth donating to a charitable food drive. (Keep in mind that when someone is routinely hungry, they generally need calories regardless of where those calories come from, but you might not be doing anyone a favor by giving them especially unhealthy foods. Simply discard the worst of the worst.)

Take a good, hard look at the foods you've been eating to identify added sugars, fats, and salts. These additives can be just as harmful to your health as unidentifiable chemicals, perhaps even more so! By eating more fresh and fewer processed foods, you will be eliminating a lot of additives. Many of the whole foods you will be preparing are natural sources of fat, sugar, and sodium, so your goal is to eliminate the excess that sneaks into your diet when you eat highly processed foods. Even when it comes to the minimally processed convenience foods you'll still keep in stock, like broths and beans, it's important to compare products and choose those with the least amount of added sodium, fats, or sugar in any form.

Review the menu plans and recipes you'll be using in the upcoming weeks, just to get a sense of what you'll be eating and what types of ingredients you'll need. Use the recipes and menus provided (or your own menus) to make a shopping list for Week 2, so that you can replenish your pantry and freezer with any convenience foods, condiments, and seasonings you will be using.

Check out different supermarkets, health food stores, and other food markets in your area to see where you can get the best variety of fresh and minimally processed foods at prices you can afford. While everything you buy doesn't have to be organic or completely free of additives, you may be surprised to find, for instance, that one store sells organic canned goods such as black beans and tomato paste for the same price that another store sells conventional brands. Or you might discover that different stores sometimes sell the same foods for vastly different prices.

For this week's meals, simply be conscious of the fact that you are trying to eat better-quality foods. Experiment with at least one or two new whole foods, such as a papaya or red cabbage or other fresh fruit or vegetable you've rarely or never prepared at home, or try out a new whole grain food, like quinoa, spelt, or short-grain brown rice for a side dish.

Spend time thinking not only about the food you eat but also about your food *behavior*. No doubt about it, we are all creatures of habit. Single out any eating patterns that may be getting in your way of switching to a real food diet. For instance, do you wait too long to eat between meals, and find yourself grabbing random fast foods to satisfy a raging hunger? See if you can adjust your schedule so that you can sit down to three meals within 3 to 5 hours of each other. What do you need to do to ensure that you always have healthful foods on hand for all meals and snacks?

Choose from the Real Quick & Healthy Snack Combos listed on page 50, or come up with some of your own ideas for healthier snack

Week 2: Break Your Breakfast Routine

This is the week you start climbing out of your breakfast rut. Replace the doughnuts, cinnamon buns, and sugary cold cereals with a real food breakfast at the start of each day. If you've been skipping breakfast, this is the week to start up again. Studies show that eating breakfast is one of the most important health habits for adults and children alike, because skipping the first meal of the day can compromise both your physical and mental health.[35]

No one has a lot of time to spend in the kitchen before heading to work, school, or other scheduled activities first thing in the morning, so Monday-to-Friday breakfasts need to be the simplest and quickest of all the meals you prepare. At the same time, breakfast must provide the energy balance you need to start your day and see it through until lunchtime. That means the best breakfasts should include a good variety of nutritious foods that provide energy immediately *and* for several hours to come. Grabbing a pastry with your coffee on the way to work just doesn't make the grade.

Sometimes you just need to get where you're going in the morning, and there's no time to eat breakfast at home. But that doesn't mean you should resort to cookies from the vending

What's the Difference between Use-By, Sell-By, or Best-By Dates?

Ninety percent of Americans say in surveys that, at least once, they've thrown out food because it was past its use-by or sell-by date. Here's why that's a waste of your money and your food: The dates, which are completely arbitrary, relate to a food's freshness, not whether it will make you sick, and were first used back in the 1970s to inform an increasingly urban public how fresh-from-the- farm their food was. Despite the fact that some states require certain foods to bear them, these ubiquitous dates aren't even set by law. They are set entirely at the discretion of the food companies making your food and are based on when the companies think the quality of their food will have reached its peak, not on any scientific standards for freshness or evidence of food decay.

To get the real thing: Learn to pay attention to your foods' colors, odors, and textures. Those are the three most reliable indicators that a food has passed its real "best-by" date, not some meaningless date stamped on a package. Foods with a high water content tend to spoil most quickly and will develop strong odors, slimy textures, and changes in color due to microbial growth and other reactions.

Real Quick & Healthy Snack Combos

Make sure the idea of nutritional balance extends to the snacks you eat. Ideally, you should combine at least two or three foods from different food groups, just as you do in a meal, so that your snack not only provides a variety of nutrients but also a steady stream of energy from food combinations that won't cause your blood sugar to surge. Think of snacks as "mini meals" that can help fill in any nutritional gaps in your diet. Here are some easy, real food snacks worth trying:

- Unsalted raw nut mixture with raisins and string cheese

- Grapes with sliced cheese and fresh turkey roll-up

- Apple or pear slices spread with nut butter or ricotta cheese

- Multigrain crackers with cottage cheese and sliced ripe strawberries, peach, or pear

- Plain yogurt with berries and a sprinkling of muesli or granola

- Hard-cooked egg with mini carrots and cherry tomatoes

- A toasted whole grain English muffin or crumpet topped with nut butter and sliced banana

- Low-sodium vegetable juice and air-popped popcorn sprinkled with smoked paprika and just a pinch or two of salt

- Smashed avocado or hummus on a rice cake and an orange

- Fresh strawberries, raw almonds, and an ounce of dark chocolate

- Precooked shrimp and baked corn chips with refrigerated fresh tomato salsa

machine. You've heard of brown-bag lunches—what about a brown-bag breakfast? It's simple: Make up an easy-to-carry, balanced breakfast—a piece of fruit, some yogurt, a small container of granola—the night before and store it in the fridge so you can grab it and go in the morning. And if this isn't something you routinely do, you might want to leave yourself a note on the front door to remember to take your mobile breakfast out of the fridge just before you leave.

A Real, Quick Breakfast

The next time you want to start your day with something warm, consider a bowl of oatmeal. This simple grain retains its fiber even when processed into the various forms—whole, quick, and instant—available in supermarkets. That's because even though oats are flattened, sliced, and sometimes pre-steamed and dried, these processes do not separate the bran from the oat kernel. Ultimately, you get as much fiber in a bowl of whole grain oats as you do in a bowl of instant.

But fiber in and of itself isn't the only reason to choose whole grains for breakfast. Researchers now know that, unlike refined-grain cereals, whole grain, high-fiber cereals also contain phytochemicals and other bioactive substances that can help with insulin regulation, fat metabolism, gastrointestinal balance, and even weight control.[36, 37] These are the natural substances found in the bran and germ of whole grain cereals that protect against diabetes, heart disease, colon cancer and other cancers, and obesity. At the same time, some of these substances help keep your liver functioning properly, protect your kidneys, and encourage new cell growth throughout your body.[38, 39]

Oats aren't the only superheroes among your breakfast options, though. When you reach for a box of cold cereal, you're helping your heart, and other important body parts, if you choose whole grain or "super grain" varieties over refined. One study found that eating 25 grams, or less than an ounce, of quinoa flakes a day for

Real Quick & Healthy Breakfast Alternatives

While certain foods have become staples of the American breakfast, there's no reason that you can't branch out. The key is to start your day by eating something from as many different food groups as possible, even if you don't choose traditional "breakfast" items. Ideally, that means choosing a combo of protein, carbohydrates, vegetables/fruit, and fat so you'll feel satisfied until lunchtime. Here are some not-so-typical breakfasts that fit the bill perfectly.

Quinoa bowl with edamame, avocado, pineapple, and cashews. If you have some leftover quinoa, you aren't limited to waiting until lunch or dinner to enjoy it. Quinoa is a superfood because it has a lot of protein and fiber, in addition to carbs. Adding edamame gets you a vegetable that also has protein, and the avocado and cashews are good fats that add texture to the bowl. Top it off with pineapple to provide a fruit and some sweetness.

Sweet potato with black beans and Cheddar cheese. Sweet potatoes are an excellent, healthy carb and a vegetable that has lots of fiber, while the beans and cheese provides protein so you'll feel fuller longer. Top it with a little salsa and guacamole to add in a good fat.

Homemade trail mix with unsalted nuts, seeds, dried fruit, and whole grain cereal. These foods offer a perfect, grab-and-go combination when you're on the go. The fiber will fill you up, and the protein will keep you full longer and may even reduce cravings and snacking later in the day. Make a few bags' worth and stash them in your purse, car, desk, or gym bag so you'll have a quick breakfast or snack on hand whenever you need it.

4 weeks reduced signs of inflammation *and* total and LDL cholesterol levels in older women, while eating corn flakes had no effect on any of these disease markers.[40] In another study, researchers who looked at the dietary records of more than 86,000 men found that those who regularly ate whole grain breakfast cereals had lower rates of premature death from any cause.[41] Similar studies show the same results for older women who get most of their fiber from whole grains rather than from refined-grain products,[42] leading researchers to emphasize the overall importance of whole grain foods in everyone's diet.

Week 3: Change Up Your Lunch

Some of the foods we traditionally eat for lunch make a perfectly good dinner, and vice versa. In fact, switching off different types of foods for different meals is a good way to help yourself adjust to change when you're trying to kick old eating habits and introduce new foods and new ways of eating into your daily diet.

Lunch may be the meal where you're most challenged to eat real food. Unless you bring it with you from home, lunch is likely to be a slice of pizza, a fast-food burger and helping of fries, or a ready-made wrap and salty soup from a deli near work. While packing up leftovers from last night's dinner is often the best solution for a quick and healthy lunch, that may not always fit into your schedule or food plan. That's why you need to have the makings of a healthy lunch on hand so you can throw something together when there are no leftovers or ready-made fresh foods available. The recipes in *Real Food, Real Fast* provide wholesome, delicious lunch ideas

for anytime and anywhere you want to eat—at home, at work, indoors or out.

This week, invest in a lunch box or reusable lunch bag, if you don't already have one. Consider a thermos for carrying homemade soups and stews. Pick lunch recipes that work with your schedule and put a plan in place for preparing these lunches in advance so you will have them at the ready throughout the week. The suggestions in "8 Ways with Salads in a Jar" on page 124 are another good place to start. The benefit of planning ahead for, say, a week's worth of meals is that you don't have to make a new decision every day about what to eat; the decision has already been made. That alone could save you more time than any convenience food would!

Week 4: Dish Out a Different Dinner

So, what's for dinner? When you have a quick answer to that question, you're well on your way to serving up real food, real fast, in your own kitchen. When you can count on an assortment of simple, easy-to-prepare dinner recipes like those you'll find in this book, you have more time to spend sitting down, relaxing at the end of each day, and enjoying an evening meal with your family.

As with any meal, a little advance planning and organization goes a long way toward simplifying everyday dinners. Look at your upcoming week and figure out what you realistically have time to do in the kitchen, then pick your recipes and menu ideas accordingly. Create a calendar-like meal plan that incorporates those recipes and ideas. Use the menu plan we provide

Not-So-Devilish Deviled Eggs

For a quick lunch, keep hard-cooked eggs on hand in the fridge to make deviled, or filled, eggs. Halve the eggs, remove the yolks, and mash them with one of these fillings before restuffing the mixture into the hollows of the whites (store any leftover filling in the refrigerator to spread on bread or crackers):

- Hummus seasoned with smoked paprika
- Half-and-half mixture of mayonnaise and low-fat plain yogurt seasoned with mustard
- Leftover mashed sweet potato or winter squash
- Avocado mashed with plain yogurt seasoned with finely chopped cilantro
- White beans seasoned with sage
- Finely chopped kimchi
- Fresh salsa
- Finely chopped kale and mayonnaise
- Grated Parmesan cheese and mustard

on page 304 for some ideas to get you started. Since your goal is to incorporate new and different types of foods into your diet, choose at least one recipe for a dish you've never tried before.

One way to be sure you'll have real, healthy food on hand during the busy workweek is to "binge-cook" on weekends. For instance, on Sunday, roast a chicken or two, broil a pound of salmon, and make sure you have plenty of easy-to-prepare side dishes on hand, such as salad greens, tomatoes, and peeled mini carrots, as well as ripe, seasonal fresh fruit for naturally sweet, nutritious desserts.

Make a plan to use those precooked ingredients (or other leftovers you may have available) in creative new ways. For instance, the mashed sweet potatoes you make on Sunday will taste just as good as a topping for your shepherd's pie on Tuesday, and your oversize pot of brown basmati rice will keep in the refrigerator until Wednesday or Thursday for a quick and easy stir-fried rice. Of course, you can also freeze intentional and unintentional leftovers to use later in the week or month. Just be sure to label the package with the name of the food and the date it was frozen.

STAYING REAL

The central problem behind adopting any type of new and healthy food plan is the question of how to stick to it. That's a matter of breaking bad habits once and for all so that you don't slip back into old ways. And we all know that's not easy!

Luckily, there are many steps you can take to change your eating behavior and break old food habits. Some of the same techniques people use when they are trying to lose weight will work for you when you're trying to eat healthier foods. Keep these tips handy and refer to them frequently so you make real food choices on a regular basis.

- Encourage family and friends to enjoy more real foods with when eating together.

- Keep plenty of healthy, real foods on hand and store them up front in your cupboard and refrigerator so you see them first thing when you open the door.

- Prepare extra food when you cook so your refrigerator stays stocked with ready-to-go ingredients for later in the week. Alternately, freeze them for later in the month.

- Never skip meals or get too hungry; otherwise, you become more vulnerable to unhealthy fast foods that are immediately available.

REMEMBER THAT NOBODY'S PERFECT

In an ideal world, there is always time to shop for and prepare fresh, wholesome foods and cook all your meals from scratch so you can have more control over what you eat and make healthier choices all the time. Alas, very few of us live in that world.

So for those times when you just can't bring yourself to do any "real" cooking, think about how you can create super-quick meals and snacks using fresh foods that require little preparation in combination with minimally processed commercial food products. For instance, many supermarkets carry fresh prepared, filled pastas like whole wheat ravioli, which you can toss with bottled tomato sauce and freshly grated Parmesan cheese, and serve with a salad made with prewashed and trimmed salad greens. That's a 15-minute meal!

Perhaps you feel like a Mexican-style dinner. Check the aisles in your supermarket for pre-pared black bean soup and multigrain tortillas you can toast in the oven while the soup is heating up. Toss together an avocado and cherry tomato salad, and finish the meal with pre-cut pineapple cubes or mango slices from the produce department.

Or head to the seafood department. Most supermarkets sell pre-cleaned, precooked shrimp that you can toss with instant brown rice and serve with a sliced cucumber and snow pea salad.

There are so many ways to put together a nutritious meal with real foods that require little or no actual cooking, especially if you shop at a market that sells pre-prepped foods like cut-up fruits and vegetables. Whenever you're out doing your weekly food shopping, look for products like those mentioned above, or others that you can keep on hand, either in your pantry or freezer, for those times when you just don't have the time or energy to cook.

(Real) Smart Eating Out

The next time you decide to eat out at a restaurant, think quality over quantity. Try to skip the fast-food joints and "all you can eat" buffets, where scrimping on dollars can also mean squandering your good health. Rather than chains, choose individually owned restaurants with menus that feature plenty of fresh vegetables, salads, seafood, and grain dishes in addition to standard meats and potatoes.

Some of your best ethnic bets include Greek, Asian, Middle Eastern, and Mexican restaurants. Contemporary American, French, and Italian restaurants can serve equally healthful fare, but sometimes require careful choices. In all cases, avoid breaded and fried foods, and instead choose grilled, roasted, steamed, or broiled fish and poultry selections; steamed, stir-fried, or lightly sautéed fresh vegetable side dishes; and brown rice or whole grains.

If you do go to a deli, fast-food chain, or inexpensive buffet-style restaurant, look for the healthiest choices, such as grilled or roasted cuts of meat, poultry, or fish; wraps and burritos made with whole grain flatbread and filled with veggies; bean dishes; pizza with a thin crust and fresh veggie toppings; and fresh vegetable salads with dressings on the side. The less dressing, sauce, or breading, the better the chance you're enjoying a meal made with all or mostly real foods.

HOW TO USE THIS BOOK

By now you should have a good understanding of the health benefits of eating real food. Now it's time to take advantage of what's in your kitchen and the flavors your family enjoys to create simple delicious and healthy meals.

Here you'll use the following mix-and-match charts for nutritious, throw-together meals that are as fun to make as they are to eat! You can also use the charts to experiment with new flavors.

Included in the next section are more than 190 delicious recipes with ingredient and nutritional comparisons to fake foods showing the surprising differences. And, discover the feature *8 Ways to . . .* , which showcases super-simple meals using only one ingredient or uncomplicated cooking technique such as ground beef or sheet-pan suppers. No matter where you start, you'll find mouthwatering recipes and photos to inspire your meals. Enjoy!

mix-and-match
GRANOLA

Choose the ingredients straight down the left side if you're craving classic granola—the farther right you go, the more adventurous the end result. Combine the first four ingredients in a bowl, mix well, and bake on a rimmed sheet pan at 325°F until golden and toasty, 30 to 40 minutes. Once the granola is cool, stir in the dried fruit and the add-in. Stored in an airtight container, the granola will last up to 2 weeks. Enjoy!

CLASSIC				➤ BOLD
WHOLE GRAIN (3 CUPS)				
Rolled oats	Quinoa flakes	Rye flakes	Barley flakes	Raw whole millet
NUTS AND SEEDS (1 CUP EACH)				
Almonds and sunflower seeds	Walnuts and sesame seeds	Hazelnuts and flaxseeds	Pecans and pumpkin seeds	Cashews and macadamia nuts
FAT (½ CUP)				
Canola oil	Olive oil	Melted butter	Grapeseed oil	Melted coconut oil
SWEETENER (½ CUP)				
Maple syrup	Honey	Molasses	Unsweetened applesauce	Brown rice syrup
DRIED FRUIT (1 CUP)				
Golden raisins	Chopped dried figs	Dried cherries	Chopped dried apricots	Chopped mango
ADD-IN (1 CUP)				
Unsweetened coconut flakes	Chopped crystallized ginger	Cacao nibs	Toasted buckwheat groats	Chopped candied orange peel (¼ cup)

⨾ mix-and-match ⨾
BREAKFAST BOWLS

Bored with your usual a.m. bowl of cereal? The tasty combos in this mix-and-match chart are so good you might actually be excited to hop out of bed in the morning. Choose straight down the left side if you're craving a classic taste—the farther right you go, the more adventurous the end result. Simmer your grains in the liquid until tender and creamy. Stir in the fruit or vegetable, nuts or seeds, and sweetener.

CLASSIC				▶ BOLD
WHOLE GRAIN BASE (½ CUP UNCOOKED)				
Rolled oats	Quinoa	Polenta	Buckwheat	Brown rice
LIQUID (1 CUP)				
Milk	Low-fat buttermilk	Unsweetened almond milk	Unsweetened coconut milk	Brewed green tea
FRUIT OR VEGETABLES (½ CUP)				
Fresh blueberries	Grated apple	Roasted grapes	Caramelized banana slices	Steamed butternut squash
NUTS OR SEEDS (2 TABLESPOONS)				
Sliced almonds	Ground flaxseeds	Chopped walnuts	Chopped pecans	Tahini
FLAVOR-BOOSTING TOPPING (1 TABLESPOON)				
Golden raisins	Dried cherries	Ricotta cheese	Toasted shredded coconut	Chopped crystalized ginger
SWEETENER (1 TABLESPOON)				
Honey	Maple syrup	Brown sugar	Molasses	Brown rice syrup

⧜ mix-and-match ⧜
BLT SANDWICHES

The bacon-lettuce-tomato combo might be classic, but that doesn't mean you have to stick with the script every single time. These variations are just as delicious, easy to make, and in every instance, healthier than the average sandwich. Just toast the bread, slather on your sauce, and pile on the protein, veggies, and greens. For a more classic taste, choose straight down the left; the farther right you go, the more adventurous the end result. Time for lunch!

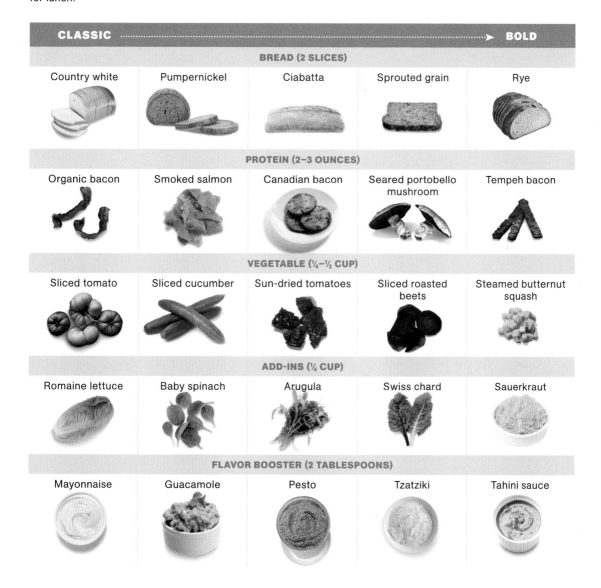

CLASSIC ·· ➤ BOLD

BREAD (2 SLICES)				
Country white	Pumpernickel	Ciabatta	Sprouted grain	Rye

PROTEIN (2–3 OUNCES)				
Organic bacon	Smoked salmon	Canadian bacon	Seared portobello mushroom	Tempeh bacon

VEGETABLE (¼–½ CUP)				
Sliced tomato	Sliced cucumber	Sun-dried tomatoes	Sliced roasted beets	Steamed butternut squash

ADD-INS (¼ CUP)				
Romaine lettuce	Baby spinach	Arugula	Swiss chard	Sauerkraut

FLAVOR BOOSTER (2 TABLESPOONS)				
Mayonnaise	Guacamole	Pesto	Tzatziki	Tahini sauce

mix-and-match
GRILLED CHEESE

Pick one ingredient per row to create your ideal grilled cheese. Choose straight down the left side if you're craving a classic taste; the farther right you go, the more adventurous the end result. To assemble: Place 1 teaspoon of the spread on the inner side of each slice of bread, then layer with a cheese, an add-in, and a flavor booster before grilling in a greased pan.

CLASSIC ······························➤ **BOLD**

BREAD (2 SLICES)

Whole wheat	Ciabatta	Seeded rye	Sourdough	Pumpernickel

CHEESE (2 OUNCES)

American	Smoked mozzarella	Swiss	Gorgonzola	Sharp Cheddar

SPREAD (2 TABLESPOONS)

Butter	Basil pesto	Russian dressing	Pecan butter	Mango chutney

ADD-IN (¼ CUP)

Crispy bacon	Sliced tomato	Raw sauerkraut	Sliced roasted beets	Grated pear

FLAVOR BOOSTER (2 TABLESPOONS)

Caramelized onions	Roasted garlic	Chopped pickles	Shredded radicchio (¼ cup)	Pickled jalapeño peppers

⁓ mix-and-match ⁓
SALADS

Pick one ingredient per row to re-create your ideal salad combos. Or choose straight down the left side if you're craving a classic taste—the farther right you go, the more adventurous the end result. Combine ingredients in a bowl and toss.

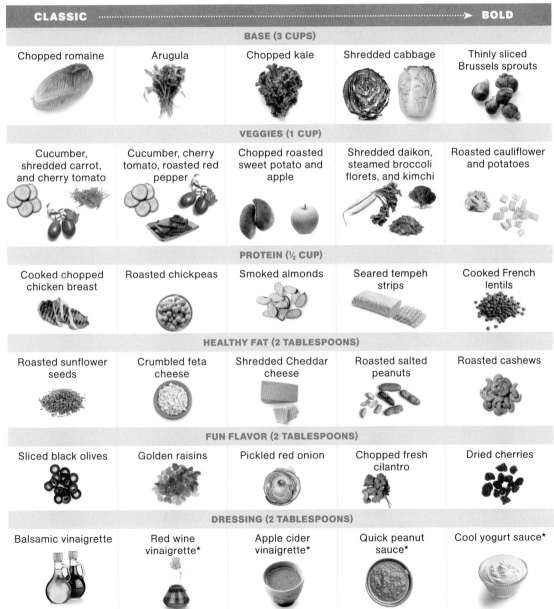

CLASSIC			⟶	BOLD
BASE (3 CUPS)				
Chopped romaine	Arugula	Chopped kale	Shredded cabbage	Thinly sliced Brussels sprouts
VEGGIES (1 CUP)				
Cucumber, shredded carrot, and cherry tomato	Cucumber, cherry tomato, roasted red pepper	Chopped roasted sweet potato and apple	Shredded daikon, steamed broccoli florets, and kimchi	Roasted cauliflower and potatoes
PROTEIN (½ CUP)				
Cooked chopped chicken breast	Roasted chickpeas	Smoked almonds	Seared tempeh strips	Cooked French lentils
HEALTHY FAT (2 TABLESPOONS)				
Roasted sunflower seeds	Crumbled feta cheese	Shredded Cheddar cheese	Roasted salted peanuts	Roasted cashews
FUN FLAVOR (2 TABLESPOONS)				
Sliced black olives	Golden raisins	Pickled red onion	Chopped fresh cilantro	Dried cherries
DRESSING (2 TABLESPOONS)				
Balsamic vinaigrette	Red wine vinaigrette*	Apple cider vinaigrette*	Quick peanut sauce*	Cool yogurt sauce*

*See page 126.

⚜ mix-and-match ⚜
SALAD DRESSINGS

Pick one ingredient per row to create your ideal salad dressing combo. Or choose straight down the left side if you're craving a classic taste—the farther right you go, the more adventurous the end result will be. Combine ingredients in a jar with a tight-fitting lid and shake to blend.

CLASSIC ···➤ BOLD

BASE (⅓ CUP)

| Extra-virgin olive oil | Flaxseed oil | Plain yogurt | Tahini |

ACID (2 TABLESPOONS)

| Apple cider vinegar | Red wine vinegar | Fresh lime juice | Fresh orange juice |

EMULSIFIER (1 TEASPOON)

| Dijon mustard | Mayonnaise | Mashed avocado | Honey |

FRESH HERBS (1 TABLESPOON)

| Chopped thyme | Chopped parsley | Chopped dill | Chopped cilantro |

WILD CARD (2 TABLESPOONS)

| Minced shallot | Crushed capers | Diced serrano pepper | Minced oil-cured olives |

✦ mix-and-match ✦
TACOS

Taco Tuesday routine getting sort of tired? Try these surprising mix-and-match picks. Warm up your favorite tortillas (corn, flour, gluten-free, or even a sturdy leafy green), then pile on your pick of protein, veggies, cheese, sauce, and flavor booster for a totally new take on the dinnertime staple. For a more classic taste, choose straight down the left; the farther right you go, the more adventurous the end result. Each portion combo makes enough for one taco.

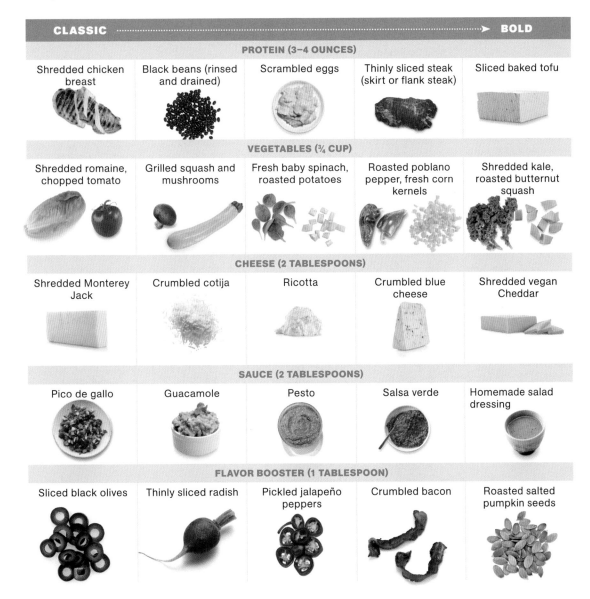

CLASSIC ···➤ BOLD				
PROTEIN (3–4 OUNCES)				
Shredded chicken breast	Black beans (rinsed and drained)	Scrambled eggs	Thinly sliced steak (skirt or flank steak)	Sliced baked tofu
VEGETABLES (¾ CUP)				
Shredded romaine, chopped tomato	Grilled squash and mushrooms	Fresh baby spinach, roasted potatoes	Roasted poblano pepper, fresh corn kernels	Shredded kale, roasted butternut squash
CHEESE (2 TABLESPOONS)				
Shredded Monterey Jack	Crumbled cotija	Ricotta	Crumbled blue cheese	Shredded vegan Cheddar
SAUCE (2 TABLESPOONS)				
Pico de gallo	Guacamole	Pesto	Salsa verde	Homemade salad dressing
FLAVOR BOOSTER (1 TABLESPOON)				
Sliced black olives	Thinly sliced radish	Pickled jalapeño peppers	Crumbled bacon	Roasted salted pumpkin seeds

⚘ mix-and-match ⚘
BURGERS

These options offer enough delicious combos to change up your traditional burger menu. Just grill or pan-sear your burger patty of choice, tuck it into your bun, pile on the toppings, and devour. For a more classic taste, choose straight down the left; the farther right you go, the more adventurous the end result.

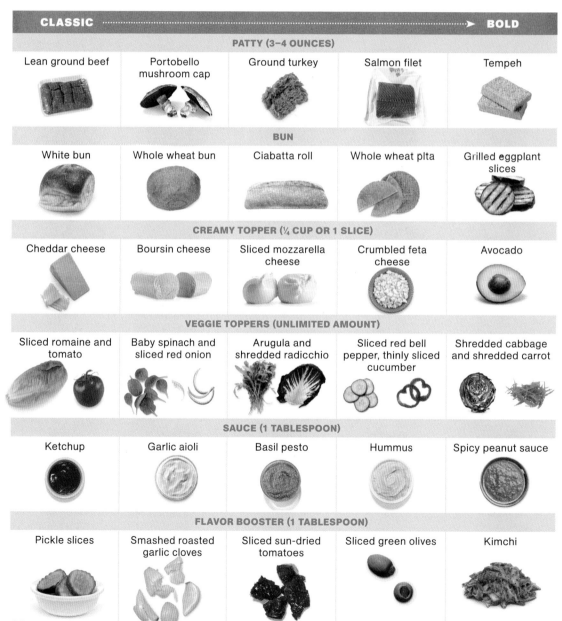

CLASSIC ⟶ BOLD				
PATTY (3–4 OUNCES)				
Lean ground beef	Portobello mushroom cap	Ground turkey	Salmon filet	Tempeh
BUN				
White bun	Whole wheat bun	Ciabatta roll	Whole wheat pita	Grilled eggplant slices
CREAMY TOPPER (¼ CUP OR 1 SLICE)				
Cheddar cheese	Boursin cheese	Sliced mozzarella cheese	Crumbled feta cheese	Avocado
VEGGIE TOPPERS (UNLIMITED AMOUNT)				
Sliced romaine and tomato	Baby spinach and sliced red onion	Arugula and shredded radicchio	Sliced red bell pepper, thinly sliced cucumber	Shredded cabbage and shredded carrot
SAUCE (1 TABLESPOON)				
Ketchup	Garlic aioli	Basil pesto	Hummus	Spicy peanut sauce
FLAVOR BOOSTER (1 TABLESPOON)				
Pickle slices	Smashed roasted garlic cloves	Sliced sun-dried tomatoes	Sliced green olives	Kimchi

mix-and-match

SHISH KEBABS

If you're craving a classic taste, choose straight down the left; the farther right you go, the more adventurous the end result.

   Pick one ingredient per row to create your ideal shish kebab. Marinate the protein and both vegetables for at least 30 minutes, or up to overnight. Thread the protein, veggies, and wild card ingredients on 8 to 10 skewers, and grill over medium-high heat until the protein is cooked through and the veggies are tender-crisp. (If using bamboo skewers, soak them in water for 30 minutes before threading.)

CLASSIC			➤	FEARLESS
MARINADE (¾ CUP)				
Tzatziki sauce	Pesto	Teriyaki sauce	Barbecue sauce	Peanut sauce
PROTEIN (1 POUND) EACH CUT INTO 1" CUBES				
Boneless, skinless chicken breast	Halloumi cheese	Skinless salmon fillet	Boneless pork loin	Extra-firm tofu
VEGGIE #1 (½ POUND)				
Red bell peppers	Cherry tomatoes	Broccoli	Green bell peppers	Sugar snap peas
VEGGIE #2 OR FRUIT (½ POUND)				
Sliced zucchini	Cubed eggplant	Cubed pineapple	Corn on the cob (sliced into ½" rounds)	Sliced sweet potatoes
WILD CARDS				
Whole rosemary sprigs	Roasted garlic cloves	Whole scallions cut into 3" pieces	Sliced red onion	Lime wedges

65

mix-and-match
NOODLE BOWLS

This isn't your typical bowl of pasta. These nutrient-dense noodle bowls use spiralized veggies and pack plenty of protein and fiber to keep you energized for hours. Use a spiralizer to spiralize your veggie noodles or purchase veggie noodles from your supermarket, then add a protein, vegetable add-ins, a sauce, and a flavor-packed topper. Choose straight down the left if you're craving a classic taste—the farther right you go, the more adventurous the end result.

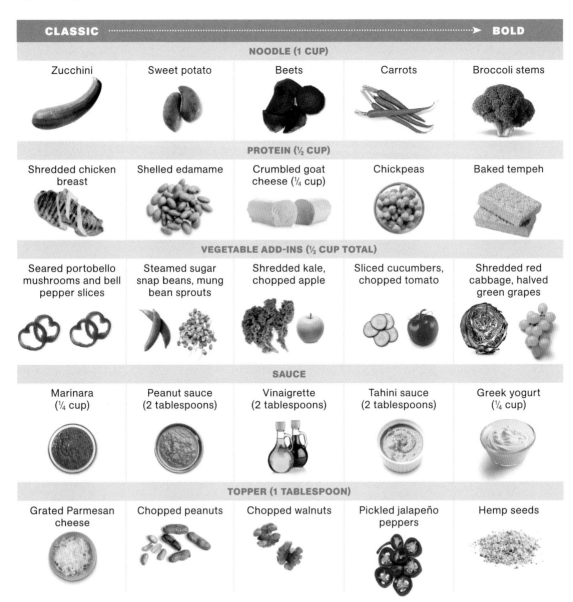

CLASSIC ⟶ BOLD

NOODLE (1 CUP)

Zucchini	Sweet potato	Beets	Carrots	Broccoli stems

PROTEIN (½ CUP)

Shredded chicken breast	Shelled edamame	Crumbled goat cheese (¼ cup)	Chickpeas	Baked tempeh

VEGETABLE ADD-INS (½ CUP TOTAL)

Seared portobello mushrooms and bell pepper slices	Steamed sugar snap beans, mung bean sprouts	Shredded kale, chopped apple	Sliced cucumbers, chopped tomato	Shredded red cabbage, halved green grapes

SAUCE

Marinara (¼ cup)	Peanut sauce (2 tablespoons)	Vinaigrette (2 tablespoons)	Tahini sauce (2 tablespoons)	Greek yogurt (¼ cup)

TOPPER (1 TABLESPOON)

Grated Parmesan cheese	Chopped peanuts	Chopped walnuts	Pickled jalapeño peppers	Hemp seeds

⚘ *mix-and-match* ⚘
CHICKEN SOUP

Pick one ingredient per row to create your ideal chicken soup, or choose straight down the left side if you're craving classic taste—the farther right you go, the more adventurous the end result.

To make: Simmer 2 quarts low-sodium chicken stock, 1½ cups cooked shredded chicken, and the raw vegetable combo of your choice until tender. Add your starch, herbs, and flavor booster, and simmer until the flavors are combined, about 5 minutes. Serve hot with your topper and eat!

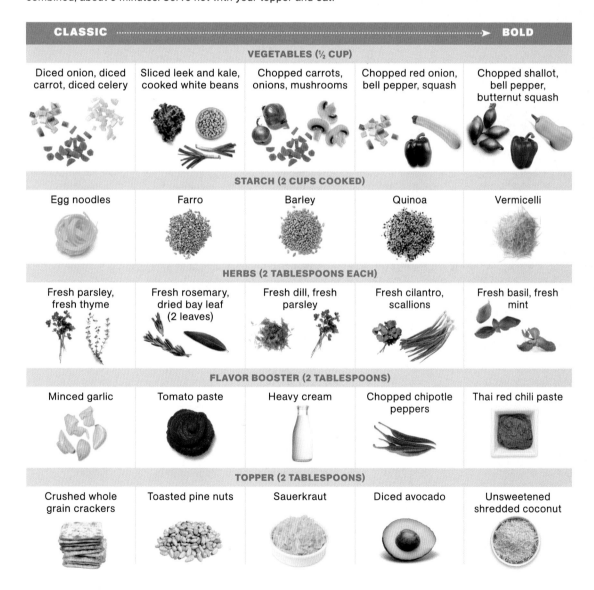

CLASSIC				➤ BOLD
VEGETABLES (½ CUP)				
Diced onion, diced carrot, diced celery	Sliced leek and kale, cooked white beans	Chopped carrots, onions, mushrooms	Chopped red onion, bell pepper, squash	Chopped shallot, bell pepper, butternut squash
STARCH (2 CUPS COOKED)				
Egg noodles	Farro	Barley	Quinoa	Vermicelli
HERBS (2 TABLESPOONS EACH)				
Fresh parsley, fresh thyme	Fresh rosemary, dried bay leaf (2 leaves)	Fresh dill, fresh parsley	Fresh cilantro, scallions	Fresh basil, fresh mint
FLAVOR BOOSTER (2 TABLESPOONS)				
Minced garlic	Tomato paste	Heavy cream	Chopped chipotle peppers	Thai red chili paste
TOPPER (2 TABLESPOONS)				
Crushed whole grain crackers	Toasted pine nuts	Sauerkraut	Diced avocado	Unsweetened shredded coconut

mix-and-match
SLOW-COOKER MEALS

Pick one ingredient per row to create your ideal slow-cooker meal. Choose straight down the left column if you're craving a classic taste—the farther right you go, the more adventurous the end result.

To cook: Sear protein in 1 tablespoon canola or olive oil until caramelized, then sauté veggies in 1 additional tablespoon oil until just tender. Add both to your slow cooker, along with the liquid, herbs and spices, and flavor booster. Cook on high heat for 4 hours or on low heat for 7 hours.

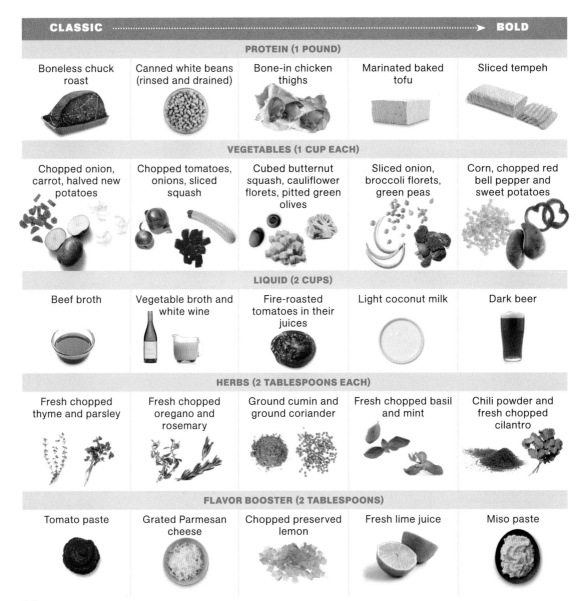

CLASSIC				➤ BOLD
PROTEIN (1 POUND)				
Boneless chuck roast	Canned white beans (rinsed and drained)	Bone-in chicken thighs	Marinated baked tofu	Sliced tempeh
VEGETABLES (1 CUP EACH)				
Chopped onion, carrot, halved new potatoes	Chopped tomatoes, onions, sliced squash	Cubed butternut squash, cauliflower florets, pitted green olives	Sliced onion, broccoli florets, green peas	Corn, chopped red bell pepper and sweet potatoes
LIQUID (2 CUPS)				
Beef broth	Vegetable broth and white wine	Fire-roasted tomatoes in their juices	Light coconut milk	Dark beer
HERBS (2 TABLESPOONS EACH)				
Fresh chopped thyme and parsley	Fresh chopped oregano and rosemary	Ground cumin and ground coriander	Fresh chopped basil and mint	Chili powder and fresh chopped cilantro
FLAVOR BOOSTER (2 TABLESPOONS)				
Tomato paste	Grated Parmesan cheese	Chopped preserved lemon	Fresh lime juice	Miso paste

⚡ mix-and-match ⚡
STIR-FRIES

Pick one ingredient per row to create your ideal stir-fry. Or choose straight down the left column if you're craving a classic taste—the farther right you go, the more adventurous the end result. To cook: Prepare the base as package directs. Cook protein in 1 tablespoon olive oil until cooked through; remove to plate. Stir-fry veggies in 1 tablespoon additional oil until just tender. Add sauce ingredients and cook to blend. Stir in protein and stir-fry for 1 minute. Place base in bowl, top with stir-fry, and sprinkle with topping.

CLASSIC ···➤ BOLD				
BASE (½ CUP)				
Brown rice	Quinoa	Millet	Farro	Buckwheat
PROTEIN (½ CUP)				
Shredded chicken breast	Shrimp	Smoked tofu	Soft-cooked egg	Steamed tempeh
VEGGIES (1½ CUPS)				
Snow peas, carrot matchsticks, water chestnuts	Cubed pineapple, broccoli florets, sliced red onion	Chopped mushrooms and bok choy, bamboo shoots	Sliced sunchokes, corn, mustard greens	Chopped green beans and pumpkin, sliced bell pepper
SAUCE (1 TABLESPOON + 1 TABLESPOON + 1 TABLESPOON)				
Low-sodium soy sauce + sesame oil + rice syrup	Teriyaki + sriracha + brown sugar	Ponzu sauce + matcha + hot chili oil	Coconut milk + fish sauce + lime juice	Orange juice + tahini + fresh basil
TOPPING (2 TABLESPOONS)				
Scallions	Chopped cashews	Black sesame seeds	Crispy shallots	Pumpkin seeds

⁓ mix-and-match ⁓
SALSAS

Why just stick to traditional tomato when there are so many much more flavorful possibilities to try? To make these mouthwatering salsas, combine all of your ingredients in a bowl, give them a good stir, and let the mixture sit for at least 30 minutes to let the flavors meld. Choose straight down the left side if you're craving a classic taste—the farther right you go, the more adventurous the end result.

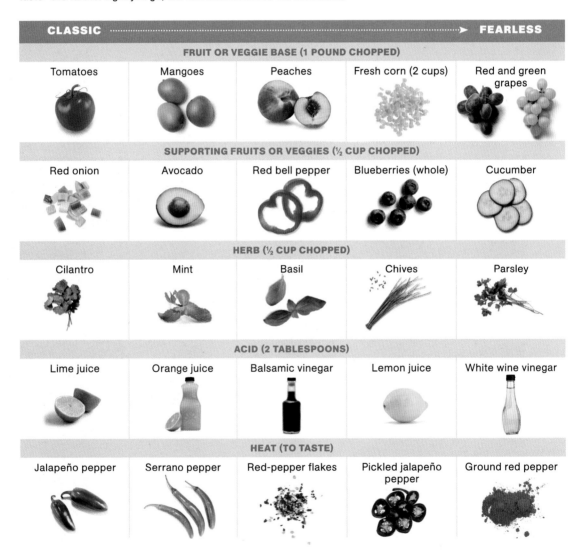

CLASSIC ···➤ FEARLESS				
FRUIT OR VEGGIE BASE (1 POUND CHOPPED)				
Tomatoes	Mangoes	Peaches	Fresh corn (2 cups)	Red and green grapes
SUPPORTING FRUITS OR VEGGIES (½ CUP CHOPPED)				
Red onion	Avocado	Red bell pepper	Blueberries (whole)	Cucumber
HERB (½ CUP CHOPPED)				
Cilantro	Mint	Basil	Chives	Parsley
ACID (2 TABLESPOONS)				
Lime juice	Orange juice	Balsamic vinegar	Lemon juice	White wine vinegar
HEAT (TO TASTE)				
Jalapeño pepper	Serrano pepper	Red-pepper flakes	Pickled jalapeño pepper	Ground red pepper

⤿ mix-and-match ⤾
PESTOS

Pesto is delicious—and very easy to make. So why stop at the traditional combo of fresh basil, Parmesan, and pine nuts when just about any veggie, cheese, and nut can combine into an awesome sauce? Simply combine your choice of greens, cheese, nuts or seeds, flavor booster, and ½ teaspoon salt (for a more classic taste, choose straight down the left; the farther right you go, the more adventurous the end result) in a food processor and pulse until finely chopped. With the motor running, add oil slowly until a smooth paste forms. Presto, pesto!

CLASSIC				➤ FEARLESS
HERBS OR GREENS (4 CUPS PACKED)				
Fresh basil	Parsley	Cilantro	Baby spinach	Kale (stems removed)
CHEESE (½ CUP)				
Grated Parmesan	Crumbled feta	Crumbled queso fresco	Crumbled Gorgonzola	Nutritional yeast
TOASTED NUTS OR SEEDS (¼ CUP)				
Pine nuts	Almonds	Pumpkin seeds	Sunflower seeds	Walnuts
FLAVOR BOOSTER (1 TABLESPOON)				
Minced garlic	Lemon juice	Chopped jalapeño pepper	Finely chopped shallot	Miso paste
OIL (½ CUP)				
Extra-virgin olive oil	Garlic-infused olive oil	Avocado oil	Grape-seed oil	Walnut oil

✿ mix-and-match ✿

TRAIL MIX

They call it trail mix for a reason: The nut-and-dried-fruit combo is packed with protein and complex carbs to keep you revved up no matter where you're running off to. And good old raisins and peanuts are just the beginning. For a more classic taste, choose straight down the left; the farther right you go, the more adventurous the end result. Use raw or roasted nuts and seeds, toss all into a bowl, portion the mix into ¼-cup servings, and head out the door.

CLASSIC				➤ BOLD
NUTS (¼ CUP)				
Peanuts	Almonds	Walnuts	Cashews	Pistachios
SEEDS (¼ CUP)				
Sunflowers	Pumpkin seeds	Sesame seeds	Hemp seeds	Chia seeds
FRUIT #1 (½ CUP)				
Raisins	Dried cherries	Chopped dried figs	Chopped dried pineapple	Sliced dried apricots
FRUIT #2 (½ CUP)				
Chopped dried apple	Dried blueberries	Chopped pitted dates	Chopped dried mango	Goji berries
ADD-INS (2¼ CUP)				
Rolled oats	Dark chocolate chunks	Chopped crystallized ginger	Unsweetened coconut flakes	Toasted buckwheat groats

BREAKFASTS

CRUSTLESS BREAKFAST QUICHE

PREP TIME: 15 MINUTES • TOTAL TIME: 45 MINUTES • MAKES 6 SERVINGS

2 tablespoons olive oil

1 onion, chopped

1 red bell pepper, chopped

1 bag (6 ounces) baby spinach

8 eggs

1 cup milk

3 or 4 drops hot sauce (optional)

¼ teaspoon salt

2 tablespoons whole wheat flour

⅔ cup shredded reduced-fat
  Cheddar cheese

1. Preheat the oven to 375°F. Coat a 9" glass pie plate with cooking spray.

2. In a large nonstick skillet, heat the oil over medium-high heat. Cook the onion and bell pepper, stirring, for 5 minutes, or until softened. Add the spinach and cook, stirring occasionally, for 2 minutes, or until the spinach begins to wilt and any liquid has evaporated. Remove from the heat.

3. In a large bowl, whisk together the eggs, milk, hot sauce (if using), and salt. Whisk in the flour until smooth. Stir in the spinach mixture and cheese until blended. Pour into the pie plate.

4. Bake for 30 minutes, or until the top is golden and a knife inserted into the center comes out clean.

Fast Fix: *You can substitute one (10-ounce) package of frozen chopped spinach, thawed. Just be sure to squeeze it dry before adding it to the onion mixture. Either way, leftovers make for quick breakfasts on the go.*

	CALORIES	PROTEIN	CARBS	FIBER	SUGARS	FAT	SAT FAT	SODIUM
REAL FOOD	219	15 g	11 g	2 g	4 g	13 g	4 g	345 mg
FAKE FOOD	490	23 g	43 g	3 g	13 g	26 g	14 g	740 mg

COMPARED TO: Nancy's Baked Quiche Lorraine

INGREDIENTS: Filling: milk, swiss cheese (part-skim milk, cheese cultures, salt, enzymes), eggs, onions, cooked bacon (bacon [cured with water, salt, sugar, sodium phosphates, sodium erythorbate, sodium nitrite], smoke flavor), corn starch, whey protein concentrate, chives, salt, spices. Pastry: enriched flour (wheat flour, niacin, reduced iron, thiamine mononitrate, riboflavin, folic acid), butter (cream, salt), canola oil, water, salt, soy lecithin.

food imposters
EGGS THAT AREN'T EGGS

Eggs are one ingredient. But substituting them takes 20. Thankfully, eggs top the ingredient list, but it goes downhill from there: The very next ingredient is a proprietary blend of "natural flavor" to conjure up egginess.

Ingredients: Egg whites (99%), less than 1% of the following: natural flavor, color (includes beta-carotene), spices, salt, onion powder, vegetable gums (xanthan gum, guar gum). *Vitamins and minerals:* calcium (sulfate), iron (ferric phosphate), vitamin E (alpha tocopherol acetate), zinc (sulfate), calcium pantothenate, vitamin B_2 (riboflavin), vitamin B_1 (thiamine mononitrate), vitamin B_6 (pyridoxine hydrochloride), vitamin B_{12}, folic acid, vitamin D_3, biotin.

CALIFORNIA-STYLE EGGS BENEDICT

PREP TIME: 5 MINUTES • TOTAL TIME: 15 MINUTES • MAKES 2 SERVINGS

½ ripe avocado

¼ cup 2% Greek yogurt

1 fresh lime or lemon, juiced

⅛ teaspoon salt

2 whole wheat English muffins, split and toasted

4 large eggs

2 cups loosely packed baby spinach

1. In a small bowl, mash the avocado with a fork. Add the yogurt, lime or lemon juice, and salt. Mash until smooth. Set aside.

2. Fill a medium saucepan with about 2" of water. Place over high heat and bring to a boil.

3. Crack the eggs into a small bowl one at a time. Slowly pour into the boiling water. Spoon some hot water over each yolk. Reduce the heat to medium and simmer for 2 minutes, or until the egg yolks are cooked to the desired consistency.

4. With a slotted spoon, remove the eggs from the water and place on a plate lined with paper towels to absorb excess water.

5. Place 2 muffin halves on each of 2 plates. Top each with one-quarter of the spinach and 1 egg. Pour the avocado mixture on top.

Fast Fix: *The most effective way to pit an avocado is to slice around the middle and through both ends with a sharp knife. Use your hands to twist the avocado to separate the halves. Sharply stick the knife blade into the pit, then lift the knife to remove it. Use caution when removing the pit from the knife.*

	CALORIES	PROTEIN	CARBS	FIBER	SUGARS	FAT	SAT FAT	SODIUM
REAL FOOD	364	22 g	35 g	8 g	7 g	17 g	4 g	578 mg
FAKE FOOD	689	31 g	42 g	1 g	7 g	45 g	18 g	1,650 mg

COMPARED TO: Perkins Classic Eggs Benedict

INGREDIENTS: Blended Soybean Oil Liquid and hydrogenated soybean oil, soy lecithin, natural and artificial flavor, beta-carotene, TBHQ and citric acid added to protect flavor, dimethylpolysiloxane (anti-foaming agent). Eggs, Large Fresh Whole egg English Muffin Bleached enriched wheat flour (flour, malted barley flour, niacin, reduced iron, thiamine mononitrate, riboflavin, folic acid), water, yeast. Contains 2% or less of yellow cornmeal, partially hydrogenated soybean oil, sugar, salt, wheat gluten, calcium sulfate, calcium propionate (to retard spoilage), citric acid, leavening (monocalcium phosphate, baking soda), datem (dough conditioner), enzymes, calcium citrate, calcium phosphate, azodicarbonamide, cornstarch, cellolose, wheat starch, non-fat milk, calcium stearate. Fresh Chopped Parsley Parsley. Ham, Off the Bone Cured with water and 2% or less of salt, sugar, potassium lactate, sodium lactate, sodium phosphates, sodium diacetate, smoke flavoring, sodium erythorbate, sodium nitrite. Hollandaise Sauce 2% milk (reduced fat milk, vitamin A palmitate, vitamin D3), butter (cream, salt), hollandaise sauce mix (modified corn starch, maltodextrin, cornstarch, partially hydrogenated soybean and cotonseed oils, whey protein concentrate, salt, autolyzed yeast extract, onion powder, hydrolyzed protein (corn, soy, wheat), citric acid, guar gum, turmeric, dextrose, paprika, thiamine hydrochloride, spice, garlic powder, natural flavors). Whipped Butter Blend Vegetable oil (soybean, palm), water, butter (cream, salt), whey solids, salt, vegetable mono- & diglycerides, soy lecithin, sodium benzoate and potassium sorbate (preservatives), buttermilk solids, citric acid, natural & artificial flavor, beta-carotene (color), vitamin A palmitate.

SAUSAGE *and* EGG MUFFINS

PREP TIME: 10 MINUTES • TOTAL TIME: 10 MINUTES • MAKES 4 SERVINGS

4 fully cooked refrigerated or thawed
frozen turkey sausage patties

1 teaspoon unsalted butter

4 eggs, lightly beaten

4 whole wheat English muffins, split
and toasted

¼ cup shredded reduced-fat
Cheddar cheese

1. Heat a large nonstick skillet coated with cooking spray over medium-high heat. Cook the sausage patties, turning once, for 5 minutes, or until browned and heated through. Transfer to a plate.

2. In the same skillet, melt the butter over medium heat. Cook the eggs, stirring, for 2 minutes, or until they're softly scrambled but still moist and creamy.

3. Top each of 4 of the muffin halves with 1 sausage patty, one-quarter of the scrambled eggs, and 1 tablespoon of the cheese. Cover the sandwiches with the remaining muffin tops.

⇒ Bonus Benefits ⇐

Eat more eggs! Researchers found a significant association between eating more than one egg per week and less advanced coronary artery disease.[1]

	CALORIES	PROTEIN	CARBS	FIBER	SUGARS	FAT	SAT FAT	SODIUM
REAL FOOD	298	20 g	28 g	4 g	6 g	13 g	4 g	628 mg
FAKE FOOD	700	23 g	41 g	2 g	5 g	50 g	20 g	1,170 mg

COMPARED TO: Dunkin' Donuts Sausage Egg & Cheese Croissant

INGREDIENTS: Croissant: dough: enriched wheat flour (flour, niacin, reduced iron, thiamin mononitrate, riboflavin, ascorbic acid, enzymes, folic acid), water, margarine [(palm oil, modified palm oil, canola oil), water, sugar, monoglycerides, soy lecithin, potassium sorbate (preservative), citric acid, artificial flavor, beta-carotene (color), vitamin a palmitate, vitamin d], sugar, contains less than 2% of the following: yeast, dough conditioner (wheat flour, datem, ascorbic acid, enzymes), salt, wheat gluten, dextrose, natural and artificial flavor; Glaze: fructose, corn syrup solids, sodium caseinate (a milk derivative), locust bean gum, sodium stearoyl lactylate, soybean and/or canola oil, soy lecithin, sodium bicarbonate; Sausage: pork, water, and contains 2% or less of: salt, caramel color, spices and flavorings, sodium tripolyphosphate, tetrapotassium pyrophosphate, sugar, monosodium glutamate, BHT, propyl gallate, citric acid; Egg Patty: egg whites, egg yolk, soybean oil, water, contains 2% or less of the following: unmodified corn starch, salt, natural flavor, xanthan gum, cellulose gum, citric acid; Cheese: american cheese (milk, cheese cultures, salt, enzymes), water, dry cream, milk fat, sodium citrate, salt, sorbic acid (preservative), annatto and oleoresin paprika color (if colored), soy lecithin (non-sticking agent).

ITALIAN EGG SANDWICHES

PREP TIME: 5 MINUTES • TOTAL TIME: 15 MINUTES • MAKES 2 SERVINGS

2 large eggs

½ cup shredded part-skim mozzarella
cheese, divided

1 teaspoon water

2 whole grain light English muffins, split
and toasted

¼ cup marinara sauce, heated

1. Coat a nonstick skillet with cooking spray and heat over medium-high heat. Break the eggs into the skillet, gently pushing the white toward the center so each egg is about the size of an English muffin. Top each egg with 2 tablespoons of the cheese. Immediately reduce the heat to low. Cook for 1 minute, or until the edges turn white. Add the water. Tightly cover the skillet.

2. Cook for 3 minutes, or until the whites are completely set and the yolks begin to thicken but are not hard.

3. Place half an English muffin on each of 2 plates. Top each with half of the sauce and the remaining 2 tablespoons cheese.

4. Place 1 egg on each muffin. Top with the remaining muffin halves.

	CALORIES	PROTEIN	CARBS	FIBER	SUGARS	FAT	SAT FAT	SODIUM
REAL FOOD	294	19 g	31 g	5g	6 g	11 g	5g	681 mg
FAKE FOOD	540	29 g	40 g	1 g	4 g	31 g	15 g	1,450 mg

COMPARED TO: Carl's Jr. Grilled Cheese Breakfast Sandwich with Bacon

INGREDIENTS: Sourdough Bread: bread, sourdough—wheat flour enriched [(niacin, ferrous sulfate, thiamine mononitrate, riboflavin, folic acid)], malted barley, ascorbic acid], water, yeast, high fructose corn syrup, sourdough base [wheat starch, bleached enriched flour (wheat flour, malted barley flour, niacin, iron, thiamine mononitrate, riboflavin and folic acid), acetic acid, citric acid, palm oil], contains 2% or less of each of the following: soybean oil, salt, datem, calcium propionate (a preservative), mono-glyceride, ascorbic acid, enzymes, prep buttery seasoning—soybean oil, hydrogenated soybean oil, Contains 2% or less of: salt, soy lecithin, artificial and natural butter flavor, vitamin a palmitate, artificial color, hydrolyzed soy protein, autolyzed yeast extract (contains barley, soy, milk, and egg components). Bacon, precooked: cured with water, salt, sugar, smoke flavoring, sodium phosphates, dextrose, sodium erythorbate and sodium nitrite. Swiss Cheese, Pasteurized Process Allergens: milk and milk products, soy protein cultured milk, skim milk, water, salt, sodium citrate, sodium phosphate, cream, citric acid, sorbic acid (preservative), enzymes, lactic acid, soy lecithin. American Cheese, Pasteurized Process Allergens: milk and milk products, soy protein cultured milk, water, cream, sodium citrate, salt, sodium phosphate, sorbic acid (preservative), artificial color, acetic acid, enzymes, soy lecithin. Egg, Liquid: whole egg, citric acid. Grill Spray: coconut oil, soy lecithin, artificial flavor, beta-carotene.

EGG BRUNCH PIZZA

SEE PHOTO ON PAGE 140.

PREP TIME: 5 MINUTES • TOTAL TIME: 15 MINUTES • MAKES 1 SERVING

1 sprouted whole wheat tortilla

¼ cup pizza sauce

¼ cup shredded mozzarella cheese

¼ cup sliced mushrooms

¼ cup sliced cherry tomatoes

1 egg

1 tablespoon chopped fresh parsley or basil leaves (optional)

1. Preheat the oven to 350°F. Line a baking sheet with parchment paper.

2. Place the tortilla on the baking sheet. Spread with the pizza sauce. Sprinkle with the cheese, mushrooms, and tomatoes. Bake for 5 minutes.

3. Break the egg into the center of the pizza. Bake for 7 minutes, or until the egg is set. Top with the parsley or basil, if using.

	CALORIES	PROTEIN	CARBS	FIBER	SUGARS	FAT	SAT FAT	SODIUM
REAL FOOD	204	15 g	9 g	2 g	3 g	12 g	5 g	395 mg
FAKE FOOD	530	25 g	40 g	3 g	4 g	30 g	15 g	1,490 mg

COMPARED TO: Steak, Egg & Cheese Biscuit from McDonald's

INGREDIENTS: Biscuit: enriched flour (bleached wheat flour, niacin, reduced iron, thiamin mononitrate, riboflavin, folic acid), cultured nonfat buttermilk (cultured skim milk, nonfat dry milk, modified food starch, salt, sodium citrate, mono- and diglycerides, locust bean gum, carrageenan), palm oil, palm kernel oil, water, leavening (sodium bicarbonate, sodium aluminum phosphate, monocalcium phosphate), contains 2% or less: salt, sugar, modified cellulose, wheat protein isolate, natural flavor, modified food starch, xanthan gum, soy lecithin. Contains: wheat, milk, soy. Breakfast Steak Pattie: beef, water, salt, sodium phosphate, natural flavor. seasoned with salt, spices, dried garlic, soybean oil, natural flavor. Folded Egg: eggs, nonfat milk, modified food starch, salt, citric acid, soy lecithin. Contains: egg, milk, soy. Pasteurized Process American Cheese: milk, cream, water, sodium citrate, cheese cultures, salt, color added, sorbic acid (preservative), citric acid, lactic acid, acetic acid, enzymes, soy lecithin. Contains: milk, soy. Caramelized Grilled Onions: slivered onions. prepared in onion reduction sauce (palm, soybean and/or cottonseed oil, salt, sugar, caramelized sugar, onion powder, natural flavors, spice). Salted Butter: cream, salt. Contains: milk Clarified Butter: pasteurized cream (butterfat). Contains: milk.

⇒ Bonus Benefits ⇐

Mushrooms help prevent a range of conditions including metabolic disease, cardiovascular disease, Alzheimer's disease, Parkinson's disease, premature aging, and various cancers.[2]

8 ways with . . . eggs

Here are some super-fast breakfast ideas that come together in minutes while giving you a hearty way to start the day. Eggs are a great source of protein, which provides energy throughout the day. The first four recipes may be served with whole grain toast.

1. **Tuscan Baked Eggs.** Preheat the oven to 350°F. Coat a 1-quart baking dish with cooking spray and crack 2 eggs into it. Top each egg with 2 tablespoons chopped tomato, ¼ teaspoon Italian seasoning, ½ teaspoon olive oil, and a pinch of salt. Bake for 10 minutes, or until the eggs are set. *Makes 1 serving.*

   Nutrition (per serving): 191 calories, 13 g protein, 3 g carbohydrates, 1 g fiber, 2 g sugars, 14 g fat, 4 g saturated fat, 304 mg sodium

2. **Herbed Scrambled Eggs.** In a small bowl, whisk together 2 eggs, ¼ teaspoon dried herb such as tarragon, basil, or thyme, and a pinch of salt and black pepper. Heat 2 teaspoons butter in a small skillet over medium heat. Add the eggs and cook, stirring, for 1 minute, or until almost set. Top with 2 tablespoons crumbled goat cheese and cook, stirring, for 1 minute, or until just set. *Makes 1 serving.*

   Nutrition (per serving): 235 calories, 14 g protein, 1 g carbohydrates, 1 g fiber, 0 g sugars, 20 g fat, 10 g saturated fat, 406 mg sodium

3. **Shiitake Omelet.** Heat 2 teaspoons butter in a medium skillet over medium heat. Cook 2 sliced scallions, 1 cup sliced shiitake mushrooms, and a pinch of salt for 5 minutes, or until lightly browned. Remove to a bowl. Coat the same skillet with cooking spray and heat over medium heat. In a small bowl, whisk together 2 large eggs and a pinch of salt and black pepper. Cook the eggs, undisturbed, for 1 minute, or until the bottom is set. Place the mushroom mixture and ¼ cup shredded Swiss cheese in the center of the eggs and fold the egg over the filling. *Makes 1 serving.*

   Nutrition (per serving): 342 calories, 22 g protein, 8 g carbohydrates, 2 g fiber, 3 g sugars, 25 g fat, 12 g saturated fat, 417 mg sodium

4. **Mediterranean Deviled Eggs.** Slice 8 hard-cooked eggs in half lengthwise, and scoop the yolks into a small bowl. Stir 2 tablespoons hummus and 2 tablespoons mayonnaise into the yolks and mix until smooth, adding 1 to 2 teaspoons water if needed. Fill each egg half with the yolk mixture and top each with a half of a pitted kalamata olive. Sprinkle with paprika, if desired. *Makes 4 servings.*

   Nutrition (per serving): 224 calories, 13 g protein, 3 g carbohydrates, 1 g fiber, 0 g sugars, 17 g fat, 4 g saturated fat, 338 mg sodium

5. **Cheesy Green Grits.** Stir 1 cup quick-cooking grits into 4 cups boiling water and cook, stirring, for 5 minutes, or until thickened. Meanwhile, soft-boil 4 eggs. Stir 1 cup shredded sharp Cheddar cheese, 3 cups chopped baby spinach, and $\frac{1}{2}$ teaspoon salt into the grits. Divide among 4 bowls and top each bowl with an egg. *Makes 4 servings.*

Nutrition (per serving): 333 calories, 16 g protein, 34 g carbohydrates, 3 g fiber, 1 g sugars, 14 g fat, 8 g saturated fat, 578 mg sodium

6. **Egg and Avocado Toast.** Toast a thick slice of whole grain bread. In a small bowl, mash half an avocado with $\frac{1}{4}$ teaspoon smoked paprika and $\frac{1}{8}$ teaspoon *each* salt and black pepper. Spread the avocado mixture on the toast, and top with a sliced hard-cooked egg. *Makes 1 serving.*

Nutrition (per serving): 385 calories, 14 g protein, 38 g carbohydrates, 8 g fiber, 3 g sugars, 21 g fat, 4 g saturated fat, 617 mg sodium

7. **Blender Dutch Baby.** Preheat the oven to 425°F and coat an 8" cast-iron skillet with cooking spray. In a blender, combine 2 large eggs, $\frac{1}{2}$ cup whole grain or whole wheat pastry flour, $\frac{1}{2}$ cup milk, 2 tablespoons melted butter, 1 tablespoon sugar, and 1 teaspoon vanilla extract. Blend until the batter is smooth, and pour into the skillet. Bake for 15 minutes, or until puffed and golden. Serve with maple syrup, if desired. *Makes 4 servings.*

Nutrition (per serving): 162 calories, 6 g protein, 14 g carbohydrates, 1 g fiber, 5 g sugars, 9 g fat, 5 g saturated fat, 99 mg sodium

8. **Savory Oatmeal.** In a medium saucepan, bring 2 cups water, 1 cup rolled oats, $\frac{1}{2}$ teaspoon salt, and $\frac{1}{4}$ teaspoon black pepper to a simmer. Reduce the heat to low, cover, and cook for 3 minutes, or until thickened. Meanwhile, soft-boil or fry 2 eggs. Stir $\frac{1}{2}$ cup shredded cheese of your choice, $\frac{1}{2}$ cup halved cherry tomatoes, and one-quarter of an avocado, chopped, into the oatmeal. Divide the oatmeal between 2 bowls, and top each with an egg. *Makes 2 servings.*

Nutrition (per serving): 451 calories, 22 g protein, 33 g carbohydrates, 8 g fiber, 3 g sugars, 26 g fat, 9 g saturated fat, 865 mg sodium

SMOKED SALMON BREAKFAST SANDWICH

PREP TIME: 10 MINUTES ● TOTAL TIME: 15 MINUTES ● MAKES 1 SERVING

3 tablespoons (1.5 ounces) Neufchâtel cheese, at room temperature

¼ teaspoon lemon-pepper seasoning (optional)

1 whole wheat bagel thin, halved and toasted

2 ounces thinly sliced smoked salmon

1/16 English cucumber, thinly cut into 4 slices

1 slice red onion

1. In a small bowl, stir together the cheese and the seasoning, if using, until well blended.

2. Spread the cheese mixture on half of the bagel thin. Top with the salmon, cucumber slices, and onion. Place the remaining bagel thin half on top.

	CALORIES	PROTEIN	CARBS	FIBER	SUGARS	FAT	SAT FAT	SODIUM
REAL FOOD	282	16 g	33 g	6 g	8 g	12 g	6 g	712 mg
FAKE FOOD	510	21 g	52 g	2 g	9 g	25 g	11 g	1,400 mg

COMPARED TO: Wendy's Honey Butter Chicken Biscuit

INGREDIENTS: Butter biscuit enriched bleached flour (wheat flour, niacin, reduced iron, thiamin mononitrate, riboflavin, folic acid), cultured buttermilk (nonfat milk, nonfat milk solids, food starch-modified, carrageenan, locust bean gum, salt, cultures), palm oil, sugar, contains less than 2%: sodium bicarbonate, buttermilk, food starch-modified, sodium aluminum phosphate, sodium acid pyrophosphate, salt, sunflower oil, sodium stearoyl lactylate, wheat starch, xanthan gum, soy lecithin, ascorbic acid, natural flavor, tricalcium phosphate, canola oil. contains allergens: wheat, milk, soy. Jr. Homestyle Chicken Fillet chicken breast fillets with rib meat containing: up to 17% of a solution of water, seasoning [salt, autolyzed yeast extract, sugar, flavor, chicken, maltodextrin, gum arabic, silicon dioxide, lactic acid, sunflower oil, canola oil, dextrose, grill flavor (from canola oil), citric acid], modified food starch, sodium phosphates. breaded with: wheat flour, water, salt, modified corn starch, leavening (sodium acid pyrophosphate, sodium bicarbonate, monocalcium phosphate), onion powder, garlic powder, autolyzed yeast extract, natural flavor, lactic acid, extractives of turmeric. breading set in vegetable oil, cooked in vegetable oil (soybean oil, vegetable oil [may contain one or more of the following: canola, corn, or cottonseed], hydrogenated soybean oil, dimethylpolysiloxane [anti-foaming agent]. cooked in the same oil as menu items that contain wheat and fish. Honey Butter Spread Butter (cream, salt), Powdered Sugar (sugar, corn starch), Honey, Soybean Oil, Natural Flavor. Contains: milk, soy.

What Is Smoked Salmon?

Typically found in the refrigerator case of your supermarket's fish section, smoked salmon is actually available in two varieties. Hot-smoked salmon is just that, processed under a higher temperature of 120° to 180°F for about 8 hours. Cold-smoked salmon is cooked at around 80°F for a few days. It has a similar texture to brined or salt-cured salmon, which is also known as lox or gravlax. Nova Scotia smoked salmon is a good choice for this recipe because its flavor is mild and not very salty.

SOUTHWESTERN BLACK BEAN WRAP

SEE PHOTO ON PAGE 142.

PREP TIME: 5 MINUTES ● TOTAL TIME: 15 MINUTES ● MAKES 1 SERVING

1 whole wheat tortilla (8" diameter)

¼ cup canned black beans, rinsed and drained

¼ cup cooked brown rice

½ cup baby spinach

1 large egg, beaten

2 tablespoons shredded Cheddar cheese

¼ avocado, sliced

2 tablespoons salsa

1 tablespoon chopped cilantro

1. Heat a medium skillet over medium heat. Cook the tortilla, turning once, for 2 minutes, or until warm. Transfer to a plate.

2. Coat the same skillet with cooking spray and heat over medium heat. Cook the beans, rice, and spinach, stirring frequently, for 2 minutes, or until the spinach begins to wilt. Spread the mixture down the center of the tortilla.

3. Recoat the skillet with cooking spray and heat over medium heat. Cook the egg, stirring frequently, for 2 minutes, or until scrambled. Place over the bean mixture.

4. Top with the cheese, avocado, salsa, and cilantro. Fold up both sides of the tortilla and roll.

⇒ Bonus Benefits ⇐

Flavonoid-rich black bean extracts have been shown to inhibit the growth of colon, breast, liver, and prostate cancer cells via apoptosis (cell death), while leaving normal cells intact.[3]

	CALORIES	PROTEIN	CARBS	FIBER	SUGARS	FAT	SAT FAT	SODIUM
REAL FOOD	441	20 g	51g	11 g	2 g	19 g	6 g	728 mg
FAKE FOOD	630	24 g	65 g	5 g	4 g	31 g	8 g	1,470 mg

COMPARED TO: Grande Scrambler Burrito from Taco Bell

INGREDIENTS: Cheddar Cheese: cheddar cheese (cultured pasteurized milk, salt, enzymes, annatto (vc)), anti-caking agent. contains: milk [certified vegetarian], Eggs: whole eggs, soybean oil, salt, citric acid, pepper, flavor (sunflower oil, flavors), xanthan gum, guar gum. Contains: egg [certified vegetarian], Flour Tortilla: enriched wheat flour, water, vegetable shortening (soybean, hydrogenated soybean and/or cottonseed oil), sugar, salt, leavening (baking soda, sodium acid pyrophosphate), molasses, dough conditioner (fumaric acid, distilled monoglycerides, enzymes, vital wheat gluten, cellulose gum, wheat starch, calcium carbonate), calcium propionate, sorbic acid, and/or potassium sorbate (P). Contains: wheat. [certified vegan], Nacho Cheese Sauce: nonfat milk, cheese whey, water, vegetable oil (canola oil, soybean oil), modified food starch, maltodextrin, natural flavors, salt, dipotassium phosphate, jalapeño puree, vinegar, lactic acid, cellulose gum, potassium citrate, sodium stearoyl lactylate, citric acid, annatto and oleoresin paprika (VC). Contains: milk, Pico de Gallo: Tomatoes, onion, cilantro, water, vinegar, lemon juice concentrate, salt, xanthan gum. [certified vegan], Potato Bites: Potatoes, soybean oil, enriched wheat flour, tapioca starch, salt, rice flour, dextrin, spices, baking powder, onion powder, garlic powder, natural flavor, modified food starch, guar gum, paprika and turmeric (VC), dextrose. Prepared in canola oil. Contains: wheat, Reduced-Fat Sour Cream: milk, cream, modified corn starch, lactic acid, maltodextrin, citric acid, sodium phosphate, natural flavor, cellulose gel, potassium sorbate (P), cellulose gum, guar gum, locust bean gum, carrageenan, vitamin A. Contains: milk [certified vegetarian], USDA Select Marinated Grilled Steak: beef, water, seasoning (modified potato starch, natural flavors, salt, brown sugar, dextrose, carrageenan, dried beef stock, cocoa powder, onion powder, disodium inosinate & guanylate, tomato powder, corn syrup solids, maltodextrin, garlic powder, spice, citric acid, lemon juice powder), sodium phosphates. sauce: water, seasoning (natural flavors, dextrose, brown sugar, salt, dried beef stock, onion powder, tomato powder, corn syrup solids, maltodextrin, disodium inosinate & guanylate, garlic powder, spices, cocoa powder, citric acid, lemon juice powder).

APPLE-BACON PANCAKES

SEE PHOTO ON PAGE 137.

PREP TIME: 10 MINUTES • TOTAL TIME: 20 MINUTES • MAKES 4 SERVINGS

2 strips bacon

1 cup whole grain pastry or whole wheat flour

¾ teaspoon baking powder

½ teaspoon ground cinnamon

¼ teaspoon salt

¾ cup milk

½ cup unsweetened applesauce

1 egg

2 tablespoons safflower oil

6 tablespoons maple syrup, divided

1. Preheat the oven to 200°F. Place the bacon on 3 paper towels on a microwaveable plate. Cover with 1 paper towel. Microwave on high power for 3 minutes, or until cooked through. Crumble.

2. In a large bowl, whisk together the flour, baking powder, cinnamon, and salt. Add the milk, applesauce, egg, oil, and 2 tablespoons of the syrup. Stir just until blended.

3. Heat a griddle coated with cooking spray over medium heat. In batches, drop heaping table-spoonfuls of batter onto the griddle to form 3" pancakes. Cook for 2 minutes, or until bubbles form on the tops. Evenly sprinkle with the bacon. Turn and cook for 2 minutes, or until lightly browned.

4. Remove the pancakes to a plate and keep warm in the oven. Repeat with the remaining batter, making a total of 12 pancakes. Divide the pancakes and remaining 4 tablespoons maple syrup among 4 plates.

Fast Fix: *These pancakes will freeze well for a quick breakfast another day. Place the cooled pancakes, separated with parchment or waxed paper, in an airtight container. To use, remove from the freezer 15 minutes before heating. Microwave on medium power for 1 minute, or until heated through.*

	CALORIES	PROTEIN	CARBS	FIBER	SUGARS	FAT	SAT FAT	SODIUM
REAL FOOD	293	7 g	44 g	3 g	25 g	11 g	2 g	393 mg
FAKE FOOD	360	9 g	32 g	1 g	11 g	22 g	7 g	630 mg

COMPARED TO: Jimmy Dean Griddle Cake Maple Pancakes & Sausage

INGREDIENTS: Maple Pancakes: water, enriched flour (wheat flour, malted barley flour, ferrous sulfate, niacin, reduced iron, thiamine mononitrate, riboflavin, folic acid), sugar, maple flavored bits (sugar, corn cereal, modified corn starch, corn flour, artificial flavor, caramel color), soybean and/or canola oil, eggs, buttermilk solids, cultured wheat flour, salt, sodium bicarbonate, sodium acid pyrophosphate, monocalcium phosphate, mono- and diglycerides, potassium sorbate, calcium propionate, natural and artificial flavor. Cooked Sausage Patty: pork, water, Contains 2% or less: potassium lactate, salt, sugar, spices, sodium phosphate, monosodium glutamate, sodium diacetate, caramel color. Contains egg, milk, soy, and wheat.

≥ food imposters ≤
MAPLE SYRUP THAT'S NOT MAPLE SYRUP

Check out the syrup in your pantry before you pour it on your stack of pancakes: Chances are good you won't find anything close to resembling maple syrup, but you'll find plenty of corn syrup (two types!) and artificial flavorings. Here, treat your pancakes to another squeeze of sodium hexametaphosphate!

Ingredients: Corn syrup, high-fructose corn syrup, water, cellulose gum, caramel color, salt, sodium benzoate and sorbic acid (preservatives), artificial and natural flavors, sodium hexametaphosphate.

RICOTTA PANCAKES
with BLUEBERRIES

PREP TIME: 15 MINUTES • TOTAL TIME: 30 MINUTES • MAKES 4 SERVINGS

2 large eggs

¾ cup buttermilk

⅔ cup part-skim ricotta cheese

⅔ cup whole grain or whole wheat pastry flour

1 tablespoon sugar

1 teaspoon baking powder

¼ teaspoon baking soda

¼ teaspoon salt

1 cup blueberries

½ cup maple syrup

1. Preheat the oven to 200°F.

2. In a medium bowl, whisk together the eggs, buttermilk, and ricotta. Stir in the flour, sugar, baking powder, baking soda, and salt until well blended. Heat a griddle or large nonstick skillet coated with cooking spray over medium heat.

3. Drop the batter by scant ¼ cupfuls onto the griddle or skillet. Cook for 2 minutes, or just until bubbles form on the tops and the bottoms brown. Turn and cook for 2 minutes, or until browned and cooked through. Remove the pancakes to a plate and keep warm in the oven. Repeat with additional cooking spray and the remaining batter, making a total of 12 pancakes. Serve with the blueberries and syrup.

	CALORIES	PROTEIN	CARBS	FIBER	SUGARS	FAT	SAT FAT	SODIUM
REAL FOOD	332	12 g	53 g	3 g	35 g	9 g	5 g	447 mg
FAKE FOOD	610	12 g	72 g	1 g	30 g	31 g	9 g	1,010 mg

COMPARED TO: Burger King Pancake and Sausage Platter

INGREDIENTS: Pancakes: water, enriched bleached flour (wheat flour, niacin, reduced iron, thiamine mononitrate, riboflavin, folic acid), sugar, soybean oil, leavening (sodium aluminum phosphate, sodium bicarbonate), egg yolks, dextrose, Contains 2% or less of the following: salt, natural and artificial flavor, whey, soy lecithin, cellulose gum, xanthan gum. Mild Sausage: pork, salt, spices, corn syrup solids, dextrose, monosodium glutamate, hydrogenated soybean oil, grill flavor (from soybean oil).

DOUBLE VANILLA FRENCH TOAST

SEE PHOTO ON PAGE 138.

PREP TIME: 5 MINUTES • TOTAL TIME: 15 MINUTES • MAKES 2 SERVINGS

3 large eggs

¼ cup milk

1 teaspoon vanilla extract

4 slices whole grain bread

½ cup organic vanilla yogurt

2 tablespoons maple syrup

1 cup mixed berries

1. In a pie plate or shallow bowl, whisk together the eggs, milk, and vanilla. Dip the bread in the egg mixture, turning once, allowing it to soak up the liquid.

2. Heat a large nonstick skillet over medium heat. Cook the bread for 5 minutes, turning once, or until browned.

3. Place 2 slices of French toast on 2 plates. Top each with ¼ cup of the yogurt, 1 tablespoon of the maple syrup, and ½ cup of the berries.

	CALORIES	PROTEIN	CARBS	FIBER	SUGARS	FAT	SAT FAT	SODIUM
REAL FOOD	380	18 g	56 g	5 g	27 g	9 g	3 g	445 mg
FAKE FOOD	777	36 g	84 g	3 g	12 g	32 g	4 g	1,067 mg

COMPARED TO: *Perkins Ooh-La-La French Toast Platter*

INGREDIENTS: Liquid and hydrogenated soybean oil, soy lecithin, natural and artificial flavor, beta-carotene, TBHQ and citric acid added to protect flavor, dimethylpolysiloxane (anti-foaming agent). French Toast Batter: pasteurized liquid eggs (whole eggs, citric acid), 2% milk (reduced fat milk, vitamin A palmitate, vitamin D3), sugar, vanilla extract, cinnamon. Powdered Sugar: sugar, cornstarch. Vienna Bread: unbleached enriched wheat flour (flour, malted barley flour, niacin, reduced iron, thiamine mononitrate, riboflavin, folic acid), water, yeast, wheat gluten, fully refined soybean oil, granulated sugar, salt, calcium propionate (to retain freshness), dough improver (malted wheat flour, enzymes, and 2% or less ascorbic acid), calcium sulfate, enzymes.

FRESH FRUIT SCONES

SEE PHOTO ON PAGE 141.

PREP TIME: 10 MINUTES • TOTAL TIME: 45 MINUTES + COOLING TIME • MAKES 8 SERVINGS

2¼ cups whole grain pastry flour

½ cup sugar

1½ tablespoons baking powder

¾ teaspoon baking soda

6 tablespoons cold unsalted butter, cut into pieces

1 cup buttermilk, divided

1 teaspoon vanilla extract

1 cup fresh fruit, such as diced peaches, whole blueberries, chopped cherries, or diced mango

1. Preheat the oven to 350°F. Line the bottom of a 9" round cake pan with parchment paper or coat with cooking spray.

2. In a large bowl, combine the flour, sugar, baking powder, and baking soda. Using a pastry blender or fork, cut in the butter until the butter pieces are pea-size and coated with flour. Make a well in the center of the mixture.

3. Pour ¾ cup of the buttermilk and the vanilla into the well. Stir just until combined. If the mixture seems dry, add more buttermilk. Add the fruit and mix until combined.

4. Transfer the dough to the cake pan and gently pat it into the pan. Using a butter knife, gently score the top of the batter into 8 wedges. Bake for 35 to 40 minutes, or until the scones are golden brown. Cool on a wire rack for 15 minutes.

Fast Fix: *These scones are perfect for a grab-and-go breakfast. Store in a resealable plastic freezer bag for up to 1 month. Remove from the freezer 15 minutes before eating. Eat with a hard-cooked egg or 2 ounces of cheese for a complete meal in minutes.*

⇟ Bonus Benefits ⇞

Cherries have gained a well-deserved reputation as a healing food for the treatment and prevention of certain types of arthritis.[4]

	CALORIES	PROTEIN	CARBS	FIBER	SUGARS	FAT	SAT FAT	SODIUM
REAL FOOD	281	5 g	45 g	2 g	16 g	9 g	6 g	462 mg
FAKE FOOD	340	5 g	45 g	1 g	24 g	17 g	3 g	340 mg

COMPARED TO: Supermarket Bakery Blueberry Muffins from Walmart

INGREDIENTS: Enriched wheat flour (wheat flour, ascorbic acid added as dough conditioner, niacin, reduced iron, thiamine mononitrate, riboflavin, enzymes, folic acid), sugar, soybean and/or canola oil, blueberries, eggs, water, cultured buttermilk (cultured part-skim milk, salt, sodium citrate), baking powder (sodium acid pyrophosphate, sodium bicarbonate, cornstarch, monocalcium phosphate), salt, margarine (soybean oil, modified palm oil, canola oil, water, salt, whey [milk], soy lecithin, monoglycerides of fatty acids, natural flavor, annatto extract color, vitamin A palmitate, citric acid, vitamin D3), dextrose, whey (milk), cultured wheat flour, artificial flavor, mono- and diglycerides, egg whites, cellulose gum, sodium stearoyl lactylate, xanthan gum, sodium bicarbonate, citric acid, soy lecithin.

What Is Whole Grain Pastry Flour?

Whole wheat flour is made from all three parts of the hard red wheat kernel—bran, germ, and endosperm—and it's also available as whole wheat pastry flour, which is lower in gluten and produces more tender baked goods. Whole grain pastry flour is made from white wheat grains referred to as albino wheat. It is just as nutritious as whole wheat flour but contains less protein, producing tender baked goods. Whole wheat and whole grain pastry flours are interchangeable. Look for them in the natural section of your supermarket.

8 ways with . . . mugs

When you need a meal quickly, try one of these recipes in a mug, which come together in minutes in the microwave. Make these tasty dishes in a 12- to 16-ounce mug to prevent potential spillover. Coat the mugs with cooking spray before preparing.

1. **Chocolate Raspberry French Toast.** Cube 2 slices whole grain bread. Place half the bread in the bottom of a mug. Top with ¼ cup raspberries and 1 teaspoon maple syrup; repeat layer. In a small bowl, whisk together 1 egg, ⅓ cup milk, 1 tablespoon unsweetened cocoa powder, ¼ teaspoon almond extract, and a pinch of salt. Pour over the bread in the mug; let sit 1 minute. Cover with a paper towel and microwave on high power for 2 minutes, or until puffed and set. Serve topped with 1 teaspoon maple syrup.

   Nutrition (per serving): 358 calories, 18 g protein, 51 g carbohydrates, 10 g fiber, 24 g sugars, 11 g fat, 4 g saturated fat, 428 mg sodium

2. **Peach Crisp.** In a mug, microwave 2 teaspoons coconut oil on high power for 20 seconds. Stir in 1 chopped peach (or 8 slices frozen peaches, thawed and chopped), 2 tablespoons rolled oats, 1 tablespoon chopped pecans, 2 teaspoons *each* brown sugar and whole wheat flour. Cover with a paper towel and microwave on high for 2 minutes, or until bubbling.

   Nutrition (per serving): 266 calories, 4 g protein, 32 g carbohydrates, 5 g fiber, 19 g sugars, 15 g fat, 8 g saturated fat, 2 mg sodium

3. **Quickie Banana Cake.** In a small bowl, mash together half a very ripe banana and 1 large egg. Stir in ¼ cup whole grain pastry flour, 1 tablespoon *each* brown sugar and milk, ¼ teaspoon *each* ground cinnamon, baking powder, and vanilla extract, and a pinch of salt. Pour into a mug. Cover with a paper towel and microwave on high power for 90 seconds, or until puffed and set. Let stand for 1 minute.

   Nutrition (per serving): 256 calories, 10 g protein, 42 g carbohydrates, 4 g fiber, 17 g sugars, 6 g fat, 2 g saturated fat, 348 mg sodium

4. **Egg in a Nest.** Stir together ⅓ cup frozen hash browns, thawed, 3 tablespoons shredded Swiss cheese, and ¼ teaspoon dried thyme, basil, or dill. Press into the bottom and a little bit up the sides of a mug. Crack 1 large egg in the potato mixture. Sprinkle with a pinch of salt and black pepper. Microwave on high power for 1 minute, or until the whites are just set. Let stand for 1 minute before eating to allow the yolk to set.

   Nutrition (per serving): 170 calories, 13 g protein, 7 g carbohydrates, 1 g fiber, 1 g sugar, 10 g fat, 5 g saturated fat, 259 mg sodium

5. **Omelet in a Mug.** (See photo on page 142.) In a prepared mug, whisk together 3 eggs, 2 ounces uncured chopped ham, and half a roasted red pepper, chopped. Microwave on high power for 1½ minutes, stirring after 1 minute, or until set.

Nutrition (per serving): 289 calories, 29 g protein, 2 g carbohydrates, 0 g fiber, 1 g sugars, 17 g fat, 6 g saturated fat, 571 mg sodium

6. **No-Pan Greek Omelet.** Wrap a slice of bacon in 2 paper towels and place on a microwaveable plate. Microwave on high power for 1 minute, or until the bacon is nearly crisp; crumble when cool enough to handle. In a 16-ounce greased mug, beat 2 eggs and 1 tablespoon water with a fork. Stir in ½ cup torn baby spinach, ⅛ teaspoon dried oregano, and the bacon. Cover with a paper towel and microwave on high power for 2 minutes, stirring after 1 minute. Top with 1 tablespoon crumbled feta cheese.

Nutrition (per serving): 231 calories, 18 g protein, 6 g carbohydrates, 1 g fiber, 3 g sugars, 15 g fat, 6 g saturated fat, 553 mg sodium

7. **Carrot Cake Oatmeal.** In a mug, combine 1 cup milk (coconut or dairy), ½ cup rolled oats, 1 teaspoon brown sugar, ¼ teaspoon *each* vanilla extract and ground cinnamon, and a pinch of salt. Stir in 1 finely grated small carrot and 1 tablespoon *each* raisins and unsweetened shredded coconut. Cover with a paper towel and microwave on high power for 90 seconds, or until creamy. Stir and let stand for 1 minute before topping with 1 tablespoon chopped walnuts.

Nutrition (per serving): 438 calories, 17 g protein, 56 g carbohydrates, 7 g fiber, 24 g sugars, 17 g fat, 7 g saturated fat, 288 mg sodium

8. **Chocolate Cake in a Mug.** In a mug, melt 1 tablespoon butter in the microwave on high for 20 seconds. Stir in 3 tablespoons milk and ¹⁄₁₆ teaspoon almond extract. Stir in 2½ tablespoons packed brown sugar and 1 tablespoon cocoa powder until smooth. Stir in ¼ teaspoon baking powder and 3 tablespoons whole grain pastry flour until well blended. Microwave on high for 45 to 60 seconds or until the top is no longer wet. Let stand 3 minutes or until cool enough to eat.

Nutrition (per serving): 310 calories, 5 g protein, 46 g carbohydrate, 4 g fiber, 29 g sugars, 14 g fat, 8 g saturated fat, 238 mg sodium

RASPBERRY-ALMOND STRATA

SEE PHOTO ON PAGE 138.

PREP TIME: 5 MINUTES ● TOTAL TIME: 1 HOUR ● MAKES 5 SERVINGS

½ large day-old whole wheat baguette, cut into 1½" cubes

8 ounces raspberries

8 eggs

2 cups milk

3 tablespoons honey

½ teaspoon salt

¾ cup vanilla-almond granola

1. Preheat the oven to 350°F. Coat a 2- to 2½-quart baking dish with cooking spray. Place the bread and berries in the baking dish. In a large measuring cup or bowl, whisk together the eggs, milk, honey, and salt and pour over the bread.

2. Sprinkle with the granola. Bake for 50 minutes, or until puffed and a knife inserted in the center comes out clean and hot.

⇒ Bonus Benefits ⇐

Eating almonds reduces coronary heart disease (CHD) lipid risk factors. Studies show almond intake was found to reduce CHD risk scores, increase HDL ("good") cholesterol, and decrease the overall estimated 10-year CHD risk.[5]

	CALORIES	PROTEIN	CARBS	FIBER	SUGARS	FAT	SAT FAT	SODIUM
REAL FOOD	362	17 g	41 g	6 g	26 g	15 g	5 g	356 mg
FAKE FOOD	530	8 g	73 g	2 g	47 g	23 g	14 g	420 mg

COMPARED TO: Au Bon Pain Raspberry CroisBun™

INGREDIENTS: Croissant [cheese filling ((cream cheese (cultured milk and cream and skim milk, salt, guar and xanthan and locust bean gum), sugar, eggs, water, food starch-modified, glucono-delta lactone, natural vanilla flavor, lemon juice concentrate)), enriched flour (wheat flour, niacin, thiamin mononitrate, riboflavin, folic acid), butter (cream), water, reduced fat milk (vitamins A and D added),yeast, eggs, sugar, salt, ascorbic acid, enzymes, soy lecithin], raspberry filling (sugar, water, raspberries, water, contains 2% or less of each of the following: pectin, citric acid, sodium citrate), powdered sugar (with cornstarch).

Serving for Brunch?

You may prepare this recipe the night before to pop in the oven in the morning. Without preheating the oven, prepare step 1 and cover the baking dish with plastic wrap before refrigerating. In the morning, remove the strata from the fridge. Preheat the oven, remove the plastic wrap, and continue with step 2, increasing the baking time by 15 minutes.

CHOCOLATE GLAZED DOUGHNUTS

SEE PHOTO ON PAGE 139.

PREP TIME: 10 MINUTES ● TOTAL TIME: 30 MINUTES ● MAKES 8 SERVINGS

DOUGHNUTS

1½ cups whole grain pastry flour

½ cup unsweetened cocoa powder

6 tablespoons granulated sugar

2 teaspoons baking powder

Pinch of salt

¾ cup buttermilk

2 eggs

3 tablespoons safflower oil

GLAZE

½ cup confectioners' sugar

¼ cup unsweetened cocoa powder

4–6 teaspoons milk

2 tablespoons toasted sliced almonds (optional)

2 tablespoons toasted unsweetened coconut chips (optional)

1. *To make the doughnuts:* Preheat the oven to 425°F. Lightly coat a doughnut pan with cooking spray.

2. In a large bowl, whisk together the flour, cocoa, granulated sugar, baking powder, and salt. Stir in the buttermilk, eggs, and oil until just combined.

3. Using a measuring cup, divide the batter among the doughnut cups, filling each three-quarters full. Bake for 10 minutes, or until puffed and lightly browned. Transfer to a rack to cool.

4. *To make the glaze:* Meanwhile, in a small bowl, whisk together the confectioners' sugar, cocoa, and 4 teaspoons of the milk until smooth, adding more milk if necessary. Dip the doughnuts in the glaze and return to the rack. Top each with almonds and coconut chips, if using.

Fast Fix: *These doughnuts are delicious even without the glaze. If desired, freeze in a single layer in an airtight container. Remove from the freezer 15 minutes before eating.*

	CALORIES	PROTEIN	CARBS	FIBER	SUGARS	FAT	SAT FAT	SODIUM
REAL FOOD	206	6 g	33 g	4 g	16 g	8 g	2 g	145 mg
FAKE FOOD	350	4 g	41 g	1 g	23 g	19 g	9 g	140 mg

COMPARED TO: Krispy Kreme Chocolate Iced Doughnut with Kreme Filling

INGREDIENTS: Doughnut: (enriched wheat flour (wheat flour, niacin, reduced iron, thiamine mononitrate, riboflavin, folic acid, and enzyme), vegetable shortening (palm oil, fully and/or partially hydrogenated soybean oil, and/or partially hydrogenated cottonseed oil, cottonseed oil, and/or soybean oil, mono- and diglycerides and polyglycerol ester and/or BHT and/or tocopherol and/or citric acid), water, dextrose, yeast, soy flour, salt, wheat gluten, monoglycerides, cellulose gum, calcium sulfate, maltodextrin, ascorbic acid, natural and artificial flavors, sorbitan monostearate, ammonium sulfate, dicalcium, phosphate, diammonium phosphate); Filling: (sugar, palm and hydrogenated palm oil, water, corn syrup solids, soybean oil, corn starch, mono- and diglycerides, polysorbate 60, enzyme modified soy protein, sodium hexametaphosphate, soy lecithin, natural and artificial flavor, salt, sodium caseinate (milk)); Icing: (sugar, water, corn starch, cocoa powder (processed with alkali), corn syrup solids, soybean oil and/or partially hydrogenated soybean oil, palm oil, chocolate liquor, enzyme modified soy protein, polysorbate 60, salt, sodium caseinate (milk), sodium hexametaphosphate, mono- and diglycerides, soy lecithin).

ROSEMARY-LEMON DOUGHNUTS

SEE PHOTO ON PAGE 139.

PREP TIME: 10 MINUTES • TOTAL TIME: 30 MINUTES • MAKES 8 SERVINGS

DOUGHNUTS

1½ cups whole grain or whole wheat pastry flour

½ cup cornmeal

6 tablespoons granulated sugar

2 teaspoons baking powder

Pinch of salt

¾ cup buttermilk

2 eggs

3 tablespoons extra-virgin olive oil

1 teaspoon grated lemon peel

GLAZE

¾ cup confectioners' sugar

4 teaspoons lemon juice

1 tablespoon finely chopped fresh rosemary (optional)

1. *To make the doughnuts:* Preheat the oven to 425°F. Lightly coat a doughnut pan with cooking spray.

2. In a large bowl, whisk together the flour, cornmeal, granulated sugar, baking powder, and salt. Stir in the buttermilk, eggs, oil, and lemon peel until just combined.

3. Using a measuring cup, divide the batter among the doughnut cups, filling each three-quarters full. Bake for 10 minutes, or until puffed and golden. Transfer to a rack to cool.

4. *To make the glaze:* Meanwhile, in a small bowl, whisk together the confectioners' sugar and lemon juice until smooth. Dip the doughnuts in the glaze and return to the rack. Top each with the rosemary, if using.

Fast Fix: *These doughnuts are delicious even without the glaze. If desired, freeze in a single layer in an airtight container. Remove from the freezer 15 minutes before eating.*

	CALORIES	PROTEIN	CARBS	FIBER	SUGARS	FAT	SAT FAT	SODIUM
REAL FOOD	345	5 g	46 g	3 g	22 g	7 g	1 g	45 mg
FAKE FOOD	450	6 g	51 g	3 g	24 g	25 g	14 g	440 mg

COMPARED TO: Wawa Chocolate Covered Cake Donut

INGREDIENTS: Enriched flour bleached (wheat flour, malted barley flour, niacin, reduced iron, thiamine mononitrate, riboflavin, folic acid), water, sugar, palm oil, palm kernel oil, cocoa processed with alkali, soybean oil, Contains less than 2% of each of the following: soy flour, leavening (baking soda, sodium acid pyrophosphate, monocalcium phosphate), egg yolks, soy protein, salt, nonfat milk, emulsifier blend (propylene glycol monoesters of fats & fatty acids, mono- & diglycerides, sodium stearoyl lactylate), soy lecithin, lactose, natural & artificial flavors, cellulose gum, hydrogenated palm oil, xanthan gum, beta-carotene color, sorbitan tristearate.

~ What's a Doughnut Pan?

Doughnut pans make a great addition to a real food home. Used to make healthier doughnuts by baking them instead of deep-fat frying, these pans make cleanup a breeze versus the fried option.

These inexpensive, nifty pans are available wherever baking pans are sold. Besides these delicious recipes, you can use cake or muffin batter to make doughnuts.

STRAWBERRY-VANILLA DOUGHNUTS

SEE PHOTO ON PAGE 139.

PREP TIME: 10 MINUTES • TOTAL TIME: 30 MINUTES • MAKES 8 SERVINGS

DOUGHNUTS

2 cups whole grain pastry flour

6 tablespoons granulated sugar

2 teaspoons baking powder

Pinch of salt

¾ cup buttermilk

2 eggs

3 tablespoons safflower oil

½ cup strawberries, chopped

1½ teaspoons vanilla extract

GLAZE

¾ cup confectioners' sugar

2–3 teaspoons milk

½ teaspoon vanilla extract

1. *To make the doughnuts:* Preheat the oven to 425°F. Lightly coat a doughnut pan with cooking spray.

2. In a large bowl, whisk together the flour, granulated sugar, baking powder, and salt. Stir in the buttermilk, eggs, oil, strawberries, and vanilla until just combined.

3. Using a measuring cup, divide the batter among the doughnut cups, filling each three-quarters full. Bake for 10 minutes, or until puffed and golden. Transfer to a rack to cool.

4. *To make the glaze:* Meanwhile, in a small bowl, whisk together the confectioners' sugar, 2 teaspoons of the milk, and vanilla until smooth. Add additional milk if needed to reach the desired consistency. With a fork, drizzle the glaze over the doughnuts.

Fast Fix: *These doughnuts are delicious even without the glaze. If desired, freeze in a single layer in an airtight container. Remove from the freezer 15 minutes before eating.*

	CALORIES	PROTEIN	CARBS	FIBER	SUGARS	FAT	SAT FAT	SODIUM
REAL FOOD	218	5 g	34 g	2 g	16 g	7 g	1 g	143 mg
FAKE FOOD	360	3 g	44 g	1 g	25 g	19 g	8 g	360 mg

COMPARED TO: Dunkin' Donuts Strawberry Frosted Dream Donut

INGREDIENTS: Donut: enriched unbleached wheat flour (wheat flour, malted barley flour, niacin, iron as ferrous sulfate, thiamin mononitrate, enzyme, riboflavin, folic acid), palm oil, water, dextrose, soybean oil, whey (a milk derivative), skim milk, yeast, contains less than 2% of the following: salt, leavening (sodium acid pyrophosphate, baking soda), defatted soy flour, wheat starch, mono- and diglycerides, sodium stearoyl lactylate, cellulose gum, soy lecithin, guar gum, xanthan gum, artificial flavor, sodium caseinate (a milk derivative), enzyme, colored with (turmeric and annatto extracts, beta-carotene), eggs; Strawberry Kreme Filling: [vanilla flavored buttercreme filling: sugar, vegetable shortening (palm oil, canola oil, mono- and diglycerides), water, high fructose corn syrup, artificial flavor, guar gum, titanium dioxide (color), salt, polysorbate 60, potassium sorbate (preservative), citric acid; strawberry flavored icing: sugar, water, corn syrup, high fructose corn syrup, partially hydrogenated soybean and/or cottonseed oil, contains 2% or less of: maltodextrin, dextrose, soybean oil, corn starch, sodium propionate and potassium sorbate (preservatives), salt, titanium dioxide (color), citric acid, polyglycerol esters of fatty acids, agar, soy lecithin (emulsifier), natural and artificial flavor, red 40]; Strawberry Flavored Icing: sugar, water, corn syrup, high fructose corn syrup, partially hydrogenated soybean and/or cottonseed oil, Contains 2% or less of: maltodextrin, dextrose, soybean oil, corn starch, sodium propionate and potassium sorbate (preservatives), salt, titanium dioxide (color), citric acid, polyglycerol esters of fatty acids, agar, soy lecithin (emulsifier), natural and artificial flavor, red 40.

⇞ Bonus Benefits ⇞

Strawberries are a nutrient powerhouse. Longer-term consumption of strawberries is associated with an improved lipid profile, a reduction in chronic inflammation, and an improvement in cognitive performance.[6, 7]

BANANA CREAM PIE OVERNIGHT OATS

PREP TIME: 5 MINUTES • TOTAL TIME: 10 MINUTES + CHILLING TIME • MAKES 1 SERVING

½ medium very ripe banana

2 teaspoons almond butter

½ teaspoon vanilla extract

½ cup plain yogurt

½ cup milk

⅓ cup rolled oats

1. In a medium bowl, mash the banana with the almond butter and vanilla until smooth.

2. Stir in the yogurt, milk, and oats and soak for 5 minutes.

3. Cover and let sit overnight in the refrigerator. In the morning, stir and enjoy. Or, if you prefer warm oats, microwave on high power for 2 minutes, stirring every 30 seconds.

	CALORIES	PROTEIN	CARBS	FIBER	SUGARS	FAT	SAT FAT	SODIUM
REAL FOOD	342	19 g	51 g	6 g	24 g	8 g	1 g	170 mg
FAKE FOOD	610	7 g	74 g	2 g	42 g	33 g	6 g	550 mg

COMPARED TO: Banana Walnut Muffin from Wawa

INGREDIENTS: Sugar, enriched wheat flour bleached (flour, niacin, iron, thiamine mononitrate, riboflavin, folic acid), water, soybean oil, food starch-modified, dehydrated banana flakes, walnuts, eggs. Contains 2% or less of the following: whey, leavening (sodium aluminum phosphate, baking soda), salt, propylene glycol, mono- and diesters of fatty acid, vital wheat gluten, sodium stearoyl lactylate, dextrose, corn starch, natural and artificial flavors, mono- and diglycerides, soy flour, sodium acid pyrophosphate, sodium bicarbonate, monocalcium phosphate, propylene glycol, alcohol, natural and artificial flavor, glycerine, caramel color, gluten, corn syrup solids, sodium alginate, soy lecithin.

CORN MUFFINS

PREP TIME: 15 MINUTES • TOTAL TIME: 45 MINUTES • MAKES 12 SERVINGS

1 cup cornmeal

1 cup whole grain pastry flour

2 teaspoons baking powder

¼ teaspoon salt

1 cup milk

¼ cup canola oil

2 tablespoons honey

1 egg

1. Preheat the oven to 400°F. Coat a 12-cup muffin pan with cooking spray or line the cups with paper liners.

2. In a medium bowl, combine the cornmeal, flour, baking powder, and salt. Form a well in the center of the pan and combine the milk, oil, honey, and egg. Using a fork, stir just until combined.

3. Divide the batter evenly among the prepared muffin cups,. Bake for 20 minutes, or until the muffin tops a toothpick inserted in the center comes out clean. Cool in the pan on a wire rack for 10 minutes.

	CALORIES	PROTEIN	CARBS	FIBER	SUGARS	FAT	SAT FAT	SODIUM
REAL FOOD	134	3 g	18 g	2 g	4 g	6 g	0 g	149 mg
FAKE FOOD	180	3 g	28 g	1 g	8 g	6 g	3 g	358 mg

COMPARED TO: Jiffy Corn Muffins

INGREDIENTS: Wheat flour, degerminated yellow corn meal, sugar, animal shortening (contains one or more of the following: lard, hydrogenated lard, partially hydrogenated lard), contains less than 2% of each of the following: baking soda, sodium acid pyrophosphate, salt, monocalcium phosphate, niacin, reduced iron, thiamine mononitrate, riboflavin, folic acid, with added egg, milk

CITRUS-YOGURT PARFAIT

PREP TIME: 5 MINUTES ● TOTAL TIME: 5 MINUTES ● MAKES 1 SERVING

⅓ cup whole grain clusters cereal

1 small Ruby Red grapefruit, peeled and cut into sections

Pinch of ground ginger

2 teaspoons chopped fresh mint (optional)

¾ cup 2% Greek yogurt

Fill the bottom of a tall glass with half of the cereal. Top with half of the grapefruit sections, half a pinch of the ginger, 1 teaspoon of the mint (if using), and half of the yogurt. Repeat the layering.

	CALORIES	PROTEIN	CARBS	FIBER	SUGARS	FAT	SAT FAT	SODIUM
REAL FOOD	247	19 g	37 g	6 g	23 g	5 g	2 g	91 mg
FAKE FOOD	420	20 g	18 g	2 g	1 g	30 g	11 g	810 mg

COMPARED TO: Jimmy Dean Sausage Breakfast Bowl

INGREDIENTS: Precooked scrambled eggs (whole eggs, skim milk, soybean oil, modified corn starch, xanthan gum, liquid pepper extract, salt, citric acid, artificial butter flavor (soybean oil, butter, lipolyzed butter fat, flavors and artificial flavors)), diced potatoes (potatoes, vegetable oil [soybean and/or cottonseed oils], maltodextrin, salt, dextrose, tetrasodium pyrophosphate and sodium acid pyrophosphate [to maintain natural color]), cooked pork sausage crumbles (pork, water, contains 2% or less of: salt, sugar, spices, natural flavor (with maltodextrin, succinic acid), sodium phosphate, caramel color), shredded cheddar cheese (pasteurized milk, cheese culture, salt, enzymes, annatto color, cellulose (to prevent caking), may also contain natamycin (a mold inhibitor), water.

How Do You Section a Grapefruit?

To section a grapefruit or other citrus, cut a thin slice from each end of the grapefruit and stand upright on a cutting board. Following the curve of the fruit, cut away the peel and white pith from the top to bottom. Hold the grapefruit over a bowl to catch the juices, and cut between the membranes, releasing the sections into the bowl.

PB&J SMOOTHIE

PREP TIME: 5 MINUTES ● TOTAL TIME: 5 MINUTES ● MAKES 1 SERVING

½ cup milk

½ cup 2% Greek yogurt

2 tablespoons natural peanut butter

1 cup fresh or frozen strawberries

4 ice cubes

In a blender, combine the milk, yogurt, peanut butter, strawberries, and ice cubes. Blend until smooth.

Fast Fix: *Any fruit can give this smoothie a delicious flavor. Keep frozen blueberries, raspberries, or cherries in your freezer for throw-together meals.*

	CALORIES	PROTEIN	CARBS	FIBER	SUGARS	FAT	SAT FAT	SODIUM
REAL FOOD	372	21 g	23 g	3 g	16 g	22 g	6 g	212 mg
FAKE FOOD	470	7 g	113 g	2 g	103 g	1.5 g	0 g	170 mg

COMPARED TO: Orange Julius Tripleberry Premium Fruit Smoothie

INGREDIENTS: Water, Tripleberry Fruit Beverage Mix: sugar, water, strawberries, raspberry puree, blackberry puree, citric acid, fruit and vegetable juice for color, natural flavor, Minute Maid Nonfat Vanilla Liquid: yogurt nonfat yogurt (cultured grade a skim milk and condensed skim milk, Cultures of: bifidobacterium lactis, lactobacillus lactis, l. acidophilus, l. bulgaricus, s. thermophilus, sugar syrup, corn syrup, Less Than 1% Of: natural flavors, mono- and diglycerides, guar gum, polysorbate 80, dextrose, locust bean gum, carrageenan, sodium citrate.

PEACH-MANGO SMOOTHIES

PREP TIME: 5 MINUTES • TOTAL TIME: 5 MINUTES • MAKES 2 SERVINGS

2 cups frozen peach slices

1 ripe mango, peeled and chopped,
    or 1 cup frozen mango chunks

1 cup coconut milk

2–4 teaspoons lemon juice

8 ice cubes

In a blender, combine the peaches, mango, milk, and lemon juice. Blend for 8 seconds. Add the ice cubes and process for 6 to 8 seconds longer, or until smooth. Divide between 2 tall glasses and serve immediately.

	CALORIES	PROTEIN	CARBS	FIBER	SUGARS	FAT	SAT FAT	SODIUM
REAL FOOD	252	7 g	53 g	6 g	46 g	4 g	2 g	57 mg
FAKE FOOD	460	0 g	112 g	5 g	94 g	0 g	0 g	0 mg

COMPARED TO: Large Strawberry Banana Smoothie from Sheetz

INGREDIENTS: Strawberry Smoothie Puree [strawberries, sugar, water, Contains 1% or less of: fruit extract (color), lemon juice concentrate, citric acid, natural flavor, ascorbic acid (vitamin C)], Banana Smoothie Puree [banana puree, water, sugar, natural flavor, citric acid, ascorbic acid (vitamin C)]. Contains no major allergens.

PINEAPPLE-BERRY SMOOTHIES

PREP TIME: 5 MINUTES • TOTAL TIME: 5 MINUTES • MAKES 2 SERVINGS

½ cup unsweetened crushed pineapple with juice

½ cup frozen unsweetened raspberries

½ cup frozen unsweetened strawberries

1 cup vanilla 0% Greek yogurt

In a blender, combine the pineapple, raspberries, strawberries, and yogurt. Blend until smooth.

	CALORIES	PROTEIN	CARBS	FIBER	SUGARS	FAT	SAT FAT	SODIUM
REAL FOOD	190	10 g	38 g	4 g	28 g	0 g	0 g	33 mg
FAKE FOOD	320	5 g	76 g	2 g	56 g	0 g	0 g	70 mg

COMPARED TO: Burger King Tropical Mango Smoothie

INGREDIENTS: Smoothie mix- tropical mango: water, cultured skim milk, sugar, concentrated pear juice, apple puree concentrate, mango puree concentrate, pineapple juice concentrate, orange juice concentrate, apple juice concentrate, citric acid, pectin, xanthan gum, glycerin, sodium carboxymethylcellulose, natural and artificial flavor, maltodextrin, guar gum, arabic, sunflower oil, beta-carotene color, ascorbic acid (vitamin c), mixed tocopherols.

CHAPTER 5

LUNCH *and* LIGHT MEALS

TOMATO BEEF SOUP

SEE PHOTO ON PAGE 152.

PREP TIME: 15 MINUTES • TOTAL TIME: 25 MINUTES • MAKES 6 SERVINGS

1 tablespoon canola oil

1 pound lean ground beef

1 onion, chopped

1 carrot, sliced

1 can (28 ounces) diced tomatoes with basil, garlic, and oregano

1 quart reduced-sodium beef broth

2 tablespoons Worcestershire sauce (optional)

1 cup elbow or other small pasta

¼ teaspoon ground black pepper

2 tablespoons grated Parmesan cheese

1. In a large soup pot, heat the oil over medium-high heat. Cook the beef, onion, and carrot, stirring, for 10 minutes, or until browned.

2. Add the tomatoes (with their juice), broth, and Worcestershire sauce, if using. Increase the heat to high and bring the soup to a boil. Stir in the pasta and pepper. Reduce the heat to medium-low and simmer for 10 minutes, or until the pasta is tender. Serve with the cheese.

⋛ Bonus Benefits ⋚

Want to lose weight? Eat tomatoes. Researchers asked a group of 35 women, ages 18 to 20, to eat a raw, ripe tomato every day before lunch for 4 weeks. Participants lost an average of more than 2 pounds, and their body fat decreased by an average of 1.54 percent. What's more, their fasting blood glucose, triglycerides, total cholesterol, and uric acid levels all decreased.[1]

	CALORIES	PROTEIN	CARBS	FIBER	SUGARS	FAT	SAT FAT	SODIUM
REAL FOOD	300	23 g	24 g	2 g	7 g	12 g	4 g	483 mg
FAKE FOOD	340	20 g	25 g	6 g	6 g	17 g	6 g	960 mg

COMPARED TO: Firehouse Subs Chili

INGREDIENTS: Ground beef, kidney beans (cooked), diced tomatoes, onions, tomato sauce (water, tomato paste, vegetable base [vegetable puree (onion, carrot, celery, garlic), salt, corn syrup, corn starch, autolyzed yeast extract, corn oil, sugar, tomato powder, natural flavor and wine], beef base [beef with natural juices and beef broth, salt, corn syrup, corn oil, yeast extract, chicken fat, dried potato, caramel color, natural flavor, and wine], chicken base [chicken meat, natural chicken juices, salt, chicken fat, corn syrup, yeast extract, natural flavoring, wine, turmeric]), water, green pepper, celery, onion powder, corn oil, chili powder (chili pepper, spices, salt, garlic powder), seasonings, jalapeño pepper (jalapeño pepper, vinegar, salt), salt, cayenne pepper, potassium sorbate and sodium benzoate (less than .01%).

MEXICAN BEAN SOUP

SEE PHOTO ON PAGE 147.

PREP TIME: 15 MINUTES ● TOTAL TIME: 30 MINUTES ● MAKES 12 SERVINGS

1 tablespoon extra-virgin olive oil

1 pound ground pork

1 large onion, chopped

1 large carrot, chopped

1 quart reduced-sodium chicken broth

4 red potatoes, cut into ½" pieces

1 cup salsa

1 can (15 ounces) black beans, rinsed and drained

1 can (15 ounces) white beans, rinsed and drained

1. In a saucepot, heat the oil over medium-high heat. Cook the pork, onion, and carrot, stirring, for 5 minutes, or until the pork is no longer pink.

2. Add the broth and potatoes and bring to a boil. Reduce the heat to medium-low and simmer for 10 minutes, or until the potatoes are tender.

3. Stir in the salsa and beans. Cook for 10 minutes, or until the flavors meld.

⇌ Bonus Benefits ⇌

Onions not only add great flavor to food but also health benefits. Compounds in onions have been shown to have anticancer effects, antiplatelet activity, antithrombotic activity, antiasthmatic activity, antibiotic effects,[2] and cholesterol-lowering effects.

	CALORIES	PROTEIN	CARBS	FIBER	SUGARS	FAT	SAT FAT	SODIUM
REAL FOOD	220	12 g	22 g	4 g	2 g	9 g	3 g	309 mg
FAKE FOOD	330	14 g	28 g	1 g	9 g	20 g	10 g	1,180 mg

COMPARED TO: Culver's Potato au Gratin Soup

INGREDIENTS: Milk, water, dehydrated potatoes (potatoes, sodium acid pyrophosphate), pasteurized process cheese spread (american cheese [milk, cheese culture, salt, enzymes], water, whey [milk], sodium phosphate, whey protein concentrate [milk], skim milk, salt, milk fat, artificial color [soybean oil]), heavy cream, modified cornstarch, rendered bacon fat, contains 2% or less of: soybean oil, salt, cheese type flavor (maltodextrin [corn], modified cornstarch, hydrolyzed corn gluten, natural flavoring, salt, mixed triglycerides, potato starch, lactic acid, butter [cream, annatto], gelatin carboxymethylcellulose, sodium benzoate [soy, egg]), emulsifier (distilled monoglycerides [soy], distilled propylene glycol, monoesters [soy], citric acid, ascorbic acid), cream flavor (lactose, whey protein concentrate [milk], cream powder [cream, nonfat milk, soy lecithin], modified cornstarch, milk fat, mannitol, xanthan gum, artificial color, salt, natural flavoring), cheddar cheese flavor (aged cheddar cheese [milk, cheese cultures, salt, enzymes], autolyzed yeast extract, natural flavors, disodium phosphate, artificial colors [yellow 5, yellow 6]), annatto color (refined soybean oil, annatto extract, mono- and diglycerides [soy]), white pepper, parsley, disodium inosinate and guanylate, yellow 5, canthaxanthin (color).

More Than a Dip?

Salsa is more than just a healthy dip. When stirred into a dish like this soup, it includes all the flavors you need. No additional chopping or measuring spices. Use it as a flavoring for chicken breasts, pork chops or tenderloin, or even fish fillets—just top the meat or poultry with some salsa before baking, and you have a delicious two-ingredient meal.

CODFISH CHOWDER

SEE PHOTO ON PAGE 145.

PREP TIME: 5 MINUTES ● TOTAL TIME: 25 MINUTES ● MAKES 6 SERVINGS

1 tablespoon olive oil

3 carrots, chopped

1 onion, chopped

½ teaspoon dried thyme

1 quart reduced-sodium vegetable broth

½ pound sweet potatoes, peeled and chopped

1 pound skinless cod, cut into 1" pieces

½ cup half-and-half

1. In a large saucepan, heat the oil over medium-high heat. Cook the carrots, onion, and thyme for 5 minutes, or until lightly browned.

2. Add the broth and sweet potatoes and bring to a boil. Reduce the heat to low, cover, and simmer for 10 minutes, or until the sweet potatoes are almost tender. Add the fish and cook for 5 minutes, or until the fish flakes easily. Stir in the half-and-half and cook for 2 minutes, or until heated through.

⊰ Bonus Benefits ⊱

Sweet potato protein has been shown to exert a powerful effect against colorectal cancer cells.[3]

	CALORIES	PROTEIN	CARBS	FIBER	SUGARS	FAT	SAT FAT	SODIUM
REAL FOOD	174	15 g	15 g	3 g	5 g	5 g	2 g	185 mg
FAKE FOOD	240	6 g	20 g	2 g	4 g	15 g	2 g	790 mg

COMPARED TO: Campbell's Slow Kettle Style Soups
Kickin' Crab & Sweet Corn Chowder

INGREDIENTS: water, corn, crab, vegetable oil (corn, cottonseed, canola, and/or soybean), celery, cream (milk), green peppers, red peppers, modified cornstarch, contains less than 2% of: onions**, sugar, salt, wheat flour, whey protein concentrate, flavoring, pollock, spice, yeast extract, crab,** celery seed, mustard seed, paprika, cod extract, potato flour, clam extract, garlic,** shrimp extract,** dried.

~ Which Broth to Buy?

There are so many brands of broth on market shelves these days that it's a challenge to know which ones to select. Those in packages or boxes are the best since they are not exposed to the BPA found in cans and they store so easily in the refrigerator. Organic brands tend to have less sodium, which is preferred, but again, reading labels will provide the best information. Use a marker to write the date on the package after you've opened it so you can be sure to use the broth while it's fresh. If you won't use all of it within a few days, pouring the remainder into ice cube trays and freeze. Thaw as needed.

8 ways with . . . canned chickpeas

Chickpeas are a versatile real food ingredients that's always at the ready. Just pop open a can, and you're on your way to easy protein-packed salads, snacks, and main dishes.

1. **Satisfying Chickpea Salad.** In a medium bowl, combine 2 cans (15 ounces each) rinsed and drained chickpeas, 1 chopped yellow bell pepper, 1 chopped small English cucumber, half a small thinly sliced red onion, ½ cup chopped basil, 3 tablespoons olive oil, 2 tablespoons fresh lemon juice, 1 minced clove garlic, and ½ teaspoon *each* salt and black pepper. Top with 2 tablespoons freshly grated Parmesan cheese. *Makes 4 servings.*

Nutrition (per serving): 252 calories, 10 g protein, 24 g carbohydrates, 8 g fiber, 2 g sugars, 14 g fat, 2 g saturated fat, 739 mg sodium

2. **One-Pan Veggie Curry.** In a saucepan, heat 2 tablespoons coconut oil over medium-high heat. Cook 1 chopped onion for 5 minutes, or until softened. Add 1 tablespoon curry powder and 1 teaspoon *each* minced garlic and minced ginger. Cook for 1 minute. Add 2 cups vegetable broth, 1 cup canned coconut milk, 1 can (14.5 ounces) petite diced tomatoes, and 1 cup instant brown rice. Increase heat and bring to a boil. Reduce heat, cover, and cook for 10 minutes, or until the rice is tender. Stir in 4 cups baby spinach and 1 can (15 ounces) rinsed and drained chickpeas and cook for 2 minutes, or until heated through. *Makes 4 servings.*

Nutrition (per serving): 432 calories, 10 g protein, 55 g carbohydrates, 9 g fiber, 6 g sugars, 22 g fat, 17 g saturated fat, 539 mg sodium

3. **Chickpea Minestrone.** In a 4- or 6-quart slow cooker, combine 1 quart vegetable broth, 1 can (14.5 ounces) diced tomatoes, 3 sliced carrots, 2 sliced ribs celery, 1 small chopped onion, 3 sliced cloves garlic, 1 tablespoon dried oregano, and ¼ teaspoon salt. Cover and cook on low for 6 to 8 hours or on high for 3 to 4 hours. Remove cover and add 1 can (15 ounces) rinsed and drained chickpeas, 1 can (15 ounces) rinsed and drained red kidney beans, 1 cup cut petite frozen green beans, and 1 cup ditalini pasta. Cover and cook on high for 30 minutes, or until the pasta is tender. Sprinkle each serving with grated Parmesan cheese, if desired. *Makes 6 servings.*

Nutrition (per serving): 203 calories, 9 g protein, 38 g carbohydrates, 8 g fiber, 7 g sugars, 2 g fat, 0 g saturated fat, 203 mg sodium

4. **Zesty Oven-Fried Chickpeas.** Preheat the oven to 400°F. On a large rimmed baking sheet, toss together 2 cans (15 ounces each) rinsed and drained chickpeas, 2 tablespoons olive oil, ¼ teaspoon *each* ground cumin, coriander, and salt, and 2 teaspoons grated lime peel. Bake for 30 minutes, or until crisp. *Makes 8 servings.*

Nutrition (per serving): 91 calories, 3 g protein, 10 g carbohydrates, 3 g fiber, 0 g sugars, 5 g fat, 3 g saturated fat, 312 mg sodium

5. **Orzo and Chickpea Salad with Pesto.** Prepare 8 ounces orzo according to package directions. Meanwhile, in a large bowl, combine 1 can (15 ounces) rinsed and drained chickpeas, 1 pint halved cherry tomatoes, ¾ cup small fresh mozzarella balls, and ½ teaspoon salt. Drain the pasta, reserving ¼ cup of the pasta cooking water. Transfer the orzo to the bowl with the tomato mixture and add 3 tablespoons prepared pesto, 2 tablespoons balsamic vinegar, and the reserved pasta water. Toss gently to combine. *Makes 4 servings.*

Nutrition (per serving): 425 calories, 19 g protein, 57 g carbohydrates, 6 g fiber, 6 g sugars, 14 g fat, 6 g saturated fat, 597 mg sodium

6. **Baked Halibut with Tomatoes and Chickpeas.** Preheat the oven to 400°F. In a 9" x 9" baking dish, combine 1 can (14.5 ounces) diced tomatoes with juice, 1 can (15 ounces) rinsed and drained chickpeas, and 1 teaspoon Italian seasoning. Top with four 6-ounce halibut fillets. Drizzle 1 tablespoon olive oil on the fish and sprinkle with ½ teaspoon black pepper. Bake for 15 minutes, or until the fish is opaque and flakes with a fork. *Makes 4 servings.*

Nutrition (per serving): 270 calories, 36 g protein, 14 g carbohydrates, 4 g fiber, 3 g sugars, 7 g fat, 1 g saturated fat, 537 mg sodium

7. **Chickpea Couscous.** Prepare ⅔ cup plain wheat couscous according to package directions. Meanwhile, in a skillet, heat 1 tablespoon olive oil over medium heat. Cook 1 thinly sliced small bulb fennel and 1 thinly sliced small shallot, stirring occasionally, for 5 minutes, or until softened. Add 1 can (15 ounces) rinsed and drained chickpeas and ½ teaspoon *each* salt and black pepper. Cook for 2 minutes, or until heated through. Transfer to a large bowl and gently toss with the couscous and 2 cups baby arugula. Top with sections from 2 mandarin oranges. *Makes 4 servings.*

Nutrition (per serving): 342 calories, 13 g protein, 63 g carbohydrates, 10 g fiber, 9 g sugars, 6 g fat, 1 g saturated fat, 552 mg sodium

8. **Chickpea Vegetable Bake.** Preheat the oven to 400°F. In a roasting pan, combine 1 wedge medium red onion, 1 thinly sliced bell pepper, 1 bunch trimmed and halved asparagus, and 8 ounces sliced mushrooms. Toss with 2 tablespoons olive oil, 1 minced clove garlic, and ½ teaspoon black pepper. Roast for 35 minutes, or until browned. Remove from the oven and toss in 1 can (15 ounces) rinsed and drained chickpeas. *Makes 2 servings.*

Nutrition (per serving): 336 calories, 15 g protein, 37 g carbohydrates, 12 g fiber, 8 g sugars, 17 g fat, 2 g saturated fat, 412 mg sodium

HOT-AND-SOUR SOUP

PREP TIME: 10 MINUTES • TOTAL TIME: 25 MINUTES • MAKES 8 SERVINGS

1 tablespoon olive oil

1 package (3.5 ounces) sliced shiitake mushrooms

2 scallions, thinly sliced

1 quart reduced-sodium vegetable broth

¼ cup rice vinegar

3 tablespoons reduced-sodium soy sauce

¼ teaspoon red-pepper flakes

7 ounces (½ of 14-ounce package) firm tofu, drained and cut into ½" pieces

3 ounces (½ of 6-ounce bag) baby spinach, coarsely chopped (about 4 cups)

1. In a large nonstick saucepan, heat the oil over medium-high heat. Cook the mushrooms and scallions, stirring occasionally, for 5 minutes, or until lightly browned.

2. Add the broth, vinegar, soy sauce, and red-pepper flakes. Bring to a boil over high heat. Reduce the heat to low and simmer for 5 minutes. Add the tofu and spinach. Cook for 3 minutes, or until the tofu is heated through and the spinach is wilted.

Fast Fix: *The variations on this classic Asian soup are endless. Leave out the tofu if you like, and add strips of left-over cooked pork or chicken. Or add ¼ pound peeled and deveined small shrimp along with the spinach during the last 3 minutes of cooking time.*

	CALORIES	PROTEIN	CARBS	FIBER	SUGARS	FAT	SAT FAT	SODIUM
REAL FOOD	60	3 g	5 g	1 g	1 g	3 g	1 g	289 mg
FAKE FOOD	290	7 g	39 g	2 g	2 g	12 g	6 g	1,120 mg

COMPARED TO: Maruchan Instant Lunch Ramen Noodle Soup Shrimp Flavor

INGREDIENTS: enriched wheat flour (wheat flour, niacin, reduced iron, thiamine mononitrate, riboflavin, folic acid), vegetable oil (contains one or more of the following: canola, cottonseed, palm) preserved by TBHQ, salt, dehydrated vegetables (carrot, green peas, garlic), maltodextrin, contains less than 2% of: monosodium glutamate, freeze dried shrimp, sugar, hydrolyzed corn, wheat and soy protein, yeast extract, dehydrated soy sauce (wheat, soybeans, salt), spices, caramel color, potassium carbonate, sodium (mono, hexameta, and/or tripoly) phosphate, natural flavors, sesame oil, sodium carbonate, disodium inosinate, disodium guanylate, chicken broth, soya lecithin, lactose, turmeric.

food imposters

WASABI THAT'S NOT WASABI

Last year, the *Washington Post* reported that 99 percent of all "wasabi" served in the United States is just horseradish with some food dyes added. That's because real wasabi is much more expensive, and if you want the real thing, restaurants would have to shell out lots more dough—we're talking $70 for ½ pound. Next time you're forking over hard-earned cash for sushi, it might be worth asking if you're also getting the real wasabi.

Ingredients: horseradish, sorbitol, rice bran oil, sugar, modified food starch, salt, water, cellulose, wasabi, artificial flavor, citric acid, turmeric, xanthan gum, artificial color.

LENTIL *and* SPINACH SOUP

PREP TIME: 5 MINUTES • TOTAL TIME: 40 MINUTES • MAKES 6 SERVINGS

1 tablespoon olive oil

1 large onion, chopped

2 carrots, chopped

2 cups lentils, picked over and rinsed

3 cloves garlic, minced

1 tablespoon ground cumin

½ teaspoon salt

7 cups reduced-sodium vegetable broth

4 cups baby spinach

1. In a large saucepan, heat the oil over medium-high heat. Cook the onion and carrots, stirring occasionally, for 5 minutes, or until softened. Stir in the lentils, garlic, cumin, and salt. Cook for 1 minute, stirring.

2. Add the broth and bring to a boil over high heat. Reduce the heat to low, cover, and simmer, stirring occasionally, for 25 minutes, or until the lentils are tender.

3. Stir in the spinach and cook for 2 minutes, or until wilted.

	CALORIES	PROTEIN	CARBS	FIBER	SUGARS	FAT	SAT FAT	SODIUM
REAL FOOD	289	18 g	48 g	17 g	7 g	3 g	1 g	403 mg
FAKE FOOD	510	9 g	46 g	4 g	2 g	33 g	16 g	1,400 mg

COMPARED TO: Au Bon Pain Baked Stuffed Potato Soup

INGREDIENTS: water, potatoes, heavy cream, onions, cream cheese (milk and cream, cheese culture, salt, carob bean gum), contains less than 2% of the following: enriched flour (wheat flour, niacin, reduced iron, thiamine mononitrate, riboflavin, folic acid), canola oil, cooked bacon topping (bacon cured with: water, salt, sugar, sodium phosphate, sodium erythorbate, sodium nitrite), modified corn starch, green onions, salt, chicken base (chicken meat including chicken juices, hydrolyzed soy and corn protein, potato flour, flavorings, autolyzed yeast extract, carrot powder, turmeric), parmesan cheese (cultured part-skim milk, salt, enzymes), chives, pepper sauce (vinegar, red pepper, salt), spices, sugar

GAZPACHO

PREP TIME: 15 MINUTES • TOTAL TIME: 15 MINUTES + CHILLING TIME • MAKES 6 SERVINGS

2 large tomatoes, chopped, divided

1 English (seedless) cucumber, chopped, divided

1 yellow bell pepper, chopped, divided

6 scallions, chopped, divided

1 bottle (46 ounces) spicy vegetable juice

3 tablespoons lime juice

1½ teaspoons smoked paprika

½ teaspoon salt

1. In a food processor, combine half the tomatoes, half the cucumber, half the bell pepper, and half the scallions. Pulse into a chunky puree.

2. Transfer the mixture to a large bowl. Stir in the vegetable juice, lime juice, paprika, salt, and the remaining tomatoes, cucumber, bell pepper, and scallions. Cover and refrigerate for at least 2 hours.

Fast Fix: *This soup is perfect as a first course on a hot night. Serve with grilled cheese quesadillas for a light lunch or dinner.*

	CALORIES	PROTEIN	CARBS	FIBER	SUGARS	FAT	SAT FAT	SODIUM
REAL FOOD	75	3 g	17 g	4 g	10 g	0 g	0 g	731 mg
FAKE FOOD	170	7 g	15 g	2 g	1 g	9 g	2 g	880 mg

COMPARED TO: Campbell's Chunky Creamy Chicken & Dumplings Soup

INGREDIENTS: water, chicken stock, spaetzle dumplings (water, enriched wheat flour [wheat flour, malted barley flour, niacin, ferrous sulfate, thiamine mononitrate, riboflavin, folic acid], eggs, enriched durum wheat flour [durum wheat flour, niacin, ferrous sulfate, thiamine mononitrate, riboflavin, folic acid], salt, spices, natural flavor, turmeric for color), chicken meat, carrots, celery, vegetable oil, Contains less than 2% of: green beans, peas, modified food starch, salt, wheat flour, soy protein concentrate, monosodium glutamate, sugar, onion,** sodium phosphate, soy protein isolate, beta-carotene for color, flavorings, spice, chicken,** butter (cream [milk]), cream (cream, soy lecithin),** chicken fat,** dehydrated

8 ways with . . . salad in a jar

Assemble one of these salads on a Sunday night, and you'll have 4 days of delicious grab-and-go lunches. Each recipe makes enough to fill 4 quart-size jars with lids. Just before eating, with the lid still tightly on the jar, shake the jar to evenly distribute the salad and dressing.

1. **Niçoise Salad in a Jar.** In a glass measuring cup or small bowl, whisk together $\frac{1}{3}$ cup olive oil, $\frac{1}{4}$ cup white wine vinegar, 1 tablespoon Dijon mustard, half a small chopped shallot, and $\frac{1}{2}$ teaspoon black pepper. Divide the dressing among the jars and divide the following in order: $\frac{1}{4}$ cup pitted kalamata olives, 2 cans (5 ounces each) drained tuna, 4 chopped hard-cooked eggs, 4 chopped plum tomatoes, and 4 cups chopped romaine lettuce. Cover tightly and refrigerate.

Nutrition (per serving): 395 calories, 24 g protein, 10 g carbohydrates, 3 g fiber, 3 g sugars, 30 g fat, 5 g saturated fat, 617 mg sodium

2. **Cobb Salad in a Jar.** In a glass measuring cup or small bowl, whisk together $\frac{1}{3}$ cup olive oil, $\frac{1}{4}$ cup red wine vinegar, 2 tablespoons Dijon mustard, and $\frac{1}{2}$ teaspoon *each* salt and black pepper. Divide the dressing among the jars and divide the following in order: $\frac{1}{2}$ chopped avocado, 2 cups shredded cooked chicken, 4 slices cooked and crumbled uncured bacon, 4 chopped plum tomatoes, 2 chopped hard-cooked eggs, $\frac{1}{2}$ cup crumbled blue cheese, and 4 cups chopped romaine lettuce. Cover tightly and refrigerate.

Nutrition (per serving): 482 calories, 36 g protein, 8 g carbohydrates, 3 g fiber, 3 g sugars, 33 g fat, 7 g saturated fat, 830 mg sodium

3. **Waldorf Salad in a Jar.** In a glass measuring cup or small bowl, whisk together $\frac{1}{2}$ cup buttermilk, $\frac{1}{4}$ cup Greek yogurt, $\frac{1}{4}$ cup fresh lemon juice, $\frac{1}{4}$ cup chopped chives, and $\frac{1}{4}$ teaspoon *each* salt and black pepper. Divide the dressing among the jars and divide the following in order: 2 chopped ribs celery, 1 chopped Granny Smith apple, 2 cups chopped cooked chicken, 1 cup halved grapes, $\frac{1}{2}$ cup chopped walnuts, and 4 cups chopped green leaf lettuce. Cover tightly and refrigerate.

Nutrition (per serving): 319 calories, 32 g protein, 20 g carbohydrates, 3 g fiber, 14 g sugars, 13 g fat, 2.5 g saturated fat, 269 mg sodium

4. **Spinach Bacon Salad in a Jar.** In a glass measuring cup or small bowl, whisk together ½ cup olive oil, ¼ cup red wine vinegar, 2 tablespoons mustard, and ¼ teaspoon *each* salt and black pepper. Divide the dressing among the jars and then divide the following in order: 1 chopped red onion, 2½ cups (8 ounces) sliced fresh mushrooms, 4 chopped hard-cooked eggs, 8 slices cooked and crumbled uncured bacon, and 4 cups baby spinach. Cover tightly and refrigerate until ready to eat.

Nutrition (per serving): 383 calories, 15 g protein, 8 g carbohydrates, 2 g fiber, 3 g sugars, 32 g fat, 8 g saturated fat, 613 mg sodium

5. **Apple Ranch Salad in a Jar.** In a glass measuring cup or small bowl, whisk together ½ cup mayonnaise, ¼ cup Greek yogurt, and ½ teaspoon *each* onion powder, dried dill, salt, and black pepper. Divide the dressing among the jars and divide the following in order: 1 chopped Granny Smith apple, 1 can (14.5 ounces) rinsed and drained chickpeas, ½ cup dried cranberries, ¼ cup sliced almonds, and 4 cups mixed greens. Cover tightly and refrigerate.

Nutrition (per serving): 425 calories, 10 g protein, 42 g carbohydrates, 9 g fiber, 19 g sugars, 26 g fat, 4 g saturated fat, 491 mg sodium

6. **Raspberry Chicken Salad in a Jar.** In a glass measuring cup or small bowl, whisk together ½ cup olive oil, ¼ cup raspberry vinegar, ¼ cup chopped fresh raspberries, and ¼ teaspoon *each* salt and black pepper. Divide the dressing among the jars and divide the following in order: 1 peeled and chopped cucumber, 2 cups chopped cooked chicken breasts, ½ cup fresh raspberries, 2 tablespoons chopped pecans, and 4 cups baby spinach. Cover tightly and refrigerate.

Nutrition (per serving): 436 calories, 28 g protein, 10 g carbohydrates, 3 g fiber, 2 g sugars, 33 g fat, 5 g saturated fat, 249 mg sodium

7. **Mexicali Salad in a Jar.** In a glass measuring cup or small bowl, whisk together ½ cup prepared fresh salsa, ¼ cup olive oil, ¼ cup fresh lime juice, ½ teaspoon ground cumin, and ½ teaspoon *each* salt and black pepper. Divide the dressing among the jars and divide the following in order: 1 chopped red bell pepper, 1 chopped avocado, 1 can (14.5 ounces) rinsed and drained black beans, 1 peeled and chopped cucumber, half a chopped red onion, 1 cup shredded Cheddar cheese, ¼ cup cilantro leaves, and 4 cups mixed greens. Cover tightly and refrigerate.

Nutrition (per serving): 457 calories, 16 g protein, 32 g carbohydrates, 12 g fiber, 5 g sugars, 31 g fat, 9 g saturated fat, 665 mg sodium

8. **Italian Roast Beef Salad in a Jar.** In a glass measuring cup or small bowl, whisk together ⅓ cup olive oil, ¼ cup balsamic vinegar, 2 tablespoons Dijon mustard, and ½ teaspoon *each* salt and black pepper. Divide the dressing among the jars and divide the following in order: 8 ounces sliced roast beef or leftover steak, 1 cup tiny fresh mozzarella balls, 1 cup halved cherry tomatoes, 4 cups shredded radicchio, and ½ cup fresh basil. Cover tightly and refrigerate.

Nutrition (per serving): 458 calories, 26 g protein, 8 g carbohydrates, 1 g fiber, 4 g sugars, 35 g fat, 12 g saturated fat, 539 mg sodium

STEAK and PEACH SALAD

SEE PHOTO ON PAGE 151.

PREP TIME: 15 MINUTES • TOTAL TIME: 15 MINUTES • MAKES 4 SERVINGS

1 pound sirloin steak

¾ teaspoon salt, divided

¾ teaspoon ground black pepper, divided

3 peaches, halved

¼ cup olive oil

1½ tablespoons balsamic vinegar

2 teaspoons Dijon mustard

1 package (5 ounces) baby spinach

1 cucumber, chopped

1 red bell pepper, sliced

1. Preheat a grill or grill pan on high heat. Coat the steak with cooking spray and sprinkle with ½ teaspoon each of the salt and black pepper. Coat the peaches with cooking spray. Grill the steak for 7 minutes, turning once, or until a thermometer inserted in the center registers 145°F for medium-rare. Grill the peaches for 4 minutes. Place on a cutting board and let sit for 5 minutes. Slice the steak and peaches.

2. Meanwhile, in a large bowl, whisk together the oil, vinegar, mustard, and remaining ¼ teaspoon salt and black pepper. Add the spinach, cucumber, and bell pepper. Divide among 4 plates and top each with one-quarter of the steak and peaches.

Want to Change Up the Flavors?

Keeping the base of a salad and changing the flavors of the dressing is an easy way to bring variety to your meals. Change this classic vinaigrette—¼ cup olive oil, 1½ tablespoons balsamic vinegar, 1 teaspoon mustard, and ¼ teaspoon each salt and pepper—with a few tweaks:

Red Wine Vinaigrette: Use red wine vinegar instead of the balsamic and add ½ teaspoon fresh oregano.

Apple Cider Vinaigrette: Use apple cider vinegar instead of the balsamic and add ½ teaspoon smoked paprika.

Here are two additional creamy options.

Quick Peanut Sauce: Whisk together 3 tablespoons creamy peanut butter with 1 teaspoon each soy sauce and sesame oil. Add water to thin.

Cool Yogurt Sauce: Whisk together 3 tablespoons cream peanut butter with 1 tablespoon lemon juice and 1 teaspoon olive oil. Add water to thin.

	CALORIES	PROTEIN	CARBS	FIBER	SUGARS	FAT	SAT FAT	SODIUM
REAL FOOD	363	28 g	21 g	5 g	13 g	19 g	4 g	621 mg
FAKE FOOD	570	38 g	51 g	7 g	40 g	25 g	8 g	1,070 mg

COMPARED TO: Wendy's Apple Pecan Chicken Salad

INGREDIENTS: Apple Pecan Salad Base Blend: iceberg lettuce, romaine lettuce, spring mix (baby lettuces [red & green romaine, red & green oak, red & green leaf, lolla rosa, tango], spinach, mizuna arugula, tatsoi, red chard, green chard), Apple Chunks (fresh apples, calcium ascorbate [to maintain freshness and color]), Dried cranberries (cranberries, sugar, sunflower oil). Grilled Chicken Breast: chicken breast, water, seasoning (salt, natural flavors, corn maltodextrin, dextrose, spices, dehydrated garlic powder, dehydrated onion powder, paprika, gum arabic, yeast extract, canola oil, sodium citrate, sugar), potato starch, carrageenan, xanthan gum, soy lecithin. Grilled, homestyle, and spicy chicken breasts are cut on a common cutting board. Contains: soy. Blue Cheese Crumbles: blue cheese (pasteurized milk, cheese cultures, salt, enzymes, penicillium roqueforti), powdered cellulose (to prevent caking), natamycin (to protect flavor). Contains: milk. Pomegranate Vinaigrette Dressing: water, sugar, pomegranate juice concentrate, white wine vinegar, soybean oil, orange juice concentrate, balsamic vinegar, distilled vinegar, sea salt, extra virgin olive oil, orange flavedo (orange peel, sugar, orange oil), shallots, xanthan gum, natural flavor, spice. Roasted Pecans: sugar, honey, corn starch, calcium stearate (anti-caking agent), soy lecithin, maltodextrin, lactose, xanthan gum, soybean oil, sea salt, cayenne pepper.

⇾ Bonus Benefits ⇽

Feeling blue? Sprinkle pepper on your foods. Studies have shown that piperine has strong potential as a natural antidepressant. It works by elevating brain serotonin and brain-derived neurotrophic factor (BDNF) levels and positively modulating the hypothalamus–pituitary–adrenal axis.[4]

BACON *and* EGG SALAD

SEE PHOTO ON PAGE 144.

PREP TIME: 20 MINUTES • TOTAL TIME: 20 MINUTES • MAKES 4 SERVINGS

- 4 slices bacon
- ½ pound asparagus, trimmed
- ¼ cup olive oil
- ¼ cup balsamic vinegar
- ½ teaspoon ground black pepper
- 1 package (5 ounces) baby arugula
- 4 large eggs
- 2 tablespoons shaved Parmesan cheese (optional)

1. Place the bacon on 3 paper towels on a microwaveable plate. Cover with another paper towel. Microwave on high power for 2 minutes, checking every 30 seconds, or until crisp. Crumble and set aside.
2. Fill a large saucepan halfway with water and bring to a low simmer. Cook the asparagus for 3 minutes, or until tender-crisp. Remove and set aside.
3. In a large bowl, whisk together the oil, vinegar, and pepper. Add the bacon, arugula, and asparagus. Divide among 4 plates.
4. Return the water to a simmer; crack in 2 eggs. Cook for 4 minutes, or until the white is set but the yolk is still runny. Remove with a slotted spoon and place 1 egg on each plate. Repeat with the remaining 2 eggs. Top each plate with some of the cheese, if using.

Bonus Benefits

Eggs and greens make a perfect pair. Eating whole cooked eggs along with carotenoid-rich foods such as arugula, which fight against the risk of certain cancers and eye disease, enhances carotenoid absorption.[5]

	CALORIES	PROTEIN	CARBS	FIBER	SUGARS	FAT	SAT FAT	SODIUM
REAL FOOD	260	11 g	7 g	2 g	4 g	21 g	5 g	194 mg
FAKE FOOD	520	28 g	46 g	8 g	9 g	25 g	6g	960 mg

COMPARED TO: McDonald's Southwest Buttermilk Crispy Chicken Salad

INGREDIENTS: Buttermilk Crispy Chicken Fillet Chicken Breast: fillets with rib meat, water, vegetable oil (canola oil, corn oil, soybean oil, hydrogenated soybean oil), wheat flour, bread crumbs (wheat flour, vinegar, sea salt, baking soda, inactive yeast, natural flavor), potato starch, buttermilk (cultured nonfat milk, salt, sodium citrate, vitamin a palmitate, vitamin d3), salt, citric acid, rice starch, palm oil, corn starch, rice flour, yellow corn flour, natural flavors, spices, baking soda, sugar, garlic powder, xanthan gum, maltodextrin. Contains: wheat, milk. Salad Blend: romaine lettuce, baby spinach, carrots, baby kale, lollo rossa lettuce, red leaf lettuce, red oak lettuce, red tango lettuce, red romaine lettuce, red butter lettuce. Ingredients That May Vary: Southwest Vegetable Blend: roasted corn, black beans, roasted tomato, poblano pepper, lime juice (water, lime juice concentrate, lime oil), cilantro. Cilantro Lime Glaze: water, corn syrup solids, high fructose corn syrup, sugar, distilled vinegar, olive oil, soybean oil, freeze-dried orange juice concentrate, cilantro, salt, freeze-dried lime juice concentrate, xanthan gum, sodium benzoate and potassium sorbate (preservatives), garlic powder, propylene glycol alginate, spice, onion powder, citric acid. shredded. Cheddar/Jack Cheese: cheddar cheese (pasteurized milk, cheese culture, salt, enzymes, annatto [color]), monterey jack cheese (pasteurized milk, cheese culture, salt, enzymes), potato starch, corn starch, dextrose, powdered cellulose (prevents caking), calcium sulfate, natamycin (natural mold inhibitor), enzyme. Contains: milk. Lime Ingredients: lime. Chili Lime Tortilla Strips: corn, vegetable oil (corn, soybean and sunflower oil), salt, maltodextrin, sugar, dried tomato, dextrose, spices, onion powder, green bell pepper powder, citric acid, autolyzed yeast extract, malic acid, paprika extract (color), disodium inosinate, disodium guanylate, natural flavor, lemon extract, spice extractive.

CHICKEN CAESAR SALAD

PREP TIME: 15 MINUTES ● TOTAL TIME: 15 MINUTES ● MAKES 4 SERVINGS

3 slices whole grain bread, cut into cubes

3 tablespoons olive oil, divided

¼ cup 2% Greek yogurt

2 tablespoons grated Parmesan cheese

2 tablespoons lemon juice

½ teaspoon Worcestershire sauce

⅛ teaspoon ground black pepper

⅛ teaspoon garlic powder

6 cups torn romaine lettuce

2 cups shredded cooked chicken

1. Preheat the oven to 450°F. In a small bowl, toss the bread cubes with 1 tablespoon of the oil. Spread onto a rimmed baking sheet and bake for 5 minutes, or until browned.

2. Meanwhile, in a large bowl, whisk together the yogurt, cheese, lemon juice, Worcestershire sauce, pepper, garlic powder, and the remaining 2 tablespoons oil.

3. Add the lettuce, chicken, and croutons and toss to coat well.

	CALORIES	PROTEIN	CARBS	FIBER	SUGARS	FAT	SAT FAT	SODIUM
REAL FOOD	292	27 g	12 g	3 g	3 g	15 g	3 g	182 mg
FAKE FOOD	444	g	15 g	4 g	9 g	40 g	12 g	1,290 mg

COMPARED TO: Subway Chicken & Bacon Salad

INGREDIENTS: Monterey Cheese Blend (shredded): monterey jack cheese (cultured pasteurized milk, salt, enzymes), cheddar cheese (cultured pasteurized milk, salt, enzymes, annatto color), potato starch and powdered cellulose added to prevent caking, natamycin (a natural mold inhibitor). Contains milk. Lettuce: fresh iceberg variety Olives: ripe olives, water, salt, ferrous gluconate Cucumbers: fresh ripe cucumbers Green Peppers: fresh green bell peppers Onions: jumbo red onions Tomatoes: fresh red ripe tomatoes Ranch: soybean oil, water, sugar, liquid egg yolks, vinegar, salt, buttermilk (cultured skim milk and milk, sodium citrate, salt), modified corn starch, dehydrated garlic, dehydrated onion, phosphoric acid, xanthan gum, polysorbate 60, buttermilk solids, autolyzed yeast extract, sodium benzoate (a preservative), potassium sorbate (a preservative), spice, dehydrated parsley, whey protein concentrate, calcium disodium EDTA (to protect flavor). Contains: eggs and milk. Chicken Breast Strips: boneless skinless chicken breast with rib meat, water, contains 2% or less soy protein concentrate, modified potato starch, sodium phosphate, potassium chloride, salt, maltodextrin, yeast extract, flavors, natural flavors, dextrose, caramelized sugar, paprika, vinegar solids, paprika extract, chicken broth. Contains: soy.

GAZPACHO CHICKEN SALAD

SEE PHOTO ON PAGE 146.

PREP TIME: 15 MINUTES • TOTAL TIME: 15 MINUTES • MAKES 6 SERVINGS

⅓ cup extra-virgin olive oil

⅓ cup fresh basil, chopped

2 tablespoons red wine vinegar

¼ teaspoon salt

¼ teaspoon ground black pepper

1 cucumber

6 cups mixed baby greens

4 cups shredded rotisserie chicken

2 peaches, chopped

1 pint cherry tomatoes, halved

1 yellow bell pepper, sliced

2 ounces crumbled soft goat cheese

1. In a large bowl, whisk together the oil, basil, vinegar, salt, and black pepper.
2. Using a vegetable peeler, shave the cucumber into long strips, stopping at the seedy core. With a paper towel, squeeze out any excess water. Add to the bowl with the dressing, along with the greens, chicken, peaches, tomatoes, bell pepper, and goat cheese. Toss to coat well.

	CALORIES	PROTEIN	CARBS	FIBER	SUGARS	FAT	SAT FAT	SODIUM
REAL FOOD	338	30 g	12 g	3 g	7 g	20 g	5 g	563 mg
FAKE FOOD	580	16 g	42 g	2 g	7 g	39 g	11 g	850 mg

COMPARED TO: Dunkin' Donuts Chicken Salad Croissant Sandwich

INGREDIENTS: Croissant: dough: enriched wheat flour (flour, niacin, reduced iron, thiamin mononitrate, riboflavin, ascorbic acid, enzymes, folic acid), water, margarine [(palm oil, modified palm oil, canola oil), water, sugar, monoglycerides, soy lecithin, potassium sorbate (preservative), citric acid, artificial flavor, beta-carotene (color), vitamin a palmitate, vitamin d], sugar, contains less than 2% of the following: yeast, dough conditioner (wheat flour, datem, ascorbic acid, enzymes), salt, wheat gluten, dextrose, natural and artificial flavor; glaze: fructose, corn syrup solids, sodium caseinate (a milk derivative), locust bean gum, sodium stearoyl lactylate, soybean and/or canola oil, soy lecithin, sodium bicarbonate; Chicken Salad: chicken meat (boneless, skinless chicken breast with rib meat, water, modified food starch, sodium phosphates, salt), mayonnaise [soybean oil, water, whole eggs and egg yolks, vinegar, salt, sugar, lemon juice (from concentrate), oleoresin paprika, natural flavors, calcium disodium edta used to protect quality], white chicken pieces (white chicken, water, salt, modified food starch, sodium phosphates), celery, salad dressing [water, soybean oil, sugar, distilled vinegar, modified corn starch, egg yolk, contains less than 2% of mustard (distilled vinegar, water, mustard seed, salt), salt, spices, torula yeast, paprika (color), natural flavors, xanthan gum, potassium sorbate (preservative)], Bread Crumbs (bleached wheat flour, yeast, sugar, salt), seasoning (maltodextrin, cultured dextrose, sodium diacetate, salt, egg white lysozyme, nisin), dried vinegar (preservative), salt, sugar, citric acid (antioxidant), cider vinegar (cider and white), spice.

Bonus Benefits

Bell peppers add a crunchy sweetness to dishes. These nutrient powerhouses are an abundant source of the flavonoids quercetin, luteolin, apigenin, and flavonoid glycosides, which exert antioxidant, anti-inflammation, and anti-allergy effects.[6]

CHICKEN PAD THAI

PREP TIME: 10 MINUTES • TOTAL TIME: 25 MINUTES • MAKES 4 SERVINGS

4 ounces flat rice noodles

¼ cup organic ketchup

1 tablespoon fish sauce

1 teaspoon sugar

3 teaspoons peanut oil, divided

1 egg, lightly beaten

2 cloves garlic, minced

2 cups cooked shredded chicken

3 scallions, cut into 1" pieces

½ cup unsalted peanuts, finely chopped

Lime wedges (optional)

1. Prepare the noodles according to package directions. In a small bowl, combine the ketchup, fish sauce, and sugar.

2. In a large nonstick skillet, heat 1 teaspoon of the oil over medium-high heat. Cook the egg, stirring occasionally, for 2 minutes, or until scrambled. Transfer to a plate.

3. In the same skillet, heat the remaining 2 teaspoons oil over medium heat. Cook the garlic for 1 minute. Stir in the noodles and cook for 1 minute, or until hot. Add the chicken and the ketchup mixture and cook, tossing, for 1 minute. Stir in the scallions and the reserved egg and remove from the heat.

4. Divide among 4 plates and top with the peanuts. Serve with lime wedges, if using.

	CALORIES	PROTEIN	CARBS	FIBER	SUGARS	FAT	SAT FAT	SODIUM
REAL FOOD	382	27 g	34 g	3 g	6 g	16 g	2 g	475 mg
FAKE FOOD	990	64 g	85 g	0 g	35 g	20 g	4 g	4,760 mg

COMPARED TO: Bd's Mongolian Grill Chicken Pad Thai

INGREDIENTS: Oil: cottonseed oil, soybean oil, TBHQ and citric acid added to protect flavor, dimethyloplysiloxane, an anti-foaming agent added. Bd's seasoning (seasoned salt [salt, sugar, spices {including paprika and turmeric}, onion, cornstarch, garlic triacalcium phophate {prevents caking}, paprika oleoresin {for color}, natural flavor], white pepper, black pepper, granulated garlic) protein: choice of (beef, chicken, pork, shrimp or tofu) vegetables: bean sprouts, carrots, pea pods, green onions, cilantro and jalapenos rice noodles (rice flour and water), egg pad thai: soy sauce (water, wheat, soybeans, salt, sodium benzoate as preservative), sugar, ketchup (tomato concentrate, distilled vinegar, high fructose corn syrup, corn syrup, salt, spice, onion powder, natrual flavoring), rice vinegar, white vinegar, water, chili paste (chili, salt, distilled vinegar, potassium sorbate and sodium bisulfite as preservatives), contains 2% or less of: modified food starch, soybean oil, ginger xanthan gum, water. veggie base thickener: water, veggie base (sauteed pureed carrots, celery, and onions, [with canola oil], salt, sugar, hydrolyzed corn protein, onion powder, autolyzed yeast extract, food starch-modified carrot powder, tumeric [color], spice extractives, citric acid), corn starch chopped peanuts, lime wedge

Why Organic?

This recipe calls for organic ketchup because it contains only natural ingredients like tomatoes, sugar, and vinegar. In contrast, conventional versions often contain high-fructose corn syrup. Likewise, the organic version of mayonnaise is free of additives. As with everything, compare the labels.

BEEF LETTUCE WRAPS *with* MANGO

SEE PHOTO ON PAGE 145.

PREP TIME: 5 MINUTES • TOTAL TIME: 20 MINUTES • MAKES 2 SERVINGS

½ pound sirloin steak

2 tablespoons orange juice

2 tablespoons soy sauce

8 small leaves Bibb or Boston lettuce

½ mango, peeled, seeded, and chopped

¼ cup cilantro and/or mint sprigs

1. Place the steak in a shallow bowl and drizzle with the orange juice and soy sauce, turning to coat. Let stand for 5 minutes.

2. Preheat an oiled grill or grill pan. Grill the steak for 5 minutes, turning once, or until a thermomcter inserted in the center registers 145°F for medium-rare. Transfer to a plate and let stand for 5 minutes before slicing.

3. Arrange the lettuce leaves on a serving platter. Divide the steak, mango, and cilantro and/or mint among the leaves.

⇥ Bonus Benefits ⇤

Sweet, succulent mangoes contain 122 milligrams of vitamin C per fruit, more than an orange. They're also a potent source of zeaxanthin, an antioxidant that helps keep your eyes healthy by filtering out harmful blue light rays that contribute to macular degeneration.[7]

	CALORIES	PROTEIN	CARBS	FIBER	SUGARS	FAT	SAT FAT	SODIUM
REAL FOOD	208	26 g	13 g	2 g	12 g	6 g	2 g	155 mg
FAKE FOOD	640	21 g	65 g	5 g	4 g	33 g	12 g	1400 mg

COMPARED TO: Taco Bell Beef Quesarito

INGREDIENTS: Flour Tortilla: enriched wheat flour, water, vegetable shortening (soybean, hydrogenated soybean and/or cotton-seed oil), sugar, salt, leavening (baking soda, sodium acid pyrophosphate), molasses, dough conditioner (fumaric acid, distilled monoglycerides, enzymes, wheat starch, calcium carbonate), calcium propionate, sorbic acid, and/or potassium sorbate (P). Contains: wheat [certified vegan], Seasoned Beef: beef, water, seasoning [cellulose, chili pepper, maltodextrin, salt, oats (contains wheat), soy lecithin, spices, tomato powder, sugar, onion powder, citric acid, natural flavors (including smoke flavor), torula yeast, cocoa, disodium inosinate & guanylate, dextrose, lactic acid, modified corn starch], salt, sodium phosphates. Contains: soy, wheat, Premium Latin Rice: enriched long grain rice, water, canola oil, seasoning (salt, natural flavor, sugar, maltodextrin, parsley, garlic and onion powder, cilantro, disodium guanylate & inosinate). [certified vegan], Cheddar Cheese: cheddar cheese (cultured pasteur-ized milk, salt, enzymes, annatto (VC)), anti-caking agent. Contains: milk [certified vegetarian], Nacho Cheese Sauce: Nonfat milk, cheese whey, water, vegetable oil (canola oil, soybean oil), modified food starch, maltodextrin, natural flavors, salt, dipotassium phosphate, jalapeño puree, vinegar, lactic acid, cellulose gum, potassium citrate, sodium stearoyl lactylate, citric acid, annatto and oleoresin paprika (VC). Contains: milk [certified vegetarian], Reduced-Fat Sour Cream: milk, cream, modified corn starch, lactic acid, maltodextrin, citric acid, sodium phosphate, natural flavor, cellulose gel, potassium sorbate (P), cellulose gum, guar gum, locust bean gum, carrageenan, vitamin A. Contains: milk [certified vegetarian], Creamy Chipotle Sauce: soybean oil, water, vinegar, egg yolk, chipotle peppers, contains 1% or less of sugar, roasted garlic, xanthan gum, chili peppers, natural flavor (including smoke flavor), potassium sorbate and sodium benzoate (P), propylene glycol alginate, garlic powder, onion powder, oleoresin paprika, calcium disodium EDTA (PF), canola and sesame seed oil. Contains: egg [certified vegetarian]

More Than Just for Salad

Lettuce cups make a delicious alternative to bread or rolls for sandwiches. Fill with chili, leftover sliced meat and coleslaw, or chicken salad for a quick lunch.

MEXICAN MEATBALL HEROS

PREP TIME: 15 MINUTES ● TOTAL TIME: 35 MINUTES ● MAKES 4 SERVINGS

1 pound ground lean chicken breast

2 tablespoons chopped cilantro

1 teaspoon no-salt taco seasoning

1 teaspoon olive oil

1½ cups low-sodium pasta sauce

4 small whole wheat Italian hard rolls, split

¼ cup shredded reduced-fat Mexican cheese blend

1. In a medium bowl, combine the chicken, cilantro, and taco seasoning just until blended. With damp hands, shape into 8 meatballs.

2. In a large nonstick skillet, heat the oil over medium-high heat. Cook the meatballs, turning occasionally, for 10 minutes, or until browned. Add the sauce and bring to a boil over high heat. Reduce the heat to low, cover, and simmer for 10 minutes, or until the meatballs are no longer pink.

3. Spoon the meatballs and sauce on the bottom half of the rolls. Top with the cheese and cover with the top halves of the rolls.

Fast Fix: *Since the meatball mixture can be sticky to work with, keep a small bowl of water handy and wet your hands as you shape the meatballs to cut down on stickiness.*

	CALORIES	PROTEIN	CARBS	FIBER	SUGARS	FAT	SAT FAT	SODIUM
REAL FOOD	367	32 g	39 g	6 g	9 g	7 g	1 g	577 mg
FAKE FOOD	560	25 g	56 g	5 g	11 g	25 g	11 g	1,310 mg

COMPARED TO: Subway Footlong Meatball Marinara

INGREDIENTS: Italian Herbs & Cheese Bread: Subway® Italian Bread, Monterey Jack cheese blend [(Monterey Jack cheese (cultured pasteurized milk, salt, enzymes), cheddar cheese (cultured pasteurized milk, salt, enzymes, annatto color), potato starch and powdered cellulose added to prevent caking, natamycin (a natural mold inhibitor)], corn maltodextrin, ground rice, toasted bread crumbs [enriched wheat flour (niacin, reduced iron, thiamine mononitrate, riboflavin, folic acid), sugar, sea salt, yeast], salt, spices (including oregano), dehydrated garlic, parmesan cheese (part skim milk, cheese cultures, salt, enzymes), modified corn starch, sunflower oil, citric acid, yeast extract, lactic acid, natural flavor, and not more than 2% silicon dioxide added (as anticaking agent). Contains milk and wheat. Meatballs: beef, water, bread crumbs [toasted wheat crumbs (enriched wheat flour {wheat flour, niacin, reduced iron, thiamine mononitrate, riboflavin, folic acid}, sugar, salt, soybean oil, yeast)], textured soy protein concentrate, seasoning (dehydrated onion and garlic, salt, spice, dehydrated parsley, soybean oil), soy protein concentrate, romano cheese (made from pasteurized part-skim cow's milk, cheese cultures, salt, enzymes). Marinara Sauce: tomatoes, tomato puree (water, tomato paste), sugar, soybean oil, modified food starch, salt, dehydrated onions, spices, onion powder. Contains milk, soy, and wheat. Provolone Cheese: cultured pasteurized milk, salt, enzymes. Contains: milk.

Apple-Bacon Pancakes ⨪ Page 88

Raspberry-Almond Strata ✕ Page 96

Double Vanilla French Toast ✕ Page 91

Rosemary-Lemon Doughnuts
Page 100, Strawberry-Vanilla
Doughnuts Page 102, and
Chocolate Glazed Doughnuts
Page 98

Egg Brunch Pizza ✂ Page 81

Fresh Fruit Scones ⟍ Page 92

Southwestern Black Bean Wrap
⌇ Page 86

Omelet in a Mug ⌇ Page 95

BLT Pizza ⚲ Page 170

Bacon and Egg Salad ⤳ Page 128

Codfish Chowder ꒦ Page 116

Beef Lettuce Wraps with Mango ꒦ Page 134

Gazpacho Chicken Salad ⌇ Page 131

Mexican Bean Soup ✈ Page 114

Shrimp Tacos with Lemon-Soy Slaw ⤙ Page 158

Pizza in a Flash ✗ Page 172

Peach and Arugula Grilled Cheese Sandwich ✗ Page 168

Fish Tacos with Pineapple Slaw ↙ Page 160

Steak and Peach Salad 〰 Page 126

Tomato Beef Soup ✧ Page 112

ROAST BEEF SANDWICHES *with* BALSAMIC ONIONS *and* PEPPERS

PREP TIME: 10 MINUTES ● TOTAL TIME: 20 MINUTES ● MAKES 4 SERVINGS

1 tablespoon olive oil

1 large onion, thinly sliced

1 red bell pepper, thinly sliced

2 tablespoons balsamic vinegar

4 whole wheat kaiser rolls, split

4 small leaves green leaf lettuce

½ pound thinly sliced lean deli roast beef

1. In a large nonstick skillet, heat the oil over medium-high heat. Cook the onion and bell pepper, stirring occasionally, for 5 minutes, or until softened. Add the vinegar and bring to a boil. Reduce the heat to medium-low and cook, stirring occasionally, for 5 minutes, or until the onion mixture is tender and glazed.

2. Place the bottom half of each roll on 4 plates. Top with a lettuce leaf, one-quarter of the roast beef, and one-quarter of the onion mixture. Cover with the top halves of the rolls.

Fast Fix: *If preparing for fewer than 4 servings, stop after step 1 and place the unused mixture in an airtight container. Refrigerate for up to 5 days. Great for a topping on burgers, steak, or sandwiches.*

	CALORIES	PROTEIN	CARBS	FIBER	SUGARS	FAT	SAT FAT	SODIUM
REAL FOOD	375	20 g	55 g	8 g	12 g	10 g	2 g	811 mg
FAKE FOOD	495	30 g	24 g	3 g	5 g	31 g	13 g	652 mg

COMPARED TO: Arby's Beef 'n Cheddar Mid

INGREDIENTS: Roast Beef: beef, water, salt, sodium phosphates. cheddar cheese sauce: water, canola oil, modified corn starch, cheddar cheese (milk, cheese cultures, salt, enzymes), maltodextrin, contains 2% or less of the following: salt, sodium phosphate, nonfat dry milk, sodium citrate, yeast extract, acetic acid, sodium stearoyl lactylate, sodium hexametaphosphate, mono- and diglycerides, annatto color, citric acid, cream, natural flavors, paprika color, carotenal color, yellow 6. Contains: milk. Red Ranch Sauce: high fructose corn syrup, soybean oil, corn-cider vinegar, tomato paste, distilled vinegar, water, salt, paprika, spice, beet juice (for color), onion (dehydrated), natural flavor, xanthan gum, propylene glycol alginate, garlic (dehydrated). onion roll: wheat flour, malted barley flour, water, high fructose corn syrup, yeast, vegetable oil (contains one or more of the following: soybean, cottonseed, canola), wheat gluten, contains 2% or less of the following: salt, dough conditioners (contains one or more of the following: mono- and diglycerides, ethoxylated mono- and diglycerides, calcium peroxide, calcium stearoyl lactylate, sodium stearoyl lactylate, DATEM, ascorbic acid, calcium iodate, soy lecithin, enzymes), Yeast Nutrients (contains one or more of the following: calcium carbonate, ammonium chloride, ammonium sulfate, calcium sulfate, monocalcium phosphate), dextrose, distilled vinegar, polysorbate 60, natural and artificial flavors, color (contains one or more of the following: extracts of annatto, turmeric, paprika), L-cysteine, diammonium phosphate, tricalcium phosphate, corn starch, yellow corn flour, soy flour, sesame seeds, preservatives (contains one or more of the following: calcium propionate, propionic acid, phosphoric acid). Topped with onions, poppy seeds.

TURKEY ROLL-UPS

PREP TIME: 10 MINUTES • TOTAL TIME: 10 MINUTES • MAKES 2 SERVINGS

3 tablespoons Greek yogurt

1 tablespoon rice vinegar

½ teaspoon curry powder

½ teaspoon lime juice

2 whole grain tortillas (8" diameter)

4 ounces thinly sliced cooked turkey breast or chicken

2 leaves green leaf lettuce

½ cucumber, peeled, seeded, and cut into strips

1 apple, cored and cut into thin wedges

1. In a small bowl, stir together the yogurt, vinegar, curry powder, and lime juice.

2. Lay the tortillas on a work surface and spread with half of the yogurt mixture. Top with the turkey or chicken and the lettuce. Arrange the cucumber and apple on the bottom third of each tortilla and roll up.

	CALORIES	PROTEIN	CARBS	FIBER	SUGARS	FAT	SAT FAT	SODIUM
REAL FOOD	293	24 g	38 g	5 g	13 g	4 g	0 g	215 mg
FAKE FOOD	670	39 g	51 g	2 g	6 g	35 g	11 g	1,690 mg

COMPARED TO: Wendy's Spicy Sriracha Chicken Sandwich

INGREDIENTS: Sriracha Jack Cheese: pasteurized milk, cheese culture, salt, red bell peppers, sriracha flavor (salt, maltodextrin, garlic powder, natural flavor, paprika, contains less than 2% of vinegar, modified food starch), enzymes. Contains: milk. Spicy Chicken Breast: chicken breast, water, seasoning (salt, spice, sodium phosphate [sodium tripolyphosphates, sodium polyphosphates], modified corn starch, paprika, spice extractives, extractives of paprika, and extractives of turmeric). Breaded with: wheat flour, water, modified corn starch, salt, bleached wheat flour, wheat gluten, spice, gum arabic, egg white solids, yellow corn flour, spice extractives, leavening (sodium acid pyrophosphates, sodium bicarbonate, monocalcium phosphate), extractives of paprika. Cooked in vegetable oil (soybean oil, corn oil, cottonseed oil, hydrogenated soybean oil, citric acid [preservative], dimethylpolysiloxane [anti-foaming agent]). Cooked in the same oil as menu items that contains fish (where available). Contains: egg, wheat. Applewood Smoked Bacon Pork Cured with: water, salt, sugar, sodium phosphates, sodium erythorbate, and sodium nitrite. Spring mix baby lettuces (red & green romaine, red & green oak, red & green leaf, Lolla Rosa, tango), spinach, mizuna, arugula, tatsoi, red chard, green chard. red onion. Sriracha Aioli (soybean oil, hot chili sauce (chili peppers, sugar, vinegar, salt, garlic, xanthan gum, beet powder, natural flavor), water, egg yolk, distilled vinegar, chili garlic sauce (salted chili pepper [chili peppers, salt], water, sugar, rice vinegar, dehydrated garlic, modified corn starch, acetic acid), rice vinegar, salt, spice, garlic, lime juice concentrate, sugar, xanthan gum, natural flavor, dehydrated garlic, dehydrated onion). Contains: egg. Sriracha Bun: (enriched wheat flour (wheat flour, malted barley flour, niacin, iron, thiamine mononitrate, riboflavin, folic acid), water, sugar, yeast, palm oil, dough conditioner (wheat flour, diacetyl tartaric acid esters of mono- and diglycerides [datem]. Contains 2% or less of: soybean oil, enzymes [wheat], ascorbic acid [vitamin c], l-cysteine hydrochloride), sriracha seasoning (sugar, spices, salt, corn maltodextrin, paprika, sriracha sauce [chili pepper, vinegar, garlic, sugar, salt, natural flavor, xanthan gum], yeast extract, citric acid, dehydrated garlic, modified corn starch, natural flavor, extractives of paprika, Contains less than 2% of: silicon dioxide [anticaking agent]), salt, calcium propionate, dough extender (wheat flour, monoglycerides, guar gum, corn syrup solids, contains 2% or less of: silicon dioxide [flow aid], soybean oil, enzymes, calcium sulfate, salt), red chile peppers, dry malt (barley malt flour, dextrose, wheat flour), dough conditioner (yellow corn flour, turmeric [color], mono-and diglycerides, contains 2% or less of: paprika [color], artificial flavors).

TURKEY PANINI

PREP TIME: 10 MINUTES • TOTAL TIME: 20 MINUTES • MAKES 4 SERVINGS

4 ounces reduced-fat goat cheese

⅓ cup apricot all-fruit spread

2 teaspoons stone-ground mustard

8 slices whole grain bread

½ pound thinly sliced deli turkey breast

1 firm, ripe pear, sliced into 8 wedges

1. In a small bowl, mash the goat cheese, chutney, and mustard until blended. Evenly spread the mixture on 4 slices of the bread. Layer the bread evenly with the turkey and pear wedges. Top with the remaining 4 slices of bread.

2. Heat a large nonstick skillet coated with cooking spray over medium heat. Add the sandwiches. Place a heavy pan over the top of the sandwiches and cook, turning once, for 6 minutes, or until browned.

Fast Fix: *Panini are pressed sandwiches that require no special equipment to make. A panini press or ridged grill pan will give nice markings to the sandwiches, but a regular nonstick skillet or a cast-iron skillet will work just as well.*

	CALORIES	PROTEIN	CARBS	FIBER	SUGARS	FAT	SAT FAT	SODIUM
REAL FOOD	323	23 g	44 g	5 g	19 g	7 g	2 g	640 mg
FAKE FOOD	400	22 g	42 g	2 g	4 g	16 g	7 g	700 mg

COMPARED TO: Stouffer's Classics Southwest-Style Chicken Panini

INGREDIENTS: Bread (enriched flour [wheat flour, malted barley flour, reduced iron, niacin, thiamin mononitrate, riboflavin, folic acid], water, sugar, yeast, oat fiber, soybean oil, cultured wheat starch, grain vinegar, salt, wheat starch, acetic acid, soy lecithin, citric acid), cooked grill marked white meat chicken strips (white meat chicken, water, isolated soy protein, modified rice starch, chicken flavor [dehydrated chicken broth, chicken powder, natural flavor], sodium phosphate, salt), pasteurized process monterey jack cheese (cultured milk, water, cream, salt, potassium citrate, sodium citrate, sodium pyrophosphate, sorbic acid [preservative], enzymes, lactic acid), water, seasoning (modified food starch, buttermilk powder, cheese powder [semi-soft cheese {cultured milk, salt, enzymes}, salt, lactic acid], vinegar powder [maltodextrin modified food starch, vinegar], nonfat dry milk, spices, salt, paprika, flavor [sesame oil, canola oil, flavoring], flavor [propylene glycol, alcohol, natural flavors], flavor [soybean oil, natural butter flavor, turmeric, annatto], xanthan gum, lemon juice powder [corn syrup solids, lemon juice solids, flavors], flavor [contains canola oil], natural smoke flavor), cooked bacon (bacon cured with water, salt, sugar, dextrose, sodium erythorbate, sodium nitrite), seasoning (soybean oil, salt, 2% or less of natural flavor, lactic acid, turmeric, annatto), 2% or less of modified cornstarch and natural flavors.

8 ways with . . . pasta sauce

These super-fast recipes all come together in the time it takes to boil water and cook 8 ounces of pasta—15 minutes or less! Remember that thicker and chunkier sauces pair better with a large-shaped pasta; thinner sauces are perfect for long, slender-shaped pasta. But whatever you choose, try to stick to a whole grain pasta, which offers the benefits of fiber and whole grains.

1. **Sage and Brown Butter.** In a small saucepan, melt 1/4 cup butter over medium heat. Cook the butter for 5 minutes, or until golden brown. Increase the heat to high and stir in 1/4 cup sage leaves (or 2 teaspoons rubbed sage) and cook for 2 minutes, or until crispy. Add hot pasta to the sauce and toss to coat. *Makes 4 servings.*

   Nutrition (per serving): 194 calories, 3 g protein, 18 g carbohydrates, 1 g fiber, 0 g sugars, 12 g fat, 8 g saturated fat, 102 mg sodium

2. **Creamy Pesto Sauce.** In a small saucepan, heat 3/4 cup heavy cream or half-and-half over medium heat for 3 minutes, or until hot but not boiling. Stir in 1/3 cup prepared pesto. Add hot pasta to the sauce and toss to coat. Sprinkle with 2 tablespoons grated Parmesan cheese. *Makes 4 servings.*

   Nutrition (per serving): 359 calories, 9 g protein, 20 g carbohydrates, 2 g fiber, 0 g sugars, 27 g fat, 14 g saturated fat, 215 mg sodium

3. **Quick Tomato Sauce.** In a large skillet, heat 1/4 cup olive oil over medium-high heat. Cook 1 pint cherry tomatoes, 1 minced clove garlic, and 1/2 teaspoon *each* dried oregano and salt for 5 minutes, or until the tomatoes burst and release their juices. Add hot pasta to the sauce and toss to coat. *Makes 4 servings.*

   Nutrition (per serving): 225 calories, 4 g protein, 21 g carbohydrates, 2 g fiber, 2 g sugars, 14 g fat, 2 g saturated fat, 295 mg sodium

4. **Garlic-Oil Sauce.** In a large skillet, heat 1/2 cup olive oil over medium heat. Cook 3 minced cloves garlic, 1/2–1 teaspoon red-pepper flakes, and 1/2 teaspoon salt for 5 minutes, or until the garlic is very tender but not browned. Add hot pasta to the sauce and toss to coat. *Makes 4 servings.*

   Nutrition (per serving): 332 calories, 3 g protein, 18 g carbohydrates, 1 g fiber, 0 g sugars, 28 g fat, 4 g saturated fat, 292 mg sodium

5. **Quick Alfredo Sauce.** In a small saucepan, melt 3 tablespoons salted butter over medium heat. Cook 1 minced clove garlic for 3 minutes, or until tender. Add $2/3$ cup heavy cream and cook for 3 minutes, or until heated through. Stir in $1/2$ cup Parmesan cheese. Add hot pasta to the sauce and toss gently to coat. *Makes 4 servings.*

Nutrition (per serving): 348 calories, 8 g protein, 25 g carbohydrates, 2 g fiber, 5 g sugars, 18 g fat, 9 g saturated fat, 679 mg sodium

6. **Hearty Meat Sauce.** In a large skillet over medium-high heat, cook 1 pound lean ground beef, 1 small chopped onion, and $1/2$ teaspoon *each* dried oregano and salt for 5 minutes, or until the meat is no longer pink. Drain if necessary. Stir in 1 can (14.5 ounces) diced tomatoes with basil, garlic, and oregano and 1 tablespoon tomato paste and cook for 10 minutes, or until the flavors meld. Remove from the heat and stir in 2 tablespoons butter until melted. Add hot pasta to the sauce and toss to coat. *Makes 4 servings.*

Nutrition (per serving): 374 calories, 27 g protein, 25 g carbohydrates, 2 g fiber, 5g sugars, 18 g fat, 9 g saturated fat, 679 mg sodium

7. **Red Pepper Sauce.** In a medium saucepan, melt 2 tablespoons butter over medium-high heat. Cook 1 small chopped onion and $1/4$ teaspoon dried basil for 5 minutes, or until tender. Add 1 jar (16 ounces) drained and chopped roasted red peppers and cook for 3 minutes. With an immersion blender or in a blender, process the mixture until smooth. Return to the pan and add $1/2$ cup heavy cream or half-and-half and cook for 5 minutes to heat through. Add hot pasta to the sauce and toss to coat. *Makes 4 servings.*

Nutrition (per serving): 269 calories, 4 g protein, 25 g carbohydrates, 3 g fiber, 5 g sugars, 17 g fat, 11 g saturated fat, 118 mg sodium

8. **Buttery Shrimp Sauce.** In a large skillet, melt $1/4$ cup butter over medium heat. Cook 1 pound peeled and deveined shrimp and $1/4$ teaspoon *each* garlic powder and black pepper for 3 minutes, or until the shrimp are opaque. Add 2 cups spinach and cook, stirring, for 1 minute, or until wilted. Add hot pasta to the sauce and toss to coat. *Makes 4 servings.*

Nutrition (per serving): 265 calories, 17 g protein, 19 g carbohydrates, 1 g fiber, 0 g sugars, 13 g fat, 8 g saturated fat, 671mg sodium

SHRIMP TACOS *with* LEMON-SOY SLAW

SEE PHOTO ON PAGE 148.

PREP TIME: 15 MINUTES • TOTAL TIME: 15 MINUTES • MAKES 4 SERVINGS

8 egg roll wrappers

1½ tablespoons reduced-sodium soy sauce

2 teaspoons dark sesame oil

2 teaspoons fresh lemon juice or water

½ teaspoon ground ginger

1 pound cooked, peeled, and deveined large (21–30 count) shrimp, chopped

1½ cups coleslaw mix

2 teaspoons sesame seeds (optional)

1. Preheat the oven to 375°F. Lightly coat a roasting rack and the egg roll wrappers with cooking spray. Lay each wrapper over a bar of the rack, creating triangle-shaped taco shells. Bake for 4 minutes, or until golden and crisp. Set aside.

2. In a medium bowl, whisk together the soy sauce, sesame oil, lemon juice or water, and ginger. Add the shrimp, coleslaw mix, and sesame seeds, if using. Toss to coat well. Divide the shrimp mixture among the shells.

⇒ Bonus Benefits ⇐

An easy way to include cabbage in your diet is with coleslaw mix. Be sure to include it often because it's a source of sulforaphane, a compound that's responsible for cabbage's sulfurous smell. But any aroma is well worth it: Sulforaphane has been shown to inhibit the growth of cancer cells.[8]

	CALORIES	PROTEIN	CARBS	FIBER	SUGARS	FAT	SAT FAT	SODIUM
REAL FOOD	335	32 g	40 g	2 g	1 g	5 g	1 g	854 mg
FAKE FOOD	500	20 g	41 g	5 g	4 g	28 g	10 g	840 mg

COMPARED TO: Taco Bell Cheesy Gordita Crunch

INGREDIENTS: Cheddar Cheese: cheddar cheese (cultured pasteurized milk, salt, enzymes, annatto (VC)), anti-caking agent. Contains: milk [certified vegetarian], Gordita Flatbread: enriched wheat flour, malted barley flour, water, soybean oil, yeast, sugar, vital wheat gluten, contains 1% or less of salt, corn syrup solids, oat fiber, dough conditioners (sodium stearoyl lactylate, mono- and diglycerides), baking powder, soy protein isolate, enzymes, calcium propionate (P). Contains: wheat, soy [certified vegan], Lettuce: fresh iceberg lettuce [certified vegan], Seasoned Beef: beef, water, seasoning [cellulose, chili pepper, maltodextrin, salt, oats (contains wheat), soy lecithin, spices, tomato powder, sugar, onion powder, citric acid, natural flavors (including smoke flavor), torula yeast, cocoa, disodium inosinate & guanylate, dextrose, lactic acid, modified corn starch], salt, sodium phosphates. Contains: soy, wheat, Spicy Ranch Sauce: soybean oil, buttermilk, water, vinegar, egg yolk, sour cream, sugar, contains 1% or less of salt, garlic powder, onion powder, dried red & habañero peppers, spice, potassium sorbate and sodium benzoate (P), glucono delta lactone, xanthan gum, natural flavor, lactic acid, propylene glycol alginate, calcium disodium EDTA (PF). Contains: egg, milk [certified vegetarian], Taco Shell: ground corn, vegetable oil (soybean, corn and/or cottonseed oil), oat fiber. [certified vegan], Three Cheese Blend: part skim mozzarella cheese, cheddar cheese, monterey pepper jack cheese (cultured pasteurized milk, salt, enzymes, water, cream, sodium citrate, jalapeno peppers, sodium phosphate, lactic acid, sorbic acid (P)), anti-caking agent. Contains: milk [certified vegetarian].

FISH TACOS *with* PINEAPPLE SLAW

SEE PHOTO ON PAGE 150.

PREP TIME: 15 MINUTES ● TOTAL TIME: 15 MINUTES ● MAKES 4 SERVINGS

4 cups coleslaw mix

½ red onion, thinly sliced

½ cup chopped pineapple

¾ cup chopped cilantro

2 tablespoons olive oil

2 tablespoons lime juice

½ teaspoon ground cumin

1 pound skinless, firm-fleshed fish, such as mahi mahi, cod, or halibut

8 corn tortillas (6")

1 avocado, thinly sliced

1. In a large bowl, stir together the coleslaw mix, onion, pineapple, cilantro, oil, lime juice, and cumin. Toss to coat well. Set aside.

2. Preheat a grill or grill pan over high heat. Coat the fish with cooking spray. Grill the fish, turning once, for 5 minutes, or until it flakes easily. Remove to a plate and cut into bite-size pieces.

3. Meanwhile, wrap the tortillas in a paper towel and microwave on high power for 30 seconds, or until warmed. Place 2 tortillas on 4 plates. Evenly divide the fish and coleslaw mixture among the tortillas. Top with the avocado.

⇥ Bonus Benefits ⇤

Beat afternoon munchies with avocados. A study of overweight individuals found that adding half a Hass avocado to a normal lunch increased satisfaction by 23 percent and decreased the desire to eat by 28 percent compared to a lunch without avocado. Though the avocado added about 112 calories, the effect of feeling full lasted for up to 5 hours, discouraging between-meal snacking.[9]

	CALORIES	PROTEIN	CARBS	FIBER	SUGARS	FAT	SAT FAT	SODIUM
REAL FOOD	359	25 g	34 g	7 g	5 g	14 g	2 g	125 mg
FAKE FOOD	580	16 g	41 g	2 g	2 g	39 g	10 g	1,330 mg

COMPARED TO: Long John Silver's Baja Fish Taco

INGREDIENTS: Battered Alaskan Pollock: fish (pollock), corn starch, rice flour, white corn meal, modified corn starch. Contains: pollock, wheat batter wheat flour (may be bleached and enriched with niacin, reduced iron, thiamin mononitrate, riboflavin, folic acid), corn starch, yellow corn flour, salt, monosodium glutamate, spices, sodium bicarbonate, sodium aluminum phosphate, monocalcium phosphate, garlic powder, natural flavoring, guar gum, spice extract. Baja Sauce: soybean oil, water, egg yolks, distilled vinegar, salt, contains less than 2% of sugar, garlic,* lime juice concentrate, egg yolk solids, spices, monosodium gluta-mate, lactic acid, xanthan gum, sodium benzoate and potassium sorbate (as preservatives), onion,* paprika, natural and artificial flavors, calcium disodium EDTA added to protect flavor. *dehydrated Contains: egg. Baja Fish Taco Flour Tortilla: enriched bleached wheat flour (wheat flour, niacin, reduced iron, thiamine mononitrate, riboflavin, folic acid), water, vegetable shortening, contains 2% or less of each of the following: salt, leavening, battered Alaskan pollock strips, iceberg lettuce, crumblies, Baja Sauce contains: pollock, wheat, egg.

Who Has Time to Chop?

Opting for pre-chopped vegetables makes meal prep a breeze. Whether they're from the salad bar or the produce section, grabbing pre-cut vegetables allows you to cook healthfully with less time and effort. Produce that's especially helpful pre-cut includes cubed butternut squash, coleslaw and broccoli slaw, and spiralized vegetables, which make a delicious pasta substitute.

8 ways with . . . muffin pans

Muffin pans are a great way to make real food fast—whatever you make, you've already portioned into perfect servings. That not only helps you bake everything a little faster, but it's also easier to make ahead for those times when you need a quick meal for one.

1. **Meat Loaf Muffins.** Preheat the oven to 375°F. Coat a 6-cup large muffin pan with cooking spray. Cook ½ cup rinsed and drained quinoa according to package directions. Transfer to a large bowl. Meanwhile, in a large skillet, heat 1 tablespoon olive oil over medium heat. Cook 1 finely chopped onion, 2 grated carrots, 1 finely chopped rib celery, and 2 teaspoons Italian seasoning for 5 minutes, or until tender. Transfer the vegetables to the bowl with the quinoa. Stir in 1½ pounds lean ground beef, 2 large eggs, 2 tablespoons Worcestershire sauce, and ½ teaspoon *each* salt and black pepper until just combined. Press the mixture into the muffin cups. Top each with 1 tablespoon ketchup, if desired. Bake for 25 minutes, or until a thermometer inserted in the center registers 160°F. Let stand for 15 minutes before removing. *Makes 6 servings.*

Nutrition (per serving): 360 calories, 27 g protein, 20 g carbohydrates, 2 g fiber, 7 g sugars, 19 g fat, 7 g saturated fat, 564 mg sodium

2. **Fluted Egg Cups.** Preheat the oven to 350°F. Coat a 12-cup muffin pan with cooking spray. With a rolling pin, slightly flatten 6 slices of whole wheat bread. Using a 3" round cookie cutter, cut 12 bread circles. Line each cup with a bread round. Bake for 15 minutes, or until the edges are browned. Meanwhile, in a large skillet, heat 2 tablespoons olive oil over medium heat. Cook 3 chopped scallions and 1 teaspoon dried basil for 2 minutes. Add 8 lightly beaten eggs and cook, stirring with a wooden spoon, for 2 minutes, or until almost set. Top with ⅓ cup shredded Cheddar cheese and cook until the eggs are set. Spoon the egg mixture into the bread cups and top each with ½ teaspoon grated Parmesan cheese. Broil 4" from the heat source for 2 minutes, or until hot and lightly browned. Let stand 2 minutes. *Makes 4 servings.*

Nutrition (per serving): 330 calories, 20 g protein, 19 g carbohydrates, 3 g fiber, 3 g sugars, 19 g fat, 6 g saturated fat, 483 mg sodium

3. **Veggie Stratas.** Preheat the oven to 350°F. Coat a 12-cup muffin pan with cooking spray. Remove the crust from 7 slices of whole wheat bread and cut into ½" cubes. In a large skillet, heat 1 tablespoon olive oil over medium-high heat. Cook 1 chopped onion and 1 chopped red bell pepper for 10 minutes, or until golden. Add 5 ounces coarsely chopped baby spinach and cook, stirring, for 1 minute, or until wilted. Let cool. In a large bowl, whisk together 6 large eggs, 1½ cups milk, and ¼ teaspoon *each* salt and black pepper. Stir in ¾ cup shredded Cheddar cheese and cooked spinach mixture. Gently fold in bread cubes and let stand for 15 minutes. Divide the mixture evenly among the muffin cups. Bake for 20 minutes, or until puffed and set. Let stand for 5 minutes before removing. *Makes 6 servings.*

Nutrition (per serving): 263 calories, 16 g protein, 23 g carbohydrates, 3 g fiber, 7 g sugars, 8 g fat, 13 g saturated fat, 477 mg sodium

4. **Cheesy Pepperoni Puffs.** Preheat the oven to 325°F. Coat a 12-cup muffin pan with olive oil. In a large bowl, whisk together 6 large eggs and ¼ cup milk. Add 2 cups shredded mozzarella cheese, ⅓ cup ricotta cheese, ¼ cup whole grain pastry flour, ½ teaspoon baking powder, and ¼ teaspoon salt; whisk until blended. Stir in 1 package (4 ounces) uncured turkey pepperoni,

coarsely chopped. Evenly divide the batter among the muffin cups. Bake for 25 minutes, or until a knife inserted in the center comes out clean. Let stand for 10 minutes before removing. *Makes 12 servings.*

Nutrition (per serving): 245 calories, 20 g protein, 5 g carbohydrates, 0 g fiber, 1 g sugars, 16 g fat, 8 g saturated fat, 556 mg sodium

5. **Tomato Tartlets.** Preheat the oven to 375°F. Coat 24 miniature muffin cups with cooking spray. Place one (17" x 11") phyllo sheet on a work surface. Brush with olive oil. Top with 3 more sheets, coating each sheet lightly with oil. Cut the sheets in thirds lengthwise and then in quarters crosswise to get 12 squares. Press each square into a muffin cup to form a shell with jagged edges. Repeat with 4 more sheets to line the remaining muffin cups. Bake for 5 minutes, or until golden. Meanwhile, in a food processor, combine ¾ cup ricotta cheese, 3 tablespoons feta cheese, and 4 eggs. Process until smooth. Add 1 chopped scallion, 2 chopped cloves garlic, and 2 chopped sun-dried tomatoes in oil. Pulse to mix. Spoon into the tart shells. Bake for 5 minutes, or until lightly puffed and heated through. Let stand 2 minutes. *Makes 12 servings.*

Nutrition (per serving): 219 calories, 12 g protein, 21 g carbohydrates, 2 g fiber, 3 g sugars, 10 g fat, 5 g saturated fat, 340 mg sodium

(continued)

8 ways with ... muffin pans (cont.)

6. **Crab Salad Bites.** Preheat the oven to 275°F. Coat a 12-cup muffin pan with cooking spray. Line each cup with a wonton wrapper (the corners will stick out). Bake for 10 minutes, or until golden brown. Transfer the wonton cups to a rack and cool completely. Meanwhile, in a large bowl, combine 2 cans (6 ounces each) drained and flaked crabmeat, half a yellow bell pepper, finely chopped, 1 chopped scallion, ¼ cup mayonnaise, ¼ cup chopped cilantro, and ¼ cup lime juice. Spoon into the cooled wrappers. *Makes 4 servings.*

Nutrition (per serving): 264 calories, 19 g protein, 16 g carbohydrates, 1 g fiber, 1 g sugars, 12 g fat, 2 g saturated fat, 497 mg sodium

7. **Mini Lasagnas.** Preheat the oven to 375°F. Coat a 12-cup muffin pan with cooking spray. Line each cup with a wonton wrapper and fill each with 1 tablespoon marinara sauce, 1 teaspoon ricotta cheese, and ¼ teaspoon pesto, spreading each ingredient to make a thin layer. Repeat to create a second layer of ingredients in each cup. Brush the edges of the wonton wrappers lightly with olive oil. Bake for 10 minutes, or until the edges are golden brown and the filling is heated through. Let stand for 1 minute before removing. *Makes 4 servings.*

Nutrition (per serving): 304 calories, 11 g protein, 43 g carbohydrates, 4 g fiber, 9 g sugars, 9 g fat, 3 g saturated fat, 766 mg sodium

8. **Asian Chicken Mini Meat Loaves.** Preheat the oven to 375°F. Coat a 12-cup muffin pan with cooking spray. In a large bowl, combine 1½ pounds ground chicken, ½ cup panko bread crumbs, 3 chopped scallions, 1 tablespoon soy sauce, 1 teaspoon dark sesame oil, and ¼ cup hoisin sauce. Press the mixture into the muffin cups and bake for 5 minutes. Top each with 1 teaspoon hoisin sauce. Return to the oven and bake for 10 minutes, or until a thermometer inserted in the center registers 165°F. Let stand for 10 minutes before removing. *Makes 12 servings.*

Nutrition (per serving): 220 calories, 21 g protein, 10 g carbohydrates, 1 g fiber, 4 g sugars, 11 g fat, 3 g saturated fat, 415 mg sodium

VEGGIE-HUMMUS PITA

PREP TIME: 5 MINUTES • TOTAL TIME: 5 MINUTES • MAKES 1 SERVING

⅓ cup prepared hummus

2 teaspoons chia seeds

2 tablespoons chopped kalamata olives

2 teaspoons white wine vinegar

1 small whole wheat pita, halved

¼ small cucumber, thinly sliced

½ vine-ripe tomato, sliced

1 leaf romaine lettuce, sliced

1. In a small bowl, stir together the hummus, chia seeds, olives, and vinegar.

2. Spoon and spread the hummus mixture in each pita half and stuff with the cucumber, tomato, and lettuce.

	CALORIES	PROTEIN	CARBS	FIBER	SUGARS	FAT	SAT FAT	SODIUM
REAL FOOD	298	8 g	39 g	9 g	6 g	14 g	1 g	918 mg
FAKE FOOD	1,470	49 g	98 g	3 g	13 g	97 g	23 g	2,670 mg

COMPARED TO: Sheetz 12" MTO Italian Meat Combo Sub

INGREDIENTS: MTO Subz-12" (white sub roll: enriched bleached flour (bleached wheat flour, malted barley flour, niacin, reduced iron, thiamine mononitrate, riboflavin, folic acid), water, sugar, wheat flour, Contains 2% or less of: soybean oil, yeast, salt, sponge extract (water, fermented wheat flour), vital wheat gluten, malted barley flour (contains sulfites), enzymes, ascorbic acid, Italian Meat Combo: capicolla ham (pork, water, salt, modified food starch, sugar, dextrose, potassium lactate, sodium phosphate, carrageenan, sodium diacetate, sodium ascorbate, sodium nitrite, flavoring), peppered ham (pork, water, salt, modified food starch, sugar, dextrose, potassium lactate, sodium phosphate, carrageenan, sodium diacetate, sodium ascorbate, sodium nitrite, flavoring), hard salami (pork, salt, contains 2% or less of: dextrose, natural flavoring, wine, natural smoke flavor, garlic, lactic acid starter culture, sodium ascorbate, potassium nitrate, sodium nitrite), Tomato Slices: tomatoes, Lettuce, Shredded: lettuce, Provolone Cheese: cultured pasteurized milk, salt, enzymes, mayonnaise: soybean oil, whole egg, water, distilled vinegar, Contains 2% or less of the following: egg yolks, salt, sugar, lemon juice concentrate, calcium disodium edta, natural flavor, olive oil: olive oil, Red Wine Vinegar: water, distilled vinegar, Contains 2% or less of: natural & artificial flavor, dimethylpolysiloxane (an antifoaming agent), red 40, blue 1, red onions: red onions).

EGG SALAD SANDWICH *with* SPINACH *and* TOMATO

PREP TIME: 10 MINUTES • TOTAL TIME: 10 MINUTES • MAKES 1 SERVING

2 hard-cooked eggs

1 tablespoon 2% Greek yogurt

1 teaspoon mayonnaise

2 tablespoons chopped celery

Ground black pepper

Garlic powder

2 slices whole grain bread

½ cup fresh baby spinach

2 slices tomato

In a small bowl, combine the eggs, yogurt, mayonnaise, and celery. Using a fork, mash until combined. Add the pepper and garlic powder to taste. Spread the egg salad on 1 slice of bread. Top with the spinach, tomato slices, and the remaining slice of bread.

	CALORIES	PROTEIN	CARBS	FIBER	SUGARS	FAT	SAT FAT	SODIUM
REAL FOOD	350	22 g	28 g	5 g	6 g	17 g	5 g	388 mg
FAKE FOOD	630	24 g	42 g	2 g	4 g	44 g	12 g	1,120 mg

COMPARED TO: Wawa Egg Salad Sandwich

INGREDIENTS: Egg Salad: hard-cooked eggs, mayonnaise (soybean oil, egg yolks, water, distilled vinegar, contains less than 2% high fructose corn syrup, salt, spice, calcium disodium EDTA added to protect flavor, dehydrated garlic, dehydrated onion), bread crumbs (bleached wheat flour, yeast, sugar, salt), yellow onion, salt, water, black pepper, sodium benzoate, potassium sorbate, White Bread: enriched wheat flour (flour, malted barley flour, reduced iron, niacin, thiamine mononitrate [vitamin b1], riboflavin [vitamin b2], folic acid), water, yeast, high fructose corn syrup, salt, soybean oil, monoglycerides, calcium propionate (preservative), datem, calcium sulfate, soy lecithin, citric acid, grain vinegar, wheat gluten, potassium iodate, calcium phosphate, sesame seeds, Swiss Cheese: swiss cheese (pasteurized part-skim milk, cheese culture, salt, and enzymes), Tomato: sliced tomatoes, Lettuce: iceberg lettuce.)

⇒ food imposters ⇐
MAYONNAISE THAT'S NOT MAYONNAISE

This white spread doesn't technically meet the official definition of "mayonnaise," which requires at least 65 percent vegetable oil. What do you get instead? "Dressing," where the major players are water, soybean oil, and vinegar. Tasty? Sure. Mayo? No.

Ingredients: Water, soybean oil, vinegar, high fructose corn syrup, modified cornstarch, sugar, eggs, salt, natural flavor, mustard flour, potassium sorbate as a preservative, paprika, spice, dried garlic.

PEACH *and* ARUGULA GRILLED CHEESE SANDWICH

SEE PHOTO ON PAGE 149.

PREP TIME: 5 MINUTES • TOTAL TIME: 10 MINUTES • MAKES 2 SERVINGS

4 slices whole grain bread

2 ounces sliced Jarlsberg cheese

1 cup baby arugula

1 peach, pitted and sliced

1. Arrange 2 slices of the bread on a clean surface. Divide the cheese, arugula, and peach slices over the bread. Top with the remaining 2 slices of bread.

2. Heat a nonstick skillet coated with cooking spray over medium heat. Cook the sandwiches, turning once, for 5 minutes, or until the cheese is melted.

	CALORIES	PROTEIN	CARBS	FIBER	SUGARS	FAT	SAT FAT	SODIUM
REAL FOOD	299	17 g	37 g	9 g	13 g	10 g	5 g	327 mg
FAKE FOOD	600	33 g	52 g	2 g	2 g	30 g	17 g	1,050 mg

COMPARED TO: Au Bon Pain Country Grilled Cheese

INGREDIENTS: Country White Bread [enriched flour (wheat flour, malted barley flour, niacin, iron, thiamin mononitrate, riboflavin, folic acid), water, contains 1% or less of: salt, yeast, dextrose, potassium chloride, ascorbic acid, soy lecithin], Cheddar Cheese Blend [cheddar cheese (pasteurized milk, cheese culture, salt, enzymes, may contain annatto as color), chipotle cheddar ((pasteurized milk, cheese cultures, salt, chipotle peppers, taco seasoning (corn flour, salt, chili pepper, spices, garlic, autolyzed yeast, onion, citric acid, paprika, natural flavors), enzymes)), smoked cheddar cheese (pasteurized milk, cheese culture, salt, enzymes, annatto as color, liquid smoke)], tomatoes, bacon (cured with water, salt, sugar, sodium phosphates, sodium diacetate, sodium erythorbate, sodium nitrite), swiss cheese (pasteurized part-skim milk, cheese culture, salt, enzymes), Lemon Shallot Vinaigrette [water, vegetable oil (soybean and/or canola), sugar, white balsamic vinegar, shallots, extra virgin olive oil, lemon juice concentrate, Contains less than 2% of: salt, distilled vinegar, pear juice concentrate, honey, cucumber juice, spices, onion, xanthan gum, carrageenan, lemon peel, citric acid, white wine, dextrose, tartaric acid, turmeric].

⇒ *Bonus Benefits* ⇐

Wonder why the French have lower heart disease rates and smaller waistlines despite a diet high in saturated fat? Experts used to credit wine and lifestyle, but now, a new study in the *Journal of Agricultural and Food Chemistry* suggests cheese may play a role. Best of all, the study is backed up by older research corroborating cheese's potential metabolism-revving effect.[10]

SPRING ROLLS

PREP TIME: 15 MINUTES • TOTAL TIME: 20 MINUTES • MAKES 6 SERVINGS

2 ounces thin rice-flour noodles

3 ounces snow peas, cut into thin matchsticks

6 rice papers (12" diameter)

½ pound cooked, peeled, and deveined large shrimp, sliced in half lengthwise

1 cup mung bean sprouts

3 scallions, sliced

2 carrots, shredded

¼ cup fresh mint leaves

1. Bring a small pot of water to a boil. Cook the noodles and snow peas for 2 minutes, or until tender but still firm. Rinse with cold water and drain.

2. Fill a large pan with hot water. Immerse 1 sheet of rice paper in the water for 1 minute, or until soft and pliable.

3. Place the soft rice paper on a work surface and pat dry. Leaving a 2" border on each side, arrange one-sixth of the shrimp halves in a row down the center.

4. Top with some of the rice noodles, snow peas, bean sprouts, scallions, carrots, and mint. Fold the bottom and side edges of the rice paper over the filling, then fold the top toward the center to make a tight cylinder. Repeat with the remaining ingredients to make a total of 6 spring rolls. Slice the rolls in half diagonally.

	CALORIES	PROTEIN	CARBS	FIBER	SUGARS	FAT	SAT FAT	SODIUM
REAL FOOD	95	9 g	13 g	2 g	2 g	1 g	0 g	464 mg
FAKE FOOD	330	9 g	50 g	4 g	13 g	11 g	2 g	850 mg

COMPARED TO: Chung's Vegetable Egg Rolls

INGREDIENTS: Filling: cabbage, carrots, celery, soybean oil, sugar, salt, natural flavor, garlic powder, natural spice, yeast extract, textured vegetable protein, onions, sesame oil, flavor enhancer (natural flavor, maltodextrin). Crust: wheat flour, water, soybean oil, salt, vegetable shortening (partially hydrogenated soybean oil), soy lecithin, eggs, calcium propionate, cornstarch. Sauce: water, sugar, apple cider vinegar, tomato paste, cornstarch, distilled white vinegar, pineapple juice concentrate, lemon juice concentrate, citric acid.

BLT PIZZA

SEE PHOTO ON PAGE 143.

PREP TIME: 10 MINUTES • TOTAL TIME: 20 MINUTES • MAKES 6 SERVINGS

2 slices bacon

1 avocado, pitted and peeled

1 teaspoon lemon juice

¼ teaspoon salt

½ pound store-bought pizza dough

1 tablespoon olive oil

½ cup ricotta cheese

1 cup cherry tomatoes, halved

1 cup shredded romaine lettuce (optional)

1. Preheat the oven to 450°F. Place the bacon on 3 paper towels on a microwaveable plate. Cover with another paper towel. Microwave on high power for 1½ minutes, checking every 30 seconds, or until crisp. Crumble and set aside.

2. In a medium bowl, mash the avocado with the lemon juice and salt.

3. Roll the dough into a 12" x 9" rectangle. Brush with the olive oil.

4. Spread the avocado mixture over the dough, leaving a 1" border. Spread the ricotta over the avocado. Sprinkle with the tomatoes and bacon.

5. Bake for 10 minutes, or until the crust is golden and crisp. Top with the lettuce, if using.

⇒ Bonus Benefits ⇐

Ward off cancer with dark green leafy vegetables including romaine lettuce. Studies find that frequent consumption of green, leafy vegetables is associated with a reduced incidence of lung, esophageal, nasopharyngeal, breast, skin, and stomach cancer.[11, 12]

	CALORIES	PROTEIN	CARBS	FIBER	SUGARS	FAT	SAT FAT	SODIUM
REAL FOOD	212	6 g	20 g	3 g	1 g	12 g	3 g	446 mg
FAKE FOOD	430	14 g	46 g	3 g	5 g	21 g	7 g	830 mg

COMPARED TO: Stouffer's French Bread Pizza Deluxe

INGREDIENTS: Bread (enriched bleached flour [wheat flour, malted barley flour, niacin, reduced iron, thiamine mononitrate, riboflavin, folic acid], water, Contains less than 2% of : yeast, salt, soybean oil, sugar, cultured wheat flour, vinegar, fumaric acid, acetic acid, citric acid, lactic acid, ascorbic acid, wheat gluten, calcium sulfate, enzymes, calcium propionate [preservative], soy lecithin), water, Low Moisture Part Skim Mozzarella Cheese (pasteurized part-skim milk, cheese cultures, salt, enzymes), Tomato Paste, Cooked Italian Sausage (pork, water, spices, salt, sugar, flavorings), Pepperoni Made With Pork, Chicken, And Beef (Pork, Mechanically Separated Chicken, Beef, Salt, Contains 2% or less of: spices, dextrose, pork stock, lactic acid starter culture, oleoresin of paprika, flavoring, sodium nitrite, sodium ascorbate, paprika, natural smoke flavor, BHA, BHT, citric acid), Margarine (soybean oil, water, vegetable mono- & diglycerides, salt, natural flavor [includes milk], vitamin A Palmitate added, vitamin D3), Contains 2% or less of: green bell peppers, red bell peppers, mushrooms (mushrooms, water, salt), onions, seasoning (sugar, spices, salt, potassium chloride, garlic powder, corn starch, onion powder, paprika, xanthan gum), soybean oil, natural flavors.

PIZZA IN A FLASH

SEE PHOTO ON PAGE 149.

PREP TIME: 10 MINUTES • TOTAL TIME: 15 MINUTES • MAKES 4 SERVINGS

1 pound whole wheat store-bought
pizza dough

1 tablespoon olive oil

1 cup prepared pizza sauce

4 ounces fresh mozzarella cheese, sliced

6 large basil leaves, roughly torn

1. Preheat the oven to 500°F. Lightly coat a baking sheet with cooking spray.

2. Roll the dough into a 12" x 9" rectangle or a 12" round and transfer to the baking sheet. Brush the dough with the oil.

3. Spread the pizza sauce over the dough, leaving a 1" border. Top the sauce with the cheese.

4. Bake for 10 minutes, or until the crust is golden and crisp and the cheese is bubbling. Top with the basil.

Fast Fix: *Look for whole wheat pizza dough in the frozen section of your supermarket. Some stores also offer prepared pizza dough in the refrigerated section near the cheese.*

	CALORIES	PROTEIN	CARBS	FIBER	SUGARS	FAT	SAT FAT	SODIUM
REAL FOOD	363	15 g	53 g	9 g	1 g	13 g	4 g	639 mg
FAKE FOOD	820	30 g	84 g	4 g	12 g	40 g	16 g	1,440 mg

COMPARED TO: Pizza Hut BBQ Bacon Cheeseburger Pizza—Large Original Pan Slice (2)

INGREDIENTS: Applewood Smoked Bacon: bacon (cured with water, salt, sugar, sodium phosphates, sodium erythorbate, sodium nitrite), may contain: smoke flavoring, brown sugar. barbeque drizzle: high fructose corn syrup, corn syrup, water, sugar, tomato paste, distilled vinegar, honey, molasses, salt, maltodextrin, natural flavors including natural smoke flavor, citric acid, modified corn starch, spices, dehydrated garlic, dehydrated onion, caramel, potassium sorbate and sodium benzoate added as preservatives, disodium inosinate, disodium guanylate, beet juice concentrate, mustard seed, dehydrated jalapeño pepper. Barbeque Pizza Sauce: high fructose corn syrup, corn syrup, water, sugar, tomato paste, distilled vinegar, honey, molasses, salt, maltodextrin, natural flavors including natural smoke flavor, citric acid, modified corn starch, spices, dehydrated garlic, dehydrated onion, caramel, potassium sorbate and sodium benzoate added as preservatives, disodium inosinate, disodium guanylate, beet juice concentrate, mustard seed, dehydrated jalapeño pepper. Beef: beef, salt, seasoning (mustard, sugar, spice, sunflower oil, natural flavors, grill flavor [from sunflower oil], natural smoke flavor), sodium phosphate. cheese: mozzarella cheese (pasteurized milk, cheese cultures, salt, enzymes), modified food starch, powdered cellulose, potassium chloride, natural flavors, ascorbic acid (to protect flavor). Diced Roma Tomatoes: fresh Roma tomatoes, fresh red onions: red onions, original pan crust (large): dough: enriched flour (bleached wheat flour, malted barley flour, niacin, ferrous sulfate, thiamin mononitrate, riboflavin, folic acid), water, yeast. Contains 2% or less of: salt, soybean oil, vital wheat gluten, sugar, enzymes, ascorbic acid, sodium stearoyl lactylate. Pan Oil: soybean oil, TBHQ added to protect freshness. Pan Spray: soybean oil, soy lecithin, non-chlorofluorocarbon propellant. Toasted Cheddar Crust Flavor (medium or large pizza): cheddar cheese [pasteurized milk, cheese culture, salt, enzymes, annatto (vegetable color)], potato starch and powdered cellulose (to prevent caking), natamycin (a natural mold inhibitor).

food imposters

CHEESE THAT'S NOT CHEESE

Pick up one of those flimsy individually wrapped slices, and you'll uncover the mystery that is a "processed cheese product." True, "cheese" is usually listed as the first ingredient, but it's all the other stuff after it that gives us pause. Some brands have a total of 15 ingredients, including preservatives and emulsifiers to alter texture. Real cheese delivers the same melty deliciousness with only four.

Ingredients: Cheddar cheese (milk, cheese culture, salt, enzymes), whey, milk, milk protein concentrate, milk fat, whey protein concentrate, sodium citrate, contains less than 2% calcium phosphate, salt, lactic acid, annatto and paprika extract (color), natamycin (a natural mold inhibitor), enzymes, cheese culture, vitamin D_3.

Bonus Benefits

When shopping for olive oil, opt for extra-virgin. Besides the fact that it adds great flavor, research is revealing the power of extra-virgin olive oil's phenolic compounds to prevent the progression of Alzheimer's disease.[13]

CHAPTER 6

DINNERS

BEEF TENDERLOIN *with* SPINACH *and* SWEET POTATOES

SEE PHOTO ON PAGE 218.

PREP TIME: 15 MINUTES • TOTAL TIME: 30 MINUTES • MAKES 4 SERVINGS

4 beef tenderloin steaks (4 ounces each)

¼ teaspoon salt

⅛ teaspoon ground black pepper

2 tablespoons olive oil, divided

1 pound sweet potatoes, peeled and cut into ¾" cubes

⅓ cup water

2½ tablespoons sherry or red wine vinegar

1 tablespoon honey

2 cloves garlic, minced

6 cups baby spinach

¼ cup pumpkin seeds, toasted

1. Sprinkle both sides of the steaks with the salt and pepper. In a large nonstick skillet, heat 1 tablespoon of the oil over medium-high heat. Cook the steaks, turning once, for 6 minutes, or until a thermometer inserted in the center registers 145°F for medium-rare. Transfer to a plate, cover, and keep warm.

2. To the same skillet, add the sweet potatoes and water. Cover and cook for 5 minutes, or until just tender. Uncover and cook for 2 minutes, or until the water evaporates.

3. Add the remaining 1 tablespoon oil. Stir in the vinegar, honey, and garlic. Cook for 2 minutes. Add the spinach and cook, stirring, for 2 minutes, or until just wilted.

4. Evenly divide the spinach mixture, steak, and pumpkin seeds among 4 plates.

Fast Fix: *Save prep time and buy baby spinach, which has tender stems that do not need to be removed.*

	CALORIES	PROTEIN	CARBS	FIBER	SUGARS	FAT	SAT FAT	SODIUM
REAL FOOD	411	31 g	29 g	6 g	10 g	20 g	5 g	348 mg
FAKE FOOD	520	21 g	37 g	6 g	10 g	32 g	11 g	1,250 mg

COMPARED TO: Hungry-Man Grilled Beef Patty

INGREDIENTS: Grilled beef patty (beef, water, soy flour (soy flour, soybean oil, soy lecithin), textured vegetable protein (soy flour, caramel coloring), salt, sodium phosphates, spice, onion powder, eggs, spice extract). Mashed potatoes (water, dehydrated potato flakes [potatoes, mono- and diglycerides, sodium acid pyrophosphate, citric acid], seasoning sauce [vegetable oil (partially hydrogenated soybean oil [TBHQ and citric acid to preserve freshness]), water, mono- and diglycerides with BHT and citric acid to protect flavor, beta-carotene for color [corn oil, dl-alphatocopherol]), contains 2% or less of: salt, dried dairy blend [whey, calcium caseinate]). Mixed vegetables (carrots, corn, cut green beans). Beer gravy (water, beer [water, malt, hops, yeast], modified corn starch, sugar, beef flavor [maltodextrin, salt, autolyzed yeast extract, cultured whey, caramel color, gelatin, disodium guanylate and disodium inosinate, natural flavors lactic acid, beef stock, gum arabic, torula yeast, potassium sorbate, ascorbic acid], butter flavor [butter (cream, salt), natural flavor], tomato paste, salt, natural flavor (salt, maltodextrin [corn, potato, tapioca], flavoring, autolyzed yeast extract, beef fat, gum acacia, sugar, beef broth, brown sugar, beef extract, honey, succinic acid, grill flavor [from vegetable oil], sunflower oil, citric acid, ascorbic acid), xanthan gum, caramel color, enriched wheat flour [wheat flour, niacin, reduced iron, thiamine mononitrate, riboflavin, folic acid], soy protein concentrate). Seasoning sauce (water, sugar, seasoning sauce (vegetable oil (partially hydrogenated soybean oil [TBHQ and citric acid to preserve freshness]), water, mono- and diglycerides with BHT and citric acid to protect flavor. beta-carotene for color (corn oil, dl-alpha-tocopherol)), salt, vegetable oil (partially hydrogenated soybean oil [TBHQ and citric acid to preserve freshness])).

⇒ Bonus Benefits ⇐

Garlic reduces inflammation, lowers serum cholesterol and triglycerides, and displays some of the most potent cancer-preventing effects of any food. It also reduces blood glucose levels, protects your liver from various toxins, strengthens your immune system, potentially reduces the frequency of the common cold and cuts its duration, and, believe it or not, improves the aroma of sweat.[1]

8 ways with ... ground beef

To get the most real food bang for your buck, opt for lean grass-fed ground beef in the following recipes. Despite its lower fat content, grass-fed beef will impart a meatier flavor in your finished dish. Plus, you'll benefit from more heart-healthy omega-3 fats when you choose grass-fed over corn-fed beef.

1. **Cuban Picadillo.** In a large skillet, heat 1 tablespoon olive oil over medium heat. Cook 1 pound ground beef, 1 chopped onion, 1 chopped red bell pepper, and 2 minced cloves garlic, stirring, for 8 minutes, or until the beef is no longer pink. Pour off any excess liquid. Stir in 1 can (8 ounces) tomato sauce and 1 teaspoon *each* ground cumin and dried oregano. Reduce the heat and simmer, covered, for 10 minutes. Stir in ½ cup raisins and ¼ cup halved Spanish olives, and simmer for 5 minutes, or until the flavors meld and raisins soften. Serve over brown rice, if desired. *Makes 4 servings.*

   Nutrition (per serving): 434 calories, 22 g protein, 24 g carbohydrates, 3 g fiber, 15 g sugars, 28 g fat, 9 g saturated fat, 593 mg sodium

2. **Quickie Zoodle Bolognese.** In a 4-quart saucepan over medium heat, cook 1 pound ground beef with 1 tablespoon Italian seasoning, stirring, for 8 minutes, or until the beef is no longer pink. Pour off any excess liquid. Stir in 1 jar (24 ounces) marinara sauce and cook, covered, for 5 minutes, or until the flavors meld. Meanwhile, spiralize 4 medium zucchini (or use a vegetable peeler to make thin, noodlelike ribbons). Stir ½ cup half-and-half into the sauce. Add the zucchini noodles and cook, stirring gently, for 3 minutes, or until heated through. Top with ¼ cup grated Parmesan cheese. *Makes 4 servings.*

   Nutrition (per serving): 366 calories, 28 g protein, 17 g carbohydrates, 3 g fiber, 11 g sugars, 12 g fat, 9 g saturated fat, 318 mg sodium

3. **Asian Beef Lettuce Wraps.** In a large skillet, heat 2 teaspoons toasted sesame oil over medium heat. Cook 1 pound ground beef, 2 thinly sliced scallions, 2 minced cloves garlic, and 2 teaspoons grated ginger, stirring, for 8 minutes, or until the beef is no lon-

ger pink. Pour off any excess liquid. Stir in 2 cups coleslaw mix and 2 tablespoons soy sauce. Cook for 3 minutes, or until the coleslaw mix has wilted. Serve the beef divided among 12 to 16 large Bibb lettuce leaves. *Makes 4 servings.*

Nutrition (per serving): 259 calories, 24 g protein, 4 g carbohydrates, 1 g fiber, 1 g sugars, 17 g fat, 6 g saturated fat, 528 mg sodium

4. **Bacon Mini Meat Loaves.** Preheat the oven to 400°F. In a large bowl, combine 1 pound ground beef, $1/2$ cup rolled oats, 1 egg, 1 finely chopped small onion, 1 finely chopped carrot, and $1/2$ teaspoon *each* garlic powder, salt, and black pepper. Divide the mixture into 4 portions and place on a large rimmed baking sheet. Shape each portion into a 2" x 4" loaf. Cut 4 strips uncured bacon in half and lay 2 pieces over the top of each loaf. Bake for 15 minutes, or until the bacon is browned and a thermometer inserted in the center registers 160°F and the meat is no longer pink. Serve with roasted potato wedges, if desired. *Makes 4 servings.*

Nutrition (per serving): 324 calories, 28 g protein, 10 g carbohydrates, 2 g fiber, 2 g sugars, 19 g fat, 7 g saturated fat, 554 mg sodium

5. **Salisbury Steaks in Mushroom Sauce.** In a large bowl, combine 1 pound ground beef, $1/3$ cup fine whole grain bread crumbs, 1 tablespoon Worcestershire sauce, and 1 teaspoon dry mustard. Shape into four $3/4$"-thick

oval patties. In a large skillet, heat 1 tablespoon olive oil over medium-high heat. Cook the patties, turning once, for 6 minutes, or until browned. Transfer to a plate and reduce the heat to medium-low. Cook 1 thinly sliced shallot, stirring, for 2 minutes, or until it softens. Whisk in 1 box (12 ounces) organic cream of mushroom soup (such as Pacific) and $2/3$ cup water and bring to a simmer. Return the patties to the skillet and cook, covered, for 10 minutes, or until a thermometer inserted in the center registers 160°F and the meat is no longer pink. Serve over mashed potatoes, if desired. *Makes 4 servings.*

Nutrition (per serving): 355 calories, 25 g protein, 11 g carbohydrates, 1 g fiber, 2 g sugars, 20 g fat, 7 g saturated fat, 618 mg sodium

6. **Ground Beef Stroganoff.** In a large saucepan, heat 2 tablespoons olive oil over medium-high heat. Cook 8 ounces sliced brown mushrooms, 1 chopped medium onion, and $1/2$ teaspoon dried thyme, stirring frequently, for 10 minutes, or until browned. Add 1 pound ground beef and $1/2$ teaspoon *each* salt and black pepper, and cook, stirring, for 8 minutes, or until no longer pink. Sprinkle $1/4$ cup whole grain flour over the meat and cook, stirring occasionally, for 3 minutes. Stir in 4 cups beef broth and bring to a boil. Stir in 8 ounces dried pappardelle, campanelle, or penne pasta. Cover and cook, stirring occasionally, for

(continued)

8 ways with … ground beef (cont.)

10 minutes, or until the pasta is tender. Remove the pan from the heat and stir in ½ cup sour cream. *Makes 6 servings.*

Nutrition (per serving): 402 calories, 24 g protein, 36 g carbohydrates, 2 g fiber, 4 g sugars, 19 g fat, 7 g saturated fat, 643 mg sodium

7. **Bar Nachos.** Preheat the oven to 425°F. Coat a large rimmed baking sheet with cooking spray. Arrange 1 bag (8 to 10 ounces) tortilla chips on the sheet. In a large skillet, heat 2 teaspoons olive oil over medium-high heat. Cook 1 pound ground beef, stirring, for 5 minutes, or until browned. Stir in 1 can (15 ounces) rinsed and drained red kidney beans, 1 tablespoon chili powder, 1 teaspoon *each* ground cumin and garlic powder, and ½ teaspoon salt. Reduce the heat to low and simmer for 5 minutes, or until the flavors meld. Top the chips with 1 cup shredded Mexican cheese mix. Spread the meat mixture over the top and sprinkle with another 1 cup shredded cheese. Bake for 5 minutes, or until the cheese is melted. Meanwhile, in a large bowl, combine 1 pitted, peeled, and chopped avocado, half a chopped small red onion, ¼ cup chopped fresh cilantro, and 2 tablespoons lime juice. Remove the nachos from the oven and top with the avocado mixture. *Makes 8 servings.*

Nutrition (per serving): 457 calories, 23 g protein, 32 g carbohydrates, 7 g fiber, 1 g sugars, 26 g fat, 9 g saturated fat, 470 mg sodium

8. **Beefy Pasta Bake.** Preheat the oven to 425°F. Coat a 13" x 9" baking dish with cooking spray. In a large bowl, cover 2 pounds frozen cheese ravioli with very hot tap water; set aside. Meanwhile, in a large skillet over medium heat, cook 1 pound ground beef and 1 teaspoon *each* garlic powder, onion powder, and dried oregano, stirring, for 5 minutes, or until browned. Place 1 of 3 cans (14 ounces each) fire-roasted diced tomatoes in the dish. Remove half the ravioli from the water and place on top of the tomatoes, followed by half the meat, 1 can of tomatoes, and ½ cup shredded mozzarella cheese. Continue adding layers with the remaining ravioli, meat, and 1 can of tomatoes. Top with 1 cup shredded mozzarella, cover with foil, and bake for 25 minutes, or until the ravioli are cooked through. Remove the foil and bake for 10 minutes, or until browned. Let stand for 10 minutes before serving. *Makes 8 servings.*

Nutrition (per serving): 478 calories, 29 g protein, 46 g carbohydrates, 4 g fiber, 8 g sugars, 19 g fat, 10 g saturated fat, 737 mg sodium

SIRLOIN *and* SNOW PEA STIR-FRY

SEE PHOTO ON PAGE 232.

PREP TIME: 10 MINUTES ● TOTAL TIME: 15 MINUTES ● MAKES 4 SERVINGS

8 ounces whole grain spaghetti

1 tablespoon olive oil

¾ pound sirloin steak, thinly sliced into 2" pieces

½ pound snow peas, trimmed

3 tablespoons soy sauce

3 tablespoons rice wine vinegar

1 tablespoon toasted sesame oil

1 can (5 ounces) sliced water chestnuts, drained

1. Prepare the pasta according to package directions.

2. Meanwhile, in a large skillet, heat the olive oil over medium-high heat. Cook the beef, stirring frequently, for 3 minutes, or until lightly browned.

3. Add the snow peas and cook, stirring, for 3 minutes. Add the soy sauce, vinegar, sesame oil, water chestnuts, and cooked pasta. Cook for 3 minutes, stirring to coat well.

	CALORIES	PROTEIN	CARBS	FIBER	SUGARS	FAT	SAT FAT	SODIUM
REAL FOOD	435	30 g	49 g	9 g	6 g	13 g	3 g	606 mg
FAKE FOOD	650	36 g	105 g	6 g	15 g	11 g	2.5 g	840 mg

COMPARED TO: Au Bon Pain Teriyaki Steak Harvest Hot Bowl

INGREDIENTS: Noodles [water, bleached enriched flour (wheat flour, niacin, thiamine mononitrate, riboflavin, reduced iron, folic acid, ascorbic acid, enzyme), potassium carbonate, sodium benzoate (preservative)], Seasoned Beef Steak [beef rib meat, water, sodium lactate, sodium diacetate, modified potato starch, salt, butter flavor (maltodextrin, butter flavor, annatto and turmeric (color)), modified food starch, garlic powder, natural flavor. coated with: salt, dextrose, sugar, flavorings (garlic powder, onion powder, spice), hydrolyzed corn gluten, caramel color (black caramel color, salt, dextrose, onion powder, citric acid, spice extractives, tricalcium phosphate, soybean oil)], Teriyaki Sauce [tamari sauce (water, soybeans, salt, vinegar), mirin wine (water, rice, dextrose, corn syrup, salt), water, dark brown sugar, ginger, rice vinegar ((rice vinegar (water, rice, sugar cane), sugar, salt)), sugar, sesame oil, corn starch, xanthan/guar gum blend, garlic, red pepper, black pepper], edamame (soybeans), carrots, water, sesame seeds.

⇢ Bonus Benefits ⇠

Beef may keep you independent longer. A research study examined the role of beef in stimulating muscle growth in older Americans, which is critical to helping people avoid bone fractures and live well and independently as they age. The study found that consuming 4 ounces of lean beef protein can help enhance muscle development by 50 percent.[2]

OPEN-FACED STEAK SANDWICHES *and* SALAD

SEE PHOTO ON PAGE 223.

PREP TIME: 10 MINUTES • TOTAL TIME: 20 MINUTES • MAKES 2 SERVINGS

2 New York strip steaks (about 4 ounces each), trimmed

½ teaspoon salt

½ teaspoon ground black pepper

2 slices (½" thick) whole grain Italian bread

1 small red onion, cut into thick slices

2 cups baby arugula

3 radishes, cut into thin strips

1 tablespoon extra-virgin olive oil

1 tablespoon white wine vinegar

1. Preheat a grill or grill pan over high heat. Coat the steaks with cooking spray and sprinkle with the salt and pepper. Coat the bread slices and onion slices with cooking spray.

2. Grill the steak, bread, and onion, turning once, for 5 minutes, or until a thermometer inserted in the center of a steak registers 145°F for medium-rare.

3. Divide the bread, steak, and onion between 2 plates. Arrange the arugula and radishes on the plates and drizzle each with half of the oil and vinegar.

⇞ Bonus Benefits ⇞

Extra-virgin olive oil helps protect you from type 2 diabetes. A 22-year study found that substituting olive oil (8 grams per day) for margarine, butter, or mayonnaise was associated with a 5, 8, and 15 percent lower risk of type 2 diabetes, respectively.[3]

	CALORIES	PROTEIN	CARBS	FIBER	SUGARS	FAT	SAT FAT	SODIUM
REAL FOOD	389	31 g	29 g	3 g	3 g	15 g	4 g	644 mg
FAKE FOOD	1,200	48 g	109 g	8 g	7 g	65 g	20 g	3,000 mg

COMPARED TO: Arby's Three Cheese Steak Sandwich with Medium Curly Fries

INGREDIENTS: Angus Beef: black angus beef, water, sea salt, raw sugar, sodium phosphate, yeast extract. coated with: black pepper, caramel color, salt, dextrose, onion powder, spices, garlic powder, citric acid, hydrolyzed soy protein, spice extractives. Smoked Gouda Cheese: gouda cheese (pasteurized milk, cheese cultures, enzymes, salt), water, sodium phosphate, potassium sorbate (preservative), apo-carotenal (for color). Swiss Cheese (Natural Slice): part skim milk, cheese culture, salt, enzymes. Cheddar Cheese (Sharp Slice): cultured pasteurized milk, salt, enzymes, annatto color. Steakhouse Peppercorn Sauce: soybean oil, water, worcestershire sauce (distilled vinegar, molasses, corn syrup, water, salt, caramel color, garlic powder, sugar, spice, tamarind, natural flavor), raisin juice concentrate, onion, egg yolk, distilled vinegar, sugar, corn syrup, contains 2% or less of the following: buttermilk powder, whey protein, tomato paste, salt, garlic, high fructose corn syrup, garlic powder, whey protein concentrate, chile powder, yeast extract, natural flavor, spice, xanthan gum, propylene glycol alginate, potassium sorbate and sodium benzoate (preservatives), calcium disodium EDTA (to protect flavor). Crispy Onions: onions, wheat flour, vegetable oil (soybean and/or canola oil), corn starch, Contains 2% Or Less Of: annatto extract (color), dried egg whites, dried garlic, dried onion, paprika extract (color), salt, spices, spice extract, sugar, turmeric extract (color), water, whey, yellow corn flour. breading set in vegetable oil. cooked in corn oil. Star Cut Bun: enriched wheat flour (wheat flour, malted barley flour, niacin, iron, thiamine mononitrate, riboflavin, folic acid), water, sugar, palm oil, yeast, salt, dough conditioner (wheat flour, wheat gluten, hydrolyzed wheat gluten, Contains 2% or less of the following: enzyme, ascorbic acid), calcium propionate, dry malt, dough strengthener (sodium stearoyl lactylate), dough conditioner (calcium sulfate, wheat starch, wheat flour, Contains 2% or less of the following: enzymes [wheat], salt), ascorbic acid, artificial color (water, propylene glycol, yellow 5, yellow 6, red 40), citric acid, sodium benzoate and propylparaben (preservatives), caramel color, shine agent (modified starch, sodium alginate, mono- and diglycerides, soy lecithin, polysorbate 60). Curly Fries: potatoes, vegetable oil (contains one or more of the following: canola oil, soybean oil, cottonseed oil, sunflower oil, corn oil, palm oil), enriched bleached flour (wheat flour, niacin, reduced iron, thiamine mononitrate, riboflavin, folic acid), salt, corn starch, onion powder, yellow corn meal, spices, garlic powder, leavening (sodium acid pyrophosphate, sodium bicarbonate), modified corn starch, dextrose, spice and coloring, natural flavor, dried torula yeast, xanthan gum, sodium acid pyrophosphate (to preserve natural color).

How Do You Prevent a Steak from Curling as It Cooks?

To prevent curling, slash through the edge of the steak every ¾". If it's already begun to curl, slash the steak, then flip it so that the curled side is now facing down. If necessary, cover with a heavy weight such as a cast-iron skillet or a foil-wrapped brick.

STEAK KEBABS

SEE PHOTO ON PAGE 265.

PREP TIME: 15 MINUTES ● TOTAL TIME: 25 MINUTES + MARINATING TIME ● MAKES 4 SERVINGS

1 pound top sirloin steak or sirloin steak, trimmed, cut into 1½" cubes

2 red and/or yellow bell peppers, each cut into 12 chunks

1 small eggplant, cut into 12 cubes

1 red onion, cut into 12 chunks

3 tablespoons olive oil

3 tablespoons balsamic vinegar

1 teaspoon Dijon mustard

¼ teaspoon salt

1. In a large resealable plastic bag, combine the steak, bell peppers, eggplant, onion, oil, vinegar, mustard, and salt. Seal and toss to coat well. Refrigerate for 1 hour or overnight, tossing occasionally.

2. Coat a grill rack or grill pan with cooking spray and preheat the grill or grill pan over medium-high heat. Thread four 12" metal skewers with the steak, peppers, eggplant, and onion, leaving ⅛" between each. Grill the kebabs, turning occasionally, for 8 minutes, or until cooked through.

Fast Fix: *Shorten the marinating time for tough cuts of meat by adding more acid, like citrus juices or soy sauce, to your marinade to help break down the meat's fibers faster.*

÷ Bonus Benefits ÷

Eggplant is a flavonoid-rich food that contains anthocyanins, which can help lower risk of cardiovascular disease. One study revealed that people who consumed more than three servings of fruits and vegetables containing anthocyanins per week had 34 percent less risk of heart disease.[4]

	CALORIES	PROTEIN	CARBS	FIBER	SUGARS	FAT	SAT FAT	SODIUM
REAL FOOD	397	25 g	14 g	4 g	8 g	27 g	8 g	228 mg
FAKE FOOD	940	50 g	69 g	7 g	3 g	51 g	12 g	1,140 mg

COMPARED TO: Perkins Top Sirloin Steak Dinner with French Fries and Side Salad

INGREDIENTS: Blended Soybean Oil Liquid and hydrogenated soybean oil, soy lecithin, natural and artificial flavor, beta-carotene, TBHQ and citric acid added to protect flavor, dimethylpolysiloxane (anti-foaming agent). Allergens: Soy. Sirloin Beef Steak, Choice: Beef, Allergens: None. French Fries: Potatoes, vegetable oil, (soybean, canola, cottonseed and/or sunflower), modified food starch. Contains 2% or less of: dextrose, leavening (sodium acid pyrophosphate, sodium bicarbonate), rice flower, salt, xanthan gum, disodium dihydrogen pyrophosphate (to maintain natural color). Allergens: None. Salad, Side: Homestyle Seasoned Croutons: Wheat flour, canola and/or olive oil, water, garlic powder, romano cheeses from cow's milk (pasteurized milk, cultures, salt, enzymes), parsley, onion, spices, citric acid, disodium inosinate and disodium guanylate, niacin, ascorbic acid, reduced iron, thiamine mononitrate, riboflavin, folic acid. Allergens: Dairy, Wheat. Lettuce Blend: Iceberg lettuce, romaine lettuce, carrots, red cabbage. Allergens: None. Onions, Yellow. Allergens: None. Shredded American Cheese: Pasteurized milk, cheese cultures, salt, enzymes, powdered cellulose (to prevent caking). Allergens: Dairy. Tomatoes, Diced Tomatoes. Allergens: None.

PAN-SEARED PORK CHOPS
and APPLES

SEE PHOTO ON PAGE 225.

PREP TIME: 5 MINUTES • TOTAL TIME: 35 MINUTES • MAKES 2 SERVINGS

2 bone-in pork chops (6 ounces each)

¼ teaspoon salt

¼ teaspoon ground black pepper

2 tablespoons olive oil

2 sturdy, sweet apples such as Pink Lady or Honeycrisp, cored and cut into 1" slices

¼ cup reduced-sodium chicken broth

1 teaspoon pumpkin pie spice

1 tablespoon fresh tarragon (optional)

1. Heat the oven to 400°F. Season the pork chops with the salt and pepper.

2. In a large ovenproof skillet, heat the oil over medium-high heat. Cook the pork chops, turning once, for 6 minutes, or until browned. Transfer to a plate.

3. Reduce the heat to medium and cook the apples, broth, and pumpkin pie spice, stirring, for 2 minutes. Return the pork to the skillet.

4. Place the skillet in the oven and roast for 8 minutes, or until a thermometer inserted in the center of a chop registers 160°F and the juices run clear. Sprinkle with the tarragon, if using.

Fast Fix: *To core an apple quickly, slice the apple in half from top to bottom. Scoop out the core with a melon baller. Or, if the shape of the final apple slices is not important, use a paring knife to make two deep cuts angled inward—one along each side of the core on each apple half. This cuts out the core in a V shape.*

	CALORIES	PROTEIN	CARBS	FIBER	SUGARS	FAT	SAT FAT	SODIUM
REAL FOOD	425	38 g	23 g	4 g	16 g	20 g	4 g	399 mg
FAKE FOOD	990	50 g	22 g	0 g	20 g	75 g	24 g	2,270 mg

COMPARED TO: Boston Market St. Louis Style BBQ Ribs Half Rack, Individual Meal

INGREDIENTS: Pork Ribs (contains up to an 11% solution with juices. Smoke flavoring added. Rubbed with salt, sugar, spices, paprika. Contains up to 11% of water, salt, sodium phosphates, liquid smoke), Zesty BBQ Sauce (water, sugar, tomato paste, cider vinegar, brown sugar, molasses, modified corn starch, sea salt, natural smoke flavor, distilled vinegar, rochester sauce* [corn syrup solids, salt, garlic, sugar, spices, soy sauce solids (naturally fermented wheat and soybeans, salt, maltodextrin, caramel color), palm oil, tamarind, natural flavor], worcestershire sauce concentrate (distilled vinegar, water, molasses, corn syrup, salt, caramel color, garlic,* sugar, tamarind, spices), spices, chili pepper, potassium sorbate and sodium benzoate added as preservatives, soybean oil, garlic,* salt, onion,* caramel color, citric acid, jalapeño pepper,* xanthan gum, calcium disodium edta added to protect flavor, water.) *dehydrated

FIRE-ROASTED PORK *and* BROWN RICE

SEE PHOTO ON PAGE 220.

PREP TIME: 5 MINUTES • TOTAL TIME: 25 MINUTES • MAKES 4 SERVINGS

1 tablespoon olive oil

1 onion, chopped

1 red bell pepper, chopped

1 pork tenderloin (about ¾ pound), cut into 2" cubes

1 can (28 ounces) diced fire-roasted tomatoes

1 teaspoon dried thyme

2 cups cooked brown rice

1. In a large saucepan, heat the oil over medium heat. Cook the onion, bell pepper, and pork for 5 minutes, turning the pork to brown on all sides.

2. Add the tomatoes and thyme. Cook, stirring occasionally, for 10 minutes, or until the flavors meld. Stir in the rice and cook for 5 minutes, or until heated through.

	CALORIES	PROTEIN	CARBS	FIBER	SUGARS	FAT	SAT FAT	SODIUM
REAL FOOD	307	22 g	36 g	4 g	9 g	8 g	2 g	494 mg
FAKE FOOD	590	23 g	50 g	5 g	20 g	34 g	12 g	1,360 mg

COMPARED TO: Hungry-Man Salisbury Steak with Mashed Potatoes and Green Beans

INGREDIENTS: Gravy (water, mushrooms, onions, modified corn starch, sherry wine, flavor [salt, beef stock, beef fat, maltodextrin, potassium chloride, hydrolyzed soy, corn and wheat gluten protein, yeast extract, vegetable stock (carrot, onion, celery), natural and artificial flavors, potassium lactate, onion powder, dextrose, sugar, disodium inosinate, disodium guanylate, Soy Sauce (soybeans, salt, wheat), modified corn starch, tomato powder and citric acid], wheat flour, onion powder, sugar, Cream Powder Blend [heavy cream, whey protein concentrate, whey], caramel color, salt, yeast extract, spice), Cooked Salisbury Steak Patty (beef, water, pork, textured soy protein concentrate with caramel color, Bread Crumbs [enriched bleached wheat flour (enriched with niacin, ferrous sulfate, thiamine mononitrate, riboflavin, folic acid), dextrose, Contains 2% or less of yeast, partially hydrogenated vegetable oil (soybean and/or cottonseed), salt], soy protein concentrate, seasoning blend [maltodextrin, salt, grill flavor (soybean and cottonseed oils), modified food starch, corn syrup solids, smoke flavoring], salt, dehydrated onion, caramel color, sodium phosphate, garlic powder, spice extract, eggs, spice), mashed potatoes (water, reconstituted potatoes (sodium acid pyrophosphate), cream, margarine [partially hydrogenated soybean oil with TBHQ and citric acid as preservatives, water, mono- and diglycerides (BHT, citric acid), beta-carotene for color (corn oil, tocopherol), vitamin A palmitate], butter concentrate [butter (cream, salt), flavor], salt, potato flavor [potatoes, water, buttermilk, butter oil, salt, natural flavors, soy lecithin, calcium chloride, tocopherol enzyme]), green beans, brownie (sugar, water, wheat flour, partially hydrogenated soybean oil with TBHQ and citric acid as preservatives, cocoa, eggs, margarine [partially hydrogenated soybean oil with TBHQ and citric acid as preservatives, water, mono- and diglycerides (BHT, citric acid), beta-carotene for color (corn oil, tocopherol), vitamin A palmitate], acacia and xanthan gums, sodium bicarbonate [hydrogenated vegetable oil], salt, natural and artificial vanilla flavor [water, propylene glycol, ethanol caramel color, vanilla extractives]), Sauce (water, sugar, margarine [soybean oil, partially hydrogenated soybean oil, water, salt, whey, soy lecithin, mono- and diglycerides, natural beta-carotene (color), flavor, vitamin A palmitate], salt, partially hydrogenated soybean oil with TBHQ and citric acid as preservatives). Contains 2% or less of: margarine (partially hydrogenated soybean oil with TBHQ and citric acid as preservatives, water, mono- and diglycerides [BHT, citric acid], beta-carotene for color [corn oil, tocopherol], vitamin A palmitate).

ZESTY ORANGE CHICKEN

SEE PHOTO ON PAGE 268.

PREP TIME: 5 MINUTES ● TOTAL TIME: 25 MINUTES ● MAKES 4 SERVINGS

2 tablespoons olive oil

2 tablespoons soy sauce

¼ –½ teaspoon red-pepper flakes

2 pounds boneless, skinless chicken thighs, trimmed

1 orange, thinly sliced

1. Preheat the oven to 425°F. In a large bowl, combine the oil, soy sauce, and red-pepper flakes. Add the chicken and toss to coat well.

2. Place the orange slices on a large rimmed baking sheet coated with cooking spray. Top with the chicken and drizzle any remaining soy mixture over the chicken.

3. Bake for 20 minutes, or until a thermometer inserted in a chicken thigh registers 165°F and the juices run clear.

	CALORIES	PROTEIN	CARBS	FIBER	SUGARS	FAT	SAT FAT	SODIUM
REAL FOOD	175	22 g	2 g	0 g	2 g	8 g	2 g	352 mg
FAKE FOOD	420	17 g	54 g	5 g	33 g	15 g	2.5 g	600 mg

COMPARED TO: P.F. Chang's Home Menu Meal for Two Orange Chicken

INGREDIENTS: Sauce (water, sugar, soy sauce [water, wheat, soybeans, salt, alcohol, vinegar], canola oil, tomato paste, garlic, ginger, corn starch, Less than 2% of: distilled vinegar, hydrogenated palm oil, chili paste [red chili peppers, distilled vinegar, salt, xanthan gum], dried orange peel, oyster flavored sauce [water, sugar, salt, oyster extractives {oyster, water, salt}, modified corn starch, caramel color], natural flavors), vegetables (carrots, water chestnuts, edamame), battered white meat chicken (chicken breast with rib meat, water, enriched wheat flour [bleached wheat flour, malted barley flour, niacin, reduced iron, thiamine mono-nitrate, riboflavin, folic acid], potato starch, corn starch, Less than 2% of: egg whites, modified food starch, salt, modified corn starch, dextrose, sodium phosphates, leavening [sodium acid pyrophosphate, sodium bicarbonate, monocalcium phosphate], maltodextrin, flavorings, xanthan gum).

✻ food imposters ✻

ORANGE JUICE THAT'S NOT ORANGE JUICE

Here's what's inside each bottle of Sunny D: high-fructose corn syrup, and less than 2 percent of concentrated orange, tangerine, apple, lime, and grapefruit juice. Fruit concentrates are basically syrup, usually added to drinks and foods as additional sweeteners.

Ingredients: Water, high fructose corn syrup, and 2 percent or less of each of the following: concentrated juices (orange, tangerine, apple, lime, grapefruit), citric acid, ascorbic acid (vitamin C), beta-carotene, thiamin hydrochloride (Vitamin B_1), natural flavors, food starch-modified, canola oil, cellulose gum, xanthan gum, sodium hexametaphosphate, sodium benzoate to protect flavor, Yellow #5, Yellow #6.

✻ Bonus Benefits ✻

Chicken is a good source of niacin (vitamin B_3), which aids in metabolism; vitamin B_6, which is important to immune system and blood sugar level maintenance; biotin (vitamin B_7), which helps cell growth; and vitamin B_{12}, which is involved in nerve cell and red blood cell maintenance. Chicken also contains iron (involved in oxygen transport and cell growth) and zinc (which helps immune system functioning and DNA synthesis).[5]

ROASTED CHICKEN THIGHS *with* LEMON *and* OLIVES

SEE PHOTO ON PAGE 226.

PREP TIME: 5 MINUTES • TOTAL TIME: 35 MINUTES • MAKES 4 SERVINGS

4 boneless chicken thighs (about 1½ pounds total), trimmed of excess skin

¼ teaspoon salt

½ teaspoon ground black pepper

1 cup reduced-sodium chicken broth

1 lemon, thinly sliced

2 tablespoons pitted kalamata olives

Fresh dill for garnish (optional)

1. Preheat the oven to 425°F. Sprinkle the chicken thighs with the salt and pepper.

2. Heat a large ovenproof skillet coated with cooking spray over medium heat. Cook the thighs for 10 minutes, or until well browned.

3. Add the chicken broth, lemon slices, and olives to the skillet. Place the skillet in the oven and roast for 10 minutes, or until a thermometer inserted in the thickest portion registers 165°F.

4. Garnish with the dill, if desired.

Fast Fix: *If you accidently bought olives with pits, here's a simple solution: To remove pits from olives, hit the olives hard with the flat side of a chef's knife to break the flesh; then cut the meat from the pit.*

	CALORIES	PROTEIN	CARBS	FIBER	SUGARS	FAT	SAT FAT	SODIUM
REAL FOOD	351	32 g	3 g	1 g	1 g	23 g	6 g	442 mg
FAKE FOOD	620	21 g	45 g	6 g	12 g	39 g	13 g	1,490 mg

COMPARED TO: KFC Basket with Original Recipe Chicken Thigh, Coleslaw, and Biscuit

INGREDIENTS: Chicken Thigh: fresh chicken marinated with: salt, sodium phosphate and monosodium glutamate. breaded with: wheat flour, salt, tricalcium phosphate, whey, nonfat milk, egg whites, corn starch, potato starch, maltodextrin, triglycerides, natural flavoring (milk), gelatin (from chicken), Colonel's secret original recipe seasoning.), Coleslaw: vegetables: chopped cabbage, carrots, and onions. sauce: sugar, soybean oil, water, distilled vinegar, whole eggs, food starch modified, salt, spice, corn vinegar, apple cider vinegar, natural and artificial flavor, xanthan gum, paprika, extractives of paprika, caramel color.), Biscuit: enriched flour bleached (wheat flour, niacin, ferrous sulfate, thiamin mononitrate, riboflavin, folic acid), water, hydrogenated palm kernel oil, buttermilk, sugar, baking soda, salt, sodium aluminum phosphate, nonfat milk, sodium caseinate, DATEM, whey protein concentrate, sodium acid pyrophosphate, whey, partially hydrogenated soybean and cottonseed oil, wheat protein isolate, natural flavor, soy lecithin. liquid and hydrogenated soybean oil, salt, soybean lecithin, natural and artificial flavor, TBHQ and citric acid added to protect flavor, beta-carotene (color), dimethylpolysidoxane, an anti-foaming agent added. or enriched flour bleached (wheat flour, niacin, reduced iron, thiamin mononitrate, riboflavin, folic acid), water, cultured buttermilk (nonfat milk, nonfat milk solids, food starch modified, carrageenan, locust bean gum, salt, cultures), hydrogenated palm kernel oil, partially hydrogenated soybean and/or cottonseed oil, sugar, sodium aluminum phosphate, sodium bicarbonate, salt, sodium acid pyrophosphate, natural flavor, soy lecithin. liquid and hydrogenated soybean oil, salt, soybean lecithin, natural and artificial flavor, TBHQ and citric acid added to protect flavor, beta-carotene (color), dimethylpolysidoxane, an anti-foaming agent added.)

food imposters
TEA THAT'S NOT TEA

Tea = tea + water. It's the easiest recipe on Earth, yet companies so often seem to lose sight of what they're brewing. See SoBe, a PepsiCo company that manages to cram 11 ingredients and no fewer than five weird extracts into their green tea. All in all, that's 21 grams of sugar and zero green tea—in our book, an extract does not a green tea make.

Ingredients: Filtered water, sugar, natural flavor, citric acid, ascorbic acid (vitamin C), green tea extract, caramel color, Reb A (purified stevia extract), guarana seed extract, panax ginseng root extract, rose hips extract.

Bonus Benefits

Lemons and other citrus fruits may lower ischemic stroke risk for women. A study revealed that those who ate the highest amounts of citrus had a 19 percent lower risk of ischemic stroke than women who consumed the least.[6]

8 ways with . . . chicken thighs

If you've grown tired of chicken because you think chicken breasts are the only virtuous part of America's favorite bird, it's time to change your thinking. Boneless, skinless chicken thighs are packed with flavor, quick to prepare, and readily available in most large groceries.

1. **Maple-Sage Roasted Chicken Thighs.** Preheat the oven to 400°F. Arrange 8 boneless, skinless chicken thighs on a large rimmed baking sheet lined with parchment paper and drizzle with 1 tablespoon olive oil. Sprinkle with 1 teaspoon dried sage and ³/₄ teaspoon salt. Roast, turning once and brushing with ¹/₄ cup maple syrup, for 20 minutes, or until a thermometer inserted in the thickest portion registers 165°F. *Makes 4 servings.*

Nutrition (per serving): 278 calories, 27 g protein, 14 g carbohydrates, 0 g fiber, 13 g sugars, 12 g fat, 2.5 g saturated fat, 561 mg sodium

2. **Tex-Mex Chicken Skillet Casserole.** In a large skillet, heat 2 tablespoons olive oil over medium-high heat. Cook 8 boneless, skinless chicken thighs, turning once, for 10 minutes, or until seared and mostly cooked through. Remove from the skillet, coarsely chop, and return to the skillet. Stir in 1³/₄ cups low-sodium chicken broth, 1 can (15 ounces) rinsed and drained black beans, 1 cup quinoa, 1 cup prepared salsa, and 1 teaspoon ground cumin. Increase the heat to high and bring to a boil. Reduce the heat to low, cover, and simmer for 25 minutes, or until the liquid is absorbed and the quinoa is tender. Fluff the quinoa with a fork and sprinkle with ¹/₃ cup shredded Cheddar cheese. *Makes 4 servings.*

Nutrition (per serving): 556 calories, 43 g protein, 52 g carbohydrates, 11 g fiber, 4 g sugars, 19 g fat, 5 g saturated fat, 403 mg sodium

3. **Buffalo Chicken Thighs.** Preheat the broiler and place a rack 6" from the heating element. Arrange 8 boneless, skinless chicken thighs cut into 3 pieces each on a broiler pan and toss with 2 tablespoons olive oil. Broil, turning once, for 5 minutes, or until cooked through. Meanwhile, in a large bowl, combine 3 tablespoons *each* melted butter and hot sauce. Remove the

thighs from the oven and toss in the sauce. Serve with carrot and celery sticks and blue cheese dressing, if desired. *Makes 4 servings.*

Nutrition (per serving): 268 calories, 27 g protein, 0 g carbohydrates, 0 g fiber, 0 g sugars, 17 g fat, 9 g saturated fat, 504 mg sodium

4. **Skillet Thighs with Couscous.** In a large skillet, heat 2 tablespoons olive oil over medium-high heat. Cook 8 boneless, skinless chicken thighs cut into bite-size pieces, 1 *each* thinly sliced onion and bell pepper, 1 sliced zucchini, and ½ teaspoon *each* salt and black pepper. Cook, stirring, for 5 minutes, or until the chicken is no longer pink and the vegetables are tender. Add 1 cup chicken broth and bring to a boil. Stir in ⅔ cup whole wheat couscous, cover, remove from the heat, and let sit for 5 minutes. Fluff the couscous just before serving. *Makes 4 servings.*

Nutrition (per serving): 362 calories, 32 g protein, 28 g carbohydrates, 3 g fiber, 3 g sugars, 13 g fat, 2.5 g saturated fat, 440 mg sodium

5. **Chili-Lime Chicken Thighs.** Preheat the oven to 425°F. In a large bowl, combine 3 tablespoons olive oil, 1 tablespoon grated lime peel, 2 teaspoons *each* chili powder and garlic powder, and ¾ teaspoon salt. Toss 8 boneless, skinless chicken thighs in the seasoning mixture and arrange on a baking sheet lined with parchment paper. Roast for 15 minutes, or until a thermometer inserted in the thickest portion registers 165°F. Remove from the

oven and squeeze half a lime over the top. *Makes 4 servings.*

Nutrition (per serving): 274 calories, 27 g protein, 5 g carbohydrates, 1 g fiber, 0 g sugars, 16 g fat, 3 g saturated fat, 561 mg sodium

6. **Chicken Thighs with Creamy Spinach Artichoke Sauce.** Season 8 boneless, skinless chicken thighs with ½ teaspoon *each* salt and black pepper. In a large skillet, heat 2 tablespoons olive oil over medium-high heat. Cook the chicken thighs, turning once, for 5 minutes, or until browned. Remove to a plate. To the skillet, add 1 bag (12 ounces) frozen, thawed artichoke heart quarters, 1 box (10 ounces) frozen, thawed chopped spinach, 1 cup half-and-half or heavy cream, and ½ cup chicken broth and bring to a simmer. Place the chicken thighs in the sauce and simmer for 8 minutes, or until a thermometer inserted in the thickest portion of a thigh registers 165°F. *Makes 4 servings.*

Nutrition (per serving): 394 calories, 35 g protein, 20 g carbohydrates, 7 g fiber, 3 g sugars, 21 g fat, 7 g saturated fat, 555 mg sodium

7. **Chicken Primavera Pasta.** Prepare 12 ounces orecchiette, or shell pasta, according to package directions. Meanwhile, preheat a gas or charcoal grill to medium-high heat and brush and oil the grill grates. (Alternatively, use a grill pan over medium-high heat and work in batches.) Season 8 boneless, skinless chicken thighs with ½ teaspoon *each* salt, black pepper,

(continued)

8 ways with ... chicken thighs (cont.)

and garlic powder. In a large bowl, toss 1 bunch trimmed asparagus with 1 tablespoon olive oil. Grill the thighs, turning once, for 14 minutes, or until a thermometer inserted in the thickest portion registers 165°F, and the asparagus for 7 minutes, or until tender-crisp. Cut the chicken and asparagus into bite-size pieces. Toss into a large bowl with $\frac{1}{2}$ cup Italian dressing, 1 pint halved grape tomatoes, 1 cup fresh mozzarella pearls, $\frac{1}{2}$ cup chopped roasted red pepper, and $\frac{1}{4}$ cup torn basil leaves. Add the drained pasta and toss well to combine. *Makes 6 servings.*

Nutrition (per serving): 454 calories, 29 g protein, 49 g carbohydrates, 4 g fiber, 6 g sugars, 16 g fat, 5 g saturated fat, 495 mg sodium

8. **Oven "Fried" Buttermilk Chicken Thighs.** Preheat the oven to 425°F and place a rack in a large rimmed baking sheet. In a large bowl, combine 1 cup buttermilk, 1 tablespoon hot sauce, and $\frac{1}{2}$ teaspoon *each* garlic powder, dried thyme, and salt. Add 8 boneless, skinless chicken thighs, turning to thoroughly coat. In a resealable plastic bag, crush 4 cups corn flakes and transfer to a wide, shallow dish. Remove the chicken from the marinade, letting the excess drip off. Dredge the chicken in the corn flake crumbs, pressing the crumbs to the chicken to adhere, and arrange on the rack. Drizzle the chicken with 4 tablespoons melted butter and bake for 25 minutes, or until golden, crispy, and a thermometer inserted in the thickest portion registers 165°F. *Makes 4 servings.*

Nutrition (per serving): 355 calories, 29 g protein, 20 g carbohydrates, 1 g fiber, 3 g sugars, 18 g fat, 9 g saturated fat, 572 mg sodium

PEACH-GLAZED CHICKEN BREASTS

SEE PHOTO ON PAGE 225.

PREP TIME: 10 MINUTES • TOTAL TIME: 30 MINUTES • MAKES 6 SERVINGS

¼ cup peach all-fruit spread

2 tablespoons grainy or Dijon mustard

¼ teaspoon ground ginger

4 boneless, skinless chicken breasts

Pinch of salt

Pinch of ground black pepper

1. Preheat the oven to 375°F. In a small bowl, stir together the fruit spread, mustard, and ginger. Season the chicken with the salt and pepper.

2. Place the chicken in a medium roasting pan and spread with the peach mixture. Bake for 20 minutes, or until a thermometer inserted in the thickest portion registers 165°F and the juices run clear.

Fast Fix: *This peach-mustard mixture turns ordinary chicken, pork, or fish into a tasty, quick meal. You can change it up by using garlic powder, soy sauce, or thyme instead of the ginger or opting for apricot or orange fruit spread.*

	CALORIES	PROTEIN	CARBS	FIBER	SUGARS	FAT	SAT FAT	SODIUM
REAL FOOD	170	24 g	10 g	0 g	8 g	3 g	1 g	268 mg
FAKE FOOD	395	38 g	33 g	1 g	13 g	17 g	3 g	370 mg

COMPARED TO: Chick-fil-A Chick-n-Strips with Honey Mustard Sauce

INGREDIENTS: Strips: (whole chicken tenderloins seasoning [sea salt, autolyzed yeast, maltodextrin, spice, natural flavor, chicken fat, garlic powder, sugar cane syrup, onion powder, paprika, molasses, sodium diacetate, tomato powder, silicon dioxide {anticaking agent}, sugar, oleoresin paprika {color}, citric acid, smoke flavor, caramel color], seasoned coater [enriched bleached wheat flour {with malted barley flour, niacin, iron, thiamine mononitrate, riboflavin, folic acid}, sugar, salt, monosodium glutamate, nonfat milk, leavening {baking soda, sodium aluminum phosphate, monocalcium phosphate}, spice, soybean oil, color {paprika}], milk wash [water, nonfat milk, egg], peanut oil [fully refined peanut oil, with dimethylpolysiloxane, an anti-foam agent added]). Honey Mustard Sauce: (water, honey, sugar, distilled vinegar, modified corn starch, mustard seed, salt, garlic,* spices, soybean oil, turmeric, natural flavors, onion,* sodium benzoate added as preservative, xanthan gum, guar gum, molasses, corn syrup, caramel color, tamarind) *dehydrated

ITALIAN-STYLE CHICKEN
and MUSHROOMS

SEE PHOTO ON PAGE 222.

PREP TIME: 10 MINUTES ● TOTAL TIME: 30 MINUTES ● MAKES 4 SERVINGS

2 tablespoons olive oil, divided

½ pound sliced mushrooms

1 onion, chopped

3 tablespoons whole grain pastry flour

¼ teaspoon salt

¼ teaspoon ground black pepper

1 pound chicken breast cutlets

½ cup Marsala wine or chicken broth

¾ cup reduced-sodium chicken broth

2 tablespoons chopped parsley, for garnish

1. In a large nonstick skillet, heat 1 tablespoon of the oil over medium-high heat. Cook the mushrooms and onion for 5 minutes, or until browned. Transfer to a bowl.

2. On a plate, combine the flour, salt, and pepper. Coat the chicken in the flour mixture, shaking off the excess.

3. In the same skillet, heat the remaining 1 tablespoon oil over medium-high heat. Cook the chicken, turning, for 3 minutes, or until browned. Add the ½ cup wine or broth and cook for 1 minute, stirring up any brown bits.

4. Add the ¾ cup broth and bring to a simmer. Return the mushroom mixture to the skillet and simmer for 3 minutes, or until the chicken is no longer pink and the juices run clear. Sprinkle with the parsley, if using.

Fast Fix: *Clean a large amount of mushrooms in minutes. Place them in a large bowl and spray with cold water to loosen as much dirt as possible. Once the bowl is filled with water, swish the mushrooms back and forth for no more than 30 seconds. Quickly lift out the mushrooms with your hand and transfer them to paper towels to absorb any excess moisture. Slice and use immediately.*

	CALORIES	PROTEIN	CARBS	FIBER	SUGARS	FAT	SAT FAT	SODIUM
REAL FOOD	264	26 g	7 g	1 g	2 g	10 g	2 g	368 mg
FAKE FOOD	460	22 g	58 g	4 g	7 g	15 g	5 g	890 mg

COMPARED TO: Stouffer's Chicken Parmigiana Large Family Size

INGREDIENTS: Blanched Spaghetti (water, semolina, wheat gluten), Cooked Breaded Chicken Breast Patty With Rib Meat (chicken breast with rib meat, water, seasoning [modified corn starch, whey protein concentrate], isolated soy protein, sodium phosphates, seasoning [yeast extract, salt, soy sauce solids {soybeans, wheat, salt}, sugar, maltodextrin, chicken powder, flavor, vegetable oil, chicken broth, tapioca starch, thiamine hydrochloride, lactic acid, citric acid, chicken fat], pre-dusted and battered with [modified food starch, wheat flour, yellow corn flour, salt, spices, xanthan gum, extractives of paprika], Breaded With [enriched wheat flour {enriched with niacin, reduced iron, thiamine mononitrate, riboflavin, folic acid}, dextrose, sea salt, salt, soybean oil, yeast, mono- and diglycerides, spice, extractive of paprika], breading set in vegetable oil), tomato puree (water, tomato paste), water, tomatoes (diced tomatoes, tomato juice, citric acid, calcium chloride), mozzarella cheese and modified cornstarch (mozzarella cheese [cultured milk, salt, enzymes], modified cornstarch, sodium citrate, flavors, annatto), onions, 2% or less of soybean oil, modified cornstarch, sugar, sea salt, garlic puree, spices, yeast extract, potassium chloride, xanthan gum.

Bonus Benefits

Can mushrooms keep you slim? One study showed that mushroom consumers are less likely to be overweight or obese and less likely to have metabolic syndrome.[7]

CHICKEN ENCHILADAS

SEE PHOTO ON PAGE 218.

PREP TIME: 15 MINUTES • TOTAL TIME: 50 MINUTES • MAKES 6 SERVINGS

2¼ cups salsa, divided

1 can (15 ounces) no-salt-added black beans, rinsed and drained

1½ cups frozen corn kernels, thawed

1½ teaspoons ground cumin

2 cups shredded cooked chicken breast

¾ cup shredded reduced-fat pepper Jack cheese, divided

¾ cup shredded reduced-fat Cheddar cheese, divided

12 whole wheat tortillas (6" diameter)

1. Preheat the oven to 375°F. Coat a 13" x 9" baking dish with cooking spray. Spread ½ cup of the salsa in the dish.

2. In a large bowl, stir together the beans, corn, cumin, and ¾ cup of the salsa. Reserve ½ cup of the bean mixture and set aside.

3. On a clean work surface, divide the chicken, the remaining bean mixture, ½ cup of the pepper Jack, and ½ cup of the Cheddar among the tortillas. Roll up to enclose the filling and arrange seam side down in the dish. Spoon the remaining 1 cup salsa and the ½ cup reserved bean mixture over the top.

4. Cover with foil. Bake for 25 minutes. Uncover and sprinkle with the remaining ¼ cup pepper Jack and ¼ cup Cheddar. Bake for 10 minutes, or until the cheese is melted and the enchiladas are heated through.

	CALORIES	PROTEIN	CARBS	FIBER	SUGARS	FAT	SAT FAT	SODIUM
REAL FOOD	422	32 g	46 g	20 g	1 g	11 g	4 g	997 mg
FAKE FOOD	980	42 g	90 g	12 g	6 g	52 g	10 g	2,220 mg

COMPARED TO: Del Taco Epic Bacon Ranch Chicken Avocado Burrito

INGREDIENTS: Tortilla (epic burritos): enriched bleached wheat flour (wheat flour, niacin, reduced iron, thiamine mononitrate, riboflavin, folic acid), water, vegetable shortening (interesterified soybean oil, hydrogenated soybean oil and/or palm oil), contains 2% or less of the following: vital wheat gluten, salt, sugar, margarine (interesterified soybean oil, hydrogenated cottonseed oil, water, salt, mono- and diglycerides, soy lecithin, sodium benzoate [preservative], artificial flavor, beta-carotene [color], vitamin A palmitate), leavening (sodium bicarbonate, sodium aluminum sulfate, corn starch, monocalcium phosphate and/or sodium acid pyrophosphate, calcium sulfate), yeast, guar gum, cellulose gum, dough conditioners (fumaric acid, sodium metabisulfite, DATEM, enzyme blend), preservatives (calcium propionate, sorbic acid and/or citric acid). Black Beans: water, black beans, garlic and water, canola oil, seasoning (salt, spices, yeast extract, paprika, and not more than 2% silicon dioxide to prevent caking), modified food starch, flavor (cooked vegetables [carrot, celery, onion], tomato paste, corn oil, natural yeast extract, potato flour, salt, onion powder, garlic powder and flavoring), onion juice (onion juice, vinegar, salt), tomato paste, chipotle sauce (chipotle pepper, water, tomato puree, vinegar, soybean oil, salt, sugar, onion, spices), salt. Fresca Lime Rice: water, rice, canola oil, vegetable base (salt, dextrose, dehydrated potato, shortening powder (partially hydrogenated soybean oil, partially hydrogenated cottonseed oil, corn syrup solids, sodium caseinate, mono- and diglycerides, citric acid), disodium inosinate, disodium guanylate, natural vegetable flavor, spices, natural vegetable powder, dehydrated yeast (yeast extract, partially hydrogenated cottonseed and soybean oils), vegetable shortening, dehydrated mushrooms, oleoresin turmeric, oleoresin paprika, oleoresin celery, lecithin, caramel color), onions, salt, garlic powder. Lime Seasoning: crystallized lime (citric acid, malic acid, lactic acid, tartaric acid, lime oil, lime juice, ascorbic acid [vitamin C]), maltodextrin, organic evaporated cane juice, sodium citrate, color added. Grilled Marinated Chicken: chicken breast with rib meat, and, boneless skinless chicken thigh meat, water, seasoning (modified food starch, salt, garlic powder, spices, dried whey protein concentrate, onion powder, soy sauce (naturally fermented from wheat and soybeans), sugar, corn syrup solids, maltodextrin, lime juice solids, autolyzed yeast extract, citric acid, natural flavors, chicken fat, dextrose, hydrolyzed corn gluten, caramel color, chicken broth, oleoresin paprika, hydrolyzed soy protein, gelatin), sodium phosphates. Creamy Ranch: soybean oil, buttermilk, water, vinegar, maltodextrin, egg yolk, contains less than 2% of: sugar, salt, corn starch, spice, garlic, buttermilk solids (milk), onion, lactic acid, guar gum, xanthan gum, yeast extract, natural flavor, sunflower oil. Bacon Strips: pork belly, water, salt, sugar, smoke flavor, sodium phosphates, sodium erythorbate, sodium nitrite. Avocado: avocado.

⇒ Bonus Benefit ⇐

Black beans contain higher amounts of saponins and flavonoids than most other types of beans. Saponins have been shown to induce cell death in several types of cancer and to inhibit cancer cell proliferation, especially when combined with flavonoids.[8]

CHICKEN and VEGGIE STIR-FRY

SEE PHOTO ON PAGE 219.

PREP TIME: 20 MINUTES • TOTAL TIME: 40 MINUTES • MAKES 4 SERVINGS

2 tablespoons peanut or olive oil, divided

1 pound ground chicken breast

¼ teaspoon ground ginger

1 red onion, cut into wedges

½ pound trimmed green beans, cut in half

3 cups broccoli florets (about ½ pound)

2 cups shredded coleslaw mix

3 tablespoons reduced-sodium soy sauce

1 tablespoon rice wine vinegar

1 tablespoon toasted sesame oil

¼ cup chopped peanuts (optional)

1. In a large skillet or wok, heat 1 tablespoon of the peanut or olive oil over medium-high heat. Cook the chicken and ginger for 5 minutes, or until no longer pink. Remove to a bowl and set aside.

2. Add the remaining 1 tablespoon peanut or olive oil to the skillet and cook the onion, green beans, broccoli, and coleslaw for 7 minutes, or until tender-crisp.

3. Add the soy sauce, vinegar, and sesame oil and cook for 2 minutes, or until reduced slightly.

4. Return the chicken to the skillet and cook, stirring, for 1 minute, or until heated through. Garnish with the peanuts, if using.

Fast Fix: *Cut a head of broccoli in no time. Simply cut off the stalk crosswise as close to the florets as possible, cutting through the small stems that attach the bottom layer of the florets to the stalk. The bottom layer of florets will fall away from the stalk. Continue cutting across the stalk through the stems on the next layer of florets. Repeat until all florets have been removed.*

	CALORIES	PROTEIN	CARBS	FIBER	SUGARS	FAT	SAT FAT	SODIUM
REAL FOOD	278	28 g	12 g	4 g	4 g	14 g	2 g	552 mg
FAKE FOOD	640	20 g	104 g	3 g	35 g	16 g	2 g	1,720 mg

COMPARED TO: Boston Market Sweet & Sour Chicken (frozen meal)

INGREDIENTS: Cooked long grain rice, water, breaded chicken breast chunks with rib meat (chicken breast meat with rib meat, water, enriched wheat flour [wheat flour, niacin, reduced iron, thiamine mononitrate, riboflavin, folic acid], bleached enriched wheat flour [wheat flour, niacin, reduced iron, thiamine mononitrate, riboflavin, folic acid], salt, yellow corn flour, modified food starch, dextrose, soy flour, sodium phosphates, leavening [sodium bicarbonate, monocalcium phosphate, sodium aluminum phosphate], nonfat dry milk, wheat gluten, garlic powder, onion powder, spices, malted barley flour, extractives of paprika, carrageenan), sugar, soy sauce (water, wheat, soybeans, salt, lactic acid and less than $\frac{1}{10}$% sodium benzoate as a preservative), peas, carrots, scrambled eggs (whole eggs, skim milk, soybean oil, corn starch, salt, xanthan gum, citric acid), Less than 2% of red bell pepper, canola oil, white distilled vinegar, tomato paste, pineapple juice concentrate, modified corn starch, chicken broth, orange juice concentrate, burgundy wine (wine, salt), salt, sesame oil, granulated garlic, dehydrated soy sauce (soy sauce [soybeans, wheat, salt, vinegar, lactic acid], maltodextrin), granulated onion, spices, citric acid, rendered chicken fat, paprika, xanthan gum.

÷ Bonus Benefits ÷

Reduce osteoarthritis pain with ginger. Studies found that ginger consumption produced a significant reduction in pain and disability.[9]

TURKEY MINI MEAT LOAVES

SEE PHOTO ON PAGE 269.

PREP TIME: 10 MINUTES • TOTAL TIME: 30 MINUTES • MAKES 4 SERVINGS

1 pound ground turkey breast

⅓ cup whole wheat panko bread crumbs

⅓ cup chopped cilantro

2 cloves garlic, minced

2 tablespoons reduced-sodium soy sauce

1 tablespoon dark sesame oil

¼ teaspoon ground ginger

4 bags bok choy, halved and steamed

2 cups cooked brown rice

1. Preheat the oven to 375°F. Coat 4 miniature loaf pans or 1 roasting pan with cooking spray.

2. In a large bowl, combine the turkey, bread crumbs, cilantro, garlic, soy sauce, oil, and ginger. Mix just until combined.

3. Evenly divide into 4 portions and place in the loaf pans or form into 4 mini loaves about 5" x 3" on the pan. Bake for 20 minutes, or until a thermometer inserted in the center registers 165°F and the meat is no longer pink. Serve with the bok choy and rice.

⌇ How Can You Save Time Chopping Garlic?

Use a garlic press. Don't bother peeling the garlic; just place the unpeeled clove in the chamber of the press, close it with gentle pressure, and scrape off the emerging garlic paste with a knife.

	CALORIES	PROTEIN	CARBS	FIBER	SUGARS	FAT	SAT FAT	SODIUM
REAL FOOD	301	32 g	31 g	6 g	1 g	5 g	1 g	379 mg
FAKE FOOD	660	26 g	61 g	5 g	25 g	35 g	12g	1,660 mg

COMPARED TO: Hungry-Man Home-Style Meatloaf

INGREDIENTS: Cooked Meatloaf Patty (beef, pork, water, seasoning [bread crumbs {enriched bleached wheat flour (niacin, reduced iron, thiamin mononitrate, riboflavin, folic acid), salt, durum flour, vegetable oil shortening (soybean), leavening (sodium bicarbonate, sodium acid pyrophosphate, monocalcium phosphate), dextrose, yeast, spice extractive}, maltodextrin, dehydrated onion, natural flavor (with hydrolyzed soy protein, hydrolyzed corn protein, dextrose, autolyzed yeast extract), tomato powder, salt, worcestershire sauce solids (molasses, vinegar, corn syrup, salt, caramel color, garlic, sugar, spice tamarind, natural flavor), spices, green bell pepper powder, garlic powder, onion powder, dried beef stock, yellow corn flour, lactic acid, chili pepper, calcium lactate, dehydrated parsley, autolyzed yeast extract, disodium inosinate, disodium guanylate, natural flavor], textured soy protein concentrate with caramel color, green pepper, onions, soy protein concentrate, bread crumbs (bleached wheat flour, salt, dextrose, yeast, partially hydrogenated soybean oil), salt, caramel color, sodium phosphate, eggs, spice extract), Meatloaf Gravy (water, tomatoes [tomato juice, calcium chloride, citric acid], natural flavor [sugar, salt, maltodextrin, onion powder, modified corn starch, tomato powder, caramel color, autolyzed yeast extract, garlic powder, spices, partially hydrogenated soybean and cottonseed oil, natural flavors, disodium guanylate and disodium inosinate, dried jalapeno puree, dried mushroom, bell pepper juice solids, carrot juice solids, vinegar solids, soy lecithin, grill flavor (from partially hydrogenated soybean and cottonseed oil), ascorbic acid, smoke flavor, egg yolk powder], modified food starch, high fructose corn syrup, wheat flour, salt, flavor [corn syrup, hydrolyzed corn protein, autolyzed yeast extract, sugar, salt, beef stock, onion powder, propylene glycol, natural flavors, monosodium glutamate, beef fat, carrot juice concentrate, hydrolyzed soy protein, hydrolyzed wheat gluten, celery juice concentrate, onion broth, thiamine hydrochloride, tomato powder, spices, garlic powder, succinic acid, partially hydrogenated soybean and cottonseed oil, soy lecithin, caramel color, potassium sorbate], tomato puree [water, tomato paste], worcestershire sauce concentrate without anchovies [vinegar, molasses, corn syrup, water, salt, caramel color, garlic powder, sugar, spices, tamarind, natural flavor, sulfiting agent], beef tallow flavor [beef fat, flavors], parsley), mashed potatoes (water, reconstituted potatoes [mono- and diglycerides, sodium acid pyrophosphate, citric acid], heavy cream, butter [cream, salt], salt, margarine [partially hydrogenated soybean oil with TBHQ and citric acid as preservatives, water, mono- and diglycerides (BHT, citric acid), beta-carotene for color (corn oil, tocopherol), vitamin A palmitate], potato flavor [potatoes, water, buttermilk, butter oil, salt, natural flavors, soy lecithin, calcium chloride, tocopherol, enzyme]), mixed vegetables (corn, carrots, peas, cut green beans), brownie (sugar, water, wheat flour, partially hydrogenated soybean oil with TBHQ and citric acid as preservatives, cocoa, eggs, margarine [partially hydrogenated soybean and/or soybean oils, water, mono- and diglycerides, beta-carotene for color, may also contain vitamin a palmitate, salt, whey, soy lecithin, natural flavor], acacia and xanthan gums, sodium bicarbonate [hydrogenated cottonseed oil], salt, natural and artificial vanilla flavor [water, propylene glycol, ethanol, caramel color]), sauce (water, sugar, margarine [soybean oil, partially hydrogenated soybean oil, water, salt, whey, soy lecithin, mono- and diglycerides, natural flavor, beta-carotene (color), vitamin A palmitate], salt, partially hydrogenated soybean oil with TBHQ and citric acid as preservatives). Contains 2% or less of: margarine (partially hydrogenated soybean oil with TBHQ and citric acid as preservatives, water, mono- and diglycerides [BHT, citric acid], beta-carotene for color [corn oil, tocopherol], vitamin A palmitate).

8 ways with . . . turkey cutlets

Turkey isn't just for Thanksgiving anymore. Because cutlets are essentially naturally lean turkey breast, these dishes afford an opportunity to splurge with other healthy fats and add a delicious boost of real flavor to your cooking.

1. **Turkey Cutlets Milanese with Salsa Cruda.** Season 4 turkey cutlets (about 1 pound) with ¼ teaspoon *each* salt and black pepper. In a shallow bowl, beat together 1 egg and 2 tablespoons water. In another shallow bowl, place ½ cup dry whole wheat bread crumbs. Dredge the cutlets in the bread crumbs, followed by the egg, and in the bread crumbs again. In a large skillet, heat ¼ cup olive oil over medium heat. Cook the cutlets, turning once, for 10 minutes, or until golden brown and no longer pink. Meanwhile, in a medium bowl, combine 2 chopped plum tomatoes, ¼ cup chopped fresh basil, a quarter of a finely chopped red onion, 2 tablespoons olive oil, 1 minced clove garlic, and ¼ teaspoon salt. Serve the cutlets on a bed of 2 cups baby arugula and topped with the tomato mixture. *Makes 4 servings.*

   Nutrition (per serving): 378 calories, 32 g protein, 11 g carbohydrates, 2 g fiber, 2 g sugars, 23 g fat, 3 g saturated fat, 500 mg sodium

2. **Turkey Fajitas.** In a medium bowl, stir together 1 pound turkey cutlets sliced into 1" strips, 2 teaspoons ground cumin, 1 teaspoon *each* chili powder and brown sugar, and ½ teaspoon salt. In a large skillet, heat 2 tablespoons olive oil over medium-high heat. Cook the turkey, 1 sliced onion, and 1 sliced bell pepper, stirring occasionally, for 10 minutes, or until the turkey is no longer pink and the vegetables are tender. Serve with 12 warm corn tortillas and dollops of sour cream. *Makes 4 servings.*

   Nutrition (per serving): 391 calories, 33 g protein, 39 g carbohydrates, 6 g fiber, 4 g sugars, 12 g fat, 3 g saturated fat, 437 mg sodium

3. **Turkey with Lemon Caper Sauce.** Season 4 turkey cutlets (about 1 pound) with ½ teaspoon *each* salt and black pepper. Place ¼ cup whole grain flour in a shallow dish. Dredge the cutlets in the flour. In a large skillet, heat 1 tablespoon *each* butter and olive oil over medium heat. Cook the cutlets, turning

once, for 8 minutes, or until golden brown and no longer pink. Stir in ½ cup chicken broth, 2 tablespoons capers, and 2 tablespoons fresh lemon juice, stirring to scrape up the bits on the bottom of the pan. Bring to a simmer. Cook for 5 minutes, or until the sauce is slightly reduced. Serve over 2 cups cooked brown rice. *Makes 4 servings.*

Nutrition (per serving): 313 calories, 32 g protein, 28 g carbohydrates, 3 g fiber, 1 g sugars, 8 g fat, 3g saturated fat, 549 mg sodium

4. **Turkey Marsala.** Prepare 8 ounces whole wheat linguine according to package directions. Meanwhile, in a large skillet, heat 2 tablespoons olive oil over medium heat. Cook 1 pound turkey cutlets cut into 1" pieces, turning occasionally, for 4 minutes, or until golden. Transfer to a plate. In the same skillet, cook 1½ pounds sliced wild mushrooms, 1 minced clove garlic, and ½ teaspoon *each* salt and black pepper for 8 minutes, or until the mushrooms are golden and the liquid has evaporated. Add ½ cup sweet Marsala wine and cook for 4 minutes, or until reduced by half. Add ½ cup chicken broth and the reserved turkey and cook for 5 minutes, or until the flavors meld. Stir in 1 tablespoon butter. Serve over cooked linguine. *Makes 4 servings.*

Nutrition (per serving): 514 calories, 40 g protein, 57 g carbohydrates, 5 g fiber, 7 g sugars, 12 g fat, 3 g saturated fat, 445 mg sodium

5. **Grilled Turkey Cutlet Club.** Coat a grill rack with cooking spray and pre-heat the grill to medium-high heat. In a small bowl, combine 1½ tablespoons olive oil and ½ teaspoon *each* salt, black pepper, and garlic powder to make a paste. Rub over 4 turkey cutlets (about 1 pound). Grill the cutlets, turning once, for 8 minutes, or until no longer pink. Spread 1 teaspoon mayonnaise on each of 8 slices 100 percent whole wheat bread. On each of 4 slices of the bread, layer 1 leaf romaine lettuce, 2 thin slices of tomato, and 1 turkey cutlet. Top with the remaining bread. *Makes 4 servings.*

Nutrition (per serving): 441 calories, 36 g protein, 42 g carbohydrates, 7 g fiber, 7 g sugars, 17 g fat, 2 g saturated fat, 732 mg sodium

6. **Mediterranean Turkey.** Prepare ¾ cup quinoa according to package directions. Meanwhile, in a large bowl, toss 1 pound turkey cutlets cut into 1" pieces, 1 tablespoon olive oil, 1 teaspoon dried oregano, and ¼ teaspoon salt. In a large skillet, heat 1 tablespoon olive oil over medium heat. Cook 1 chopped red onion and 2 minced cloves garlic, stirring, for 5 minutes, or until the vegetables soften. Add the turkey and cook for 5 minutes, or until it begins to brown. Add 1 can (14.5 ounces) diced tomatoes and 2 tablespoons thinly sliced black olives and bring to a simmer. Cook, stirring, for 5 minutes, or until the turkey is no longer pink. Serve over the quinoa. *Makes 4 servings.*

Nutrition (per serving): 361 calories, 34 g protein, 30 g carbohydrates, 3 g fiber, 4 g sugars, 12 g fat, 1 g saturated fat, 646 mg sodium

(continued)

8 ways with … turkey cutlets (cont.)

7. Almond-Crusted Turkey Cutlets with Broccoli Slaw. Preheat the oven to 400°F. Line a rimmed baking sheet with parchment paper. Season 1 pound turkey cutlets with ½ teaspoon *each* salt and black pepper. In a shallow bowl, beat 1 large egg. Place ½ cup ground almonds in another shallow bowl. Dip the turkey cutlets in the egg, coat completely in the almond mixture, and arrange on the baking sheet. Bake, turning once, for 10 minutes, or until the turkey is golden and no longer pink. Meanwhile, in a large bowl, whisk together ¼ cup mayonnaise and ¼ cup sweet pickle brine (the liquid from a jar of pickles). Add 1 bag (10 or 12 ounces) broccoli slaw and toss to coat well. Serve the turkey with the slaw. *Makes 4 servings.*

Nutrition (per serving): 346 calories, 34 g protein, 12 g carbohydrates, 3 g fiber, 6 g sugars, 19 g fat, 2 g saturated fat, 505 mg sodium

8. Honey Dijon Turkey with Potatoes. Preheat the oven to 400°F and line a rimmed baking sheet with parchment paper. On the baking sheet, toss 2 pounds halved baby potatoes (such as Yukon Gold) with 2 tablespoons olive oil and ½ teaspoon *each* salt and black pepper. Bake for 10 minutes, or until the potatoes begin to soften. Meanwhile, in a small bowl, combine 1 tablespoon *each* Dijon mustard and olive oil, and 2 teaspoons honey. Spread the mixture over 1 pound turkey cutlets. Arrange the cutlets on top of the potatoes and bake for 10 minutes, or until the potatoes are completely tender and the turkey is no longer pink. *Makes 4 servings.*

Nutrition (per serving): 390 calories, 32 g protein, 45 g carbohydrates, 4 g fiber, 5 g sugars, 11 g fat, 1g saturated fat, 553 mg sodium

COD IN TURMERIC BROTH

SEE PHOTO ON PAGE 217.

PREP TIME: 5 MINUTES • TOTAL TIME: 15 MINUTES • MAKES 4 SERVINGS

1 tablespoon olive oil

4 cod, haddock, flounder, or other
white fish (about 5 ounces each)

1½ cups chicken broth

¼ teaspoon ground turmeric

Chopped fresh dill for garnish

1. In a large skillet, heat the oil over medium heat. Cook the fish, turning once, for 4 minutes.
Transfer to a plate and set aside.

2. Add the broth and turmeric to the skillet. Bring to a simmer. Return the fish to the skillet and
cook for 2 minutes, or until it flakes easily. Sprinkle with dill, if using.

	CALORIES	PROTEIN	CARBS	FIBER	SUGARS	FAT	SAT FAT	SODIUM
REAL FOOD	174	27 g	1 g	0 g	0 g	7 g	1 g	419 mg
FAKE FOOD	430	20 g	60 g	4 g	6 g	12 g	3.5 g	1,140 mg

COMPARED TO: Marie Callender's® Golden Battered Fish Fillet

INGREDIENTS: Cooked rice (water, white rice), battered fish fillet (pollock, water, enriched bleached flour [wheat, niacin, reduced iron, thiamine mononitrate, riboflavin, folic acid], yellow corn flour, modified food starch, contains 2% or less of: salt, baking powder [sodium acid pyrophosphate, sodium bicarbonate, corn starch, monocalcium phosphate], spice, dextrose, natural flavor, yeast extract, extractives of paprika and turmeric [color], parfried in soybean oil), broccoli, water, contains 2% or less of: cheddar club cheese (pasteurized cultured milk, salt, enzymes, annatto [color]), soybean oil, maltodextrin, butter (cream, salt), cheddar cheese flavor (cheddar and colby cheese [pasteurized milk, cheese cultures, salt, enzymes], water, lactic acid, yeast extract, sodium citrate, sodium phosphate, salt, enzymes), whey, salt, nonfat dry milk, modified corn starch, yeast extract, vegetable powder (vegetable stock [carrot, onion, celery], maltodextrin, flavorings), spices including turmeric, disodium phosphate, dehydrated garlic, dehydrated onion, citric acid, xanthan gum, potassium chloride, guar gum, annatto (color), beta-carotene (color).

ROASTED MACKEREL *and* VEGGIES

SEE PHOTO ON PAGE 224.

PREP TIME: 15 MINUTES ● TOTAL TIME: 1 HOUR 20 MINUTES ● MAKES 4 SERVINGS

2 small orange bell peppers, cut into 1" pieces

1 large onion, cut into 1" pieces

2 small zucchini, quartered and cut into 1" pieces

1½ tablespoons olive oil, divided

1 teaspoon salt, divided

1 pint cherry tomatoes

1¼ pounds mackerel, cod, or flounder fillets

¼ cup fresh basil leaves, thinly sliced (optional)

1. Preheat the oven to 400°F. On a rimmed baking sheet or roasting pan, place the bell peppers, onion, and zucchini and drizzle with 1 tablespoon of the oil. Sprinkle with ½ teaspoon of the salt. Toss to combine.

2. Roast for 15 minutes, or until browned. Stir in the tomatoes and sprinkle with ¼ teaspoon of the salt. Roast, stirring occasionally, for 20 minutes, or until tender. Remove from the oven. Turn on the broiler.

3. Place the fish on the vegetables and drizzle with the remaining ½ tablespoon oil. Sprinkle with the remaining ¼ teaspoon salt. Broil on the top rack for 6 minutes, or until the fish flakes easily. Top with the basil, if using.

	CALORIES	PROTEIN	CARBS	FIBER	SUGARS	FAT	SAT FAT	SODIUM
REAL FOOD	429	31 g	17 g	3 g	9 g	27 g	6 g	633 mg
FAKE FOOD	720	21 g	82 g	6 g	5 g	34 g	6 g	800 mg

COMPARED TO: McDonald's Filet-O-Fish with Medium World Famous Fries

INGREDIENTS: Fish Filet Patty: pollock, water, vegetable oil (canola oil, corn oil, soybean oil, hydrogenated soybean oil), wheat flour, modified food starch, contains 2% or less: yellow corn flour, bleached wheat flour, salt, whey (milk), dextrose, dried yeast, sugar, cellulose gum, paprika and turmeric extract (color), natural flavors. Contains: fish (pollock), wheat, milk. Regular Bun: enriched unbleached flour (wheat flour, malted barley flour, niacin, reduced iron, thiamine mononitrate, riboflavin, folic acid), water, high fructose corn syrup, yeast, soybean oil, Contains 2% or less: salt, wheat gluten, leavening (calcium sulfate, ammonium sulfate), may contain one or more dough conditioners (sodium stearoyl lactylate, datem, ascorbic acid, mono- and diglycerides, monocalcium phosphate, enzymes, calcium peroxide), calcium propionate (preservative). Contains: wheat. Tartar Sauce: soybean oil, pickle relish (diced pickles, vinegar, salt, capers, xanthan gum, potassium sorbate [preservative], calcium chloride, spice extractives, polysorbate 80), egg yolks, water, onions, distilled vinegar, sugar, spice, salt, xanthan gum, potassium sorbate (preservative), parsley. Contains: egg. Pasteurized Process American Cheese Half Slice: milk, cream, water, sodium citrate, cheese cultures, salt, color added, sorbic acid (preservative), citric acid, lactic acid, acetic acid, enzymes, soy lecithin. French Fries: potatoes, vegetable oil (canola oil, corn oil, soybean oil, hydrogenated soybean oil, natural beef flavor [wheat and milk derivatives]*), dextrose, sodium acid pyrophosphate (maintain color), salt. *Natural beef flavor contains hydrolyzed wheat and hydrolyzed milk as starting ingredients.

SCALLOPS *with* SPINACH *and* BACON

SEE PHOTO ON PAGE 230.

PREP TIME: 15 MINUTES • TOTAL TIME: 15 MINUTES • MAKES 4 SERVINGS

2 slices thick-cut uncured bacon, chopped
1 pound large scallops, muscle removed
¼ teaspoon salt
¼ teaspoon ground black pepper
1 large clove garlic, thinly sliced
1 bag (10 ounces) fresh spinach

1. In a large skillet over medium-high heat, cook the bacon for 5 minutes, or until crisp. Transfer to a plate with a slotted spoon and set aside. Season the scallops with the salt and pepper and add to the skillet. Cook, turning once, for 5 minutes, or until opaque. Transfer to the plate with the bacon.
2. Add the garlic to the skillet and cook for 2 minutes, or until translucent. Add the spinach and cook, stirring, for 3 minutes, or until wilted. Stir in the bacon.
3. Divide the spinach mixture among 4 plates and top with the scallops.

	CALORIES	PROTEIN	CARBS	FIBER	SUGARS	FAT	SAT FAT	SODIUM
REAL FOOD	188	19 g	10 g	2 g	1 g	8 g	3 g	685 mg
FAKE FOOD	330	15 g	41 g	0 g	6 g	12 g	2 g	820 mg

COMPARED TO: Gorton's New England Style Haddock

INGREDIENTS: Haddock fillets: Haddock, sodium tripolyphosphate (to retain fish moisture). Breadcrumb coating: Enriched bleached wheat flour (flour, niacin, iron, thiamin mononitrate, riboflavin, folic acid), canola oil, water, wheat flour, maltodextrin, yellow corn flour, vinegar, natural butter flavor, salt, sugar, nonfat milk, whey, cultured buttermilk, brown sugar, butterfat, baking powder (baking soda, sodium aluminum phosphate), dextrose, soybean oil, cheddar cheese (milk, cheese cultures, salt enzymes), colored with paprika, annatto, and turmeric extracts, yeast, caramel color, garlic powder, onion powder, palm oil, citric acid, butter (cream, salt), modified corn starch, sunflower oil. Canola oil

Bonus Benefit

Garlic is good for you! Studies revealed that garlic has a significant lowering effect on both systolic and diastolic blood pressure.[10]

TILAPIA FISH *and* CHIPS *with* MALT VINEGAR DIP

SEE PHOTO ON PAGE 267.

PREP TIME: 5 MINUTES • TOTAL TIME: 40 MINUTES • MAKES 4 SERVINGS

3 large Yukon Gold potatoes, sliced into ½" strips

¾ cup whole grain pastry flour

3 large eggs

1½ cups panko bread crumbs, toasted until golden

3 tablespoons chopped fresh parsley

¾ teaspoon kosher salt

½ teaspoon ground black pepper

3 tilapia fillets, quartered

⅓ cup 0% Greek yogurt

⅓ cup light mayonnaise

3 tablespoons malt or cider vinegar

1. Preheat the oven to 425°F. Coat 2 baking sheets with cooking spray. Arrange the potatoes on 1 sheet and bake for 35 minutes, or until golden and tender.

2. Meanwhile, place the flour in a shallow dish. Whisk the eggs in another shallow dish. In a third shallow dish, combine the bread crumbs, parsley, salt, and pepper.

3. Dust the fish in the flour, dip in the eggs, and roll in the bread crumb mixture. Arrange the fish on the second baking sheet and coat with cooking spray. Bake for 20 minutes, or until it flakes easily.

4. Meanwhile, in a small bowl, combine the yogurt, mayonnaise, and vinegar. Serve the fish and chips with the dip.

⇌ Bonus Benefits ⇌

Parsley does more than add color to dishes or brighten one's breath. A review of the pharmacological benefits of parsley identified antioxidant, liver-protecting, brain-protective, antidiabetic, analgesic, smooth muscle spasm relief, and immuno-suppressant benefits, just to name a few caused by this delicious common herb.[11]

	CALORIES	PROTEIN	CARBS	FIBER	SUGARS	FAT	SAT FAT	SODIUM
REAL FOOD	**450**	**37 g**	**51 g**	**4 g**	**4 g**	**11 g**	**2 g**	**529 mg**
FAKE FOOD	**1,320**	**38 g**	**107 g**	**8 g**	**10 g**	**87 g**	**18 g**	**2,530 mg**

COMPARED TO: Perkins Fish 'n Chips

INGREDIENTS: French Fries: potatoes, vegetable oil (soybean, canola, cottonseed and/or sunflower), modified food starch. Contains 2% or less of dextrose, leavening (sodium acid pyrophosphate, sodium bicarbonate), rice flower, salt, xanthan gum, disodium dihydrogen pyrophosphate (to maintain natural color). Garden Side Salad mix: (iceberg lettuce, romaine lettuce, green leaf hearts, romaine hearts, red cabbage, carrots), diced tomatoes, red onions, asiago cheese croutons (enriched wheat flour [flour, malted barley flour, niacin, reduced iron, thiamine mononitrate, riboflavin, folic acid], canola and extra virgin olive oil, salt. Contains 2% or less of whey, natural flavor, sugar, butter [cream, salt], spice, nonfat milk, asiago cheese powder [asiago cheese flavor {milk, cultures, salt, enzymes}, whey, maltodextrin], dehydrated parsley and garlic, yeast, garlic powder, spice extractive, ascorbic acid), shredded American cheese (pasteurized milk, cheese cultures, salt, enzymes, powdered cellulose to prevent caking). Lemon Wedge Milwaukee Style Breaded Cod Fillets: cod, enriched wheat flour (flour, niacin, reduced iron, thiamine mononitrate, riboflavin, folic acid), vegetable oil (canola, cottonseed and/or soybean), bleached wheat flour, water. Contains 2% or less of modified corn starch, sweet whey powder, salt, sugar, spices, dextrose, whole egg powder, yeast, nonfat milk, disodium inosinate, disodium guanylate, defatted soy flour, iodized salt, enriched yellow corn flour (corn flour, niacin, reduced iron, thiamine mononitrate, riboflavin, folic acid), leavening (sodium acid pyrophosphate, sodium bicarbonate, monocalcium phosphate), sodium tripolyphosphate to retain moisture. Tartar Sauce: soybean oil, pickle relish (cucumbers, vinegar, water, salt, natural flavor, xanthan gum), water, vinegar, corn syrup, egg yolk, modified food starch. Contains 2% or less of salt, spices, xanthan gum, garlic, onion, red bell pepper, sodium benzoate (preservative).

⊰ food imposters ⊱
CRAB THAT'S NOT CRAB

We have to hand it to imitation crab—at least the label actually says it's not the real thing. So what is it really? Most brands are made of ground-up white fish like pollock, plus a laundry list of flavoring and texturizing additives, sugars, and food dye (that pink color has to come from somewhere!). Some brands use wild and sustainably harvested fish—but then, why not just buy the fish whole and skip the "crab" masquerade?

Ingredients: Alaska pollock, water, egg whites, cornstarch, sugar, sorbitol, contains 2 percent or less of king crab meat, natural and artificial flavor (extracts of blue crab, snow crab, lobster, and Alaska pollock), refined fish oil (anchovy, sardine), rice wine (water, rice, koji), modified tapioca starch, sea salt, carrageenan, yam flour, potassium chloride, disodium inosinate, sodium pyrophosphate, soy lecithin, carmine, paprika, color added.

SHRIMP *with* WHITE BEANS *and* TOMATOES

SEE PHOTO ON PAGE 231.

PREP TIME: 10 MINUTES • TOTAL TIME: 25 MINUTES • MAKES 4 SERVINGS

2 tablespoons olive oil

1 pound peeled and deveined medium shrimp

1 can (14.5 ounces) diced tomatoes with basil, garlic, and oregano

1 tablespoon tomato paste

2 cans (15 ounces each) white beans, rinsed and drained

2 tablespoons chopped fresh parsley (optional)

In a large skillet, heat the oil over medium-high heat. Cook the shrimp for 2 minutes, or until pink. Stir in the tomatoes, tomato paste, and beans. Reduce the heat to low, cover, and simmer for 3 minutes, or until the flavors meld. Sprinkle with the parsley, if using.

⇾ Bonus Benefits ⇽

While fresh summer tomatoes are wonderful in salads and sandwiches, heating lycopene-rich tomatoes instigates a chemical change that makes the heart-healthy nutrient much easier for your body to absorb.[12]

	CALORIES	PROTEIN	CARBS	FIBER	SUGARS	FAT	SAT FAT	SODIUM
REAL FOOD	327	27 g	36 g	8 g	1 g	9 g	1 g	652 mg
FAKE FOOD	1,030	38 g	96 g	5 g	8 g	53 g	17 g	1,530 mg

COMPARED TO: Uno Pizzeria & Grill Shrimp Scampi

INGREDIENTS: Shrimp 26/20 tail off shrimp, salt, sodium tripolyphosphate, scampi sauce (water, chablis wine (chablis wine, salt, potassium sorbate, potassium metabisulfite), unsalted butter, contains 2% or less of modified cornstarch, chopped garlic (water, garlic, phosphoric acid, potassium sorbate, xanthan gum, guar gum), garlic puree (garlic, high fructose corn syrup), flavor enhancer (hydrolyzed corn gluten, wheat protein and soy protein, autolyzed yeast extract), roasted garlic puree (roasted garlic, citric acid), salt, enriched flour (wheat flour, niacin, reduced iron, thiamine mononitrate, riboflavin, folic acid) cooked mechanically separated chicken, natural butter flavor (milk), lemon juice concentrate, soybean oil, rendered chicken fat (chicken fat, natural flavoring), potassium chloride, chicken broth, sugar, disodium inosinate and guanylate, hydrolyzed corn protein (contains soybeans), flavor (potassium lactate, autolyzed yeast extract, water, natural flavors), guar and xanthan gum blend (guar gum, xanthan gum), vermicelli (semolina [wheat], niacin, iron [ferrous sulfate], thiamin mononitrate, riboflavin, folic acid), tomatoes, soybean oil, Contains less than 2% of basil, chili pepper, red pepper, diamond crystal kosher salt, garlic, parsley, shredded parmesan.

8 ways with . . .
sheet-pan meals

These super-easy dishes come together directly on your baking sheet pan—no extra bowls or pots to clean! For even easier cleanup, line the baking sheet with parchment paper or foil (if broiling).

1. **Lemon Chicken with Broccoli.** Preheat the oven to 400°F. Toss 1 pound broccoli florets on a baking sheet with 1 tablespoon *each* olive oil and grated lemon peel and spread evenly around the edges. Place four 6-ounce chicken breast cutlets in the center and drizzle with 1 tablespoon olive oil and the juice of half a lemon. Sprinkle 1 teaspoon *each* garlic powder, salt, and black pepper over the chicken and broccoli. Bake for 25 minutes, or until the broccoli is tender and the chicken is no longer pink and the juices run clear. *Makes 4 servings.*

   Nutrition (per serving): 292 calories, 40 g protein, 8 g carbohydrates, 4 g fiber, 0 g sugars, 12 g fat, 2 g saturated fat, 810 mg sodium

2. **Sausage Bake with Onions and Peppers.** Preheat the oven to 400°F. On a baking sheet, combine 2 bell peppers, cut into strips, 1 onion, cut into wedges, 2 coarsely chopped tomatoes, and 1 pound Italian turkey sausages cut into 2" pieces. Drizzle with 2 tablespoons olive oil and sprinkle with 1 teaspoon dried Italian seasoning and ¼ teaspoon salt. Toss to combine. Roast for 20 minutes, or until the sausages are no longer pink and the vegetables are tender. Serve in hero rolls, if desired. *Makes 4 servings.*

   Nutrition (per serving): 240 calories, 15 g protein, 10 g carbohydrates, 2 g fiber, 6 g sugars, 16 g fat, 1 g saturated fat, 692 mg sodium

3. **Pork Chops with Potatoes, Apples, and Thyme.** Preheat the oven to 400°F. On a baking sheet, combine 8 quartered small red potatoes with 1 teaspoon olive oil and bake for 10 minutes. Add 2 cored apples cut into 8 wedges each. Sprinkle with ½ teaspoon dried thyme and drizzle with 1 teaspoon olive oil. Toss to combine and spread evenly to the edges. Rub 1 teaspoon olive oil over four 1"-thick boneless pork chops (1¼ pounds) and sprinkle with ½ teaspoon *each* salt and black pepper. Place the chops in the center. Bake for

10 minutes, or until the potatoes and apples are tender and a thermometer inserted in the center of a chop registers 160°F and the juices run clear. Drizzle with 1 tablespoon balsamic vinegar before serving. *Makes 4 servings.*

Nutrition (per serving): 435 calories, 25 g protein, 68 g carbohydrates, 8 g fiber, 14 g sugars, 8 g fat, 2 g saturated fat, 405 mg sodium

4. Pork Fajitas. Preheat the oven to 400°F. Rub a 1-pound pork tenderloin with 1 teaspoon olive oil and sprinkle with ½ teaspoon *each* ground cumin, salt, and chili powder. Place in the middle of a baking sheet and scatter 1 pint cherry tomatoes; 1 onion, cut into wedges; and 1 green bell pepper, cut into strips, around the pork. Roast for 15 minutes, or until a thermometer inserted in the center of the tenderloin reaches 160°F, the juices run clear, and the vegetables are soft. Let the pork rest for 5 minutes before slicing. Serve with 8 whole wheat flour tortillas and ¼ cup shredded Cheddar cheese. *Makes 4 servings.*

Nutrition (per serving): 342 calories, 33 g protein, 47 g carbohydrates, 6 g fiber, 4 g sugars, 7 g fat, 3 g saturated fat, 743 mg sodium

5. Broiled Steak and Roasted Potatoes with Green Beans. Preheat the oven to 400°F and position a rack in the upper third of the oven. On a baking sheet, combine 1 pound quartered baby potatoes and 1 tablespoon olive oil. Roast for 10 minutes, or until almost tender. Remove the baking sheet from the oven and turn on the broiler. Push the potatoes to one side and add 1 pound trimmed green beans and 1 pound flank steak, cut into 4 equal pieces. Drizzle the beans and steak with 1 tablespoon olive oil. Sprinkle the potatoes, beans, and steak with 1 teaspoon *each* salt and black pepper. Broil, turning once, for 6 minutes for medium-rare, or until a thermometer inserted in the center of a steak registers 145°F. *Makes 4 servings.*

Nutrition (per serving): 333 calories, 27 g protein, 26 g carbohydrates, 5 g fiber, 5 g sugars, 14 g fat, 4 g saturated fat, 654 mg sodium

6. Baked Salmon with Spring Vegetables. Preheat the oven to 400°F. On a baking sheet, combine 1 trimmed bunch asparagus, 1 pound halved baby gold potatoes, and 1 small red onion cut into wedges. In a small bowl, whisk together 3 tablespoons olive oil, 1½ teaspoons herbes de Provence, ¾ teaspoon salt, and ½ teaspoon black pepper. Drizzle half the oil mixture over the vegetables, toss, and bake for 15 minutes. Remove from the oven and place four 5-ounce salmon fillets on top of the vegetables. Brush with the remaining herb mixture. Roast for 10 minutes, or until the potatoes are tender and the fish is opaque. *Makes 4 servings.*

Nutrition (per serving): 501 calories, 34 g protein, 28 g carbohydrates, 5 g fiber, 4 g sugars, 29 g fat, 6 g saturated fat, 559 mg sodium

(continued)

8 ways with...sheet-pan meals (cont.)

7. Roasted Shrimp with Tomatoes and Zucchini. Preheat the oven to 425°F. On a baking sheet, combine 1 medium zucchini, halved lengthwise and sliced, and 1 teaspoon olive oil. Roast for 10 minutes, or until tender-crisp. Meanwhile, in a large bowl, whisk together 2 teaspoons olive oil, juice of half a lemon, 1 minced clove garlic, and 2 teaspoons chopped fresh dill. Add 1 pound peeled and deveined shrimp, 1 can (15 ounces) rinsed and drained cannellini beans, and 1 pint halved grape tomatoes. Toss the shrimp mixture with the zucchini and roast for 10 minutes, or until the shrimp are opaque. Sprinkle with 2 tablespoons crumbled feta cheese. *Makes 4 servings.*

Nutrition (per serving): 196 calories, 20 g protein, 17 g carbohydrates, 5 g fiber, 4 g sugars, 6 g fat, 1g saturated fat, 803 mg sodium

8. Roasted Sweet Potatoes with Green Olives. Preheat the oven to 425°F. On a baking sheet, combine 2 pounds scrubbed sweet potatoes, chopped into 1" pieces, 1 can (15 ounces) rinsed and drained chickpeas, and 1 red onion, cut into wedges, with 3 tablespoons olive oil. Sprinkle with 1 teaspoon smoked paprika and ¼ teaspoon salt. Roast, tossing occasionally, for 25 minutes, or until the sweet potatoes are tender. Top with ¼ cup green olives, chopped, and 1 tablespoon sherry vinegar (optional). *Makes 4 servings.*

Nutrition (per serving): 357 calories, 7 g protein, 53 g carbohydrates, 10 g fiber, 15 g sugars, 13 g fat, 1g saturated fat, 528 mg sodium

Cod in Turmeric Broth ⚓ Page 207

217

Beef Tenderloin with Spinach and Sweet Potatoes
✍ Page 176

Chicken Enchiladas ✍ Page 198

Chicken and Veggie Stir-Fry ✄ Page 200

Fire-Roasted Pork and Brown Rice ↗ Page 187

Green Bean, Tomato, and Olive Salad ∽ Page 244

Mac & Cheese Page 234

Italian-Style Chicken and Mushrooms
Page 196

Open-Faced Steak Sandwiches and Salad ✍ Page 182

Roasted Mackerel and Veggies
⤴ Page 208

Pan-Seared Pork Chops and Apples
⤴ Page 186

Peach-Glazed Chicken Breasts
⤴ Page 195

Roasted Chicken Thighs with Lemon and Olives ⟋ Page 190

Roasted Vegetables ✄ Page 239

Roasted Curry
Cauliflower 🍃 Page 238

Sautéed Baby Kale and Pine Nuts ⌇ Page 242

Hearty Red Scalloped Potatoes ⌇ Page 236

Scallops with Spinach and Bacon ꝊꝊ Page 209

Shrimp with White Beans and Tomatoes ⁓ Page 212

Sirloin and Snow Pea Stir-Fry ✗ Page 181

PARMESAN FETTUCCINE ALFREDO

SEE PHOTO ON PAGE 266.

PREP TIME: 10 MINUTES • TOTAL TIME: 30 MINUTES • MAKES 6 SERVINGS

1 pound fettuccine

1 tablespoon butter

1 clove garlic, minced

1 cup Greek yogurt

½ cup grated Parmesan cheese

2 tablespoons chopped basil

Basil leaves for garnish (optional)

1. Prepare the pasta according to package directions. Drain, reserving 1 cup cooking water.

2. Meanwhile, in a large skillet, melt the butter over medium heat. Cook the garlic for 1 minute, or until fragrant. Whisk in the yogurt, cheese, and chopped basil. Add the pasta and toss to coat, adding reserved water as needed to thin. Garnish with basil leaves, if desired.

Fast Fix: *To save boiling time, add salt to the pasta water after it comes to a boil. Salted water takes longer to come to a boil than unsalted water.*

	CALORIES	PROTEIN	CARBS	FIBER	SUGARS	FAT	SAT FAT	SODIUM
REAL FOOD	370	18 g	58 g	3 g	5 g	8 g	4 g	182 mg
FAKE FOOD	560	16 g	53 g	3 g	6 g	31 g	12 g	900 mg

COMPARED TO: Stouffer's Classics Fettuccini Alfredo

INGREDIENTS: Blanched fettuccini (water, semolina, wheat gluten), cream, skim milk, soybean oil, parmesan cheese (cultured milk, salt, enzymes), 2% or less of water, asiago cheese (cultured milk, salt, enzymes), modified cornstarch, romano cheese ([made from cow's milk], pasteurized milk, cheese culture, salt, enzymes), salt, enzyme modified parmesan cheese (cultured milk, water, salt, enzymes), whey protein concentrate, lactose (contains milk), DATEM, black pepper, xanthan gum, lactic acid, calcium lactate, seasoning (maltodextrin, flavor, enzyme modified butterfat), seasoning (wheat starch, extracts of annatto and turmeric color, natural flavor).

⇾ Bonus Benefit ⇽

Be sure to include creamy yogurt during winter months. It contains zinc, vitamin B_6, protein, and healthy probiotics, which help to enhance your immune system. Studies have shown that probiotics alone enhance innate immunity, reduce the severity and duration of respiratory infections, and improve gut-associated immunity.[13]

MAC & CHEESE

SEE PHOTO ON PAGE 222.

PREP TIME: 10 MINUTES • TOTAL TIME: 40 MINUTES • MAKES 8 SERVINGS

1 package (16 ounces) whole grain pasta shells

2 tablespoons butter

1 small onion, finely chopped

3 tablespoons whole grain pastry flour

2 cups milk

8 ounces shredded Cheddar cheese

1 package (10 ounces) frozen pureed squash, thawed

½ teaspoon salt

½ cup whole wheat bread crumbs (optional)

1. Preheat the oven to 350°F. Prepare the pasta according to package directions. Coat 1 large cast-iron skillet or 4 small cast-iron skillets (or a 3-quart baking dish) with cooking spray.

2. Meanwhile, in a medium saucepan, melt the butter over medium-high heat. Cook the onion for 5 minutes, or until tender. Add the flour and cook for 1 minute, or until bubbling.

3. Whisk in the milk and cook for 4 minutes, or until thick. Stir in the cheese, squash, and salt, and cook for 3 minutes, or until the cheese melts. Stir in the pasta.

4. Place the mixture in the skillet and top with the bread crumbs, if using. Bake for 20 minutes, or until heated through.

Fast Fix: *Here's a great way to sneak nutritious butternut squash into a comfort food favorite. Use orange cheese, and no one will notice the difference.*

	CALORIES	PROTEIN	CARBS	FIBER	SUGARS	FAT	SAT FAT	SODIUM
REAL FOOD	**419**	**17 g**	**54 g**	**8 g**	**4 g**	**16 g**	**9 g**	**332 mg**
FAKE FOOD	**710**	**32 g**	**54 g**	**2 g**	**7 g**	**41 g**	**17 g**	**1,200 mg**

COMPARED TO: Devour White Cheddar Mac & Cheese with Bacon

INGREDIENTS: Cooked enriched macaroni product (water, enriched macaroni product [semolina wheat flour, niacin, ferrous sulfate, thiamin mononitrate, riboflavin, folic acid], carrageenan), sauce (water, pasteurized process white cheddar cheese [cheddar cheese (cultured milk, salt, enzymes), water, sodium phosphate, milk fat, salt], fully cooked applewood smoked bacon pieces [bacon cured with water, salt, sugar, sodium nitrite, applewood smoke flavor. may contain sodium phosphate, smoke flavor, sodium erythorbate, sodium ascorbate, dextrose], soybean oil, whey protein concentrate, nonfat milk, parmesan cheese [cultured part-skim milk, salt, enzymes], cheddar cheese [cultured milk, salt, enzymes], modified cornstarch, modified cellulose, spices, potassium chloride, salt, sodium phosphate, enzymes), white cheddar cheese (cultured milk, salt, enzymes).

Bonus Benefits

A 1-cup serving of butternut squash contains nearly half of your daily dose of vitamin C, which has been linked to healthier skin: A study published in the *American Journal of Clinical Nutrition* observed links between vitamin C and skin aging in 4,025 women ages 40 to 74, and found that higher intakes of the vitamin were linked to a lower likelihood of wrinkles and dryness.[14]

HEARTY RED SCALLOPED POTATOES

SEE PHOTO ON PAGE 229.

PREP TIME: 5 MINUTES ● TOTAL TIME: 50 MINUTES + STANDING TIME ● MAKES 6 SERVINGS

6 red potatoes, cut into ½" slices

3 tablespoons whole grain pastry flour

1½ ounces Parmesan cheese, grated

1½ ounces Gruyère cheese, shredded

½ teaspoon garlic salt

Pinch of ground black pepper

1 cup milk, warmed

1. Preheat the oven to 400°F. Coat the bottom of a 2-quart baking dish with cooking spray.

2. Line the baking dish with one-third of the potatoes. Sprinkle with 1 tablespoon of the flour, onc-third of the Parmesan, one-third of the Gruyère, one-third of the garlic salt, and a sprinkle of pepper. Repeat the layers 2 more times.

3. Pour the milk over the top. Cover with foil and bake for 25 minutes. Uncover and bake for 20 minutes, or until the potatoes are tender and the cheese is browned. Let stand for 10 minutes before serving.

Bonus Benefit

Potatoes are high in potassium, which may help lower blood pressure. Studies have linked high potassium intake with reduced risk of hypertension and heart disease.[15, 16, 17]

	CALORIES	PROTEIN	CARBS	FIBER	SUGARS	FAT	SAT FAT	SODIUM
REAL FOOD	169	10 g	21 g	2 g	4 g	5 g	3 g	281 mg
FAKE FOOD	230	7 g	19 g	2 g	3 g	14 g	8 g	520 mg

COMPARED TO: Bob Evans Oven Bake Scalloped Potatoes

INGREDIENTS: Potatoes, milk, cheddar cheese (pasteurized milk, cheese culture, salt, enzymes and annatto [vegetable color], potato starch and powdered cellulose [to prevent caking]), butter (cream, salt), sour cream (cultured cream, skim milk, modified food starch [corn], lactic and citric acid gelatin, mono- and diglycerides, guar gum, potassium sorbate [preservative], carrageenan, sodium phosphate, natural and artificial flavor), onion, water, cheese (cheddar cheese [pasteurized milk, cheese culture, salt, enzymes], water, salt), parmesan and romano cheese (pasteurized milk, cheese culture, salt, enzymes, powdered cellulose [to prevent caking]), Contains less than 2% of the following: modified food starch, dextrose, salt, gelatin, onion powder, potassium sorbate (preservative), sodium acid pyrophosphate, black pepper.

⇒ food imposters ⇐
POTATOES THAT AREN'T POTATOES

Meet the mashed-potato-in-a-box, whose first ingredient is, thankfully, potatoes. (Dehydrated potato flakes, to be exact.) But they also come with preservatives, emulsifiers, flavorings, and even trans fat. At that point, good luck trying to convince anyone of potato realness.

Ingredients: Potato flakes (sodium bisulfite, BHA, and citric acid added to protect color and flavor), contains 2 percent or less of: monoglycerides, partially hydrogenated cottonseed oil, natural flavor, sodium acid pyrophosphate, butteroil.

ROASTED CURRY CAULIFLOWER

SEE PHOTO ON PAGE 228.

PREP TIME: 5 MINUTES • TOTAL TIME: 25 MINUTES • MAKES 4 SERVINGS

1 head cauliflower (2½–3 pounds), cored
and cut into bite-size pieces

1 tablespoon olive oil

1 teaspoon curry powder

½ teaspoon salt

¼ teaspoon ground black pepper

1. Preheat the oven to 450°F.

2. Spread the cauliflower on a rimmed baking sheet. Drizzle with the oil. Sprinkle with the curry powder, salt, and pepper. Toss well to coat. Roast for 20 minutes, or until the cauliflower is tender and browned.

	CALORIES	PROTEIN	CARBS	FIBER	SUGARS	FAT	SAT FAT	SODIUM
REAL FOOD	76	3 g	9 g	4 g	3 g	4 g	1 g	342 mg
FAKE FOOD	330	6 g	36 g	2 g	7 g	18 g	3 g	610 mg

COMPARED TO: Carl's Jr. Fried Zucchini

INGREDIENTS: Zucchini, bleached wheat flour, water, modified corn starch, salt, whey, sugar, spices, garlic powder, onion powder, yeast, leavening (sodium acid pyrophosphate, sodium bicarbonate), partially hydrogenated soybean oil (a processing aid), dried parsley, citric acid, maltodextrin, gum arabic, natural flavor. Fried in: vegetable oil (soybean oil, hydrogenated soybean oil with TBHQ and citric acid to protect flavor, dimethylpolysiloxane (as an antifoaming agent)).

Bonus Benefit

Consuming cruciferous vegetables, such as cauliflower, at least once per week has been shown to significantly decrease the risk of cancers of the oral cavity and pharynx, esophagus, colon and rectum, breast, and kidney.[18]

ROASTED VEGETABLES

SEE PHOTO ON PAGE 227.

PREP TIME: 15 MINUTES • TOTAL TIME: 50 MINUTES • MAKES 6 SERVINGS

1½ pounds butternut squash, peeled, halved, seeded, and cut into 1½" pieces

4 bell peppers, such as red and yellow, cut into chunks

4 small red onions, cut into wedges

4 medium parsnips, cut into 2" sticks

4 medium carrots, cut into 2" sticks

2 tablespoons olive oil

½ teaspoon salt

½ teaspoon ground black pepper

1. Heat the oven to 450°F with racks in the upper and lower thirds of the oven.

2. In a large bowl, stir together the squash, bell peppers, onions, parsnips, carrots, oil, salt, and black pepper.

3. Divide between 2 large rimmed baking sheets. Roast, stirring occasionally, for 35 minutes, or until golden brown and tender.

	CALORIES	PROTEIN	CARBS	FIBER	SUGARS	FAT	SAT FAT	SODIUM
REAL FOOD	153	3 g	29 g	7 g	10 g	4 g	1 g	180 mg
FAKE FOOD	260	7 g	33 g	1 g	3 g	11 g	5 g	990 mg

COMPARED TO: HORMEL® Cheddar Broccoli Rice

INGREDIENTS: Cooked rice (water, parboiled long-grain rice), milk with vitamin D3, broccoli, cheddar cheese blend (cheddar cheese [pasteurized milk, cheese cultures, salt, enzymes], butter [cream, salt], water, whey, natural flavors, nonfat milk, salt, annatto extract [color], and disodium phosphate), pasteurized process cheese spread (american cheese [pasteurized milk, cheese culture, salt, enzymes], water, whey, sodium phosphate, whey protein concentrate, skim milk, salt, milk fat, artificial color), liquid margarine (liquid and hydrogenated soybean oil, water, salt, vegetable mono- and diglycerides, soy lecithin, citric acid, natural and artificial flavor, vitamin a palmitate added), contains 2% or less of antimicrobial blend (maltodextrin, cultured dextrose, sodium diacetate, salt, nisin preparation [salt, nisin], egg white lysozyme), hydrolyzed corn protein, monosodium glutamate, modified cornstarch, salt, disodium phosphate, annatto color, onion powder, potassium sorbate (preservative). Milk ingredients present, egg ingredients present, soy ingredients present

Bonus Benefit

Carrots can play a role in reducing your risk of age-related macular degeneration and its associated vision loss.[19]

8 ways with . . . grain bowls

Take a stroll along the grain section of your grocery, and you'll likely find an abundant selection of precooked grains to make these bowl-inspired dishes a snap to put together. Alternately, save a little money by cooking your grains on the weekend for these quick weeknight meals.

1. **Asian Salmon Bowl.** In a medium bowl, whisk together 2 tablespoons olive oil, 1 tablespoon *each* warm water, white or yellow miso paste, rice vinegar, 2 teaspoons *each* toasted sesame oil and soy sauce, and ½ teaspoon grated fresh ginger. Divide 1 cup precooked wild rice between 2 bowls and top each with half of the following: 1 can (6 ounces) drained Alaskan pink salmon, 2 shredded carrots, and ½ cup snow peas. Drizzle with the dressing. *Makes 2 servings.*

   Nutrition (per serving): 394 calories, 20 g protein, 33 g carbohydrates, 4 g fiber, 6 g sugars, 21 g fat, 3 g saturated fat, 723 mg sodium

2. **Bacon, Egg, and Kale Bowl.** In a large skillet over medium heat, cook 4 chopped slices uncured bacon for 8 minutes, or until crisp. Add 4 cups packed torn kale leaves and ½ teaspoon *each* salt and black pepper. Cook, stirring, for 2 minutes, or until the kale wilts. Stir in 2 cups cooked brown rice and cook for 1 minute, or until the rice is heated through. Divide the mixture among 4 bowls. Wipe the skillet and heat 2 teaspoons olive oil over medium heat. Cook 4 eggs sunny-side up until desired doneness. Top each bowl with an egg and one-quarter of a chopped avocado. Serve with hot sauce, if desired. *Makes 4 servings.*

   Nutrition (per serving): 339 calories, 16 g protein, 38 g carbohydrates, 6 g fiber, 0 g sugars, 15 g fat, 4 g saturated fat, 529 mg sodium

3. **Chicken and Apple Bowl.** In a large bowl, whisk together ⅓ cup Greek yogurt, 3 tablespoons fresh lemon juice, 1 tablespoon *each* extra-virgin olive oil and Dijon mustard, and ¼ teaspoon *each* salt and black pepper. Add 2 cups cooked wheat berries, 2 cups chopped cooked skinless chicken breast, 2 chopped apples, and 1 chopped rib celery. Toss to coat well. Divide among 4 bowls and top each with 1 tablespoon chopped pecans. *Makes 4 servings.*

   Nutrition (per serving): 393 calories, 29 g protein, 43 g carbohydrates, 8 g fiber, 11 g sugars, 12 g fat, 2 g saturated fat, 442 mg sodium

4. **Morning Millet Bowl.** In a medium dry saucepan over medium heat, toast ½ cup millet for 4 minutes, or until fragrant. Add 1½ cups unsweetened coconut milk and a pinch *each* of salt and ground ginger or cardamom. Bring to a boil, reduce the heat to low, cover, and simmer for 15 minutes, or until the millet is tender (will be creamy). Divide the millet between 2 bowls and top

each with 2 sliced prunes and 2 table-spoons chopped almonds. *Makes 2 servings.*

Nutrition (per serving): 375 calories, 10 g protein, 53 g carbohydrates, 8 g fiber, 8 g sugars, 15 g fat, 5 g saturated fat, 51 mg sodium

5. **Pesto Grain Bowl.** Place a steamer basket in a large skillet with 1" of water over medium-high heat. Place 1 pound asparagus cut into 2" pieces in the basket and bring to a boil. Reduce the heat to low, cover, and simmer for 5 minutes, or until tender. Remove from the heat and let cool. Meanwhile, in a large bowl, whisk together 3 tablespoons Greek yogurt, 2 tablespoons prepared pesto, and 1 tablespoon balsamic vinegar. Add 1 cup cooked brown rice, 1 cup shred-ded cooked chicken breast, $\frac{1}{2}$ cup thawed frozen peas, 2 cups baby aru-gula or spinach, and the asparagus. *Makes 2 servings.*

Nutrition (per serving): 338 calories, 10 g protein, 39 g carbohydrates, 9 g fiber, 4 g sugars, 16 g fat, 4 g saturated fat, 503 mg sodium

6. **Quick Turkey Taco Bowl.** Cook $\frac{1}{3}$ cup quinoa according to package directions. Meanwhile, in a large skil-let, heat 1 tablespoon olive oil over medium-high heat. Cook $\frac{1}{2}$ pound ground turkey, stirring, for 5 minutes, or until no longer pink. Stir in 1 cup prepared salsa and $\frac{1}{2}$ teaspoon ground cumin and cook for 5 minutes, or until the flavors meld. Divide the quinoa and turkey mixture between 2 bowls. Top each bowl with half of *each* of the following: $\frac{1}{4}$ cup shredded Cheddar cheese, $\frac{1}{2}$ cup shredded

romaine lettuce, and half a chopped tomato. *Makes 2 servings.*

Nutrition (per serving): 398 calories, 37 g protein, 29 g carbohydrates, 7 g fiber, 7 g sugars, 15 g fat, 4 g saturated fat, 539 mg sodium

7. **Roasted Veggie Bowl.** Preheat the oven to 425°F. Place 1 sweet potato, cut into $\frac{3}{4}$" pieces, and 1 cup *each* halved Brussels sprouts and small cauliflower florets on a large rimmed baking sheet lined with parchment paper. Toss with 1 tablespoon olive oil and $\frac{1}{2}$ teaspoon *each* salt and dried thyme. Roast, turn-ing occasionally, for 20 minutes, or until browned and tender. Meanwhile, in a small saucepan, prepare $\frac{1}{2}$ cup quick-cooking barley according to pack-age directions. Stir in 1 tablespoon *each* olive oil and balsamic vinegar. Divide the barley and vegetables between 2 bowls and top each with 2 ounces chopped smoked baked tofu. *Makes 2 servings.*

Nutrition (per serving): 380 calories, 17 g protein, 52 g carbohydrates, 9 g fiber, 9 g sugars, 8 g fat, 2 g saturated fat, 595 mg sodium

8. **Mediterranean Bulgur Bowl.** Cook $\frac{1}{3}$ cup bulgur according to package directions. Meanwhile, in a large bowl, whisk together 1 minced small shallot, 2 tablespoons olive oil, 2 teaspoons red wine vinegar, and $\frac{1}{4}$ teaspoon *each* salt and black pepper. Add the bulgur, 1 small chopped cucumber, 1 cup halved cherry tomatoes, and $\frac{1}{4}$ small chopped onion. Evenly divide between 2 bowls and top with 2 tablespoons *each* pistachios and crumbled feta. *Makes 2 servings.*

Nutrition (per serving): 325 calories, 11 g protein, 32 g carbohydrates, 8 g fiber, 7 g sugars, 19 g fat, 5 g saturated fat, 518 mg sodium

SAUTÉED BABY KALE *and* PINE NUTS

SEE PHOTO ON PAGE 229.

PREP TIME: 5 MINUTES • TOTAL TIME: 15 MINUTES • MAKES 4 SERVINGS

2 tablespoons olive oil

2 large cloves garlic, smashed and peeled

½ teaspoon red-pepper flakes

¼ cup pine nuts

16 ounces baby kale leaves

2 tablespoons water

¼ teaspoon salt

1. In a large, deep skillet, heat the oil over medium heat. Cook the garlic and red-pepper flakes for 1 minute, or until the garlic is golden.

2. Discard the garlic. Add the pine nuts and cook, stirring constantly, for 1 minute, or until lightly toasted.

3. Add the kale, water, and salt. Cover and cook over high heat, tossing with a fork occasionally, for 10 minutes, or just until wilted and tender.

	CALORIES	PROTEIN	CARBS	FIBER	SUGARS	FAT	SAT FAT	SODIUM
REAL FOOD	178	6 g	12 g	3 g	0 g	14 g	2 g	189 mg
FAKE FOOD	270	7 g	51 g	2 g	4 g	5 g	2 g	960 mg

COMPARED TO: Green Giant Steamers Cheesy Rice & Broccoli

INGREDIENTS: Cooked long grain white rice and broccoli in a sauce containing water, whey, soybean oil, wheat flour, modified corn starch, buttermilk, salt, dried cheddar cheese (milk, cheese cultures, salt, enzymes), partially hydrogenated soybean oil, nonfat milk, sodium phosphate, natural flavor, sodium hexametaphosphate, sodium alginate, dried parmesan cheese (milk, cheese cultures, salt, enzymes), hydrolyzed corn gluten, dried blue cheese (milk, cheese cultures, salt, enzymes), maltodextrin, onion powder, cream, monoglycerides, torula yeast, garlic powder, yeast, lactic acid, autolyzed yeast extract, colored with beta-carotene, turmeric and annatto extract, ascorbyl palmitate (preservative), disodium inosinate, disodium guanylate.

SLAW *with* BUTTERMILK DRESSING

PREP TIME: 10 MINUTES • TOTAL TIME: 10 MINUTES • MAKES 4 SERVINGS

⅓ cup Greek yogurt

¼ cup buttermilk

1 tablespoon apple cider vinegar

2 teaspoons sugar

¼ teaspoon salt

1 package (14 ounces) coleslaw mix (about 6 cups)

1 Granny Smith apple, cut into matchsticks

In a large bowl, whisk together the yogurt, buttermilk, vinegar, sugar, and salt until blended. Add the coleslaw mix and apple. Toss to coat well.

Fast Fix: *This slaw is great with barbecue, or as a crunchy topping for sandwiches or burgers. Refrigerate for at least 30 minutes for the best flavor. Refrigerate any unused slaw in an airtight container for up to 5 days.*

	CALORIES	PROTEIN	CARBS	FIBER	SUGARS	FAT	SAT FAT	SODIUM
REAL FOOD	70	3 g	15 g	3 g	11 g	1 g	0 g	186 mg
FAKE FOOD	200	1 g	18 g	0 g	15 g	14 g	12 g	180 mg

COMPARED TO: Grandma's Original Recipes Cole Slaw

INGREDIENTS: Cabbage, slaw base (mayonnaise [soybean oil, egg yolks [egg yolks, salt], high fructose corn syrup, distilled vinegar, mustard [distilled vinegar, mustard seed, salt, spices], water, salt, color [water, yellow 5 and 6, blue 1, citric acid]), fructose, sugar, carrots, water, pea vegetable extract, erythorbic acid (to retain color), potassium sorbate (to retard spoilage), natural flavor, salt, citric acid, xanthan gum. Contains: egg.

⇒ *food imposters* ⇐
CREAM THAT ISN'T CREAM

"Cream" that doesn't have to be refrigerated? Yeah, right. The only thing even partially resembling dairy in most shelf-stable coffee creamers is something called sodium caseinate, a "milk derivative." The rest of the ingredient list is usually composed of a nutritionally empty blend of sugar, oil, and natural and artificial flavors—definitely not the best way to start your day.

Ingredients: Water, sugar, hydrogenated coconut oil, less than 2 percent of: sodium caseinate, dipotassium phosphate, mono- and diglycerides, salt, natural and artificial flavor.

GREEN BEAN, TOMATO, *and* OLIVE SALAD

SEE PHOTO ON PAGE 221.

PREP TIME: 15 MINUTES • TOTAL TIME: 15 MINUTES • MAKES 4 SERVINGS

1 tablespoon extra-virgin olive oil

½ pound green beans

1 red onion, sliced

6 plum tomatoes, cut into quarters

¼ cup pitted kalamata olives, halved

¼ teaspoon salt

¼ teaspoon ground black pepper

1 tablespoon balsamic vinegar

1. In a large skillet, heat the oil over medium-high heat. Cook the green beans and onion, stirring, for 10 minutes, or until browned and the green beans are crisp-tender.

2. Add the tomatoes, olives, salt, and pepper. Cook, stirring, for 2 minutes, or just until the tomatoes are hot. Add the vinegar and cook for 1 minute, or until blended.

⇒ *Bonus Benefit* ⇐

Olives contain lots of heart-healthy fats. Oleic acid, the main fatty acid in olives, may regulate cholesterol levels and protect the LDL cholesterol from oxidation.[20, 21]

	CALORIES	PROTEIN	CARBS	FIBER	SUGARS	FAT	SAT FAT	SODIUM
REAL FOOD	133	2 g	12 g	4 g	6 g	9 g	1 g	478 mg
FAKE FOOD	270	3 g	22 g	2 g	1 g	19 g	5 g	390 mg

COMPARED TO: Wal-Mart Deli Red Skin Potato Salad

INGREDIENTS: Red potatoes, sour cream (milk, cream and nonfat milk, whey, modified food starch, guar gum, sodium phosphate, locust bean gum, sodium citrate, carrageenan, culture, coagulant, natamycin [natural preservative], potassium sorbate [to preserve freshness], and enzyme), mayonnaise (soybean oil, water, egg yolks, vinegar, corn syrup, salt, spice, calcium disodium edta to protect flavor), dillweed, vinegar, seasoning (salt, monosodium glutamate, onion powder, garlic powder, spices, hydrolyzed soy protein), water, potassium sorbate and sodium benzoate to protect flavor, modified corn starch.

Should You Seed Your Tomatoes?

Skip seeding your tomatoes. It may reduce a small amount of bitterness but wastes much of the bulk of the tomatoes. It also drains away the flavorful tomato gel along with the seeds.

8 ways with . . . rice

1. Cool Rice Salad. In a large bowl, whisk together ⅓ cup *each* smooth natural peanut butter and warm water, 2 teaspoons *each* soy sauce, honey, toasted sesame oil, and rice vinegar. Stir in 2 cups cooked brown rice and 2 cups shredded cooked chicken. Top with 2 tablespoons *each* chopped fresh mint and cilantro, if desired. *Makes 4 servings.*

Nutrition (per serving): 381 calories, 28 g protein, 31 g carbohydrates, 3 g fiber, 4 g sugars, 16 g fat, 2 g saturated fat, 471 mg sodium

2. Unstuffed Cabbage "Rolls." Preheat the oven to 350°F. Steam 1 head sliced cabbage (about 12 cups) in a steamer basket set inside a large saucepan with 2" of water for 10 minutes, or until tender. Meanwhile, in a large skillet, heat 1 tablespoon olive oil over medium heat. Cook 1 pound grass-fed ground beef and 1 chopped onion for 8 minutes, or until no longer pink. Drain excess liquid. In a 13" x 9" baking dish, combine 1 can (28 ounces) tomato puree, 2 cups cooked brown rice, ½ cup water, and 1 teaspoon *each* garlic powder and dried thyme. Add the cabbage and the meat mixture, mixing until well combined. Cover with foil and bake for 20 minutes, or until hot. *Makes 6 servings.*

Nutrition (per serving): 314 calories, 21 g protein, 38 g carbohydrates, 8 g fiber, 12 g sugars, 11 g fat, 4 g saturated fat, 607 mg sodium

3. Quick Coconut Rice Pudding. In a medium saucepan over medium-low heat, combine 2 cups cooked brown rice, 1 can (13.5 ounces) coconut milk, ¼ cup sugar, ¼ teaspoon ground cinnamon, and a pinch of salt. Bring to a simmer and cook, stirring occasionally, for 10 minutes, or until thick and creamy. *Makes 4 servings.*

Nutrition (per serving): 347 calories, 5 g protein, 38 g carbohydrates, 3 g fiber, 13 g sugars, 21 g fat, 18 g saturated fat, 54 mg sodium

4. Brown Rice Pilaf. In a large skillet, heat 1 tablespoon olive oil over medium heat. Cook 1 chopped small onion for 5 minutes, or until softened. Add 1 cup uncooked brown rice, 1 minced clove garlic, and ¼ teaspoon *each* ground cinnamon, ginger, and turmeric. Cook for 1 minute, or until fragrant. Add 3 cups low-sodium chicken broth and bring to a boil. Reduce the heat to medium-low, cover, and simmer for 40 minutes, or until the rice is tender. Mix in ¼ cup raisins and 3 tablespoons sliced almonds. *Makes 4 servings.*

Nutrition (per serving): 278 calories, 6 g protein, 49 g carbohydrates, 4 g fiber, 6 g sugars, 7 g fat, 1 g saturated fat, 649 mg sodium

5. Emerald Rice with Shrimp. In a large skillet, heat 1 tablespoon olive oil over medium-high heat. Cook 1 cup brown basmati rice, stirring, for 2 minutes. Stir in 2½ cups chicken broth or water. Bring to a boil, reduce the heat to medium-low, cover, and simmer for 35 minutes, or until the broth is absorbed and the rice is tender. Stir in 2½ cups finely chopped baby spinach, 2 finely chopped scallions, 2 tablespoons chopped fresh parsley, and 1 cup thawed frozen shelled edamame (or peas). Top each portion with 4 large cooked shrimp. *Makes 4 servings.*

Nutrition (per serving): 264 calories, 14 g protein, 39 g carbohydrates, 5 g fiber, 2 g sugars, 7 g fat, 1 g saturated fat, 292 mg sodium

6. **Quick Paella.** Preheat the oven to 325°F. In a large ovenproof skillet, heat 1 tablespoon olive oil over medium heat. Cook half a chopped onion and 2 ounces chopped chorizo for 5 minutes, or until the onion softens and the chorizo browns. Add 1 cup Arborio rice and 1 teaspoon paprika and cook, stirring, for 1 minute. Add 3 cups low-sodium chicken broth and bring to a boil. Reduce the heat to medium-low and simmer for 10 minutes. Stir in ½ cup frozen peas. Place 1½ pounds mixed seafood (such as peeled and deveined shrimp, cleaned mussels, and calamari) in the mixture. Bake for 20 minutes, or until the mussels open and the shrimp and calamari are opaque. *Makes 4 servings.*

Nutrition (per serving): 440 calories, 34 g protein, 48 g carbohydrates, 3 g fiber, 2 g sugars, 12 g fat, 3 g saturated fat, 607 mg sodium

7. **Easy Chicken and Rice Soup.** In a large saucepot, heat 1 tablespoon olive oil over medium heat. Cook 1 large thinly sliced carrot, 1 thinly sliced rib celery, 1 small chopped onion, and ½ teaspoon thyme, stirring occasionally, for 8 minutes, or until the vegetables are tender. Add 4 cups chicken broth and 1 cup cooked brown rice. Bring to a boil; reduce heat to medium-low. Simmer for 10 minutes, or until the flavors combine. Stir in 2 cups shredded cooked chicken. Season with ½ teaspoon salt. *Makes 4 servings.*

Nutrition (per serving): 269 calories, 22 g protein, 18 g carbohydrates, 2 g fiber, 2 g sugars, 12 g fat, 3 g saturated fat, 568 mg sodium

8. **Mexican Cheesy Rice Casserole.** Preheat the oven to 375°F. Lightly coat a 13" x 9" baking dish with cooking spray and add 1 bag (10 ounces) frozen brown rice, 1 can (15 ounces) rinsed and drained black beans, 1 can (10 ounces) diced tomatoes with green chiles, and 1 cup shredded Mexican cheese blend. Stir to combine and sprinkle with ½ cup additional cheese. Bake for 15 minutes, or until the cheese is melted and bubbly. Sprinkle with 1 tablespoon chopped cilantro, if desired. *Makes 4 servings.*

Nutrition (per serving): 335 calories, 17 g protein, 39 g carbohydrates, 6 g fiber, 3 g sugars, 13 g fat, 7 g saturated fat, 832 mg sodium

SPICED SWEET POTATO WEDGES

PREP TIME: 10 MINUTES • TOTAL TIME: 50 MINUTES • MAKES 4 SERVINGS

3 sweet potatoes (about 1½ pounds), scrubbed and cut lengthwise into 8 wedges

1 tablespoon olive oil

1 teaspoon ground cumin

½ teaspoon ground coriander

¼ teaspoon salt

⅛ teaspoon ground cinnamon

1. Preheat the oven to 400°F. Coat a large rimmed baking sheet with cooking spray. Add the potatoes, oil, cumin, coriander, salt, and cinnamon and toss to mix well. Spread evenly in the pan.

2. Roast, turning occasionally, for 40 minutes, or until the potatoes are tender and lightly browned.

Fast Fix: *Coated in fragrant spices of cumin, coriander, and cinnamon, these fries are a perfect accompaniment to turkey or veggie burgers. Roast the potatoes with their skins on for extra fiber and vitamins. Another bonus—you'll save on prep time.*

	CALORIES	PROTEIN	CARBS	FIBER	SUGARS	FAT	SAT FAT	SODIUM
REAL FOOD	116	2 g	20 g	3 g	4 g	4 g	1 g	200 mg
FAKE FOOD	230	2 g	23 g	2 g	1 g	14 g	2.5 g	390 mg

COMPARED TO: Ore-Ida Crispers! Crispy, Shaped Potatoes

INGREDIENTS: Potatoes, vegetable oil (sunflower, cottonseed, soybean and/or canola), dehydrated potatoes (potatoes, mono- and diglycerides, sodium acid pyrophosphate, citric acid), salt, monoglycerides, xanthan gum, dextrose, yeast, disodium dihydrogen pyrophosphate, dehydrated onions.

⇌ Bonus Benefit ⇌

Does coriander have any impact on diabetes? Antidiabetic effects have been observed from ingesting coriander essential oil. It appears to stimulate insulin secretion and enhance glucose uptake and metabolism by muscles.[22]

CREAMY MASHED CAULIFLOWER

PREP TIME: 5 MINUTES • TOTAL TIME: 30 MINUTES • MAKES 4 SERVINGS

1 head cauliflower, cut into florets

3 tablespoons reduced-fat cream cheese

1 tablespoon butter

½ teaspoon salt

¼ teaspoon garlic powder

Place a steamer basket in a large saucepan with 2" of water. Place the cauliflower in the basket. Over high heat, bring the water to a simmer. Reduce the heat to medium, cover, and simmer for 25 minutes, or until very tender. Drain and return the cauliflower to the saucepan. Add the cream cheese, butter, salt, and garlic powder. Using a potato masher, mash the mixture until smooth.

	CALORIES	PROTEIN	CARBS	FIBER	SUGARS	FAT	SAT FAT	SODIUM
REAL FOOD	88	4 g	9 g	3 g	4 g	5 g	3 g	416 mg
FAKE FOOD	170	4 g	22 g	3 g	1 g	18 g	4 g	430 mg

COMPARED TO: Giant Fresh Side Loaded Mashed Potatoes

INGREDIENTS: Potatoes, milk, butter (sweet cream, salt), cheese powder (palm oil, cheddar cheese [pasteurized milk, cheese cultures, salt, enzymes], corn syrup solids, natural flavors, salt, sugar, lactic acid, sodium caseinate, disodium phosphate, monoglycerides), margarine (liquid and hydrogenated soybean oil, water, salt, contains less than 2% of vegetable mono- and diglycerides, soy lecithin, citric acid, natural and artificial flavor, vitamin a palmitate), water, bacon bits (bacon [cured with water, salt, sugar, sodium erythorbate, sodium nitrate], may also contain potassium chloride, dextrose, smoke flavoring, sodium phosphates, honey, sodium diacetate), salt, potassium sorbate (to protect flavor), mono- and diglycerides, chives, ascorbic acid, citric acid.

≈ food imposters ≈
BUTTER THAT'S NOT BUTTER

Serve this on your popcorn, and you'll have people believing it's not butter in no time. "Butter" spray is as artificial as it gets.

Ingredients: Water, soybean oil, salt, sweet cream buttermilk, xanthan gum, soy lecithin, polysorbate 60, lactic acid (potassium sorbate, calcium disodium EDTA) used to protect quality, natural and artificial flavor, vitamin A palmitate, beta-carotene (color).

WHOLE GRAIN BREAD

SEE PHOTO ON PAGE 269.

PREP TIME: 15 MINUTES • TOTAL TIME: 2 HOURS 20 MINUTES • MAKES 10 SERVINGS

1⅔ cups lukewarm water

2 teaspoons honey

1½ teaspoons active dry yeast

2¼ cups whole grain pastry flour

¾ cup rye flour

⅓ cup steel-cut oats

1 teaspoon salt

1. Line a 6-quart slow cooker with parchment paper and coat with cooking spray.

2. In a small measuring cup, stir together the water, honey, and yeast until the yeast dissolves. Let stand for 10 minutes; the yeast should be bubbly and foamy.

3. In a large bowl, combine the pastry and rye flours, oats, and salt. Stir the yeast mixture into the dry ingredients until a dough forms. Transfer to a lightly floured surface and knead 3 or 4 times, or until the dough is cohesive and smooth. Form into a ball.

4. Place the dough in the slow cooker, cover, and cook on high for 2 to 3 hours, or until a thermometer inserted in the center registers 200°F.

5. Preheat the broiler to high. Position a rack 6" from the broiler. Place the bread on the rack and broil for 2 minutes, or until golden brown and crisp. Cool completely before slicing.

	CALORIES	PROTEIN	CARBS	FIBER	SUGARS	FAT	SAT FAT	SODIUM
REAL FOOD	150	5 g	32 g	3 g	1 g	1 g	0 g	193 mg
FAKE FOOD	340	12 g	67 g	5 g	7 g	3 g	0 g	630 mg

COMPARED TO: Dunkin' Donuts Everything Bagel

INGREDIENTS: Bagel: enriched wheat flour (wheat flour, niacin, reduced iron, thiamin mononitrate, riboflavin, folic acid), water, sugar, malt extract, degermed yellow corn meal, yeast, salt, natural ferment flavor (cultured wheat and wheat malt flours, vinegar, salt), molasses, dough conditioner (malted barley flour, enzymes, dextrose), soy (trace); Topping: sesame and poppy seeds, dehydrated onion, dehydrated garlic, rolled oats.

⇥ Bonus Benefit ⇤

Add oats to your meals when dieting. Oats and oatmeal can help with weight management by increasing satiety and improving appetite control. In a study of volunteers who ate either oatmeal or a cold breakfast cereal, oatmeal resulted in a greater increase in fullness, greater reduction in hunger, less desire to eat, and less food intake.[23]

DESSERTS
and SNACKS

LEMON PUDDING CAKE

SEE PHOTO ON PAGE 276.

PREP TIME: 15 MINUTES ● TOTAL TIME: 2 HOURS 15 MINUTES ● MAKES 4 SERVINGS

½ teaspoon butter

½ cup sugar + extra for dusting

¼ cup whole grain pastry flour

¼ teaspoon salt

2 large eggs, separated

⅔ cup plain yogurt

3 tablespoons fresh lemon juice

3 teaspoons freshly grated lemon peel

Fresh pomegranate seeds (arils) and whipped cream (optional)

1. Butter and lightly sugar four 6-ounce ramekins. In a small bowl, whisk together the ½ cup sugar, flour, and salt. Set aside.

2. In a large bowl, with an electric mixer on high speed, beat the egg whites until stiff peaks form. Transfer to a small bowl and set aside.

3. In the same bowl, with an electric mixer on medium speed, beat the egg yolks, yogurt, lemon juice, and lemon peel until well combined. Reduce the speed to low. Slowly add the reserved flour mixture until just combined. Fold in the reserved egg whites.

4. Divide the batter among the ramekins. Arrange in a 6-quart slow cooker. Add enough water to come halfway up the sides of the ramekins. Cover and cook on low for 2 hours, or until the cakes spring back when pressed. Remove to a rack and let cool slightly. Invert the cakes onto plates. Serve with pomegranate arils and whipped cream, if using.

	CALORIES	PROTEIN	CARBS	FIBER	SUGARS	FAT	SAT FAT	SODIUM
REAL FOOD	216	6 g	35 g	0 g	29 g	6 g	6 g	185 mg
FAKE FOOD	360	7 g	62 g	1 g	52 g	9 g	4.5 g	270 mg

COMPARED TO: Edwards' Lemon Meringue Pie

INGREDIENTS: Reduced fat sweetened condensed milk (milk, skim milk, sugar, vitamin a palmitate), corn syrup, water, enriched flour (wheat flour, niacin, reduced iron, thiamine mononitrate, riboflavin, folic acid), egg whites, sugar, vegetable shortening (palm oil and soybean oil), egg yolks, contains 2% or less of: lemon juice concentrate, enriched bleached flour (bleached wheat flour, malted barley flour, niacin, reduced iron, thiamine mononitrate, riboflavin, folic acid), lemon pulp cells, sodium bicarbonate, salt, cornstarch, carob bean gum, agar, lemon oil, sodium silicoaluminate, monosodium phosphate, soy lecithin, cream of tartar, artificial flavor.

⇒ food imposters ⇐
LEMONADE THAT ISN'T LEMONADE

Even if life doesn't give you lemons, you can still make lemonade. Their lemonade drink mix ingredient list mentions nary a lemon, but plenty else! Because nothing captures the color of summer quite like yellow #5.

Ingredients: Sugar, fructose, citric acid, contains less than 2% of maltodextrin, natural flavor, ascorbic acid (vitamin C), sodium acid pyrophosphate, sodium citrate, magnesium oxide, calcium fumarate, soy lecithin, artificial color, yellow 5 lake, tocopherol (preserves freshness). Contains soy.

CHOCOLATE CUPCAKES *with* PEANUT BUTTER FROSTING

PREP TIME: 25 MINUTES • TOTAL TIME: 60 MINUTES • MAKES 24 SERVINGS

1¼ cups whole grain pastry flour

½ cup unsweetened cocoa powder

1 teaspoon baking soda

1 teaspoon baking powder

½ teaspoon salt

¾ cup granulated sugar

3 eggs

3 tablespoons canola oil

1 teaspoon vanilla extract

1½ cups plain yogurt

¾ cup creamy natural peanut butter

¾ cup confectioners' sugar

3 ounces cream cheese (6 tablespoons), at room temperature

¼ cup milk or half-and-half

Ground walnuts (optional)

1. Preheat the oven to 350°F. Coat 24 muffin cups with cooking spray or line with paper liners.

2. In a medium bowl, whisk together the flour, cocoa, baking soda, baking powder, and salt. Set aside.

3. In a large bowl, with an electric mixer on medium speed, beat together the granulated sugar and egg for 5 minutes, or until thick and pale. Beat in the oil and vanilla. Alternately add the reserved flour mixture and yogurt and beat on low just until incorporated.

4. Divide the batter among the muffin cups, filling just over half full. Bake for 15 minutes, or until a wooden pick inserted in the center comes out clean. Cool on a rack.

5. Meanwhile, in a medium bowl, working with a mixer or whisk, beat the peanut butter, confectioners' sugar, cream cheese, and milk or half-and-half until well blended. Spread 1 tablespoon over each cupcake. Garnish cupcakes with ground walnuts, if using.

Fast Fix: *Get a head start on any cake by assembling the dry and/or wet ingredients hours or even days ahead. Then you can easily combine and bake them closer to serving for a fresher cake.*

	CALORIES	PROTEIN	CARBS	FIBER	SUGARS	FAT	SAT FAT	SODIUM
REAL FOOD	157	5 g	18 g	1 g	11 g	8 g	2 g	177 mg
FAKE FOOD	290	2 g	56 g	1 g	36 g	6.5 g	3.5 g	475 mg

COMPARED TO: Betty Crocker Super Moist Chocolate Fudge Cake Mix with Betty Crocker Rich & Creamy Chocolate Frosting

INGREDIENTS: Cake: enriched flour bleached (wheat flour, niacin, iron, thiamin mononitrate, riboflavin, folic acid), sugar, corn syrup, cocoa processed with alkali, leavening (baking soda, sodium aluminum phosphate, monocalcium phosphate). Contains 2% or less of: corn starch, modified corn starch, partially hydrogenated soybean and/or cottonseed oil, propylene glycol mono- and diesters of fatty acids, distilled monoglycerides, carob powder, salt, dicalcium phosphate, sodium stearoyl lactylate, xanthan gum, cellulose gum, artificial flavor. Frosting: sugar, water, palm oil, high maltose corn syrup, corn starch, cocoa processed with alkali. Contains 2% or less of: salt, distilled monoglycerides, polysorbate 60, natural and artificial flavor, sodium stearoyl lactylate, citric acid, sodium acid pyrophosphate, color added, nonfat milk. Freshness preserved by potassium sorbate.

⇒ Bonus Benefit ⇐

A study looking at the relationship between nuts and mortality found that nut consumption was associated with lower overall mortality and cardiovascular disease mortality. Peanuts figured heavily in this study, and with their affordability, eating peanuts could be considered a cost-effective measure to improve cardiovascular health.[1]

STRAWBERRY SHORTCAKE
with WHIPPED RICOTTA

SEE PHOTO ON PAGE 279.

PREP TIME: 20 MINUTES • TOTAL TIME: 35 MINUTES • MAKES 6 SERVINGS

1½ cups whole grain pastry flour

2 teaspoons baking powder

½ teaspoon baking soda

1 tablespoon granulated sugar

½ teaspoon salt

3 tablespoons butter, cubed

¾ cup buttermilk

1 cup part-skim ricotta cheese

¼ cup confectioners' sugar

1 teaspoon vanilla extract

2 pints strawberries, hulled and sliced

1. Preheat the oven to 375°F. Lightly coat a baking sheet with cooking spray.

2. In a large bowl, combine the flour, baking powder, baking soda, granulated sugar, and salt. Cut the butter into the dry ingredients with a pastry cutter or 2 butter knives (moving the knives in opposite directions) until the mixture is crumbly. Add the buttermilk, stirring with a fork just until moistened.

3. Transfer the dough onto a floured surface. Knead a few times, or until the dough is smooth. Pat into a 6" round. Using a 2½"-round biscuit cutter, cut the dough into 6 rounds, gathering scraps and repatting as necessary. Place on the baking sheet. Bake for 10 minutes, or until golden brown. Cool on a rack.

4. Meanwhile, in a medium bowl, combine the ricotta, confectioners' sugar, and vanilla. Beat with an electric mixer on medium-high speed for 1 minute, or until smooth. When the biscuits are cool, split crosswise in half. Top 1 biscuit half with about ¼ cup strawberries and ¼ cup whipped ricotta, followed by the other biscuit half.

⁒ Bonus Benefit ⁒

Eat more berries! Greater intake of strawberries and blueberries is associated with slower rates of cognitive decline. Frequent berry consumption has been shown to delay cognitive aging by as much as 2.5 years.[2]

	CALORIES	PROTEIN	CARBS	FIBER	SUGARS	FAT	SAT FAT	SODIUM
REAL FOOD	269	9 g	37 g	4 g	14 g	10 g	6 g	618 mg
FAKE FOOD	470	12 g	75 g	0 g	63 g	14 g	9 g	180 mg

COMPARED TO: Dairy Queen Strawberry Sundae (Medium)

INGREDIENTS: Artificially Flavored Vanilla Reduced Fat Ice Cream: milk fat and nonfat milk, sugar, corn syrup, whey, mono- and diglycerides, artificial flavor, guar gum, polysorbate 80, carrageenan, vitamin A palmitate, Strawberry Topping: sliced strawberries, sugar, cellulose gum, citric acid, sodium benzoate (preservative), potassium sorbate (preservative), red #40.

⇒ food imposters ⇐

BLUEBERRIES THAT AREN'T BLUEBERRIES

What goes best with fake maple syrup? Fraudulent pancakes, of course. Read the tiny print that says "with imitation blueberries," and you'll be dying to hear how to fake a fruit. Here's the secret: Take some dextrose, fractionated palm kernel oil, flour, citric acid, cellulose gum, maltodextrin, artificial flavors, two types of blue, one part red, and you're set.

Ingredients: Enriched bleached flour (wheat flour, niacin, reduced iron, thiamin mononitrate, riboflavin, folic acid, may contain malted barley flour), imitation blueberry pieces (dextrose, fractionated palm kernel oil, enriched flour [wheat flour, niacin, reduced iron, thiamin mononitrate, riboflavin, folic acid], citric acid, cellulose gum, maltodextrin, artificial flavor, red 40, blue 1, blue 2), sugar, soy flour, leavening (sodium bicarbonate, monocalcium phosphate, sodium aluminum sulfate), canola or soybean oil, dextrose, salt, mono- and diglycerides, guar gum, artificial flavor.

CHOCOLATE TART *with* BERRIES

SEE PHOTO ON PAGE 272.

PREP TIME: 10 MINUTES • TOTAL TIME: 1 HOUR 45 MINUTES • MAKES 8 SERVINGS

18 organic cream-filled chocolate sandwich cookies, crushed

3 tablespoons butter, melted

1 cup heavy cream

8 ounces cream cheese, at room temperature

¼ cup + 1 tablespoon sugar

1 tablespoon lemon juice

1 pint blackberries

1 pint raspberries

1 tablespoon water

1. Coat a 9" tart pan or pie pan with cooking spray. In a medium bowl, combine the cookie crumbs and butter. Press onto the bottom and sides of the pan.

2. In a large bowl, with an electric mixer on high speed, beat the cream until soft peaks form. Transfer to another bowl and set aside.

3. In the same bowl with the same beaters, beat the cream cheese, ¼ cup of the sugar, and the lemon juice until smooth. Fold in the whipped cream. Spread in the tart shell and chill for at least 1 hour.

4. In a medium bowl, combine the berries with the remaining 1 tablespoon sugar and the water. Cover and chill until ready to serve. Top the tart with the berries just before serving.

Fast Fix: *To crush the cookies, either place in a food processor and pulse until crumbs form or place in a resealable plastic bag and crush with a rolling pin.*

⇾ Bonus Benefit ⇽

Raspberries to the rescue! Raspberries have been shown to reduce the risk of type 2 diabetes by as much as 35 percent.[3]

	CALORIES	PROTEIN	CARBS	FIBER	SUGARS	FAT	SAT FAT	SODIUM
REAL FOOD	218	2 g	19 g	2 g	11 g	16 g	9 g	132 mg
FAKE FOOD	330	4 g	41 g	2 g	30 g	17 g	7 g	310 mg

COMPARED TO: Hershey's Chocolate Mousse Cake

INGREDIENTS: Sugar, bleached enriched flour (wheat flour, niacin, reduced iron, thiamine mononitrate, riboflavin, folic acid), whole eggs, vegetable shortening (palm oil, canola oil, partially hydrogenated palm kernel oil), water, cake base (cocoa [processed with alkali], nonfat dry milk, whey [milk], salt, modified corn starch, egg whites, sodium acid pyrophosphate, sodium bicarbonate, soybean oil. Contains 2% or less of each of the following: carboxymethylcellulose, artificial flavors, sodium stearoyl lactylate {ssl}, monocalcium phosphate, xanthan gum), soybean oil, cream cheese (pasteurized milk and cream, cheese culture, salt, carob bean gum), high fructose corn syrup. Contains 2% or less of each of the following: cocoa (processed with alkali), vanilla creme (sugar, soybean oil, palm oil, palm kernel oil, milk, soy lecithin, natural flavor, vanilla), chocolate chips (sugar, chocolate, cocoa butter, cocoa [processed with alkali], milk fat. Contains 2% or less of each of: vanillin [artificial flavor], milk), cocoa, bittersweet chocolate (chocolate liquor [processed with potassium carbonate], sugar, cocoa butter, soy lecithin), milk chocolate (sugar, chocolate, nonfat milk, cocoa butter, milk fat, soy lecithin, vanillin [artificial flavor]), white chips (sugar, nonfat milk, partially hydrogenated palm kernel oil, partially hydrogenated soybean oil, palm kernel oil, corn starch, artificial flavor, salt, hydrogenated palm oil, soy lecithin), dextrose, heavy whipping cream (milk), corn syrup solids, corn syrup, soy lecithin, emulsifier (water, sorbitan monostearate, polysorbate 60, monoglycerides, with phosphoric acid and sodium propionate [preservatives]), sweetened condensed milk (milk, sugar), corn starch, sodium caseinate (milk), salt, polysorbate 60, mono- and diglycerides, gum arabic, soy protein concentrate, potassium sorbate (preservative), cellulose gum, citric acid, chocolate liquor, polyglycerol esters of fatty acids, guar gum, xanthan gum, natural and artificial flavors, propylene glycol, vanillin, beta-carotene (color).

⇒ food imposters ⇐
CHOCOLATE THAT'S NOT CHOCOLATE

A chocolate chip cookie, by any other name, is a total red flag. See the chocolate-chip-flavored cookie. Why is it called "flavored"? To be called chocolate, the FDA requires that a food contain cocoa butter, and these use cheaper vegetable oils as substitutes. And yes—that partially hydrogenated palm kernel oil is code for trans fat. Better bake your own.

Ingredients: Enriched flour bleached (wheat flour, niacin, iron, thiamin mononitrate, riboflavin, folic acid), sugar, chocolate flavored chips (sugar, partially hydrogenated palm kernel oil, cocoa, cocoa processed with alkali, dextrose, soy lecithin), partially hydrogenated soybean and/or cottonseed oil, water, contains 2% or less of: molasses, wheat protein isolate, baking powder (baking soda, sodium aluminum phosphate), salt, eggs, artificial flavor, nonfat milk.

"BAKED" GRANOLA APPLES

SEE PHOTO ON PAGE 270.

PREP TIME: 5 MINUTES • TOTAL TIME: 10 MINUTES • MAKES 4 SERVINGS

2 large crisp apples, such as Gala, halved and cored

2 tablespoons chopped dried tart cherries

1 tablespoon firmly packed light brown sugar

¼ teaspoon ground cinnamon

⅛ teaspoon ground nutmeg

4 teaspoons butter

½ cup granola

1. In a microwaveable dish, arrange the apple halves cut side up.

2. Top each half with the cherries and sugar. Sprinkle with the cinnamon and nutmeg. Dot each with 1 teaspoon of the butter. Cover and microwave on high power for 4 minutes, or until tender.

3. Transfer the apples to serving bowls. Sprinkle with the granola. Drizzle any juices in the cooking dish on top.

⇥ Bonus Benefit ⇤

Eating an apple a day is great advice! Apples have been shown to positively affect lipid metabolism, weight management, vascular function, and inflammation, and to lower total cholesterol.[4,5]

	CALORIES	PROTEIN	CARBS	FIBER	SUGARS	FAT	SAT FAT	SODIUM
REAL FOOD	185	2 g	29 g	5 g	20 g	8 g	3 g	36 mg
FAKE FOOD	230	2 g	32 g	4 g	13 g	10 g	5 g	160 mg

COMPARED TO: McDonald's Baked Apple Pie

INGREDIENTS: Apples (apples, salt, citric acid, ascorbic acid), enriched flour (bleached wheat flour, niacin, reduced iron, thiamine mononitrate, riboflavin, folic acid), water, palm oil, sugar, high fructose corn syrup, Contains 2% or less: modified food starch, sorbitol, dextrose, brown sugar, yeast, salt, cinnamon, apple powder (dehydrated apples, citric acid), sodium alginate, spice, trisodium citrate, dicalcium phosphate, natural and artificial flavors, hydroxylated soy lecithin, yeast extract, enzyme, L-cysteine, color (annatto, turmeric, beta-carotene, caramel color).

⇒ food imposters ⇐
CARAMEL THAT'S NOT CARAMEL

Caramel syrup may look and taste like the gross approximation of caramel, but industrial caramel is way different from the kind you make at home using a sugar base. Some "caramel color" is processed with ammonia, and California even added the compound that makes it up—4-methylimidazole—to its list of known carcinogens. Companies don't have to disclose whether they use ammonia in their caramel color, so it's best to make your own caramel.

Ingredients: Corn syrup, high fructose corn syrup, sweetened condensed skim milk (skim milk and sugar), water. Contains 2% or less of: disodium phosphate, sodium citrate, salt, artificial flavor, caramel color, xanthan gum, artificial color (yellow 6, yellow 5).

CHOCOLATE-BERRY CRISP

SEE PHOTO ON PAGE 271.

PREP TIME: 10 MINUTES • TOTAL TIME: 50 MINUTES • MAKES 8 SERVINGS

2 bags (12 ounces each) frozen mixed berries, such as strawberries, blackberries, raspberries, and blueberries, thawed and drained

3 tablespoons cornstarch

2 tablespoons honey

1⅓ cups old-fashioned rolled oats

½ cup firmly packed brown sugar

1 cup chopped almonds

⅓ cup dark or bittersweet chocolate chips

Vanilla ice cream (optional)

1. Preheat the oven to 350°F. In a medium bowl, mix the berries and cornstarch. Pour into an 8" x 8" glass baking dish.

2. In a small bowl, combine the honey, oats, sugar, and almonds. Spread over the berry mixture. Bake for 30 minutes.

3. Remove the dish from the oven and top evenly with the chocolate chips. Bake for 10 minutes, or until the chocolate is melted. Serve warm topped with a small scoop of vanilla ice cream, if using.

Fast Fix: *It can be a challenge to get a proper measurement of honey when the majority of it sticks to the measuring spoon. To prevent honey from sticking to a measuring spoon or cup, coat the utensil with cooking spray or dip it in oil before measuring.*

	CALORIES	PROTEIN	CARBS	FIBER	SUGARS	FAT	SAT FAT	SODIUM
REAL FOOD	274	6 g	41 g	6 g	25 g	12 g	2 g	4 mg
FAKE FOOD	580	5 g	54 g	3 g	33 g	38 g	18 g	330 mg

COMPARED TO: Marie Callender's Chocolate Satin Pie (Frozen, Thaw & Serve)

INGREDIENTS: Sugar, partially hydrogenated soybean oil, water, eggs, enriched wheat flour (flour, niacin, iron, thiamine mono-nitrate, riboflavin, folic acid), milk, butter (cream, salt), partially hydrogenated palm kernel oil, high fructose corn syrup, cocoa. Contains less than 2% of: partially hydrogenated cottonseed oil, palm oil, cocoa (processed with alkali), sodium caseinate, salt, natural and artificial flavor, beta carotene (color), dextrose, guar gum, partially hydrogenated canola oil, polysorbate 60, sorbitan monostearate, xanthan gum, soy lecithin, cocoa butter, chocolate, caramel color, corn flour, sodium bicarbonate, whey, mono- and diglycerides, modified corn starch, sodium pyrophosphate, sodium alginate, soybean oil, calcium sulfate, dextrin, nonfat dry milk, sodium phosphate.

⇒ Bonus Benefit ⇐

Oats and oatmeal can help with weight management by increasing satiety and improving appetite control.[6] They are the only source of avenanthramides, a group of antioxidants that, in addition to anti-inflammatory activity, have been shown to exert cardioprotective benefits.[7]

RUSTIC GINGERED PEACH TART

SEE PHOTO ON PAGE 278.

PREP TIME: 10 MINUTES • TOTAL TIME: 40 MINUTES • MAKES 8 SERVINGS

4 medium peaches, pitted, peeled, and sliced

¼ cup firmly packed brown sugar

2 tablespoons whole grain pastry flour

¼ teaspoon ground ginger

1 organic whole wheat (9") pie dough, thawed if frozen

1. Preheat the oven to 400°F. Coat a baking sheet with cooking spray.

2. In a large bowl, combine the peaches, sugar, flour, and ginger, tossing to coat well.

3. Place the pie dough on a lightly floured surface and roll to 12". Place on the baking sheet. Mound the peach mixture in the center, leaving a 3" border. Fold the edges over the filling.

4. Bake for 30 minutes, or until golden brown and the juices are bubbling.

	CALORIES	PROTEIN	CARBS	FIBER	SUGARS	FAT	SAT FAT	SODIUM
REAL FOOD	183	2 g	28 g	3 g	13 g	7 g	3 g	96 mg
FAKE FOOD	270	2 g	36 g	2 g	20 g	11 g	5 g	300 mg

COMPARED TO: Tastykake Peach Pie

INGREDIENTS: Peaches, enriched flour (wheat flour, niacin, reduced iron, thiamine mononitrate-b1, riboflavin-b2, folic acid), high fructose corn syrup, palm oil, water, sugar, food starch modified, contains 2% or less of: salt, skim milk, cellulose gum, sorbic acid (to preserve freshness), sodium stearoyl lactylate, baking soda, citric acid, potassium sorbate (to preserve freshness), eggs.

What's the Easiest Way to Pit a Peach?

To pit a peach, slice around the peach, perpendicular to its crease line. Twist the two halves apart. Then, dislodge the pit out of the half that held on to it.

Bonus Benefit

Ginger is known as a natural, safe, and quite effective way to treat nausea and vomiting associated with morning sickness, postoperative recovery, and medication therapy, including chemotherapy and antiretrovirals.[8, 9, 10, 11]

Steak Kebabs ⌇ Page 184

Parmesan Fettuccine Alfredo ✍ Page 233

Tilapia Fish and Chips with Malt Vinegar Dip ⤴ Page 210

Zesty Orange Chicken ✧ Page 188

Whole Grain Bread ∝ Page 250

Turkey Mini Meat Loaves
∝ Page 202

"Baked" Granola Apples Page 260

Chocolate-Dipped Watermelon
Page 283

Chocolate-Berry Crisp ✍ Page 262

Chocolate Tart with Berries
Page 258

Coconut-Almond Energy Bars
↙ Page 296

Chocolate-Orange
Mousse with Raspberries
↙ Page 284

Cherry Frozen Dessert ✍ Page 290

Figs with Mascarpone and Honey ⤳ Page 282

Lemon Pudding Cake ⌣ Page 252

Chocolate Fudge Pops Page 288

Rustic Gingered Peach Tart ✣ Page 264

Strawberry Shortcake with Whipped Ricotta ✒ Page 256

Three-Ingredient Ice Cream
⌇ Page 286

PLUM *and* RASPBERRY CRUMBLE

PREP TIME: 15 MINUTES • TOTAL TIME: 40 MINUTES + STANDING TIME • MAKES 6 SERVINGS

TOPPING

1 cup rolled oats

¼ cup chopped walnuts

2 tablespoons whole grain pastry flour

½ teaspoon ground cinnamon

⅛ teaspoon salt

3 tablespoons maple syrup

3 tablespoons butter, melted

FILLING

4 plums, pitted and cut into ½" pieces

1 pint raspberries

2 tablespoons maple syrup

1½ tablespoons whole grain pastry flour

1. Preheat the oven to 375°F. Coat a 9" x 9" baking pan or 6 ramekins (8 ounces each) with cooking spray.

2. *To make the topping:* In a medium bowl, stir together the oats, walnuts, flour, cinnamon, and salt. Add the maple syrup and butter and stir until the mixture is crumbly.

3. *To make the filling:* In a large bowl, combine the plums, raspberries, maple syrup, and flour and toss to coat. Transfer to the pan or divide among the ramekins. Top with the topping mixture.

4. Bake for 20 minutes, or until the topping is browned and the filling is bubbly. Let stand for 10 minutes.

	CALORIES	PROTEIN	CARBS	FIBER	SUGARS	FAT	SAT FAT	SODIUM
REAL FOOD	233	5 g	32 g	5 g	18 g	10 g	4 g	44 mg
FAKE FOOD	350	3 g	47 g	1 g	21 g	17 g	8 g	290 mg

COMPARED TO: Mrs. Smith's Original Flaky Crust Cherry Pie (Frozen)

INGREDIENTS: Filling: cherries, water, sugar, corn syrup, food starch modified, salt, citric acid, xanthan gum. Crust: wheat flour, shortening butter blend (palm oil, butter [cream, salt]), palm oil, water, soybean oil, salt, dextrose, yeast, mono- and diglycerides, apple juice concentrate.

FIGS *with* MASCARPONE *and* HONEY

SEE PHOTO ON PAGE 275.

PREP TIME: 5 MINUTES • TOTAL TIME: 10 MINUTES • MAKES 2 SERVINGS

4 large fresh figs, cut into quarters

2 ounces mascarpone cheese, at room temperature

1 tablespoon honey

Divide the figs between 2 serving bowls. Top each with half of the cheese and honey.

	CALORIES	PROTEIN	CARBS	FIBER	SUGARS	FAT	SAT FAT	SODIUM
REAL FOOD	248	3 g	33 g	4 g	29 g	14 g	7 g	17 mg
FAKE FOOD	340	8 g	38 g	1 g	27 g	18 g	8 g	260 mg

COMPARED TO: Sara Lee Original Cream Classic Cheesecake (Frozen)

INGREDIENTS: Cream cheese (pasteurized milk and cream, cheese culture, salt, carob bean gum), sour cream topping (cultured skim milk, cream, modified corn and tapioca starch, carob bean gum, carrageenan, xanthan gum, potassium chloride), sugar, bakers cheese (cultured skim milk, enzymes), enriched flour (wheat flour, niacin, iron, thiamin mononitrate, riboflavin, folic acid), eggs, water, cream, high fructose corn syrup, partially hydrogenated vegetable oil (soybean and/or cottonseed oils), whole wheat flour. Contains 2% or less of each of the following: corn syrup, milk protein concentrate, skim milk, corn starch, modified corn starch, leavening (sodium acid pyrophosphate, baking soda, monocalcium phosphate, calcium sulfate), salt, lactose, vanillin (artificial flavor), molasses, cinnamon, gums (xanthan and guar), methylcellulose, citric acid, sodium caseinate, carrageenan, agar, dextrose, konjac flour, soy flour.

⇒ Bonus Benefit ⇐

Honey boasts an astonishing array of health benefits, including anti-inflammatory, antioxidant, antitumor, antifungal, antiviral, antibacterial, antiwrinkle, antitussive, anti-insomnia, antiulcer, anticaries, antigingivitis, immune-supporting, and wound-healing properties.[12, 13]

CHOCOLATE-DIPPED WATERMELON

SEE PHOTO ON PAGE 270.

PREP TIME: 10 MINUTES ● TOTAL TIME: 10 MINUTES + CHILLING TIME ● MAKES 8 SERVINGS

2 ounces dark chocolate, finely chopped

4 wedges (1" thick) watermelon

Pinch of sea salt (optional)

1. Line a baking sheet with parchment paper. In a small microwaveable bowl, microwave the chocolate on high power for 1 minute, stirring after 30 seconds, or until melted.

2. Dip the watermelon in the chocolate and place on the baking sheet. Sprinkle with the salt, if using. Chill for at least 30 minutes.

	CALORIES	PROTEIN	CARBS	FIBER	SUGARS	FAT	SAT FAT	SODIUM
REAL FOOD	82	1 g	15 g	1 g	12 g	3 g	1 g	3 mg
FAKE FOOD	160	1 g	33 g	1 g	25 g	2.5 g	1.5 g	30 mg

COMPARED TO: Friendly's Wattamelon Roll

INGREDIENTS: Milk, water, sugar, corn syrup, cream, watermelon juice concentrate, chocolate liquor, lemon puree (water, lemon pulp, concentrated lemon juice, corn syrup, natural flavor), citric acid, natural and artificial flavor, guar gum, beet juice (for color), mono- and diglycerides, carob bean gum, disodium phosphate, karaya gum, cocoa butter, soy lecithin, red 40, pectin, annatto extract and turmeric (for color), blue 1.

Researchers found that the risk of diabetes decreased as the frequency of dark chocolate intake increased, up from two to six 1-ounce servings of dark chocolate per week.[14]

CHOCOLATE-ORANGE MOUSSE
with RASPBERRIES

SEE PHOTO ON PAGE 273.

PREP TIME: 5 MINUTES • TOTAL TIME: 15 MINUTES + CHILLING TIME • MAKES 6 SERVINGS

1 cup chocolate almond milk

5 ounces bittersweet chocolate, chopped

2 tablespoons unsweetened cocoa powder
(we used Ghirardelli)

1 teaspoon grated orange peel (optional)

½ cup heavy cream

Mint leaves for garnish

Orange peel for garnish

1½ cups fresh raspberries

1. In a small saucepan, combine the milk, chocolate, and cocoa. Cook over medium heat, stirring occasionally, until the chocolate melts. Transfer to a bowl and stir in the orange peel, if using. Cool completely.

2. In a small bowl, with an electric mixer or a whisk, beat the heavy cream until soft peaks form. Fold into the chocolate mixture until smooth. Cover and chill until set, about 2 hours.

3. Spoon into 6 small serving bowls, top with the mint and additional orange peel, and serve with the raspberries.

⇟ Bonus Benefit ⇟

Leave milk chocolate for kids. According to the latest research, much of the health benefit in chocolate comes from the flavanol epicatechin, which improves heart health and is found in high concentrations in dark, but not milk, chocolate.[15]

	CALORIES	PROTEIN	CARBS	FIBER	SUGARS	FAT	SAT FAT	SODIUM
REAL FOOD	199	4 g	23 g	5 g	14 g	14 g	9 g	26 mg
FAKE FOOD	760	6 g	66 g	3 g	44 g	54 g	27 g	333 mg

COMPARED TO: Perkins Chocolate French Silk Pie

INGREDIENTS: Chocolate Curls: sugar, partially hydrogenated cottonseed and soybean oils, cocoa, chocolate liquor processed with alkali, cocoa processed with alkali, distilled monoglycerides, sorbitan monostearate, soy lecithin, artificial flavors, salt. Manufactured on equipment that processes peanuts and tree nuts. Chocolate French Silk Pie Pie Filling: sugar, whole eggs, butter, cocoa processed with alkali, palm oil. Contains 2% or less of soybean oil, corn syrup, sorbitol, water, soy lecithin, mono- & diglycerides with citric acid as a preservative, salt, polysorbate 60, citric acid, vanilla. Crust: enriched wheat flour (flour, niacin, reduced iron, thiamine mononitrate, riboflavin, folic acid), vegetable oil (soybean oil and/or palm oil, citric acid as a preservative), water. Contains 2% or less of dextrose, salt, dough conditioner (whey, L-cysteine hydrochloride), sodium propionate (preservative). Whipped Cream: cream, sugar, corn syrup, modified food starch, sodium citrate, xanthan gum, polysorbate 80, artificial flavor.

⇒ food imposters ⇐
WHIPPED CREAM THAT'S NOT WHIPPED CREAM

Imitation whipped cream is a modern marvel, though very debatably "food." How else to explain the 14 ingredients responsible for a light-as-air texture? As the old childhood expression goes, "Pretty please, with imitation whipped topping and a cherry on top."

Ingredients: Water, hydrogenated vegetable oil (coconut and palm kernel oils), high fructose corn syrup, skim milk, light cream, contains less than 2% of: sodium caseinate, natural and artificial flavor, xanthan and guar gums, polysorbate 60, sorbitan monostearate, beta-carotene (color).

THREE-INGREDIENT ICE CREAM

SEE PHOTO ON PAGE 280.

PREP TIME: 5 MINUTES ● TOTAL TIME: 5 MINUTES + FREEZING TIME ● MAKES 4 SERVINGS

4 ripe bananas, peeled and cut into thirds

1 tablespoon almond or other nut butter

2–4 tablespoons milk

Chocolate shavings for garnish (optional)

1. Freeze the bananas overnight (or longer) in a sealed container.

2. In a blender, combine the bananas and nut butter. Blend, adding milk 1 tablespoon at a time, just until combined. Scoop into bowls and top with chocolate shavings, if using.

	CALORIES	PROTEIN	CARBS	FIBER	SUGARS	FAT	SAT FAT	SODIUM
REAL FOOD	113	2 g	28 g	3 g	15 g	1 g	1 g	8 mg
FAKE FOOD	540	8 g	62 g	1 g	54 g	31 g	19 g	310 mg

COMPARED TO: Cold Stone Chocolate Layer Cake Ice Cream (Love It Size)

INGREDIENTS: Sweet Cream Ice Cream (cream, nonfat milk, milk, whey, sugar, corn syrup, guar gum, cellulose gum, carrageenan, mono- & diglycerides, polysorbate 80, annatto extract), chocolate cake (sugar, enriched bleached wheat flour (flour, niacin, reduced iron, thiamine mononitrate, riboflavin, folic acid), skim milk, egg whites, soybean oil, cocoa (processed with alkali). Contains less than 2% of the following: leavening (baking soda, sodium acid pyrophosphate, sodium aluminum phosphate, monocalcium phosphate), wheat starch, propylene glycol mono- and diesters of fats and fatty acids, natural and artificial chocolate flavor (contains natural dairy ingredients), salt, egg yolks, mono- & diglycerides, modified tapioca starch, polysorbate 60, guar gum, sodium stearoyl lactylate, soy lecithin, corn syrup solids, sodium caseinate (milk derivative), modified corn starch, xanthan gum).

food imposters

ICE CREAM THAT'S NOT ICE CREAM

Gone are the good ol' days of ice cream. Now, we're forced to shovel down spoonfuls of Frozen Dairy Dessert, which can't legally be called ice cream without containing at least 10 percent milk fat. What Breyer's Extra Creamy Vanilla Frozen Dairy Dessert (phew) does contain is plenty of corn syrup, gums, and whey.

Ingredients: Milk, sugar, corn syrup, cream, whey, mono- and diglycerides, carob bean gum, guar gum, carrageenan, natural flavor, annatto (for color), vitamin A palmitate, tara gum.

CHOCOLATE FUDGE POPS

SEE PHOTO ON PAGE 277.

PREP TIME: 5 MINUTES • TOTAL TIME: 15 MINUTES + FREEZING TIME • MAKES 9 SERVINGS

2 cups milk

½ cup sugar

⅓ cup unsweetened cocoa powder

1 teaspoon vanilla extract

1. In a small saucepan, whisk together the milk, sugar, cocoa, and vanilla. Cook over medium heat for 2 minutes, or until the sugar dissolves.

2. Divide among 9 ice-pop molds (3 ounces each). Freeze for 6 hours, or until solid.

	CALORIES	PROTEIN	CARBS	FIBER	SUGARS	FAT	SAT FAT	SODIUM
REAL FOOD	111	5 g	24 g	4 g	16 g	3 g	2 g	32 mg
FAKE FOOD	270	2 g	28 g	2 g	23 g	17 g	12 g	40 mg

COMPARED TO: Magnum Ice Cream Bar Double Chocolate Dipped in Chocolate

INGREDIENTS: Milk chocolate coating [sugar, chocolate, cocoa butter, milk, milk fat, PGPR (emulsifier) and soy lecithin (emulsifier), vanilla extract], milk, chocolatey sauce [water, sugar, corn syrup, cocoa processed with alkali, nonfat dry milk, coconut oil, modified corn starch, mono- and diglycerides, carrageenan, potassium sorbate (used to protect quality)], cream, chocolatey coating [coconut oil, sugar, cocoa, soy lecithin, vanilla extract], sugar, cocoa processed with alkali. Contains less than 1% of: whey, mono- and diglycerides, locust bean gum, guar gum, carrageenan, water, corn syrup, caramel and annatto extract (color), natural flavor.

⇒ Bonus Benefit ⇐

Research has credited dark chocolate, including cocoa, with such health benefits as reducing oxidative stress, lowering blood pressure, increasing vasodilation, increasing platelet activity, exerting antidiabetic effects, relieving stress, reducing inflammation, improving exercise recovery, and even exerting antiobesity effects.[16]

✦ *food imposters* ✦
VANILLA THAT'S NOT VANILLA

Imitation vanilla extract gets most of its vanilla flavor from vanillin, a synthetic flavoring agent. That's not so bad on its own, but manufacturers don't stop there. Most imitation vanillas also contain potentially dangerous caramel color and mysterious natural flavors, which could be almost anything (even an extract from a beaver's backside).

Ingredients: Water, alcohol, natural flavorings, vanillin and other artificial flavorings, corn syrup, and caramel color.

CHERRY FROZEN DESSERT

SEE PHOTO ON PAGE 274.

PREP TIME: 5 MINUTES • TOTAL TIME: 5 MINUTES • MAKES 4 SERVINGS

1½ cups frozen unsweetened cherries

1 cup 2% Greek yogurt

1 tablespoon confectioners' sugar

1 teaspoon vanilla extract

1. In a food processor, process the cherries for 15 seconds, or until shaved. Scrape down the sides of the bowl.

2. Add the yogurt, sugar, and vanilla and process for 15 seconds, or until blended, thick, and smooth. For a softer serve, eat immediately, or store in the freezer in an airtight container for up to 1 week. Let frozen yogurt stand at room temperature for a few minutes to soften before serving.

	CALORIES	PROTEIN	CARBS	FIBER	SUGARS	FAT	SAT FAT	SODIUM
REAL FOOD	75	5 g	11 g	1 g	9 g	1 g	1 g	19 mg
FAKE FOOD	260	4 g	27 g	1 g	23 g	15 g	9 g	40 mg

COMPARED TO: Ben & Jerry's Cherry Garcia Ice Cream

INGREDIENTS: Cream, skim milk, liquid sugar (sugar, water), water, cherries, sugar, egg yolks, coconut oil, cocoa (processed with alkali), fruit and vegetable concentrates (color), coca powder, guar gum, natural flavors, lemon juice concentrate, carrageenan, milk fat, soy lecithin.

ICED SPICED COCOA LATTE

PREP TIME: 10 MINUTES • TOTAL TIME: 10 MINUTES • MAKES 6 SERVINGS

3 cups water

¼ teaspoon ground cinnamon

5 tablespoons freshly ground coffee

2 tablespoons sugar

1 tablespoon unsweetened cocoa powder

3 cups milk

6 cinnamon sticks for garnish (optional)

1. Place the water in a coffeemaker. In the coffee basket, combine the cinnamon and coffee; brew 1 pot. Stir in the sugar and cocoa. Chill until serving.

2. Pour equal amounts of coffee into 6 glasses filled with ice. Top each with ½ cup of the milk. Garnish with the cinnamon sticks, if using.

Fast Fix: *Quickly cool hot coffee when making iced coffee by putting a few stainless steel knives into the glass of ice into which you are pouring the hot coffee. If not serving to 6 people, prepare the full recipe, use what you need, and chill the remainder for another day.*

	CALORIES	PROTEIN	CARBS	FIBER	SUGARS	FAT	SAT FAT	SODIUM
REAL FOOD	95	4 g	11 g	0 g	10 g	4 g	2 g	57 mg
FAKE FOOD	350	3 g	52 g	1 g	37 g	15 g	11 g	330 mg

COMPARED TO: Dunkin' Donuts Dunkaccino (medium)

INGREDIENTS: Water; Dunkaccino Powder: sugar, non-dairy creamer [coconut oil, sodium caseinate (a milk derivative), mono- and diglycerides, dipotassium phosphate, sugar, silicon dioxide, sodium stearoyl lactylate, soy lecithin, annatto and turmeric (colors), artificial flavor], sweet cream (sweet cream, skim milk solids, soybean oil, corn syrup solids, sodium caseinate, soy leci- thin, mono- and diglycerides), natural and artificial flavor, instant coffee, whey powder, cocoa powder processed with alkali, nonfat dry milk, cellulose gum, salt, silicon dioxide, xanthan gum.

FROSTY CHOCOLATE MILKSHAKE

PREP TIME: 5 MINUTES ● TOTAL TIME: 5 MINUTES ● MAKES 1 SERVING

2 tablespoons unsweetened dark cocoa powder

2 tablespoons confectioners' sugar

2 tablespoons boiling water

¾ cup milk

¼ cup crushed ice cubes

2 teaspoons vanilla extract

In a glass measuring cup, whisk the cocoa, sugar, and water until syrupy. Add the milk and stir to completely dissolve the syrup. Pour into a blender with the ice and vanilla. Blend for 2 minutes, or until thick and creamy.

	CALORIES	PROTEIN	CARBS	FIBER	SUGARS	FAT	SAT FAT	SODIUM
REAL FOOD	172	8 g	30 g	4 g	25 g	3 g	2 g	86 mg
FAKE FOOD	710	16 g	110 g	1 g	96 g	23 g	16 g	290 mg

COMPARED TO: Dairy Queen Chocolate Shake (Medium)

INGREDIENTS: Artificially Flavored Vanilla Reduced Fat Ice Cream: milk fat and nonfat milk, sugar, corn syrup, whey, mono- and diglycerides, artificial flavor, guar gum, polysorbate 80, carrageenan, vitamin A palmitate, milk, 2% fat, Artificially Flavored Chocolate Topping: high fructose corn syrup, water, cocoa (processed with alkali), modified food starch, salt, potassium sorbate (preservative), artificial flavors, whipped topping general label declaration, ingredients may vary by supplier. Water, partially hydrogenated palm kernel oil, sugar. Contains less than 1%: sodium caseinate* (a milk derivative), polysorbate 60, mono- and diglycerides, artificial flavor, sorbitan monostearate, disodium phosphate, hexaglyceryl distearate, carrageenan, beta-carotene (color). Propellant: nitrous oxide.

⊰ food imposters ⊱
CHOCOLATE MILK THAT'S
NOT CHOCOLATE MILK

Take a closer look: That's chocolate drink in your hand, not chocolate milk. Yoo-hoo doesn't actually contain any liquid milk, but it does come with a dose of partially hydrogenated soybean oil (hello, trans fat!).

Ingredients: Water, high fructose corn syrup, whey (from milk), sugar, corn syrup solids, cocoa (alkali process), partially hydrogenated soybean oil, sodium caseinate (from milk), nonfat dry milk, salt, tricalcium phosphate, dipotassium phosphate, xanthan gum, guar gum, natural and artificial flavors, soy lecithin, mono- and diglycerides, vitamin A palmitate, niacinamide (vitamin B_3), vitamin D_3, riboflavin (vitamin B_2).

CHOCOLATE-POMEGRANATE CLUSTERS

PREP TIME: 10 MINUTES ● TOTAL TIME: 10 MINUTES + CHILLING TIME ● MAKES 4 SERVINGS

½ cup semisweet or dark chocolate chips   1 cup pomegranate seeds (arils), patted dry

1. Line a baking sheet with parchment paper or waxed paper. In a medium microwaveable bowl, microwave the chocolate chips on high power for 1 minute. If necessary, microwave for a few more seconds to melt completely.

2. Stir in the pomegranate arils until well coated. Drop by heaping tablespoonful onto the baking sheet. Chill for 15 minutes, or until the clusters are set.

Fast Fix: *Pomegranate seeds, or arils, are loaded with antioxidants. An easy way to seed a pomegranate is to cut off the crown and score the skin into sections. Submerge the pomegranate in a large bowl of cold water, gently pry open the sections, and pull out the seeds. The seeds will sink to the bottom of the bowl, and the membranes will float to the top. Lift the seeds out of the water and transfer to a paper towel to dry. The seeds can be refrigerated in an airtight container for up to 1 week.*

	CALORIES	PROTEIN	CARBS	FIBER	SUGARS	FAT	SAT FAT	SODIUM
REAL FOOD	73	1 g	11 g	2 g	9 g	4 g	2 g	2 mg
FAKE FOOD	170	1 g	28 g	1 g	23 g	8 g	4.5 g	60 mg

COMPARED TO: Brookside Dark Chocolate Pomegranate Flavor

INGREDIENTS: Dark chocolate (sugar; chocolate; cocoa butter; milk fat; cocoa processed with alkali; lecithin (soy); milk; salt; natural vanilla flavor); sugar; corn syrup; fruit juice concentrate (pomegranate juice; apple juice; cranberry juice; lemon juice concentrates); maltodextrin; deionized apple juice concentrate; natural flavor; pectin; canola oil; malic acid; tapioca dextrin; sodium bicarbonate; sodium citrate; ascorbic acid; citric acid; resinous glaze.

BANANA-OAT ENERGY BARS

PREP TIME: 15 MINUTES • TOTAL TIME: 40 MINUTES • MAKES 12 SERVINGS

2 very overripe bananas

½ cup vegetable oil

1 cup sugar

½ teaspoon vanilla extract

1½ cups old-fashioned rolled oats

¾ cup whole grain pastry flour

¾ teaspoon baking powder

½ teaspoon salt

½ teaspoon ground cinnamon

¼ teaspoon baking soda

¾ cup chopped walnuts, toasted

¾ cup dried cranberries

1. Preheat the oven to 350°F. Coat an 8" x 8" baking pan with cooking spray.

2. In a medium bowl, mash together the bananas, oil, sugar, and vanilla until smooth.

3. In a large bowl, combine the oats, flour, baking powder, salt, cinnamon, and baking soda. Add the banana mixture and stir until just combined. Fold in the walnuts and cranberries.

4. Spoon into the pan. Bake for 25 minutes, or until a wooden pick inserted in the center comes out clean. Cool completely on a rack.

Fast Fix: *To prevent walnuts from sinking to the bottom of a batter, toast them first. This makes them lighter.*

	CALORIES	PROTEIN	CARBS	FIBER	SUGARS	FAT	SAT FAT	SODIUM
REAL FOOD	303	4 g	41 g	3 g	24 g	15 g	2 g	158 mg
FAKE FOOD	390	5 g	57 g	1 g	57 g	16 g	10 g	400 mg

COMPARED TO: Starbucks Classic Coffee Cake

INGREDIENTS: Enriched flour (wheat flour, malted barley flour, niacin, reduced iron, thiamine mononitrate, riboflavin, folic acid), sugar, sour cream (cultured cream, skim milk, modified corn starch, sodium citrate, locust bean gum, carrageenan, whey, lactic acid, citric acid, phosphoric acid), butter (cream, natural flavor), eggs, brown sugar. Contains 2% or less of: leavening (baking soda, sodium acid pyrophosphate, corn starch, monocalcium phosphate), spices, dried orange peel (orange peel, sugar, refined sunflower oil, ascorbic acid, citric acid), natural flavor, salt, soy lecithin.

MARBLED BROWNIES

PREP TIME: 15 MINUTES • TOTAL TIME: 55 MINUTES • MAKES 16 SERVINGS

½ cup butter

⅓ cups unsweetened cocoa powder

¾ cup + 2 tablespoons sugar

1 egg

2 teaspoons vanilla extract

½ cup + ½ tablespoon whole grain pastry flour

¼ teaspoon baking powder

4 ounces cream cheese, at room temperature

1 egg yolk

1. Preheat the oven to 375°F. Coat an 8" x 8" baking pan with cooking spray.

2. In a large microwaveable bowl, place the butter. Microwave on high power for 2 minutes, or until melted. Stir in the cocoa and ¾ cup of the sugar. Add the egg and stir until well blended. Stir in the vanilla, ½ cup of the flour, and the baking powder. Spread the mixture into the pan.

3. In a medium bowl, with an electric mixer on low speed, beat the cream cheese, egg yolk, the remaining 2 tablespoons sugar, and the remaining ½ tablespoon flour for 3 minutes, or until creamy. Pour the cream cheese mixture over the chocolate mixture and, using a knife, swirl to marble.

4. Bake for 40 minutes, or until a wooden pick inserted in the center comes out clean. Remove the pan to a rack to cool completely. Cut into 16 pieces.

Fast Fix: *Quickly soften chilled cream cheese by sealing the cream cheese in a resealable plastic bag and immersing in hot water.*

	CALORIES	PROTEIN	CARBS	FIBER	SUGARS	FAT	SAT FAT	SODIUM
REAL FOOD	142	2 g	15 g	1 g	11 g	9 g	5 g	87 mg
FAKE FOOD	440	4 g	62 g	2 g	39 g	21 g	6 g	240 mg

COMPARED TO: Au Bon Pain Chocolate Chip Brownie

INGREDIENTS: Sugar, vegetable oil blend [(soybean, palm and olive oils), water, salt, milk, mono- and diglycerides, soy lecithin, sodium benzoate, natural and artificial flavors, vitamin A palmitate, beta-carotene for color], pasteurized whole eggs, wheat flour (bleached, enriched with niacin, reduced iron, thiamine mononitrate, riboflavin, folic acid), chocolate (sugar, chocolate liquor, cocoa butter, milk, soy lecithin, artificial flavor), chocolate chips (sugar, chocolate liquor, cocoa butter, soy lecithin, vanilla, salt, milk), cocoa powder, potassium sorbate, artificial vanilla flavor, baking soda.

COCONUT-ALMOND ENERGY BARS

SEE PHOTO ON PAGE 273.

PREP TIME: 10 MINUTES • TOTAL TIME: 25 MINUTES • MAKES 12 SERVINGS

1½ cups natural peanut butter

1 cup honey

1 teaspoon vanilla extract

2 cups old-fashioned rolled oats

1 cup unsweetened shredded coconut

½ cup whole raw almonds

½ cup whole raw cashews or peanuts

½ cup sesame seeds

½ cup raw sunflower seeds

½ cup chopped dates or raisins

1. Preheat the oven to 350°F. Coat a 13" x 9" baking pan with cooking spray.

2. In a large microwaveable bowl, microwave the peanut butter and honey for 2 minutes, stirring every 30 seconds, or until melted. Stir in the vanilla until smooth. Stir in the oats, coconut, almonds, cashews or peanuts, sesame seeds, sunflower seeds, and dates or raisins.

3. Spread into the pan, patting into place with wet hands if needed. Bake for 15 minutes, or until the edges of the bars turn golden brown. Do not overbake. The bars will still feel tacky in the center but will firm up as they cool.

Fast Fix: *Chop sticky dates and raisins without getting them stuck to your knife by coating it with cooking spray first.*

Bonus Benefit

Almonds do the body good. They have been shown to improve oxidative status, both in the short term and after long-term consumption.[17] Reducing the effects of oxidative stress on cells helps decrease your risk of inflammatory-related conditions, some types of cancers, and premature aging.

	CALORIES	PROTEIN	CARBS	FIBER	SUGARS	FAT	SAT FAT	SODIUM
REAL FOOD	311	8 g	30 g	5 g	18 g	20 g	5 g	26 mg
FAKE FOOD	370	3 g	46 g	1 g	30 g	19 g	8 g	230 mg

COMPARED TO: Tastykake Coconut Junior (Yellow Layer Cake with Coconut Topping)

INGREDIENTS: Sugar, vegetable shortening (soybean oil, palm oil, partially hydrogenated soybean oil, cottonseed oil, partially hydrogenated cottonseed oil, and/or hydrogenated cottonseed oil with TBHQ and citric acid added to preserve freshness), bleached enriched flour (wheat flour, niacin, reduced iron, thiamine mononitrate-b1, riboflavin-B2, folic acid), eggs, water, corn syrup, coconut (prepared with sodium meta-bisulfite to maintain color), high fructose corn syrup. Contains 2 percent or less of: dextrose, skim milk, food starch modified, leavening (sodium acid pyrophosphate, baking soda, monocalcium phosphate, calcium sulfate), mono- and diglycerides, natural and artificial flavors, salt, soy lecithin, polysorbate 60, xanthan gum, coconut oil, corn flour, potassium sorbate (to preserve freshness), sorbitan monostearate, nutmeg, cinnamon.

food imposters

PEANUT BUTTER THAT'S NOT PEANUT BUTTER

Peanut-flavored sugar oil doesn't have quite the same ring to it, but it's far more accurate a name than your average peanut butter. What shouldn't contain added sugar typically has at least two types, plus partially hydrogenated oil (code for trans fat). What should be on the ingredients list? Peanuts. Period.

Ingredients: Peanut butter [roasted peanuts, sugar, hydrogenated vegetable oils (cottonseed and rapeseed), molasses, salt, partially hydrogenated cottonseed oil], sugar, and honey.

CURRIED PEANUTS

PREP TIME: 5 MINUTES • TOTAL TIME: 5 MINUTES • MAKES 8 SERVINGS

2 teaspoons canola oil

1 cup dry-roasted unsalted peanuts

1 teaspoon curry powder

¼ onion, chopped

2 tablespoons chopped cilantro

⅛ teaspoon salt

Pinch of ground red pepper

In a skillet, heat the oil over medium heat. Add the peanuts and curry powder. Cook, stirring constantly, for 2 minutes, or until golden. Add the onion, cilantro, salt, and pepper. Cook for 2 minutes.

	CALORIES	PROTEIN	CARBS	FIBER	SUGARS	FAT	SAT FAT	SODIUM
REAL FOOD	120	4 g	5 g	2 g	1 g	10 g	1 g	38 mg
FAKE FOOD	170	6 g	6 g	3 g	2 g	15 g	1 g	115 mg

COMPARED TO: Blue Diamond Almonds Bold Wasabi & Soy Sauce

INGREDIENTS: Almonds, vegetable oil (canola, safflower and/or sunflower), sugar, modified corn starch, salt, soy sauce (soybean, wheat, salt), horseradish, onion, spice, fractionated coconut oil and/or palm kernel oil, garlic, maltodextrin, yeast extract, natural flavor, citric acid, disodium guanylate and disodium inosinate.

GARLIC CHILI POPCORN

PREP TIME: 5 MINUTES • TOTAL TIME: 10 MINUTES • MAKES 10 SERVINGS

2 tablespoons extra-virgin olive oil

1 clove garlic, minced

1 teaspoon red-pepper flakes

10 cups freshly popped popcorn
(about ½ cup dry)

Pinch of salt

1. In a small skillet, heat the oil over medium-low heat. Cook the garlic and red-pepper flakes for 2 minutes, or until the garlic is soft. Cool for 5 minutes.

2. Place the popcorn in a large bowl. Pour the oil mixture over the popcorn. Sprinkle with the salt. Toss to coat well.

Fast Fix: *To avoid soggy popcorn, remove the pan lid immediately after popping so that the steam does not condense on the lid and fall back into the pot of freshly popped popcorn.*

	CALORIES	PROTEIN	CARBS	FIBER	SUGARS	FAT	SAT FAT	SODIUM
REAL FOOD	57	1 g	6 g	12 g	0 g	3 g	0 g	16 mg
FAKE FOOD	150	2 g	16 g	2 g	0 g	9 g	4.5 g	290 mg

COMPARED TO: Pop Secret Movie Theater Butter Microwave Popcorn

INGREDIENTS: Whole grain popcorn, palm oil, salt, natural and artificial flavor [milk], color added, freshness preserved by TBHQ. Contains milk.

≈ food imposters ≈
GUM THAT'S NOT GUM

Sad news for habitual gum chompers: Most major brands are made from "gum base," a proprietary blend of synthetic rubbers and plastics, not the natural gums harvested from tropical trees. Plus, they're rife with artificial sweeteners.

Ingredients: Sorbitol, gum base, xylitol, glycerol, natural and artificial flavors, less than 2% of soy lecithin, hydrogenated starch hydrolysate, acesulfame K, sucralose, colors (red 40, 40 Lake), BHT (to maintain freshness), aspartame.

PARMESAN PITA CHIPS

PREP TIME: 10 MINUTES • TOTAL TIME: 20 MINUTES • MAKES 4 SERVINGS

2 multigrain pitas (6" diameter)

4 teaspoons extra-virgin olive oil

2 tablespoons grated Parmesan cheese

¼ teaspoon ground red pepper

1. Preheat the oven to 425°F. Coat 2 large baking sheets with cooking spray.

2. Split each pita horizontally into 2 rounds. Brush the cut sides with the oil. Sprinkle with the cheese and pepper.

3. Cut each round into 8 wedges and arrange oiled sides up on the baking sheets. Bake for 10 minutes, switching the sheets halfway through baking, or until golden.

Fast Fix: *Store these chips in an airtight container at room temperature for up to 3 days.*

	CALORIES	PROTEIN	CARBS	FIBER	SUGARS	FAT	SAT FAT	SODIUM
REAL FOOD	56	2 g	6 g	1 g	0 g	3 g	1 g	68 mg
FAKE FOOD	150	2 g	18 g	2 g	1 g	8 g	1 g	180 mg

COMPARED TO: Doritos Cool Ranch Flavored Tortilla Chips

INGREDIENTS: Corn, vegetable oil (corn, canola, and/or sunflower oil), maltodextrin (made from corn), salt, tomato powder, corn starch, lactose, whey, skim milk, corn syrup solids, onion powder, sugar, garlic powder, monosodium glutamate, cheddar cheese (milk, cheese cultures, salt, enzymes), dextrose, malic acid, buttermilk, natural and artificial flavors, sodium acetate, artificial color (including red 40, blue 1, yellow 5), sodium caseinate, spice, citric acid, disodium inosinate, and disodium guanylate.

CORN TORTILLA CHIPS

PREP TIME: 10 MINUTES • TOTAL TIME: 10 MINUTES • MAKES 8 SERVINGS

6 corn tortillas, each cut into 8 wedges   ¼ teaspoon salt

1. Preheat the oven to 425°F. Coat 2 large baking sheets with cooking spray.

2. Arrange the tortillas on the baking sheets and coat lightly with cooking spray. Sprinkle with the salt. Bake for 5 minutes, switching the sheets halfway through baking, or until golden.

Fast Fix: *Store these chips in an airtight container at room temperature for up to 3 days.*

	CALORIES	PROTEIN	CARBS	FIBER	SUGARS	FAT	SAT FAT	SODIUM
REAL FOOD	80	2 g	16 g	2 g	0 g	1 g	0 g	107 mg
FAKE FOOD	150	2 g	18 g	1 g	0 g	7 g	1 g	125 mg

COMPARED TO: Tostitos Stone-Ground White Corn Tortilla Chips Hint of Lime

INGREDIENTS: Corn, vegetable oil (corn, canola, and/or sunflower oil), maltodextrin (made from corn), salt, sugar, natural flavors (including natural lime flavor), dextrose, sour cream (cultured cream, skim milk), corn bran, whey, spice, and yeast extract.

ZUCCHINI CHIPS

PREP TIME: 10 MINUTES ● TOTAL TIME: 50 MINUTES ● SERVES: 4

2 zucchini

1 tablespoon olive oil

¼ teaspoon salt

¼ teaspoon garlic powder (optional)

1. Preheat the oven to 400°F. Coat 2 baking sheets with cooking spray.

2. Thinly slice the zucchini on the diagonal, about ⅛" thick. Place the slices in a large bowl and toss well with the oil, salt, and garlic powder (if using). Arrange in a single layer on the baking sheets.

3. Bake, turning often, for 25 minutes. Reduce the oven temperature to 300°F and bake for 10 minutes or until splotchy brown and crisp. Remove to paper towels and let cool. These will keep at room temperature, uncovered, for several hours.

	CALORIES	PROTEIN	CARBS	FIBER	SUGARS	FAT	SAT FAT	SODIUM
REAL FOOD	58	2 g	5 g	1 g	4 g	4 g	1 g	145 mg
FAKE FOOD	510	21 g	52 g	2 g	9 g	25 g	11 g	1,400 mg

COMPARED TO: Lay's Potato Chips Sour Cream & Onion

INGREDIENTS: Potatoes, vegetable oil (sunflower, corn, and/or canola oil), sour cream & onion seasoning (skim milk, salt, maltodextrin [made from corn], onion powder, whey, sour cream [cultured cream, skim milk], canola oil, parsley, natural flavor, lactose, sunflower oil, citric acid, whey protein, concentrate, and buttermilk)

BEAN DIP

PREP TIME: 5 MINUTES • TOTAL TIME: 5 MINUTES • MAKES 20 (2 TABLESPOONS) SERVINGS

2 cups cooked beans, such as cannellini, pinto, or great Northern

2 tablespoons extra-virgin olive oil

2 tablespoons prepared horseradish

¼ cup finely chopped onion

¼ teaspoon salt

2 scallions, finely chopped

In a blender or food processor, combine the beans, oil, horseradish, onion, and salt. Process until smooth, adding a little water if necessary. Garnish with the scallions.

	CALORIES	PROTEIN	CARBS	FIBER	SUGARS	FAT	SAT FAT	SODIUM
REAL FOOD	35	2 g	4 g	1 g	0 g	1 g	0 g	36 mg
FAKE FOOD	60	1 g	1 g	0 g	1 g	5 g	3 g	170 mg

COMPARED TO: Heluva Good! French Onion Dip

INGREDIENTS: Cultured pasteurized milk, cream & nonfat milk, onion seasoning (salt, dehydrated onion, sugar, monosodium glutamate, parsley, spices and soybean oil), modified corn starch, gelatin, potassium sorbate (to preserve freshness) and enzyme.

MEAL PLANS

SUNDAY

BREAKFAST

Crustless Breakfast Quiche
(page 74)

Orange wedges

Hot coffee/tea

LUNCH

Lentil and Spinach Soup (page 122)

Parmesan Pita Chips (page 300)

Pear

SNACK

Coconut Almond Energy Bars
(page 296)

DINNER

Pan-seared Pork Chops and Apples
(page 186)

Hearty Scalloped Potatoes (page 236)

Steamed Broccoli

Quick Coconut Rice Pudding
(page 246)

MONDAY

BREAKFAST

PB&J Smoothie (page 107)

Hot coffee/tea

LUNCH

Waldorf Salad in a Jar (page 124)

Whole grain bread

SNACK

Hummus

Vegetable sticks

DINNER

Cuban Picadillo (page 178)

Brown rice or quinoa

Green salad with choice of dressing from
page 126

Iced Spiced Cocoa Latte (page 291)

TUESDAY

BREAKFAST

Leftover Crustless Breakfast Quiche
from Sunday

Hot coffee/tea

LUNCH

Lentil and Spinach Soup from Sunday

Parmesan Pita Chips from Sunday

Grapes

SNACK

Coconut Almond Energy Bars from Sunday

DINNER

Steak Kebabs (page 184)

Couscous

Three-Ingredient Ice Cream (page 286)

WEDNESDAY

BREAKFAST

Plain Greek yogurt with berries
and sliced almonds

Hot coffee/tea

LUNCH

Turkey Panini (page 155)

Carrot and Celery Sticks

Orange

SNACK

Bean Dip (page 303)

Corn Tortilla Chips (page 301)

DINNER

Roasted Shrimp with Tomatoes and
Zucchini (page 216)

Green salad with choice of dressing from
page 126

Chocolate-Orange Mousse with
Raspberries (page 284)

MEAL PLANS (*continued*)

THURSDAY	FRIDAY
BREAKFAST	**BREAKFAST**
Herbed Scrambled Eggs (page 82)	Egg and Avocado Toast (page 83)
Whole grain Toast	Apple
Hot coffee/tea	Hot coffee/tea
LUNCH	**LUNCH**
Lentil and Spinach Soup from Sunday	Waldorf Salad in a Jar (page 124)
Parmesan Pita Chips from Sunday	Whole Grain Bread
Grapes	
SNACK	**SNACK**
Coconut Almond Energy Bars from Sunday	Hummus
	Vegetable sticks
DINNER	**DINNER**
Chicken Thighs with Creamy Spinach Artichoke Sauce (page 193)	Chicken Pad Thai (page 132)
Whole grain pasta	Strawberry Shortcake with Whipped Ricotta (page 256)
Green salad with choice of dressing from page 126	
Chocolate Pomegranate Clusters (page 293)	

SATURDAY

BREAKFAST

Ricotta Pancakes with Blueberries
(page 90)

Hot coffee/tea

LUNCH

Leftover Chicken Pad Thai from Saturday

Orange

SNACK

Garlic Chili Popcorn (page 299)

DINNER

Whole roasted chicken with favorite
seasonings

Roasted Vegetables (page 239)

Brown Rice Pilaf (page 246)

Lemon Pudding Cake (page 252)

ENDNOTES

CHAPTER 1

1   Boelsma E, Hendriks HFJ, Roza L. Nutritional skin care: health effects of micronutrients and fatty acids. *American Journal of Clinical Nutrition* May 2001;73(5):853–64, http://ajcn.nutrition.org/content/73/5/853.full.

2   Chaput JP. Sleep patterns, diet quality and energy balance. *Physiology and Behavior* July 2014;134:86–91 [Abstract], http://www.sciencedirect.com/science/article/pii/S0031938413002862.

3   Peuhkuri K, Sihvola N, Korpela R. Diet promotes sleep duration and quality. *Nutrition Research* May 2012;32(5):309–19, http://www.sciencedirect.com/science/article/pii/S0271531712000632.

4   McMillan L, Owen L, Kras M et al. Behavioural effects of a 10-day Mediterranean diet. Results from a pilot study evaluating mood and cognitive performance. *Appetite* February 2011;56(1):143–47, http://www.sciencedirect.com/science/article/pii/S0195666310006963.

5   Rogers PJ. A healthy body, a healthy mind: long-term impact of diet on mood and cognitive function. *Proceedings of the Nutrition Society* 28 February 2007;60(1):135–43, https://www.cambridge.org/core/journals/proceedings-of-the-nutrition-society /article/a-healthy-body-a-healthy-mind -long-term-impact-of-diet-on-mood-and -cognitive-function/922E117A057B6F1 B65FF420657099522.

6   Coffey JT, Brandle M, Zhou H et al. Valuing health-related quality of life in diabetes. *Diabetes Care* Dec 2002;25(12):2238–43 [Abstract] http://care.diabetesjournals.org /content/25/12/2238.short.

7   Revicki DA, Wood M, Maton PN et al. The impact of gastroesophageal reflux disease on health-related quality of life. *American Journal of Medicine* March 1998;104(3): 252–58 [Abstract].

8   Amarantos E, Martinez A, Dwyer J. Nutrition and quality of life in older adults. *Journals of Gerontology* 2001;56(Suppl 2): 54–64.

9   Katz DL, Meller S. Can we say what diet is best for health? *Annual Review of Public Health* March 2014;35:83–103, http://www.annualreviews.org/doi/full/10.1146 /annurev-publhealth-032013-182351.

10 Mujcic R, Oswald AJ. Evolution of well-being and happiness after increases in consumption of fruit and vegetables. *American Journal of Public Health* August 2016;106(8):1504–10, http://ajph.aphapublications.org/doi /abs/10.2105/AJPH.2016.303260.

11 Lesani A, Mohammadpoorasl A, Javadi M et al. Eating breakfast, fruit and vegetable intake and their relation with happiness in college students. *Eating and Weight Disorders: Studies on Anorexia, Bulimia and Obesity* December 2016; 21(4):645–51, http://link.springer.com/article/10.1007/s40519-016-0261-0.

12 Bowman SA, Gortmaker SL, Ebbeling CB et al. Effects of fast-food consumption on energy intake and diet quality among children in a national household survey. *Pediatrics* 2004;13(1):112–18.

13 Rosenheck R. Fast food consumption and increased caloric intake: a systematic review of a trajectory towards weight gain and obesity risk. *Obesity Reviews* 14 November 2008;9(6):535–47.

14 Jabs J, Devine CM. Time scarcity and food choices: an overview. *Appetite* September 2006;47(2):196–204, http://www.sciencedirect.com/science/article/pii/S0195666306003813.

15 Scholliers P. Convenience foods: what, why and when. *Appetite* February 2015;94:2–6, http://www.academia.edu/15324881/Convenience_foods_what_why_and_when.

16 Smith LP, Ng SW, Popkin BM. Trends in US home food preparation and consumption: analysis of national nutrition surveys and time use studies from 1965–1966 to 2007–2008. *Nutrition Journal* April 11, 2013;12:45, https://www.ncbi.nlm.nih.gov/pmc/articles/PMC3639863/.

17 Okrent AM, Kumcu A. U.S. households' demand for convenience foods. USDA, July 2016, https://www.ers.usda.gov/webdocs/publications/err211/err-211.pdf.

18 McDermott AJ, Stephens MB. Cost of eating: whole foods versus convenience foods in a low-income model. *Family Medicine* April 2010;42(4):280–84, http://www.stfm.org/fmhub/fm2010/April/Andrew280.pdf.

19 Ibid.

20 Cutler DM, Glaeser EL, Shapiro JM. Why have Americans become more obese? *Journal of Economic Perspectives* Summer 2003;17(3):93–118, http://pubs.aeaweb.org/doi/pdfplus/10.1257/089533003769204371.

21 Monteiro CA. Nutrition and health. The issue is not food, nor nutrients, so much as processing. *Public Health Nutrition* May 2009;12(5):729–31, https://www.cambridge.org/core/journals/public-health-nutrition/article/nutrition-and-health-the-issue-is-not-food-nor-nutrients-so-much-as-processing/0C514FC9DB264538F83D5D34A81BB10A.

22 Stuckler D, Nestle M. Big food, food systems, and global health. *PLOS Medicine* June 19, 2012, http://journals.plos.org/plosmedicine/article?id=10.1371/journal.pmed.1001242.

23 Lerner A, Matthias T. Changes in intestinal tight junction permeability associated with industrial food additives explain the rising incidence of autoimmune disease. *Autoimmunity Reviews* June 2015;14(6):479–89.

24 Cordain L., Eaton SB, Sebastian A et al. Origins and evolution of the Western diet: health implications for the 21st century. *American Journal of Clinical Nutrition* February 2005;81(2):341–54, http://ajcn.nutrition.org/content/81/2/341.full.

25 National Heart, Lung, and Blood Institute. What is metabolic syndrome? Updated June 22, 2016, http://www.nhlbi.nih.gov/health/health-topics/topics/ms.

26 Dandona P, Aljada A, Chaudhuri A et al. Metabolic syndrome: a comprehensive perspective based on interactions between obe-

sity, diabetes, and inflammation. *Circulation* 2005;111(11):1448–53, http://circ.ahajournals .org/content/111/11/1448.full.

27 Myles, IA. Fast food fever: reviewing the impacts of the Western diet on immunity. *Nutrition Journal* 2014;13(61), https:// nutritionj.biomedcentral.com/articles /10.1186/1475-2891-13-61.

28 Mosby TT, Cosgrove M, Sarkardei S et al. Nutrition in adult and childhood cancer: role of carcinogens and anti-carcinogens. *Anti-cancer Research* October 2012;32(10):4171– 92, http://ar.iiarjournals.org/content /32/10/4171.full.

29 Calle EE, Rodriguez C, Walker-Thurmond K et al. Overweight, obesity, and mortality from cancer in a prospectively studied cohort of U.S. adults. *New England Journal of Medicine* 24 April 2003;348(17):1625–38, http://www.nejm.org/doi/full/10.1056 /NEJMoa021423#t=article.

30 Mosby TT. Nutrition in adult and childhood cancer. 4171–92.

31 D'Elia L, Rossi G, Ippolito R et al. Habitual salt intake and risk of gastric cancer: a meta-analysis of prospective studies. *Clinical Nutrition* August 2012;31(4):489–98, http://www.sciencedirect.com/science /article/pii/S0261561412000052.

32 Tsugane S. Salt, salted food intake, and risk of gastric cancer: epidemiologic evidence. *Cancer Science* 13 January 2005;96(1):1–6, http://onlinelibrary.wiley.com/doi/10 .1111/j.1349-7006.2005.00006.x/full.

33 Kiecolt-Glaser JK. Stress, food, and inflammation: psychoneuroimmunology and nutrition at the cutting edge. *Psychosomatic Medicine* May 2010;72(4):365–69, https://www.ncbi.nlm.nih.gov/pmc /articles/PMC2868080/.

34 Sears B. Anti-inflammatory diets. *Journal of the American College of Nutrition* 2015;34(Suppl. 1):14–21, https://www.ncbi .nlm.nih.gov/pubmed/26400429.

35 Simopoulos AP. Omega-3 fatty acids in wild plants, nuts and seeds. *Asia Pacific Journal of Clinical Nutrition* September 2002;11(s6):S163–73, http://onlinelibrary .wiley.com/doi/10.1046/j.1440-6047.11.s.6.5 .x/full.

36 Xie H-L, Wu B-H, Xue W-Q et al. Greater intake of fruit and vegetables is associated with a lower risk of osteoporotic hip fractures in elderly Chinese: a 1:1 matched case–controlled study. *Osteoporosis International* November 2013;24(11):2827–36, http://link .springer.com/article/10.1007/s00198-013 -2383-9.

37 Lister CE, Skinner MA, Hunter DC. Fruits, vegetables and their phytochemicals for bone and joint health. *Current Topics in Nutraceutical Research* 2007;5(2/3):67–82, http://ctnr .newcenturyhealthpublishers.com/about/pdf /ctnrv5p67_82.pdf.

38 Hooshmand S, Arjmandi BH. Viewpoint: dried plum, an emerging functional food that may effectively improve bone health. *Ageing Research Reviews* April 2009;8(2):122–27, http://www.sciencedirect.com/science/article /pii/S156816370900004X.

39 Moodie R, Stuckler D, Monteiro C et al. Profits and pandemics: prevention of harmful effects of tobacco, alcohol, and ultra-processed food and drink industries. *Lancet* 1 March 2013;381(9867):670–79, http://www .sciencedirect.com/science/article/pii /S0140673612620893.

40 Reddy MB, Love M. The impact of food processing on the nutritional quality of vitamins and minerals. In Jackson LS, Knize MG,

Morgan JN. *Advances in Experimental Medicine and Biology* (Boston, MA: Springer, 1999), 459:99–106, http://link.springer.com /chapter/10.1007/978-1-4615-4853-9_7#page-1.

41 Patras A, Brunton NP, O'Donnell C et al. Effect of thermal processing on anthocyanin stability in foods; mechanisms and kinetics of degradation. *Trends in Food Science Technology* January 2010;21(1):3–11, http://www .sciencedirect.com/science/article/pii /S0924224409002271.

42 Ismail A, Marjan ZM, Foong CW. Total antioxidant activity and phenolic content in selected vegetables. *Food Chemistry* October 2004;87(4):581–86, http://www.sciencedirect .com/science/article/pii/S0308814604000366.

43 Skrede G, Wrolstad RE, Durst RW. Changes in anthocyanins and polyphenolics during juice processing of highbush blueberries (*Vaccinium corymbosum* L.). *Journal of Food Science* March 2000;65(2):357–64, http:// onlinelibrary.wiley.com/doi/10 .1111/j.1365-2621.2000.tb16007.x/abstract.

44 Slavin JL, Lloyd B. Health benefits of fruits and vegetables. *Advances in Nutrition* July 2012;3(4):506–16, http://advances.nutrition .org/content/3/4/506.full.

45 Kaczmarczyk MM, Miller MJ, Freund GG. The health benefits of dietary fiber: beyond the usual suspects of type 2 diabetes, cardiovascular disease and colon cancer. *Metabolism* August 2012;61(8):1058–66, https://www.ncbi.nlm.nih.gov/pmc/articles /MC3399949/.

46 Fujii H, Iwase M, Ohkuma T et al. Impact of dietary fiber intake on glycemic control, cardiovascular risk factors and chronic kidney disease in Japanese patients with type 2 diabetes mellitus: the Fukuoka Diabetes Registry. *Nutrition Journal* 2013;12(159),

https://nutritionj.biomedcentral.com /articles/10.1186/1475-2891-12-159.

47 Kaczmarczyk MM. The health benefits of dietary fiber. *Metabolism*. 2012 Aug;61(8):1058–66. doi: 10.1016/j .metabol.2012.01.017

48 Poti JM, Mendez MA, Ng SW et al. Is the degree of food processing and convenience linked with the nutritional quality of foods purchased by US households? *American Journal of Clinical Nutrition* 2015;101(6): 1251–62, http://ajcn.nutrition.org/content /early/2015/05/06/ajcn.114.100925.short.

49 Schulze MB, Manson JE, Ludwig DS et al. Sugar-sweetened beverages, weight gain, and incidence of type 2 diabetes in young and middle-aged women. *JAMA* August 2004;292(8):927–34, http://jamanetwork.com /journals/jama/fullarticle/199317.

50 Blekkenhorst LC, Prince RL, Hodgson JM et al. Dietary saturated fat intake and atherosclerotic vascular disease mortality in elderly women: a prospective cohort study. *American Journal of Clinical Nutrition* June 2015;10(6):1263–68, http://ajcn.nutrition.org /content/101/6/1263.short.

51 Rosqvist F, Iggman D, Kullberg J et al. Overfeeding polyunsaturated and saturated fat causes distinct effects on liver and visceral fat accumulation in humans. *Diabetes* November 2016;65(11):2356–68, http://diabetes.diabetesjournals.org /content/63/7/2356.short.

52 Kroenke CH, Kwan ML, Sweeney C et al. High- and low-fat dairy intake, recurrence, and mortality after breast cancer diagnosis. *Journal of the National Cancer Institute* 2013;105(9):616–23, http://jnci.oxford journals.org/content/105/9/616.full.

53 Violi F, Loffredo L, Angelico F et al. Extra

virgin olive oil use is associated with improved post-prandial blood glucose and LDL cholesterol in healthy subjects. *Nutrition & Diabetes* 20 July 2015;5:e172 http://www .nature.com/nutd/journal/v5/n7/abs /nutd201523a.html.

54 Schwingshackl L, Hoffmann G. Monounsaturated fatty acids, olive oil and health status: a systematic review and meta-analysis of cohort studies. *Lipids in Health and Disease* 1 October 2014;13:154, https://lipidworld .biomedcentral.com/articles/10.1186 /1476-511X-13-154.

55 Whitney E, Rolfes SR. *Understanding Nutrition,* 13th edition (Boston, MA: Cengage Learning, 2012), 109.

56 Mensink RP, Sanders TA, Baer DJ et al. The increasing use of interesterified lipids in the food supply and their effects on health parameters. *Advances in Nutrition* July 2016;7(4):719–29, http://advances.nutrition .org/content/7/4/719.abstract.

57 Zhang H, Jacobsen C, Adler-Nissen J. Storage stability study of margarines produced from enzymatically interesterified fats compared to margarines produced by conventional methods. *European Journal of Lipid Science and Technology* 4 August 2005;107(7-8): 530–39, http://onlinelibrary.wiley.com /doi/10.1002/ejlt.200501198/full.

58 Holm HC, Cowan D. The evolution of enzymatic interesterification in the oils and fats industry. *European Journal of Lipid Science and Technology* August 2008;110(8):679–91, http://onlinelibrary.wiley.com/doi/10.1002 /ejlt.200800100/full.

59 Harrison K, Marske AL. Nutritional content of foods advertised during the television programs children watch most. *American Journal of Public Health* September 2005;95(9):1568–74,

http://ajph.aphapublications.org/doi /abs/10.2105/AJPH.2004.048058.

60 He FJ, MacGregor GA. A comprehensive review on salt and health and current experience of worldwide salt reduction programmes. *Journal of Human Hypertension* 25 December 2009;23(6):363–84, http://www .nature.com/jhh/journal/v23/n6/full /jhh2008144a.html.

61 Doyle ME, Glass KA. Sodium reduction and its effect on food safety, food quality, and human health. *Comprehensive Reviews in Food Science and Food Safety* January 2010;9(1):44–56.

62. Kiefer MV, Hern HG, Alter HJ et al. Dextrose 10% in the treatment of out-of-hospital hypoglycemia. *Prehospital and Disaster Medicine* April 2014;29(2):190–194, https://www .cambridge.org/core/journals/prehospital -and-disaster-medicine/article/dextrose -10-in-the-treatment-of-out-of-hospital -hypoglycemia/897291789681CD46755 AD6F0B7BC2E5B.

63. Murphy-Gutekunst L. Hidden phosphorus-enhanced meats: part 3. *Journal of Renal Nutrition* October 2005;15(4):e1–e4, http: //www.jrnjournal.org/article/S1051-2276 (05)00119-6/fulltext?mobileUi=0.

64. Ramsey NB, Tuano KTS, Davis CM et al. Annatto seed hypersensitivity in a pediatric patient. *Annals of Allergy, Asthma & Immunology* Sept 2016;117(3):331–33, http://www .annallergy.org/article/S1081- 1206(16)30413-6/fulltext?rss=yes.

65. Ebo DG, Ingelbrecht S, Bridts CH et al. Allergy for cheese: evidence for an IgE-mediated reaction from the natural dye annatto. *Allergy* 2009;64(10):1558–60, http://onlinelibrary .wiley.com/doi/10.1111/j.1398-9995.2009 .02102.x/full.

66. Overview of food ingredients, additives & colors. U.S. Food & Drug Administration, revised April 2010, accessed December 13, 2016, http://www.fda.gov/Food/Ingredients PackagingLabeling/FoodAdditivesIngredients /ucm094211.htm#qanatural.

67. Maffini MV, Alger HM, Olson ED et al. Looking back to look forward: a review of FDA's food additives safety assessment and recommendations for modernizing its program. *Comprehensive Reviews in Food Science and Food Safety* July 2013;12(4):439–53, http://onlinelibrary.wiley.com/doi/10.1111 /1541-4337.12020/full.

CHAPTER 2

1 Liu RH. Whole grain phytochemicals and health. *Journal of Cereal Science* November 2007;46(3):207–19, http://www.sciencedirect .com/science/article/pii/S0733521007001166.

2 Fraga CG, Oteiza PI, Litterio MC et al. Phytochemicals as antioxidants: chemistry and health effects. *Ata Horticulturae* November 2012;939:63–69, https://www.scopus.com /record/display.uri?eid=2-s2.0-84872174163 &origin=inward&txGid=9045C49F989F- 035B17AC088A705680A4.wsnAw8kcdt7 IPYLO0V48gA%3a2.

3 Liu RH. Health benefits of fruit and vegetables are from additive and synergistic combinations of phytochemicals. *American Journal of Clinical Nutrition* September 2003;78(3):517S–20S, http://ajcn.nutrition. org/content/78/3/517S.full.

4 Whitney E and Rolfes SR. *Understanding Nutrition.* 13th Ed. 2013. Wadsworth, Cenage Learning. Belmont, CA.

5 Biesalski HK. Meat as a component of a healthy diet—are there any risks or benefits if meat is avoided? *Meat Science* July 2005;70(3):509–24, http://www.sciencedirect .com/science/article/pii/S0309174005000422.

6 Potera C. Red meat and colorectal cancer: exploring potential HCA connection. *Environmental Health Perspectives* October 2016;124(10):A189, https://www.ncbi.nlm .nih.gov/pmc/articles/PMC5047788/.

7 Li F, An S, Hou L et al. Red and processed meat intake and risk of bladder cancer: a meta-analysis. *International Journal of Clinical and Experimental Medicine* August 15, 2014;7(8):2100–10, https://www.ncbi.nlm .nih.gov/pubmed/25232394.

8 Mourouti N, Kontogianni MD, Papavagelis C et al. Meat consumption and breast cancer: a case-control study in women. *Meat Science* February 2015;100:195–201, http://www .sciencedirect.com/science/article/pii /S0309174014004677.

9 Micha R, Wallace SK, Mozaffarian D. Red and processed meat consumption and risk of incident coronary heart disease, stroke, and diabetes mellitus: a systematic review and meta-analysis. *Circulation* June 2010;121(21):2271–83, http://circ.ahajournals .org/content/121/21/2271?ijkey=1d4c8b52662 d45ce6d58dcb0103b03c6e0f7d6b6& keytype2=tf_ipsecsha.

10 Wu P-Y, Yang S-H, Wong T-C et al. Association of processed meat intake with hypertension risk in hemodialysis patients: a cross-sectional study. *PLOS ONE* October 30, 2015, journals.plos.org/plosone/article ?id=10.1371/journal.pone.0141917.

11 Eat more chicken, fish and beans. American Heart Association, published December 2, 2014, accessed December 14, 2016, http://www.heart.org/HEARTORG/HealthyLiving/HealthyEating/Nutrition/Eat-More-Chicken-Fish-and-Beans_UCM_320278_Article.jsp#.WGRDqe-QxMs.

12 American Cancer Society guidelines on nutrition and physical activity for cancer prevention. American Cancer Society, published February 5, 2016, accessed December 14, 2016, http://www.cancer.org/acs/groups/cid/documents/webcontent/002577-pdf.pdf.

13 Bouchenak M, Lamri-Senhadji M. Nutritional quality of legumes and their role in cardiometabolic risk prevention: a review. *Journal of Medicinal Food* March 2013;16(3):185–98, http://online.liebertpub.com/doi/abs/10.1089/jmf.2011.0238.

14 Quigley EMM. Gut bacteria in health and disease. *Gastroenterology & Hepatology* September 2013;9(9):560–69, https://www.ncbi.nlm.nih.gov/pmc/articles/PMC3983973/.

15 Wolfram T. Prebiotics and probiotics: creating a healthier you. *Academy of Nutrition and Dietetics,* published October 10, 2016, accessed December 14, 2016, http://www.eatright.org/resource/food/vitamins-and-supplements/nutrient-rich-foods/prebiotics-and-probiotics-the-dynamic-duo.

16 Selhub EM, Logan AC, Bested AC. Fermented foods, microbiota, and mental health: ancient practice meets nutritional psychiatry. *Journal of Physiological Anthropology* 15 January 2014;33(2), http://jphysiolanthropol.biomedcentral.com/articles/10.1186/1880-6805-33-2.

17 Tillisch K, Labus J, Kilpatrick L et al. Consumption of fermented milk product with probiotic modulates brain activity. *Gastroenterology* June 2013;144(7):1394–401.e4, http://www.gastrojournal.org/article/S0016-5085(13)00292-8/abstract?referrer=http%3A%2F%2Fjphysiolanthropol.biomedcentral.com%2Farticles%2F10.1186%2F1880-6805-33-2.

18 Selhub EM, Logan AC, Bested AC. Fermented foods, microbiota, and mental health. *Journal of Physiological Anthropology.* 2014;33(1):2.

19 Jukanti AK, Gaur PM, Gowda CL et al. Nutritional quality and health benefits of chickpea (*Cicer arietinum* L.): a review. *British Journal of Nutrition* August 2012;108(S1):S11–S26, https://www.cambridge.org/core/journals/british-journal-of-nutrition/article/nutritional-quality-and-health-benefits-of-chickpea-cicer-arietinum-l-a-review/BCD8920297E987AAABBC12BFF90EB0CF.

20 Guajardo-Flores D, Serna-Saldívar SO, Gutiérrez-Uribe JA. Evaluation of the antioxidant and antiproliferative activities of extracted saponins and flavonols from germinated black beans. *Food Chemistry* 2013;141:1497–1503, http://fulltext.study/article/1187178/Evaluation-of-the-antioxidant-and-antiproliferative-activities-of-extracted-saponins-and-flavonols-from-germinated-black-beans-Phaseolus-vulgaris-L.

21 Zhang B, Deng Z, Ramdath DD et al. Phenolic profiles of 20 Canadian lentil cultivars and their contribution to the antioxidant activity and inhibitory effects on glucosidase and pancreatic lipase. *Food Chemistry* April 1, 2015;172:862–72, https://www.ncbi.nlm.nih.gov/pubmed/25442631.

22 Dahl WJ, Foster LM, Tyler RT. Review of the health benefits of peas (*Pisum sativum* L.). *British Journal of Nutrition* August 2012;108(S1):S3–S10, https://www.ncbi.nlm.nih.gov/pubmed/22916813.

23 Fulgoni VL, Dreher M, Davenort AJ. Avocado consumption is associated with better diet quality and nutrient intake, and lower metabolic syndrome risk in US adults: results from the National Health and Nutrition Examination Survey (NHANES) 2001–2008. *Nutrition Journal* 2013;12:1, http://nutritionj.biomedcentral.com/articles/10.1186/1475-2891-12-1.

24 Ashton O, Wong M, McGhie TK et al. Pigments in avocado tissue and oil. *Journal of Agricultural and Food Chemistry* 2006;54(26):10151–58, http://pubs.acs.org/doi/abs/10.1021/jf061809j.

25 Moeller SM, Parekh N, Tinker L. Associations between intermediate age-related macular degeneration and lutein and zeaxanthin in the carotenoids in age-related eye disease study (CAREDS). *JAMA Ophthalmology* 2006;124(8):1151–62, http://jamanetwork.com/journals/jamaophthalmology/fullarticle/417829.

26 Marangoni F, Poli A. Phytosterols and cardiovascular health. *Pharmacological Research* March 2010;61(3):193–99, http://www.sciencedirect.com/science/article/pii/S1043661810000150.

27 Beltran-Sanchez H, Harhay MO, Harhay MM et al. Prevalence and trends of metabolic syndrome in the adult U.S. population, 1999–2010. *Journal of the American College of Cardiology* August 2013;62(8):697–703, http://content.onlinejacc.org/article.aspx?articleid=1709463.

28 Akhtar N, Haqqi TM. Current nutraceuticals in the management of osteoarthritis: a review. *Therapeutic Advances in Musculoskeletal Disease* June 2012;4(3):181–207, https://www.ncbi.nlm.nih.gov/pmc/articles/PMC3400101/.

29 Aviram M, Rosenblat M. Pomegranate protection against cardiovascular diseases. *Evidence-Based Complementary and Alternative Medicine* November 18, 2012;382763, https://www.ncbi.nlm.nih.gov/pmc/articles/PMC3514854/.

30 Akhtar N, Haqqi T Current nutraceuticals in the management of osteoarthritis. *Therapeutic Advances in Musculoskeletal Disease* 2012 Jun; 4(3): 181–207. doi: 10.1177/1759720X11436238

31 Su X, Sangster MY, D'Souza DH. Time-dependent effects of pomegranate juice and pomegranate polyphenols on foodborne viral reduction. *Foodborne Pathogens and Disease* November 2011;8(11):1177–83, https://www.ncbi.nlm.nih.gov/pubmed/21777065.

32 Chun OK, Kim D-O, Smith N et al. Daily consumption of phenolics and total antioxidant capacity from fruit and vegetables in the American diet. *Journal of the Science of Food and Agriculture* 15 August 2005;85(10):1715–24, http://onlinelibrary.wiley.com/doi/10.1002/jsfa.2176/full.

33 Razis AFA, Noor NM. Cruciferous vegetables: dietary phytochemicals for cancer prevention. *Asian Pacific Journal of Cancer Prevention* 2013;14(3):1565–70, https://www.researchgate.net/publication/236913780_Cruciferous_Vegetables_Dietary_Phytochemicals_for_Cancer_Prevention.

34 Ares AM, Nozal MJ, Bernal J. Extraction, chemical characterization and biological activity determination of broccoli health promoting compounds. *Journal of Chromatography A* 25 October 2013;1313:78–95, http://www.sciencedirect.com/science/article/pii/S0021967313010959.

35 Yan L. Dark green leafy vegetables. USDA, published August 13, 2016, accessed December 14, 2016, https://www.ars.usda.gov

/plains-area/gfnd/gfhnrc/docs/news-2013
/dark-green-leafy-vegetables/.

36 Tighe P, Duthie G, Vaughan N et al. Effect of increased consumption of whole-grain foods on blood pressure and other cardiovascular risk markers in healthy middle-aged persons: a randomized controlled trial. *American Journal of Clinical Nutrition* August 4, 2010;92(4):733–40, http://ajcn.nutrition.org /content/92/4/733.short.

37 Ye EQ, Chacko SA, Chou EL et al. Greater whole-grain intake is associated with lower risk of type 2 diabetes, cardiovascular disease, and weight gain. *Journal of Nutrition* May 30, 2012;142(7):1304–13.

38 Jacobs DR, Pereira MA, Meyer KA et al. Fiber from whole grains, but not refined grains, is inversely associated with all-cause mortality in older women: the Iowa women's health study. *Journal of the American College of Nutrition* June 2000;19(S3):326S–30S, https://www .ncbi.nlm.nih.gov/pubmed/10875605.

39 Aune D, Norat T, Romundstad P, Vatten LJ. Whole grain and refined grain consumption and the risk of type 2 diabetes: a systematic review and dose-response meta-analysis of cohort studies. *European Journal of Epidemiology* Nov 2013;28(11):845–58, https://www .ncbi.nlm.nih.gov/pubmed/24158434.

40 Aune D, Keum N, Giovannucci E et al. Whole grain consumption and risk of cardiovascular disease, cancer, and all cause and cause specific mortality: systematic review and dose-response meta-analysis of prospective studies. *British Medical Journal* June 14, 2016;353:i2716, https://www.ncbi.nlm.nih .gov/pubmed/27301975.

41 Zhou K, Su L, Yu L. Phytochemicals and antioxidant properties in wheat bran. *Journal of Agricultural and Food Chemistry* 2004;52(20):6108–14, http://pubs.acs.org/doi /abs/10.1021/jf049214g.

42 Jensen MK, Koh-Banerjee P, Hu FB et al. Intakes of whole grains, bran, and germ and the risk of coronary heart disease in men. *American Journal of Clinical Nutrition* December 2004;80(6):1492–99, http://ajcn.nutrition. org/content/80/6/1492.full.pdf+html.

43 Jacobs DR, Pereira MA, Meyer KA, Kushi LH. Fiber from whole grains. *Journal of the American College of Nutrition* 2000 June;19(3 Suppl):326S-330S.

44 Liu RH. Whole grain phytochemicals and health. *Journal of Cereal Science* November 2007;46(3):207–19, http://www.sciencedirect .com/science/article/pii/S0733521007001166.

45 Vinson JA, Cai Y. Nuts, especially walnuts, have both antioxidant quantity and efficacy and exhibit significant potential health benefits. *Food & Function* 2012;3:134–40, http://pubs.rsc.org/en/content/articlehtml /2012/fo/c2fo10152a.

46 Yang J. Brazil nuts and associated health benefits: a review. *LWT: Food Science and Technology* December 2009;42(10):1573–80, http://www.sciencedirect.com/science/article /pii/S0023643809001522.

47 Blomhoff R, Carlsen MH, Andersen LF et al. Health benefits of nuts: potential role of antioxidants. *British Journal of Nutrition* November 2006;96(S2):S52–S60, https://www .cambridge.org/core/journals/british-journal -of-nutrition/article/health-benefits -of-nuts-potential-role-of-antioxidants /73C2B58F9AE6CC08786078548018E30D.

48 Ibid.

49 Fiedor J, Burda K. Potential role of carotenoids as antioxidants in human health and disease.

Nutrients 2014;6(2):466–88, http://www.mdpi
.com/2072-6643/6/2/466/htm.

50 Phytochemicals: the cancer fighters in the
food we eat. *American Institute for Cancer
Research*, accessed December 14, 2016,
http://www.aicr.org/reduce-your-cancer-risk
/diet/elements_phytochemicals.html
?referrer=https://www.google.com/.

51 Ho CT. Phenolic compounds in food: an
overview. American Chemical Society, October 1, 1992, doi: 10.1021/bk-1992-0506 http://
www.denver-nutrition.com/pdf
/Phenolic-Study-1992.pdf.

52 Lila MA, Raskin I. Health-related interactions of phytochemicals. *Journal of Food
Science* January 2005; 70(1):R20–R27,
http://onlinelibrary.wiley.com/doi/10.1111
/j.1365-2621.2005.tb09054.x/abstract.

53 Poyrazoglu E, Gokmen V, Artik N. Organic
acids and phenolic compounds in pomegranates (*Punica granatum* L.) grown in Turkey.
Journal of Food Composition and Analysis
October 2002;15(5):567–75, http://www
.sciencedirect.com/science/article/pii/S0889
157502910719.

54 Wang L-S, Stoner GD. Anthocyanins and
their role in cancer prevention. *Cancer Let-
ters* October 8, 2008;269(2):281–90,
http://www.sciencedirect.com/science/article
/pii/S0304383508003960.

55 Zhang Y, Vareed SK, Nair MG. Human
tumor cell growth inhibition by nontoxic
anthocyanidins, the pigments in fruits and
vegetables. *Life Sciences* February 11,
2005;76(13):1465–72, http://www.science
direct.com/science/article/pii/S0024320
504009907.

56 He J, Giusti MM. Anthocyanins: natural colorants with health-promoting properties.

*Annual Review of Food Science and Technol-
ogy* April 2010;1:163–87, http://www.annual
reviews.org/doi/full/10.1146/annurev.food
.080708.100754.

57 Bouchenak M, Lamri-Senhadji M. Nutritional quality of legumes, and their role in
cardiometabolic risk prevention: a review.
Journal of Medicinal Food February
2013;16(3), https://www.researchgate.net
/publication/235519730_Nutritional_Quality
_of_Legumes_and_Their_Role_in_Cardio
metabolic_Risk_Prevention_A_Review

58 Liu RH. Whole grain phytochemicals and
health. *Journal of Cereal Science* November
2007;46(3):207–19, http://www.science
direct.com/science/article/pii/S073352
1007001166.

59 Belobrajdic D, Bird AR. The potential role
of phytochemicals in wholegrain cereals for
the prevention of type-2 diabetes. *Nutrition
Journal* 2013;12:62, https://nutritionj.bio
medcentral.com/articles/10.1186
/1475-2891-12-62.

60 Bolling BW, Oliver Chen C-Y, McKay DL et
al. Tree nut phytochemicals. *Nutrition
Research Reviews* December 2011;24(2):
244–75, https://www.cambridge.org/core
/journals/nutrition-research-reviews
/article/tree-nut-phytochemicals
-composition-antioxidant-capacity
-bioactivity-impact-factors-a-systematic
-review-of-almonds-brazils-cashews
-hazelnuts-macadamias-pecans-pine
-nuts-pistachios-and-walnuts/F28DC9C
F2246C09ACEFBDF41623CAB63.

61 Sciullo EM, Vogel CF, Wu D et al. Effects of
selected food phytochemicals in reducing the
toxic actions of TCDD and p,p'-DDT in U937
macrophages. Archives of Toxicology Decem-

ber 2010;84(12):957–66, https://www.ncbi.nlm
.nih.gov/pmc/articles/PMC2991151/.

62 Gupta VK, Singh S, Agrawal A et al. Phytochemicals mediated remediation of neurotox-
icity induced by heavy metals. *Biochemistry
Research International* 2015;(2015)ID 534769,
https://www.hindawi.com/journals
/bri/2015/534769/.

CHAPTER 3

1 Corn muffin mix. Jiffymix.com, accessed
December 14, 2016, http://www.jiffymix
.com/product.php/12/corn_muffin_mix.

2 Description
Perdue Breaded Freshly Prepared Chicken,
Fresh 100% Perdue white meat chicken, No
Fillers, Fully Cooked, 0 grams Trans Fat
[package insert]. Salisbury, Maryland: Perdue
Farms; 2016.
Ingredients
Boneless Skinless Chicken Breast With Rib
Meat, Water, Bleached Wheat Flour, Enriched
Wheat Flour (Enriched With Niacin,
Reduced Iron, Thiamine Mononitrate, Ribo-
flavin, Folic Acid), Yellow Corn Flour, Yellow
Corn Meal. Contains 2% Or Less Of Salt,
Potassium Lactate, Sodium Lactate, Dex-
trose, Sugar, Dried Whey, Sodium Phos-
phates, Flavor, Sodium Diacetate, Leavening
(Sodium Acid Pyrophosphate, Sodium Bicar-
bonate), Yeast, Calcium Propionate (To Pro-
tect Freshness), Extractives Of Paprika,
Potassium Sorbate (To Protect Freshness),
Soybean Oil, Guar Gum, Colored With Oleo-
resin Paprika.

3 Bailey RL, Parker EA, Rhodes DG et al. Esti-
mating sodium and potassium intakes and
their ratio in the American diet: data from
the 2011–2012 NHANES. *Journal of Nutrition*
2016;146(4):745–50, http://jn.nutrition
.org/content/early/2016/03/09/jn.115.221184
.abstract.

4 Carrigan A, Klinger A, Choquette SS et al.
Contribution of food additives to sodium and
phosphorus content of diets rich in processed
foods. *Journal of Renal Nutrition* January
2014;24(1):13–19.e1, http://www.science
direct.com/science/article/pii/S105122
7613001659.

5 Buttermilk complete mix [package insert].
Aunt Jemima.com, Purchase, New York:
PepsiCo; 2016, accessed November 16, 2016,
http://www.auntjemima.com/products
/pancake_waffle_mixes/buttermilk_complete.

6 Reddy MB, Love M. The impact of food processing on the nutritional quality of vitamins
and minerals. In Jackson Lauren S, Knize
Mark G, Morgan Jeffrey N. *Advances in
Experimental Medicine and Biology* (Boston,
MA: Springer, 1999), 459:99–106, http://link
.springer.com/chapter/10.1007/978-1-4615
-4853-9_7#page-1.

7 Larson NI, Story MT, Nelson MC. Neighbor-
hood environments: disparities in access to
healthy foods in the U.S. *American Journal of
Preventive Medicine* January 2009;36(1):
74–81, http://www.sciencedirect.com/science
/article/pii/S0749379708008386.

8 Stern D, Ng SW, Popkin BM. The nutrient
content of U.S. household food purchases by
store type. *American Journal of Preventive
Medicine* February 2016;50(2):180–90
[Abstract], http://www.ajpmonline.org
/article/S0749-3797(15)00415-8/abstract.

9 Bustillos B, Sharkey JR, Anding J et al. Availability of more healthful food alternatives in
traditional, convenience, and nontraditional
types of food stores in two rural Texas coun-
ties. *Journal of the America Dietetic Association* May 2009;109(5):883–89, http://www
.sciencedirect.com/science/article/pii/S000
2822309001576.

10 http://www.mayoclinic.org/healthy-lifestyle
/nutrition-and-healthy-eating/expert-blog
/clean-eating/bgp-20200665

11 Meat and poultry labeling terms. USDA, published August 10, 2015, accessed November
14, 2016, http://www.fsis.usda.gov/wps
/portal/fsis/topics/food-safety-education
/get-answers/food-safety-fact-sheets/food
-labeling/meat-and-poultry-labeling-terms
/meat-and-poultry-labeling-terms/!ut/p/a1
/jZDNCsIwEISfxQcI2doqepSCtFVbRNS
Yi6ya1kCblCYq-vRaREHxp7unZb5hh6GcM
soVHmWGVmqFeX3z7hqm0HX6PkRJ3xlC
GC-mycj3oTfr3IDVDyB2G_q_zAD--aMG
D9rVxJ9klJdo90SqVFOWCUtQmZOoDGW
p1jtiMBX2TFLcWmL2QtiHkONG5FJllBU
Ca9eOlPqQ2-r8lIgVVWH-A0vKX-OC
c9swdmdeEMUuJN478KHPO_C9sLKYs
8t4EIAMW1dofMrM/#4.

12 Grass fed small and very small producer program. USDA, accessed December 14, 2016,
https://www.ams.usda.gov/services/auditing
/grass-fed-SVS.

13 Meat and poultry labeling terms. USDA.

14 Forman J, Silverstein J., Committee on Nutrition, Council on Environmental Health.
Organic foods: health and environmental
advantages and disadvantages. *Pediatrics*
November 2012;130(5):e1406–15,
http://pediatrics.aappublications.org
/content/130/5/e1406.short.

15 Organic labeling. USDA, accessed December
14, 2016, https://www.ams.usda.gov
/rules-regulations/organic/labeling.

16 Vinha AF, Barreira SVP, Costa ASG et al.
Organic versus conventional tomatoes: influ-
ence on physicochemical parameters, bioactive compounds and sensorial attributes.
Food and Chemical Toxicology May
2014;67:139–44, http://www.sciencedirect
.com/science/article/pii/S0278691514000982.

17 Oliveira AB, Moura CFH, Gomes-Filho E et
al. The impact of organic farming on quality
of tomatoes is associated to increased oxidative stress during fruit development. *PLOS
ONE* February 20, 2013, http://journals.plos
.org/plosone/article?id=10.1371/journal
.pone.0056354.

18 Friedman M. Anticarcinogenic, cardioprotective, and other health benefits of tomato
compounds lycopene, α-tomatine, and toma-
tidine in pure form and in fresh and processed tomatoes. *Journal of Agricultural and
Food Chemistry* 2013;61(40):9534–50,
http://pubs.acs.org/doi/abs/10.1021/jf402654e.

19 Oliveira AB. The impact of organic farming
on quality of tomatoes.

20 Williams CM. Nutritional quality of organic
food: shades of grey or shades of green? *Proceedings of the Nutrition Society* February
2002;61(1):19–24, https://www.cambridge
.org/core/journals/proceedings-of-the
-nutrition-society/article/nutritional
-quality-of-organic-food-shades-of-grey
-or-shades-of-green/FFE1784B44530E4
F9C828A265C776ABB.

21 Crecente-Campo J, Nunes-Damaceno M,
Romero-Rodríguez MA et al. Color, anthocyanin pigment, ascorbic acid and total phenolic compound determination in organic

versus conventional strawberries. *Journal of Food Composition and Analysis* November 2012;28(1):23–30, http://www.sciencedirect.com/science/article/pii/S0889157512001159.

22 He J, Guisti M. Anthocyanins: natural colorants with health-promoting properties. *Annual Review of Food Science and Technology* April 2010;1:163–87, http://www.annualreviews.org/doi/full/10.1146/annurev.food.080708.100754.

23 Shimada A, Cairns BE, Vad N et al. Headache and mechanical sensitization of human pericranial muscles after repeated intake of monosodium glutamate (MSG). *Journal of Headache and Pain* 2013;14(1):2, doi:10.1186/1129-2377-14-2, http://thejournalofheadacheandpain.springeropen.com/articles/10.1186/1129-2377-14-2.

24 Shi Z, Taylor AW, Wittert GA. Re. Association between monosodium glutamate intake and sleep-disordered breathing among Chinese adults with normal body weight: emerging opportunities for research on monosodium glutamate intake and health at a population level. Nutrition. October 2013;29(10):1276–77, doi:10.1016/j.nut.2013.04.002, https://www.ncbi.nlm.nih.gov/pubmed/23800569.

25 Holton KF, Taren DL, Thomson CA et al. The effect of dietary glutamate on fibromyalgia and irritable bowel symptoms. *Clinical and Experimental Rheumatology* 2012;30(6 Suppl 74):10–17, https://www.ncbi.nlm.nih.gov/pubmed/22766026.

26 Meat and poultry labeling terms. USDA.

27 Guidance for industry: a food labeling guide (6. Ingredient lists). U.S. FDA, published January 13, 2013, accessed December 14, 2016, http://www.fda.gov/Food/Guidance Regulation/GuidanceDocuments RegulatoryInformation/LabelingNutrition/ucm064880.htm#ingredient.

28 How to understand and use the Nutrition Facts label. U.S. FDA, published May 25, 2016, accessed December 14, 2016, http://www.fda.gov/Food/Ingredients PackagingLabeling/LabelingNutrition/ucm274593.htm.

29 Guidance for industry: a food labeling guide (6. Ingredient lists). U.S. FDA.

30 Chenhall C. Improving cooking and food preparation skills: a synthesis of the evidence to inform program and policy development. Health Canada, published 2010, accessed December 14, 2016, http://www.hc-sc.gc.ca/fn-an/nutrition/child-enfant/cfps-acc-synthes-eng.php#a42.

31 Hartmann C, Dohle S, Siegrist M. Importance of cooking skills for balanced food choices. *Appetite* June 1, 2013;65:125–31, http://www.sciencedirect.com/science/article/pii/S0195666313000457.

32 Van der Horst K, Brunner TA, Siegrist M. Ready-meal consumption: associations with weight status and cooking skills. *Public Health Nutrition* February 2011;14(2):239–45, https://www.cambridge.org/core/journals/public-health-nutrition/article/ready-meal-consumption-associations-with-weight-status-and-cooking-skills/A6CB7B703AC51F95976CD1E07965ECC8.

33 Chenhall C. Improving cooking and food preparation skills. Health Canada.

34 Yusufov M, Prochaska JO, Paiva AL et al. Baseline predictors of singular action among participants with multiple health behavior risks. *American Journal of Health Promotion* May 2016;30(5):365–73,

https://www.researchgate.net/publication
/303093622_Baseline_Predictors_of_Singular
_Action_Among_Participants_With
_Multiple_Health_Behavior_Risks.

35 Keski-Rahkonen A, Kaprio J, Rissanen A et al.
Breakfast skipping and health-compromising
behaviors in adolescents and adults.
European Journal of Clinical Nutrition
2003;57:842–53, http://www.nature.com/ejcn
/journal/v57/n7/full/1601618a.html.

36 Fardet A. New hypotheses for the health
-protective mechanisms of whole-grain cereals: what is beyond fibre? *Nutrition Research
Reviews* June 2010;23(1):65–134, https://www
.cambridge.org/core/journals/nutrition
-research-reviews/article/new-hypotheses
-for-the-health-protective-mechanisms-of
-whole-grain-cereals-what-is-beyond-fibre
/CADD660D4B3EADC44D58D
DA91C78D30D.

37 Ross AB, Bruce SJ, Blondel-Lubrano A et al.
A whole-grain cereal-rich diet increases
plasma betaine, and tends to decrease total
and LDL-cholesterol compared with a
refined-grain diet in healthy subjects. *British
Journal of Nutrition* May 2011;105(10):
1492–1502, https://www.cambridge.org/core
/journals/british-journal-of-nutrition/article/a
-whole-grain-cereal-rich-diet-increases-plasma
-betaine-and-tends-to-decrease-total-and
-ldl-cholesterol-compared-with-a-refined
-grain-diet-in-healthy-subjects/8DF164827
D817910B1A80EE5096162F8.

38 Betaine (trimethylglycine). University of
Michigan Health System, published March
24, 2015, accessed December 14, 2016,
http://www.uofmhealth.org/health-library
/hn-2807004.

39 Jacobs DR, Pereira MA, Meyer KA et al. Fiber
from whole grains, but not refined grains, is
inversely associated with all-cause mortality
in older women: the Iowa Women's Health
Study. *Journal of the American College of
Nutrition* 14 June 2013;19(Suppl 3):326S–30S,
http://www.tandfonline.com/doi/abs/10.1080
/07315724.2000.10718968.

40 De Carvalho FG, de Santos R, De Carvalho
AL et al. Quinoa or corn flakes to prevent
peripheral inflammation after menopause?
Journal of Obesity & Eating Disorders
November 2015;1(2):4, http://obesity
.imedpub.com/quinoa-or-corn-flakes-to
-prevent-peripheral-inflammation-after
-menopause.php?aid=7484.

41 Liu S, Sesso HD, Manson JE et al. Is intake of
breakfast cereals related to total and
cause-specific mortality in men? *American
Journal of Clinical Nutrition* March
2003;77(3):594–99, http://ajcn.nutrition.org
/content/77/3/594.full.

42 Jacobs DR. Fiber from whole grains.

CHAPTER 4

1   Chagas P, Caramori P, Galdino TP et al.
(2013). Egg consumption and coronary atherosclerotic burden. *Atherosclerosis* August
2013;229(2):381–84, doi:10.1016/j.athero
sclerosis.2013.05.008.

2   Kozarski M, Klaus A, Jakovljevic D et al.
Antioxidants of edible mushrooms. *Molecules*
2015;20(10):19489–525, http://www.mdpi
.com/1420-3049/20/10/19489/htm.

3   Guajardo-Flores D, Serna-Saldívar SO,

Gutiérrez-Uribe JA. (2013). Evaluation of the antioxidant and antiproliferative activities of extracted saponins and flavonols from germinated black beans (*Phaseolus vulgaris* L.). *Food Chemistry* 2013;141(2):1497–1503, doi:10.1016/j.foodchem.2013.04.010.

4   Kraus V. Faculty of 1000 evaluation for randomized double-blind crossover study of the efficacy of a tart cherry juice blend in treatment of osteoarthritis (OA) of the knee. *F1000: Post-Publication Peer Review of the Biomedical Literature* 2013, doi:10.3410/f.718016430.793482015.

5   Nishi S, Kendall CW, Gascoyne A et al. Effect of almond consumption on the serum fatty acid profile: a dose-response study. *British Journal of Nutrition* 2014;112(07):1137–46, doi:10.1017/s0007114514001640.

6   Forbes-Hernandez TY, Gasparrini M, Afrin S et al. The healthy effects of strawberry polyphenols: which strategy behind antioxidant capacity? *Critical Reviews in Food Science and Nutrition* 2015;56(Suppl 1), doi:10.1080/10408398.2015.1051919.

7   Shukitt-Hale B, Bielinski DF, Lau FC et al. The beneficial effects of berries on cognition, motor behaviour and neuronal function in ageing. *British Journal of Nutrition* 2015; 114(10):1542–49, doi:10.1017/s0007114515003451.

CHAPTER 5

1   Vinha AF, Barreira SV, Costa AS et al. Pre-meal tomato (*Lycopersicon esculentum*) intake can have anti-obesity effects in young women? *International Journal of Food Sciences and Nutrition* December 2014;65(8):1019–26, doi:10.3109/09637486.2014.950206.

2   Suleria HA, Butt MS, Anjum FM et al. Onion: Nature protection against physiological threats. *Critical Reviews in Food Science and Nutrition* 2015;55(1):50–66, doi:10.1080/10408398.2011.646364.

3   Li PG, Mu TH, Deng L. Anticancer effects of sweet potato protein on human colorectal cancer cells. *World Journal of Gastroenterology* 7 June 2013;19(21):3300–8, doi:10.3748/wjg.v19.i21.3300.

4   Bahramsoltani R, Farzaei MH, Farahani MS et al. Phytochemical constituents as future antidepressants: a comprehensive review. *Reviews in the Neurosciences* 2015;26(6):699–719, doi:10.1515/revneuro-2015-0009.

5   Kim JE, Gordon SL, Ferruzzi MG et al. Effects of egg consumption on carotenoid absorption from co-consumed, raw vegetables. *American Journal of Clinical Nutrition* 27 May 2015;102(1):75–83, doi: 10.3945/ajcn.115.111062.

6   Wahyuni Y, Ballester A-R, Sudarmonowati E et al. Secondary metabolites of *Capsicum* species and their importance in the human diet. *Journal of Natural Products* 2013;76(4):783–93, doi:10.1021/np300898z.

7   Mozaffarieh, M, Sacu, S, and Wedrich, A (2003). The role of the carotenoids, lutein, and zeaxanthin in protecting against age-related macular degeneration: A review based on controversial evidence. *Nutrition Journal* 2(1). doi:10.1186/1475-2891-2-20

8   Figueiredo SD, Binda N, Nogueira-Machado J et al. The antioxidant properties of organosulfur compounds (sulforaphane). *Recent*

Patents on Endocrine, Metabolic & Immune Drug Discovery 2015;9(1):24–39, doi:10.2174/1 872214809666150505164138.

9 Wien M, Haddad E, Oda K et al. A randomized 3x3 crossover study to evaluate the effect of Hass avocado intake on post-ingestive satiety, glucose and insulin levels, and subsequent energy intake in overweight adults. *Nutrition Journal* 2013;12(1):155, doi:10.1186/1475-2891-12-155.

10 Zheng, H. et al. (2015). Metabolomics Investigation to Shed Light on Cheese as a Possible Piece in the French Paradox Puzzle. *Journal of Agricultural and Food Chemistry*, 63(10), 2830–39. doi:10.1021/jf505878a

11 Dosil-Díaz O, Ruano-Ravina A, Gestal-Otero JJ et al. Consumption of fruit and vegetables and risk of lung cancer: a case-control study in Galicia, Spain. *Nutrition* 2008;24(5):407–13, doi:10.1016/j.nut.2008.01.005.

12 Sewram V, Sitas F, O'Connell D et al. Diet and esophageal cancer risk in the Eastern Cape Province of South Africa. *Nutrition and Cancer* 2014;66(5):791–99, doi:10.1080/016355 81.2014.916321.

13 Rigacci S. Olive oil phenols as promising multi-targeting agents against Alzheimer's disease. *Advances in Experimental Medicine and Biology* 2015;863:1–20, doi:10.1007/978-3 -319-18365-7_1.

CHAPTER 6

1 Bayan L, Koulivand PH, Gorji A. Garlic: a review of potential therapeutic effects. *Avicenna Journal of Phytomedicine* 2014;4(1): 1–14.

2 Symons T, Schutzler S, Cocke T et al. Aging does not impair the anabolic response to a protein-rich meal. *American Journal of Clinical Nutrition* 2007;86:451–6.

3 Guasch-Ferre M, Hruby A, Salas-Salvado J et al. (2015). Olive oil consumption and risk of type 2 diabetes in US women. *American Journal of Clinical Nutrition* 2015;102(2):479–86, doi:10.3945/ajcn.115.112029.

4 Cassidy A, Mukamal KJ, Liu L et al. (2013). High anthocyanin intake is associated with a reduced risk of myocardial infarction in young and middle-aged women. *Circulation* 15 January 2013;127(2):188–96, doi:10.1161 /circulationaha.112.122408.

5 Chicken: the preferred protein for your health and budget! (n.d.). Retrieved January 23, 2017, http://www.nationalchickencouncil .org/chicken-the-preferred-protein-for-your -health-and-budget/.

6 Cassidy A, Rimm EB, O'Reilly EJ et al. Dietary flavonoids and risk of stroke in women. *Stroke* 23 February 2012, doi: 10.1161 /STROKEAHA.111.637835.

7 Feeney MJ, Dwyer J, Hasler-Lewis CM et al. Mushrooms and health summit proceedings. *Journal of Nutrition* 2014;144(7):1128S–36S, http://doi.org/10.3945/jn.114.190728.

8 Guajardo-Flores D, Serna-Saldívar SO, Gutiérrez-Uribe JA. (2013). Evaluation of the antioxidant and antiproliferative activities of extracted saponins and flavonols from germinated black beans (*Phaseolus vulgaris* L.). *Food Chemistry* 15 November 2013;141(2):1497–503, doi:10.1016/j.foodchem .2013.04.010.

9 Bartels E, Folmer V, Bliddal H et al. Efficacy and safety of ginger in osteoarthritis patients:

a meta-analysis of randomized placebo-controlled trials. *Osteoarthritis and Cartilage* 2015;23(1):13–21, doi:10.1016/j.joca.2014.09.024.

10 Sahebkar A, Serban C, Ursoniu S et al. Effect of garlic on plasma lipoprotein(a) concentrations: a systematic review and meta-analysis of randomized controlled clinical trials. *Nutrition* 2016;32(1):33–40, doi:10.1016/j.nut.2015.06.009.

11 Farzaei MH, Abbasabadi Z, Ardekani MR et al. Parsley: a review of ethnopharmacology, phytochemistry and biological activities. *Journal of Traditional Chinese Medicine* 2013;33(6):815–26, doi:10.1016/s0254-6272(14)60018-2.

12 Unlu, N. et al, (2007). Lycopene from heat-induced cis-isomer-rich tomato sauce is more bioavailable than from all-trans-rich tomato sauce in human subjects. *British Journal of Nutrition* 98(1), 140–46. doi:10.1017/S0007114507685201

13 Sun J, Buys N. Effects of probiotics consumption on lowering lipids and CVD risk factors: a systematic review and meta-analysis of randomized controlled trials. *Annals of Medicine* 2015;47(6):430–40, doi:10.3109/07853890.2015.1071872.

14 Dietary nutrient intakes and skin-aging appearance among middle-aged American women. (n.d.). Retrieved March 10, 2017, from https://www.ncbi.nlm.nih.gov/pubmed/17921406

15 Turati F, Rossi M, Pelucchi C et al. Fruit and vegetables and cancer risk: a review of southern European studies. *British Journal of Nutrition* 2015;113(S2), doi:10.1017/s0007114515000148.

16 Age-Related Eye Disease Study Research Group. A randomized, placebo-controlled, clinical trial of high-dose supplementation with vitamins C and E and beta carotene for age-related cataract and vision loss. *Archives of Ophthalmology* October 2001;119(10):1439–52, doi:10.1001/archopht.119.10.1439.

17 Whelton PK, He J. Health effects of sodium and potassium in humans. *Current Opinion in Lipidology* 2014;25(1):75–79, doi:10.1097/mol.0000000000000033.

18 Lagiou P. Faculty of 1000 evaluation for salt intake, stroke, and cardiovascular disease: meta-analysis of prospective studies. *F1000: Post-Publication Peer Review of the Biomedical Literature,* doi:10.3410/f.1346961.818059.

19 Aburto NJ, Hanson S, Gutierrez H et al. Effect of increased potassium intake on cardiovascular risk factors and disease: systematic review and meta-analyses. *BMJ* 2013;346:f1378, doi:10.1136/bmj.f1378.

20 Aviram M, Eias K. Dietary olive oil reduces low-density lipoprotein uptake by macrophages and decreases the susceptibility of the lipoprotein to undergo lipid peroxidation. *Annals of Nutrition and Metabolism* 1993;37(2):75–84, doi:10.1159/000177753.

21 Sales-Campos H, Souza PR, Peghini BC et al. An overview of the modulatory effects of oleic acid in health and disease. *Mini-Reviews in Medicinal Chemistry* 2013;13(2):201–10, doi:10.2174/1389557511313020003.

22 Laribi B, Kouki K, M'hamdi M et al. Coriander (*Coriandrum sativum* L.) and its bioactive constituents. *Fitoterapia* June 2015;103:9–26, doi:10.1016/j.fitote.2015.03.012.

23 Rebello CJ, Johnson WD, Martin CK et al. Acute effect of oatmeal on subjective measures of appetite and satiety compared to a ready-to-eat breakfast cereal: a randomized crossover trial. *Journal of the American College of Nutrition* 2013;32(4):272–79, doi:10.1080/07315724.2013.816614.

CHAPTER 7

1   Luu HN, Blot WJ, Xiang YB et al. Prospective evaluation of the association of nut/peanut consumption with total and cause-specific mortality. *JAMA Internal Medicine* May 2015;175(5):755–66.

2   Devore EE, Kang JH, Breteler MM et al. Dietary intakes of berries and flavonoids in relation to cognitive decline. *Annals of Neurology* 2012;72(1):135–43, doi:10.1002 /ana.23594.

3   Mursu J, Virtanen JK, Tuomainen T et al. Intake of fruit, berries, and vegetables and risk of type 2 diabetes in Finnish men: the Kuopio Ischaemic Heart Disease Risk Factor Study. *American Journal of Clinical Nutrition* 2013;99(2):328–33, doi:10.3945/ajcn.113 .069641.

4   Hyson DA. A comprehensive review of apples and apple components and their relationship to human health. *Advances in Nutrition: An International Review Journal* 2011;2(5):408–20, doi:10.3945/an.111 .000513.

5   Koutsos A, Tuohy K, Lovegrove J. Apples and cardiovascular health—is the gut microbiota a core consideration? *Nutrients* 2015;7(6):3959–98, doi:10.3390/nu7063959.

6   Rebello CJ, Johnson WD, Martin CK et al. Acute effect of oatmeal on subjective measures of appetite and satiety compared to a ready-to-eat breakfast cereal: a randomized crossover trial. *Journal of the American College of Nutrition* 2013;32(4):272–79, doi:10.1080/07315724.2013.816614.

7   Meydani M. Potential health benefits of avenanthramides of oats. *Nutrition Reviews* 2009;67(12):731–35, doi:10.1111/j.1753-4887 .2009.00256.x.

8   Saberi F, Sadat Z, Abedzadeh-Kalahroudi M et al. Effect of ginger on relieving nausea and vomiting in pregnancy: a randomized, placebo-controlled trial. *Nursing and Midwifery Studies* 2014;3(1), doi:10.17795 /nmsjournal11841.

9   Dabaghzadeh F, Khalili H, Dashti-Khavidaki S. Ginger for prevention or treatment of drug-induced nausea and vomiting. *Current Clinical Pharmacology* 2014;9(4):387–94, doi:10.2174/1574884708666131111205736.

10 Arslan M, Ozdemir L. Oral intake of ginger for chemotherapy-induced nausea and vomiting among women with breast cancer. *Clinical Journal of Oncology Nursing* 2015;19(5), doi:10.1188/15.cjon.e92-e97.

11 Dabaghzadeh F, Khalili H, Dashti-Khavidaki S et al. Ginger for prevention of antiretroviral-induced nausea and vomiting: a randomized clinical trial. *Expert Opinion on Drug Safety* 2014;13(7):859–66, doi:10.1517/14740338.2014 .914170.

12 Ajibola A, Chamunorwa JP, Erlwanger KH. Nutraceutical values of natural honey and its contribution to human health and wealth. *Nutrition & Metabolism* 2012;9(1):61, doi:10.1186/1743-7075-9-61.

13 Eteraf-Oskouei T, Najafi M. Traditional and modern uses of natural honey in human diseases: a review. *Iranian Journal of Basic Medical Sciences* 2013;16(6):731–42.

14 Greenberg JA. Chocolate intake and diabetes risk. *Clinical Nutrition* 2015;34(1):129–33, doi:10.1016/j.clnu.2014.02.005.

15 Higginbotham E, Taub PR. Cardiovascular benefits of dark chocolate? *Current Treatment Options in Cardiovascular Medicine* 2015;17(12), doi:10.1007/s11936-015-0419-5.

16 Van Wensem J. Overview of scientific evidence for chocolate health benefits. *Integrated Environmental Assessment and Management* 2014;11(1):176–77, doi:10.1002/ieam.1594.

17 Ros E. Nuts and CVD. *British Journal of Nutrition* 2015;113(S2), doi:10.1017/s0007114514003924.

PHOTO CREDITS

PHOTO CONTRIBUTORS

page 57: Rodrigobark, Savany, Ffolas, Draconus, Lew Roberts, Rimglow, Ljupco, Corbis, Bigacis, Ajafoto, Etiennevoss, Sarahdoow, Bigacis, Ajafoto

page 58: Savany, Jasmina81, Etiennevoss, Sarahdoow, Lew Robertson, Rimglow, Ljupco,

page 59: Ghinassi, IlonaImagine, Stuart Tyson, Hydrangea100, 8vFanI, Jasmina81, The Tofurky Company

page 60: IlonaImagine, Ghinassi, Jjwithers, Thinkstock, Baibaz, Hydrangea100, Dlerick

page 61: Pincarel, Jultud, Stockdisc, Bedo, PicturePartners, Ffolas, Alisafarov, Corbis, Kamilopafilms, Joseph Graziano, Szefei

page 62: Corbis, Joseph Graziano, Savany, Robynmac, Lew Robertson, Rob Cardillo, PicturePartners

page 63: Kim Klang, Joseph Graziano

page 64: John P. Hamel, PicturePartners, IlonaImagine, Magone, Jjwithers, Alisafarov, Pincarel, Szefei, Bedo, 8vFanI

page 65: Mayakova, Szefei, Robynmac, Vikif, Stockdisc, Lepas2004

page 66: Stockdisc, Getty/Imagesource, Pincarel, Szefei, Joseph Graziano, Jasmina81, Corbis, Temmuzcan

page 67: Cheche22, Floortje, Rob Cardillo, HeavAlamy, Joxxxxjo, Phanasitti, Twing, Hydrangea100, Robynmac, PicturePartners

page 68: Cheche22, Kang Kim, Zkruger, Robynmac, Rob Cardillo, Ribeiroantonio, FotografiaBasica

page 69: Robynmac, PicturePartners, Digital Vision, Difydave, Aristotoo, Ljupco, Mayakova, Rimma Bondarenko, Baibaz, Studiocasper, Marilyna, Goodapp, Jasmina81, ThamKC, Pincarel,Digitalr

page 70: Digitalr, Digital Vision : Culinary Photo Objects

page 71: Alisafarov, Maquinotico, MonaMakela, Twing, Ffolas, FotografiaBasica

page 72: Ffolas, Johnfoto18, Draconus, Bigacis, Sarahdoow, Temmuzcan, Etiennevoss, Ajafoto

RECIPE PHOTOS

Carmen Troesser, page 145

Catherine Sears, page 218

Christopher Testani, pages 148, 222, 225, 230, 266, 267, 268, 276

Con Poulos, pages 138, 140, 144, 149, 226, 266

David Malosh, pages 270, 277

Emily Kate Roemer, page 280

Jason Varney, pages 139, 143

John Kernick, page 223

Kana Okada, pages 137, 140, 224, 278

Kate Teutsch, page 227

Laura Moss, page 272

Monica Buck, page 273

Philip Ficks, page 142

Quentin Bacon, pages 218, 222, 225

Tara Donne, page 145

All other photos by Rodale Images: Mitch Mandel, Matt Rainey, and Thomas MacDonald

RECIPE CONTRIBUTORS

Anne Egan, pages 156–157

Amy Gorin, page 86

David Santner, page 298

Khalil Hymore Quasha, pages 158, 168, 186, 209, 210, 240–241, 250, 254, 281

Liz Applegate, pages 91 236, 282

Lydia Maruniak, page 296

Matthew Kadey, pages 126, 131

Pamela Parseghian, page 208

Rodale Test Kitchen, pages 82–83, 94–95, 118–119, 124–125, 178–180, 192–194, 204–206, 214–216, 246–248, 258, 262, 284

INDEX

Underscored page references indicate sidebars. **Boldface** references indicate photographs.

sodium in, 10
stores selling, 33
Produce. *See also* Fruits; Vegetables
real food brands of, 44
Protein, 16, 18–19, 24, 42
Puddings
instant, 43
Quick Coconut Rice Pudding, 246

Q

Quiche
Crustless Breakfast Quiche, 74
Quinoa
for breakfast, 51–52, 51
Mediterranean Turkey, 205
Quick Turkey Taco Bowl, 241
Tex-Mex Chicken Skillet Casserole, 192

R

Raisins
Carrot Cake Oatmeal, 95
Raspberries
Chocolate-Orange Mousse with Raspberries, 273, 284–85
Chocolate Raspberry French Toast, 94
Chocolate Tart with Berries, 258–59, 272
health benefits of, 258
Pineapple Berry Smoothies, 109
Plum and Raspberry Crumble, 281
Raspberry-Almond Strata, 96–97, 97, 138
Raspberry Chicken Salad in a Jar, 125
Raw sugar, 9
Real foods
balanced intake of, 25–27
best sources of, 23–24
for clean eating, 33–34
convenience foods as, 39–41
cost of, 4
fats in, 8
health benefits of, 1–2
natural sugars in, 8
nutrients in, 7, 15–16, 26–27
organic, 34–35
recommended brands of, 42–44
sodium in, 10

types to eat
dairy products, 18
fruits and vegetables, 20–21
good fats, 16–17
legumes, 18–19
meats, 17–18
nuts, 23
whole grains, 22
Real Quick & Healthy Snack Combos, 48, 50
Recipe information, 45–46, 48, 56. *See also specific recipes*
Restaurant meals, 3, 4, 55
Rice, Arborio
Quick Paella, 247
Rice, brown
Bacon, Egg, and Kale Bowl, 240
Brown Rice Pilaf, 246
Cool Rice Salad, 246
Easy Chicken and Rice Soup, 247
Emerald Rice with Shrimp, 246–47
Fire-Roasted Pork and Brown Rice, 187, 220
Mexican Cheesy Rice Casserole, 247
Pesto Grain Bowl, 241
Quick Coconut Rice Pudding, 246
Southwestern Black Bean Wrap, 86–87, 142
Unstuffed Cabbage "Rolls," 246
Rice milk, 40
Rice noodles
Chicken Pad Thai, 132–33
Rosemary
Rosemary-Lemon Doughnuts, 100–101, 139

S

Sage
Maple-Sage Roasted Chicken Thighs, 192
Sage and Brown Butter, 156
Salad dressings
mix-and-match, 62, 62
processed, 43
vinaigrettes, 126
Salads
Apple Ranch Salad in a Jar, 125
Bacon and Egg Salad, 128–29, 144
Chicken Caesar Salad, 130
Cobb Salad in a Jar, 124
Cool Rice Salad, 246

Crab Salad Bites, 164
Egg Salad Sandwich with Spinach and Tomato, 166
Gazpacho Chicken Salad, 131, 146
Green Bean, Tomato, and Olive Salad, 221, 244–45
Italian Roast Beef Salad in a Jar, 125
Mexicali Salad in a Jar, 125
mix-and-match, 61, 61
Niçoise Salad in a Jar, 124
Open-Faced Steak Sandwiches and Salad, 182–83, 223
Orzo and Chickpea Salad with Pesto, 119
Raspberry Chicken Salad in a Jar, 125
Satisfying Chickpea Salad, 118
Spinach Bacon Salad in a Jar, 125
Steak and Peach Salad, 126–27, 151
Waldorf Salad in a Jar, 124
Salmon
Asian Salmon Bowl, 240
Baked Salmon with Spring Vegetables, 215
smoked
Smoked Salmon Breakfast Sandwich, 84
types of, 85
Salsas
mix-and-match, 70, 70
Tex-Mex Chicken Skillet Casserole, 192
Turkey Cutlets Milanese with Salsa Cruda, 204
versatility of, 115
Salt, 6. *See also* Sodium
Sandwiches. *See also* Wraps
Egg Salad Sandwich with Spinach and Tomato, 166
Grilled Turkey Cutlet Club, 205
Italian Egg Sandwiches, 80
Mexican Meatball Heros, 136
mix-and-match BLT, 59, 59
mix-and-match burgers, 64, 64
mix-and-match grilled cheese, 60, 60
Open-Faced Steak Sandwiches and Salad, 182–83, 223
Peach and Arugula Grilled Cheese Sandwich, 149, 168
Roast Beef Sandwiches with Balsamic Onions and Peppers, 153
Smoked Salmon Breakfast Sandwich, 84